PILGRIM'S WAY

David Winter

PILGRIM'S WAY

Journeying through the year with the Bible

Published by
The Bible Reading Fellowship
15 The Chambers, Vineyard
Abingdon OX14 3FE
Tel: +44 (0)1865 319700
Email: enquiries@brf.org.uk
Website: www.brf.org.uk

ISBN 978 1 84101 529 3
First published 2008
10 9 8 7 6 5 4 3 2 1 0

Acknowledgments

Unless otherwise stated, scripture quotations are taken from The New Revised Standard Version of the Bible, Anglicized Edition, copyright © 1989, 1995 by the Division of Christian Education of the National Council of the Churches of Christ in the USA, and are used by permission. All rights reserved.

Extracts from the Authorized Version of the Bible (The King James Bible), the rights in which are vested in the Crown, are reproduced by permission of the Crown's patentee, Cambridge University Press.

New English Bible copyright 1961, 1970 by Oxford University Press and Cambridge University Press.

A catalogue record for this book is available from the British Library

Printed in Singapore by Craft Print International Ltd

CONTENTS

Introduction 6
January: All things new 7
February: The dark days 39
March: Rescue 69
April: New life 101
May: The Helper 133
June: The good life 165
July: Refreshment 197
August: True love 229
September: The life watched over 261
October: Forgiveness and hope 293
November: The future 325
December: Living in family 357
Bible index 389

INTRODUCTION

This book is clearly intended to be read through the year, one day at a time. For the reader who does this faithfully, there are big rewards! For one thing, they will follow themes from the Bible for each month of the year. For another, due regard is paid to the changing seasons, and—as far as possible—the great festivals of the Christian calendar. But for those who can't, there is still the opportunity to read my personal selection of what we might impolitely call the Bible's 'best bits', not as tiny nuggets but in passages of reasonable length, with some comments about the background and context. Each reading ends with a short 'thought for the day', a reflection on its relevance to the present-day reader.

The scriptures exist, Paul tells us, to teach, reprove, correct and train us in righteousness (2 Timothy 3:16). They tell what we might call the 'story of God', but it is a story which is meant to change us. From first to last the Bible is a book to enrich the spirit, to introduce us to the truly good life and to draw us closer to God. My hope is that as you read it through the year, each day something of that life-giving process will be at work for you.

January: All things new

January is the month of new beginnings, and so our readings pick up a theme that is constant throughout the Bible. God, who created everything at the beginning, is also constantly at work renewing his creation.

1 January

THE FIRST DAY

In the beginning God created the heaven and the earth. And the earth was without form, and void; and darkness was upon the face of the deep. And the Spirit of God moved upon the face of the waters. And God said, Let there be light; and there was light.

GENESIS 1:1–3 (KJV)

We're all interested in 'beginnings'. 'Where did I come from?' the child asks. The cosmologist wrestles with the question of how the universe came into being. Here, in words of stark simplicity and poetic restraint, is the answer of the Bible. Before anything, there was God, and God alone is the source and origin of everything that exists.

There is significance in the choice of the verb 'create', because the author could have chosen another Hebrew word, such as 'make' or 'form', to describe what God did. A 'maker' takes what already exists and shapes it into an object. A carpenter, for instance, takes wood and glue and perhaps some nails or screws, and 'makes' a chair. But a creator starts from nothing. Before Beethoven wrote down the first chords of his seventh symphony, it didn't exist at all. Until then, there were only six of his symphonies! But from himself, out of his own will and imagination and genius, that great work was 'created'.

These verses are describing an act of creation of that kind, though infinitely greater, of course. Out of his own will, imagination and genius, God created the universe. The verses offer no arguments for his existence; they simply take it for granted. Into a formless 'void'—the Hebrew word means something like 'empty waste'—the Creator spoke, and the light of creation shone. Matter, time, space and all the endless possibilities of physical and spiritual life flow from that single creative act.

We now know, as the ancient Hebrews could not have done, the immensity of the creation. Far from being a problem for the believer, surely that is a stimulus to wonder and praise. The greater the work, the greater its Creator.

2 January

THE FIRST PEOPLE

Then God said, 'Let us make humankind in our image, according to our likeness… So God created humankind in his image, in the image of God he created them; male and female he created them. God blessed them, and God said to them, 'Be fruitful and multiply, and fill the earth and subdue it; and have dominion over the fish of the sea and over the birds of the air and over every living thing that moves upon the earth.'

GENESIS 1:26–28 (abridged)

During the first five 'days' of creation God has brought into being the universe, the earth, and then plants, birds and animals. Now, on the sixth day, the language changes. Until now the command has simply been, 'Let there be…'—a kind of remote control of events. Now, however, as though to signal a change of emphasis, God commands in a more personal and involved way: 'Let us make…' We feel that the Creator himself is now deeply and even emotionally involved.

The next act of creation is human beings, made 'in [God's] image' and 'according to our likeness'. Nothing like this had been said about the material or animal creation, but now, in a particular way, God is bringing into being a creature who shares something of his own nature and likeness. This doesn't, of course, imply that human beings are 'God-like' in their status or character—far from it. But it does suggest that humankind has a different relationship to God from that of the rest of the creation. People share his self-conscious existence. They can have a relationship with him. And one day, in the fullness of time, a human being would be born who would show the world what its Creator is like.

The first thing to know about ourselves is that we are creatures, not cosmic accidents. The second is that, however inadequately, we mirror the nature of God. The third is that privilege involves responsibility. We may have 'dominion' over the earth and its living creatures but we shall answer to the Creator for their misuse.

3 January

THE GARDEN OF EDEN

And the Lord God planted a garden in Eden, in the east... Out of the ground the Lord God made to grow every tree that is pleasant to the sight and good for food, the tree of life also in the midst of the garden, and the tree of the knowledge of good and evil... The Lord God took the man and put him in the garden of Eden to till it and keep it. And the Lord God commanded the man, 'You may freely eat of every tree of the garden; but of the tree of the knowledge of good and evil you shall not eat, for in the day that you eat of it you shall die.'

GENESIS 2:8–9, 15–17 (abridged)

In the Genesis story, the man (as yet there is no woman) is given a garden as his home—Eden. It is a place of perfection, full of trees 'pleasant to the sight and good for food'. The man is also given congenial work to do, tilling and maintaining the garden.

It seems, at first sight, a place of total contentment. We can visualize Adam the gardener whistling as he works, pausing only to help himself to a ripe fruit from the trees. His freedom to enjoy the garden is total—apart from one deceptively simple command. He may eat of every tree in the garden, except for 'the tree of the knowledge of good and evil'. If he were to eat the fruit of that tree, he is warned, he will die.

To eat of the 'tree of the knowledge of good and evil' would mean the man had usurped the unique knowledge of God. He had been created in innocence, totally unaware of evil in any form. Only God (who had declared his whole creation to be 'good') knew that what had been created good could be infected with evil. Better by far, then, for the man to stay in what we might call blissful ignorance, simply enjoying the garden and being contented with his lot. In God's good time he will learn wisdom—but there are no short cuts to it.

Contentment is one of the most elusive virtues, and even though Eden sounds very pleasant, the man foolishly wanted more.

4 January

THE CREATION OF EVE

Then the Lord God said, 'It is not good that the man should be alone; I will make him a helper as his partner' ... So the Lord God caused a deep sleep to fall upon the man, and he slept; then he took one of his ribs and closed up its place with flesh. And the rib that the Lord God had taken from the man he made into a woman and brought her to the man. Then the man said, 'This at last is bone of my bones and flesh of my flesh; this one shall be called Woman, for out of Man this one was taken.'

GENESIS 2:18, 21–23

This is not, of course, a biological or anatomical explanation of the development of human gender! Rather, it is an exploration of its meaning and significance. Without woman, man is incomplete. Surrounded by natural beauty, animals and birds, trees and fruit, there is an emptiness in his heart. 'It is not good that the man should be alone', says God. It would be equally true, we may suppose, that without man woman is incomplete. The whole thrust of this narrative is that the two human genders are two parts of a whole: 'bone of my bones and flesh of my flesh'. Because man and woman are complementary, they can become—in what we now call marriage—'one flesh' (v. 24). It is a high view of the relationship of the sexes, one endorsed by Jesus himself (Matthew 19:6).

Later we learn the woman's name, 'Eve', which resembles the Hebrew word for 'living'. So Adam's partner is seen from the start as a bearer of life. Here is responsibility indeed.

The man was given 'a helper as his partner', not a 'helpmeet' as the old translation has it. Women were not created to be a kind of subordinate species to their male overlords. Marriage is a joint enterprise, not a solo performance with an assistant.

Now, surely, the first humans will be happy and contented. Their environment is perfect. They are surrounded by rich beauty and abundant food. And now, at last, there is also the fulfilling joy of an innocent, loving relationship.

5 January

REBELLION IN THE GARDEN

Now the serpent was more crafty than any other wild animal that the Lord God had made. He said to the woman, 'Did God say, "You shall not eat from any tree in the garden"?' The woman said to the serpent, '... God said, "You shall not eat of the fruit of the tree that is in the middle of the garden, nor shall you touch it, or you shall die."' But the serpent said... 'You will not die; for God knows that when you eat of it... you will be like God, knowing good and evil.' So when the woman saw that... the tree was to be desired to make one wise, she took of its fruit and ate; and she also gave some to her husband, who was with her, and he ate.
GENESIS 3:1–6 (abridged)

Eve and the apple—everyone knows the story, or thinks they do. Perhaps as a result, it tends to get trivialized. There's the talking serpent (always good for a laugh), and gullible Eve, and Adam, unable to resist the suggestion of his beautiful wife. And later on there's Adam and Eve hiding from God in the bushes, ashamed of what they'd done. It is all too easy to see it as a comedy. Yet the writer wanted to tell a tale of the ultimate tragedy. He intended to answer the most difficult of all questions: how did evil come into a world created by a good God?

Most of us can easily understand Adam and Eve's fascination with the one forbidden tree. What did it mean that it represented 'the knowledge of good and evil'? Wasn't knowledge a good thing? And, for that matter, what was evil? The very concept was foreign to them. With those questions in mind, the dialogue between the serpent and the woman sounds remarkably like the normal pattern of what we call 'temptation'; the very questions that she and Adam may have secretly asked about God's commandment took persuasive shape.

They were made in the image of God. They weren't moral robots. He wanted their freely given love and obedience. Tragically, because they thought they knew better than their Creator, he didn't get it.

Is that the heart of all sin—thinking that we know better than God?

6 January

FAILURE—AND EXCUSES

They heard the sound of the Lord God walking in the garden at the time of the evening breeze, and the man and his wife hid... But the Lord God called to the man, and said to him, 'Where are you?' He said, 'I heard the sound of you in the garden, and I was afraid, because I was naked; and I hid myself.' [God] said, 'Who told you that you were naked? Have you eaten from the tree of which I commanded you not to eat?' The man said, 'The woman whom you gave to be with me, she gave me fruit from the tree, and I ate.' Then the Lord God said to the woman, 'What is this that you have done?' The woman said, 'The serpent tricked me, and I ate.'

GENESIS 3:8–13 (abridged)

The chronicler has already told us of the cunning snake and the gullible pair of humans. Now all three are to face the consequences. Right from the beginning, the Bible establishes the principle that decisions have consequences, actions have reactions.

The moment of truth comes 'at the time of the evening breeze'. Apparently God was accustomed to taking a stroll through Eden when the day's heat was abating, but on this day he could see no sign of his human creatures. In fact, they were hiding from him—and sporting loincloths made from fig leaves. When God called for Adam, a shame-faced man appeared from the undergrowth. His brand new loincloth gave the game away. If he 'knew' he was naked—if innocence had died and guilty shame at nakedness had replaced it—there was only one explanation: they had eaten the forbidden fruit.

The man blamed the woman ('the woman you gave me'—clever touch, that!—'gave me the fruit'). The woman blamed the serpent ('he tricked me'). And the serpent, having no one to blame, hadn't, as we might say, a leg to stand on. At least, he soon wouldn't have.

Blaming others is so much a part of life that we tend not to see it as a moral failure. Yet all through the Bible the key to blessing is repentance, and repentance is admitting that we are at fault.

7 January

SENTENCE IS PASSED

The Lord God said to the serpent, '... cursed are you among all animals... upon your belly you shall go, and dust you shall eat all the days of your life. I will put enmity between you and the woman, and between your offspring and hers; he will strike your head, and you will strike his heel.' To the woman he said, 'I will greatly increase your pangs in childbearing; in pain you shall bring forth children, yet your desire shall be for your husband, and he shall rule over you.' And to the man he said, 'Because you have listened to the voice of your wife, and have eaten of the tree... cursed is the ground because of you; in toil you shall eat of it all the days of your life; thorns and thistles it shall bring forth for you... By the sweat of your face you shall eat bread until you return to the ground.'

GENESIS 3:16–19 (abridged)

The man and the woman have disobeyed a clear command of their Creator, at the instigation of the mysterious 'serpent'. Their sin has been revealed, their lame excuses heard, and sentence is to be passed.

The serpent—clearly some kind of personification of evil—is dealt with first. Its punishment is that it will move on its belly and that there will be lifelong enmity between its descendants and those of Adam and Eve. The woman is dealt with next. Her punishment is two-fold. She will experience 'pangs' in childbirth, and be subservient to her husband. The man's punishment has to do with his daily work. It will no longer be a joy, but a sore trial.

The man and the woman (and their descendants) have acted as though they knew better than God what was good for them. Now the consequences will blight the most potentially satisfying elements of their lives—for the woman, childbearing and her relationship with her sexual partner, and for the man, his daily work. These punishments will only be lifted when a qualified person comes to effect a release.

That moment of release, of 'redemption', will come, but only at the end of the whole story of the Bible.

8 January

A NEW HOME

Now the Lord said to Abram, 'Go from your country and your kindred and your father's house to the land that I will show you. I will make of you a great nation, and I will bless you, and make your name great, so that you will be a blessing. I will bless those who bless you, and the one who curses you I will curse; and in you all the families of the earth shall be blessed.'

GENESIS 12:1–3

Most of us at some time face the dilemma: to go or to stay? When we get married, do we go far away in search of a future life in a new environment? At retirement, should we settle for a home near our children and grandchildren, or stay where friends and familiar faces are to be found? Until modern times most people stayed with their roots, generation after generation able to tend the family graves in the local churchyard. Today young people routinely take work opportunities in distant lands. Should I go, or should I stay?

In today's passage, Abram faces just that dilemma. He was a god-fearing man, living in the ancient city of Ur in the area we now call Iraq. He felt called to leave the security of the familiar—his home, his family, his country—and head westwards, to an unknown destination. He recognized in some way that this prompting was the voice and will of God, and obeyed it. As he did, a whole new door was opened for the human race. Through this one man and his obedience to God a chain of blessing would be formed. He himself would be blessed, as would the 'great nation' that would be born from him. Those who accepted him ('those who bless you') would be blessed. And one day 'all the families of the earth' would be blessed through him.

Abram left, at whatever cost in tears, wealth, or loneliness we cannot tell, and through his going a nation was born, Israel. From that nation, after many centuries, a Saviour came, called Jesus. And through him, over the past two thousand years, millions of people on every continent have been blessed. It may be difficult to go, but sometimes not going can hinder the purposes of God.

9 January

SEEING IS BELIEVING

When the queen of Sheba heard of the fame of Solomon (fame due to the name of the Lord), she came to test him with hard questions. She came to Jerusalem with a very great retinue... and when she came to Solomon, she told him all that was on her mind. Solomon answered all her questions; there was nothing hidden from the king that he could not explain to her. When the queen of Sheba had observed all the wisdom of Solomon... there was no more spirit in her. So she said to the king, 'The report was true that I heard in my own land of your accomplishments and of your wisdom, but I did not believe the reports until I came and my own eyes had seen it.'

1 KINGS 10:1–7A (abridged)

The queen of Sheba came to Jerusalem with 'hard questions', as we often do when we want to avoid recognizing or accepting an unpalatable truth—in this case, that there was a monarch richer and wiser than she was! To her astonishment, Solomon answered them all. As she looked around his court, she also recognized something very profound: that what Solomon had was not so much a great talent or a brilliant intelligence as a gift of God. She had heard of all these things by repute but now she had actually seen them, and for her (as for us) 'seeing is believing'. She recognized that 'the God of Israel' was the source of his wisdom—but the suspicion remains that she went home to tell everyone how marvellous Solomon and his court were, rather than how wonderful his God had been.

Like the queen of Sheba, we can often feel a mixture of admiration and envy when we are confronted with great talent or intelligence. But there is another way! We can turn our admiration (and even our envy) into praise to God for his generous gift.

10 January

IS NOTHING NEW?

Vanity of vanities, says the Teacher, vanity of vanities! All is vanity. What do people gain from all the toil at which they toil under the sun? ... The sun rises and the sun goes down, and hurries to the place where it rises. The wind blows to the south, and goes round to the north; round and round goes the wind, and on its circuits the wind returns. All streams run to the sea, but the sea is not full; to the place where the streams flow, there they continue to flow. All things are wearisome; more than one can express; the eye is not satisfied with seeing, or the ear filled with hearing. What has been is what will be, and what has been done is what will be done; there is nothing new under the sun.

ECCLESIASTES 1:2–3, 5–9

In the Hebrew scriptures (what we call the 'Old Testament') one category of writing is called 'Wisdom'. Included in it are the Psalms, Proverbs, Job and this rather strange but haunting book called Ecclesiastes—the book of the 'Teacher'. This unnamed person seems to have a cynical, caustic view of life, which right from the start he categorizes as 'vanity'—emptiness. For him, there is little point in life at all; it simply goes nowhere. People come and go, the streams run into the sea but never fill it, events are 'wearisome' and nothing satisfies the eye or the ear.

So why is this pessimistic and even depressing book in the Bible? Surely because, like the psalmist's 'miry bog', this experience is part of life as we know it. For many people, life is indeed an unhappy business, yet the Teacher's message is not simply a rant against our existence. We shall come back to this book later and find that, for the Teacher wisdom lies in seeking God and keeping his commandments, and that those who do so will find true fulfilment.

'Nothing new'? What about the psalmist's 'new song'? The difference is between outward events and inner experience. Even when life is wearisome, the heart tuned to its Creator can sing.

11 January

NEW EVERY MORNING

The thought of my affliction and my homelessness is wormwood and gall! My soul continually thinks of it and is bowed down within me. But this I call to mind, and therefore I have hope: The steadfast love of the Lord never ceases, his mercies never come to an end; they are new every morning; great is your faithfulness... The Lord is good to those who wait for him, to the soul that seeks him.

LAMENTATIONS 3:19–23, 25

'Lamentations' is just what its title implies—a book lamenting the dreadful fate that befell the people of Jerusalem after the capture of their city by the Babylonians. According to Jeremiah, 4600 of the leading citizens were taken into exile, the temple was burnt down and all its treasures looted, and only the poorest people were left to till the ground. This book is, for the most part, a cry of pain at their suffering. 'No one comes to the festivals; all her gates are desolate, her priests groan; her young girls grieve, and her lot is bitter' (1:4).

Yet halfway through this book is one of the Bible's most courageous statements of faith: 'The steadfast love of the Lord never ceases.' It seems entirely appropriate that this is one of the opening sentences of the funeral service, because it is a confession of trust which faces the awfulness of sorrow with hope. If God's mercies are 'new every morning', then who knows what the new day may bring?

The key word is 'faithfulness', an attribute of God that is celebrated all through the Bible. God is faithful. A very early Christian hymn puts it in its most extreme form: 'If we are faithless, he remains faithful—for he cannot deny himself' (2 Timothy 2:13). In other words, God's faithfulness does not depend on whether we have faith in him, but on his very nature. As James puts it in his letter, with 'the Father of lights' there is 'no variation or shadow due to change' (James 1:17).

'Great is thy faithfulness... morning by morning new mercies I see.'

THOMAS CHISHOLM (1866–1960)

12 January

A NEW HEART

I will... gather you from all the countries, and bring you into your own land. I will sprinkle clean water upon you... and from all your idols I will cleanse you. A new heart I will give you, and a new spirit I will put within you; and I will remove from your body the heart of stone and give you a heart of flesh. I will put my spirit within you, and make you follow my statutes... Then you shall live in the land that I gave to your ancestors; and you shall be my people, and I will be your God.

EZEKIEL 36:24–28 (abridged)

God's covenant with the people of Israel was that if they kept his commandments they would be his people and he would be their God. Sadly, the whole story of the Old Testament is of a nation that consistently failed to keep his commandments. Yet, in these prophetic words of Ezekiel, the same nation is promised that one day they will be brought back from exile and given a new start in a restored Jerusalem. More than that, their physical restoration would be matched by spiritual renewal. They would be forgiven for past sins, and their old, stubborn hearts would be replaced with gentle and obedient ones. Thus God would make it possible for them to keep his commandments, not just in the letter but in the spirit, too, and so they would indeed be 'his people' and he would be 'their God'.

In cold historical truth, it didn't happen—certainly not in Ezekiel's lifetime, nor in the records of the rest of the Old Testament. However, the idea of a 'new spirit' and a 'new heart' is central to the teaching of Jesus and the apostles, probably most powerfully expressed in the dialogue between Jesus and Nicodemus (see John 3:1–10). Certainly the whole Bible stands firm on the principle that true religion is of the heart. In the words of Jesus himself, 'It is the spirit that gives life; the flesh is useless' (John 6:63).

True religion is not a matter of ritual observance or even scrupulous attention to rules, but a glad and willing openness to the mind and will of God.

13 January

NEW WINE

[Jesus] also told them a parable: 'No one tears a piece from a new garment and sews it on an old garment; otherwise the new will be torn, and the piece from the new will not match the old. And no one puts new wine into old wineskins; otherwise the new wine will burst the skins and will be spilled, and the skins will be destroyed. But new wine must be put into fresh wineskins. And no one after drinking old wine desires new wine, but says, "The old is good."'

LUKE 5:36–39

Ezekiel and the other prophets of Israel looked to a time when God would do a 'new thing' (Isaiah 43:19). When Jesus came on the scene, 500 years later, he announced that the 'new thing' had now arrived. In these sayings he likens it to two everyday experiences of the time.

The first is patching a worn garment—to do this you wouldn't tear a piece from a new garment. If you did, you would ruin both the old and the new one. So, the argument goes, you can't pick and mix from the 'new' religion and try to patch it into the old one.

The second example has to do with wine and wineskins. In those days wine was not bottled but stored in specially prepared skins. The effect of the fermented wine was to expand the skin slowly to accommodate it. It wasn't a good idea to take an old empty wineskin and put new wine into it, because that would burst the container so that the wine would be lost. New wine had to go into new wineskins. In Jesus, God was doing the promised 'new thing' and it had to be accepted in its entirety. People couldn't have some of the gospel but not the rest.

Finally, he gives a warning. Those who are steeped in the 'old wine' won't find this easy. 'The old is good,' they will say.

'New wine' was the wine for partying and celebration. It represents the 'abundant' life that Jesus came to bring to us (John 10:10). To reject that is to reject the very heart of Christianity.

14 January

A NEW COMMANDMENT

'Little children, I am with you only a little longer. You will look for me; and as I said to the Jews so now I say to you, "Where I am going, you cannot come." I give you a new commandment, that you love one another. Just as I have loved you, you also should love one another. By this everyone will know that you are my disciples, if you have love for one another.' Simon Peter said to him, 'Lord, where are you going?' Jesus answered, 'Where I am going, you cannot follow me now; but you will follow afterwards.' Peter said to him, 'Lord, why can I not follow you now? I will lay down my life for you.' Jesus answered, 'Will you lay down your life for me? Very truly, I tell you, before the cock crows, you will have denied me three times.'

JOHN 13:33–38

This 'new commandment' does not contradict the old ones, but fulfils and amplifies them. The people of the kingdom are to love their neighbour, as commanded, but the immediate application, in the light of all that lay ahead, was to be absolutely sure that they loved each other as well. Jesus had already told them to love their enemies (Matthew 5:44) and to love God with all their heart, mind, soul and strength (Luke 10:27). This would seem to be a simpler command—love those who are already members of Christ's family. Yet it has often proved remarkably difficult, rather like the squabbles that disrupt even the closest earthly families. The 'new commandment' is still new, and still challenges the followers of Jesus. Can we even love those who love us?

We then have a dramatic instance of what such love demands. Jesus is leaving his followers and they cannot follow him for the present. 'Why can't we?' asks Peter impetuously. 'Why, I'll even lay down my life for you!' It would take less than 24 hours for that bold expression of love to be tested to breaking point.

To love our fellow members of Jesus' kingdom community means much more than being nice to them. Peter got one thing right, at least. True love means being prepared to die for the one who is loved. No wonder it's so difficult.

15 January

A NEW LIFE, A NEW FAMILY

Turn again, my daughters: why will ye go with me? are there yet any more sons in my womb, that they may be your husbands? … And they lifted up their voice, and wept again: and Orpah kissed her mother in law; but Ruth clave unto her… And Ruth said, Intreat me not to leave thee, or to return from following after thee: for whither thou goest, I will go; and where thou lodgest, I will lodge: thy people shall be my people, and thy God my God: Where thou diest, will I die, and there will I be buried.

RUTH 1:11, 14, 16–17 (KJV)

I remember a sermon on this passage by a student training for ministry. She had grown up in the Hindu religion. Her Hindu parents, both doctors, had come to hear her preach. Like everyone else in church that night, they were deeply moved by what they heard, for this is a story about a desperate choice facing two young women: a choice between different cultures and different faiths.

Orpah and Ruth, Moabite women, had married Jewish men—the sons of Naomi, who had come to Moab during a time of famine in Israel. When both the husbands died, Naomi determined to return to her own land. She advised her daughters-in-law to stay in their own country and marry again. Eventually Orpah agreed to stay in Moab. Ruth, however, even in the face of Naomi's strong arguments to the contrary, insisted on travelling with her, to share fully in the culture and faith of her late husband and his mother. Her words here are one of the great declarations of love and loyalty in ancient literature.

Orpah was not at fault in deciding to return to her roots. But Ruth had found in this formerly alien culture, and perhaps especially in the worship of the one eternal and almighty God, something wonderfully attractive and compelling.

Ruth married again in Israel and had a son, who was destined to be an ancestor of Jesus of Nazareth. Thus the love and loyalty of a Moabitess have earned her an honoured role in the great story of redemption.

16 January

SPOILT AND REMADE

The word that came to Jeremiah from the Lord: 'Come, go down to the potter's house, and there I will let you hear my words.' So I went down to the potter's house, and there he was working at his wheel. The vessel he was making of clay was spoiled in the potter's hand, and he reworked it into another vessel, as seemed good to him. Then the word of the Lord came to me: Can I not do with you, O house of Israel, just as this potter has done? says the Lord. Just like the clay in the potter's hand, so are you in my hand, O house of Israel.

JEREMIAH 18:1–6

The prophet Jeremiah is usually associated with gloom and doom, and it's true that much of his book is about the terrible things that would happen to the people of Judah if they didn't repent and turn back to God. However, it isn't all gloom. The Lord told him to go down to the potter's studio and watch him at work. The prophet saw the clay being worked on the wheel. When it didn't turn out as the potter intended—'it was spoiled in the potter's hand'—the craftsman had a simple strategy. He simply reworked the clay into a brand new vessel.

'Look', said God, 'can't I do what the potter does? Can't I take what has not worked out as I intended, and rework it into something new and good?' The people of Judah had gone astray, but that didn't mean that the Lord couldn't take them and shape from them a better future. This is an image of the God who never gives up—just like the potter. In his great patience the Creator is reluctant to see his handiwork spoilt. He is the God of new starts, always making from the raw material of failure the brand new vessels of hope.

Lord, you are the Potter; I am the clay. Please remake me according to your loving purposes.

17 January

A NEW WAY OF LIVING

Do you not know that all of us who have been baptized into Christ Jesus were baptized into his death? Therefore we have been buried with him by baptism into death, so that, just as Christ was raised from the dead by the glory of the Father, so we too might walk in newness of life. For if we have been united with him in a death like his, we will certainly be united with him in a resurrection like his... For whoever has died is freed from sin. But if we have died with Christ, we believe that we will also live with him.
ROMANS 6:3–5, 7–8

Years ago I went to Milan with a BBC crew to record material for a drama-documentary on the life of Augustine of Hippo, who was baptized there in AD387. We went down under the medieval cathedral to the remains of the fourth century church, and entered the baptistery where Augustine, his son and his friend were baptized by the great Bishop Ambrose. The baptistery is in the form of a mausoleum, with a deep pool entered down stone steps. Here, in a dramatic ceremony on Easter Eve, the candidates, stripped naked, went down into the water as a sign of dying with Christ ('buried with him by baptism') and then emerged to be clothed in white robes, given lighted candles and led along a narrow corridor into the main church. There, for the very first time, they shared in the Eucharist—the first Communion of Easter. Having symbolically 'died' with Christ, they now entered fully into his risen life.

I have always thought of that scene when I read this passage. The Christian life is about 'dying' to sin and the old life, and then 'rising' with Christ into a new life with new goals and new hopes. Like Augustine, we go down into the dark waters of death, but we emerge in new 'clothes', with a new light for our paths and refreshment and companionship on the journey.

The new life of the Christian is the life of the risen Jesus. It will be marked by his characteristics of self-giving love and genuine joy.

18 January

THE RENEWED MIND

I appeal to you therefore, brothers and sisters, by the mercies of God, to present your bodies as a living sacrifice, holy and acceptable to God, which is your spiritual worship. Do not be conformed to this world, but be transformed by the renewing of your minds, so that you may discern what is the will of God—what is good and acceptable and perfect. For by the grace given to me I say to everyone among you not to think of yourself more highly than you ought to think, but to think with sober judgment.
ROMANS 12:1–3

Paul uses daring language here, calling on the Christians in Rome to offer themselves as a 'living sacrifice'—not the offerings of dead animals or birds with which they were familiar, but a live offering to God. This is not an invitation to carry out human sacrifice in the literal sense, but to offer our lives to God as a spiritual response to his own generosity. That, says Paul, is true worship.

The heart of the passage lies in the word 'mind'. It is when human thinking becomes 'futile' that 'senseless minds are darkened' (1:21), and all kinds of evil follow. Here, the call is to correct our thinking, not to let the values of this world distort it but to allow God's values to 'transform' or 'renew' our minds. In his paraphrase of the New Testament, J.B. Phillips caught the implication beautifully: 'Don't let the world around you squeeze you into its own mould'. The answer is to allow the 'will of God' to shape our thought processes.

Paul then gives one example of the danger of wrong thinking—when we think of ourselves 'more highly than we ought'. Devoutly religious people sometimes adopt a dismissive attitude towards those who don't share their beliefs. Instead, we should judge ourselves 'soberly', recognizing that on the journey of faith we are all pilgrims and learners.

It's easier to discipline the body than the mind! Yet everything we say and do stems from what goes on in our heads. We should heed Paul's challenge: 'We take every thought captive to obey Christ' (2 Corinthians 10:5).

19 January

WAITING AND WATCHING

Out of the depths I cry to you, O Lord. Lord, hear my voice! Let your ears be attentive to the voice of my supplications! … I wait for the Lord, my soul waits, and in his word I hope; my soul waits for the Lord more than those who watch for the morning, more than those who watch for the morning. O Israel, hope in the Lord! For with the Lord there is steadfast love, and with him is great power to redeem.

PSALM 130:1–2, 5–7

'Waiting' is a great theme of the psalmist, but he doesn't have in mind the sort of waiting we do at a bus stop or for the kettle to boil. For him, to 'wait for the Lord' is to believe that what he has promised, he will do. That sort of waiting is not irksome or tedious, nor is it a waste of time. It is 'waiting in hope', which means, in biblical language, being confident of the outcome.

I particularly like the repeated phrase 'more than those who watch for the morning'. The psalmist's soul is looking for God, just as (indeed, more than) the watchmen on their posts are confidently looking for the first sign of the rising sun. But there is no hint of impatience, even though he is crying out to God from the 'depths'—presumably at a time of great spiritual need. Even then, he knows that the secret is not just to 'wait', but to wait 'in hope'.

This is one of the lovely 'Songs of Ascent', which worshippers and pilgrims sang as they made their way up the hill towards the temple in Jerusalem. It may be a prayer of need, wrung out of the depths of human longing or forgiveness, healing and reassurance; but it is also a prayer of patient and strong faith.

Perhaps, in the darkness before dawn, the pilgrims glimpsed the watchmen on the walls, gazing eagerly towards the east. As they sang these words, they may have seen that their quest for God was like looking for the rising sun—he will come to us, even though we have to wait for the appointed time.

20 January

DAYBREAK

And thou, child, shalt be called the prophet of the Highest: for thou shalt go before the face of the Lord to prepare his ways; To give knowledge of salvation unto his people by the remission of their sins, Through the tender mercy of our God; whereby the dayspring from on high hath visited us, To give light to them that sit in darkness and in the shadow of death, to guide our feet into the way of peace.

LUKE 1:76–79 (KJV)

This is one of three songs in the opening chapters of Luke's Gospel, and like the others it echoes Old Testament language and ideas. The notion of the 'dayspring'—dawn—bringing light in place of darkness is a common theme, as we have seen in Psalm 130. The 'shadow of death' may also recall the words of Psalm 23:4 ('Though I walk through the valley of the shadow of death…')

This song is voiced by Zechariah, the father of John the Baptist, after the birth and naming of his son. He was aware that John was not the promised 'mighty saviour' mentioned earlier in the song (v. 69), but would have the honour of being the prophet who prepared the way for him. That turned out to be the calling of John, whose ministry was to baptize those who repented and sought a new life, and point them to one who would come after him, the 'thong of whose sandals he was not worthy to untie' (Luke 3:16).

Zechariah and his wife Elizabeth were well prepared for the birth of John, his conception having been foretold to an astonished (and apparently sceptical) Zechariah (1:8–20). The young boy grew up into a prophet, described by Jesus later as 'more than a prophet': indeed, 'among those born of women no one is greater than John'. Yet at the same time, 'the least in the kingdom of heaven is greater than he' (7:26, 28). That seems to be saying that John was the last of the great prophets of Israel, whose task was to usher in the kingdom of God.

Through God's mercy, the new day has dawned.

21 January

WEEPING AND REJOICING

When the Lord restored the fortunes of Zion, we were like those who dream. Then our mouth was filled with laughter, and our tongue with shouts of joy; then it was said among the nations, 'The Lord has done great things for them.' The Lord has done great things for us, and we rejoiced. Restore our fortunes, O Lord, like the watercourses in the Negeb. May those who sow in tears reap with shouts of joy. Those who go out weeping, bearing the seed for sowing, shall come home with shouts of joy, carrying their sheaves.

PSALM 126

The former exiles have been liberated and have returned home. This poem captures their gratitude and joy, in words that have a universal appeal. Who has not felt that wonderful relief when a cloud of fear or suffering has been removed? Who cannot identify with the laughter and exuberance, the feeling that it is all no more than a wonderful dream? If the poet's art is to express universal emotions in language of intensity and beauty, then this must be one of the world's great poems.

The opening is full of joy, gratitude and exuberance, but the second half represents a change of emphasis. The returning exiles realize that there is work to do if their homeland is to be restored to its former glory. If the Gentiles are truly to exclaim, 'The Lord has done great things for them', and if they can truthfully respond, 'The Lord has done great things for us', they will need to share in the work. The 'Negeb', in the south of Israel, is a notoriously dry region, but suddenly its water courses fill up and the crops begin to grow. The psalmist sees this as a picture of their experience: those who bear the seed of the next harvest, even while weeping for the harvests that have been lost, will 'come home with shouts of joy', carrying their sheaves.

Sometimes our lives seem so unfruitful that we despair of ever being truly happy again. Then something unexpected happens, to get the 'water courses' flowing again—and it can turn our tears of regret into shouts of joy.

22 January

THE BEGINNING OF WISDOM

Whoever corrects a scoffer wins abuse; whoever rebukes the wicked gets hurt. A scoffer who is rebuked will only hate you; the wise, when rebuked, will love you. Give instruction to the wise, and they will become wiser still; teach the righteous and they will gain in learning. The fear of the Lord is the beginning of wisdom, and the knowledge of the Holy One is insight.
PROVERBS 9:7–10

These words are spoken by 'Wisdom', personified as a wise woman, sending out her 'servant girls' to invite the 'simple' and those 'without sense' to change their ways (v. 4). Her invitation comes from the 'highest places in the town' (v. 3) but is for everybody who lives there. Wisdom is not an optional extra, but essential for the good and godly life.

In fact, wisdom is a recurring theme of the Bible. God is 'wise', uniquely and absolutely, which gives deep significance to the fact that Paul speaks of Jesus as the one who 'became for us wisdom from God' (1 Corinthians 1:30). For humans, wisdom needs to be learnt, however. The scoffers and the wicked reject correction with abuse and even physical violence, but 'the wise, when rebuked, will love you'. Most of us find correction difficult to take, especially when we think we are right, yet true wisdom lies in accepting it as something that does not belittle us, but builds us up. We might think of a parent who corrects a child, not out of disrespect or contempt but out of love. The wise recognize the truth of this, and through correction they become 'wiser still'.

This leads into a phrase that is virtually a refrain of parts of the Old Testament: 'The fear of the Lord is the beginning of wisdom, and the knowledge of the Holy One is insight.' 'Fear' is not terror, but respect. Those who recognize the wisdom of God and revere him for it have taken the first steps on the path to true wisdom.

Wisdom is not acquiring information or skills, but gaining insight. And of that knowledge God is the only true source.

23 January

THE FRUITS OF WISDOM

I, wisdom, live with prudence, and I attain knowledge and discretion. The fear of the Lord is hatred of evil. Pride and arrogance and the way of evil and perverted speech I hate. I have good advice and sound wisdom; I have insight, I have strength. By me kings reign, and rulers decree what is just; by me rulers rule, and nobles, all who govern rightly. I love those who love me, and those who seek me diligently find me… I walk in the way of righteousness, along the paths of justice, endowing with wealth those who love me, and filling their treasuries. The Lord created me at the beginning of his work, the first of his acts of long ago.

PROVERBS 8:12–17, 20–22

Wisdom speaks, this time to set out her characteristics. Positively, wisdom involves prudence (acting with due attention to the consequences), knowledge, discretion, righteousness, insight and (mental) strength. Negatively, it hates evil, pride, arrogance and 'perverted speech'—presumably lying or deceit. Such qualities can be learnt by those who genuinely seek spiritual wisdom, who listen to her 'good advice'. Wisdom has existed with God since creation, so those who seek wisdom should seek God.

This passage is also about the fruits or rewards of wisdom. Those who are wise accrue many benefits, some practical, some spiritual. Through wisdom rulers can govern justly. Wisdom endows her followers with wealth and honour. She leads her followers along paths of righteousness and justice, and she 'loves those who love her'.

If we find this a strange concept, we should remember how the notion of God's wisdom is central to the gospel message, too. Paul speaks of Christ himself, 'in whom are hidden all the treasures of wisdom and knowledge' (Colossians 2:3). That is what fills the 'treasuries' of the spiritually wise.

Wisdom is not acquired but given, as a grace of the God who is ultimate wisdom. Just as we seek God, so we may seek his gifts, including this one.

24 January

GOOD NEWS FOR POOR PEOPLE

When he came to Nazareth, where he had been brought up, [Jesus] went to the synagogue on the sabbath day… He stood up to read, and the scroll of the prophet Isaiah was given to him. He unrolled the scroll and found the place where it was written: 'The Spirit of the Lord is upon me, because he has anointed me to bring good news to the poor. He has sent me to proclaim release to the captives and recovery of sight to the blind, to let the oppressed go free, to proclaim the year of the Lord's favour.' … The eyes of all in the synagogue were fixed on him. Then he began to say to them, 'Today this scripture has been fulfilled in your hearing.'

LUKE 4:16–21 (abridged)

This is the first recorded public statement made by Jesus after his baptism, although he had already taught in synagogues around Galilee. Thus he came to his home town, Nazareth, with something of a reputation already, so doubtless the locals packed in to see what he had to say for himself. Invited to read (and explain) the scripture, he opened the scroll of the prophet Isaiah at chapter 61 and began to read. Intentionally or by providence, the reading was the Lord's mandate for his Servant, the messianic figure who suffered for his people.

In sharp contrast to some of the teaching elsewhere in scripture, where wealth and riches are seen as marks of God's favour, the favoured ones in this ringing declaration of purpose are the poor, the captives, the blind and the oppressed.

The Messiah came to bring 'good news' to poor people, which meant most of those who heard Jesus speak. In the coming kingdom, human wealth and status would count for nothing. Among Jesus' followers, some will be rich, as the world counts riches, and some will be financially poor, but all, without distinction, are rich in Christ.

Jesus declared, 'Today this scripture has been fulfilled in your hearing'. The hearers then showed how little they understood its message by rejecting him on the grounds that he was a nobody—the village carpenter (Mark 6:3))!

25 January

LOVE LIKE THIS

[Jesus said] 'This is my commandment, That ye love one another as I have loved you. Greater love hath no man than this, that a man lay down his life for his friends. Ye are my friends, if ye do whatsoever I command you… Ye have not chosen me, but I have chosen you, and ordained you, that ye should go and bring forth fruit… These things I command you, that ye love one another.'

JOHN 15:12–14, 16–17 (KJV, abridged)

'Greater love hath no man than this…' is probably one of the best-known sayings of the Bible. Inscribed on ten thousand or more war memorials up and down the country, it is still part of the brief ritual of Remembrance Day. It states a universal truth—that there is no greater proof of love than to die for someone. The mother who sacrifices herself for her child, the lifeguard who dies trying to rescue a swimmer, the pilot who loses his life by navigating a doomed plane past a built-up area—these all demonstrate the 'greater love' of which Jesus speaks.

Yet at the war memorials we seldom read the rest of the verse: 'You are my friends, if you do whatever I command you'. Jesus sets the stakes high: there is no greater love. And then he says that he himself will demonstrate that greater love for those who are his friends, 'those who do what I command'.

If we love someone, we want to please them—to 'do what they command', as Jesus puts it. The test of discipleship, of a true love for Jesus, is our willingness to fit in with his will for us. For these disciples, it was a special appointment ('ordination', as the old version puts it) to bear fruit for the kingdom, presumably by being his special witnesses or apostles. What is certain is that they could not do this, and neither can we, if disunity and rancour divided them: 'Love one another'.

Time and again in this final discourse to his disciples, Jesus urged them to 'love one another'. He knew that the greatest hazard facing the new community of believers would be division and strife. Sadly, it still is.

26 January

EVEN OUR ENEMIES

'You have heard that it was said, "You shall love your neighbour and hate your enemy." But I say to you, Love your enemies and pray for those who persecute you, so that you may be children of your Father in heaven; for he makes his sun rise on the evil and on the good, and sends rain on the righteous and on the unrighteous. For if you love those who love you, what reward do you have? Do not even the tax collectors do the same? ... Be perfect, therefore, as your heavenly Father is perfect.'

MATTHEW 5:43–46, 48

'Loving one another' is hard enough, which is presumably why Jesus constantly urged it on his disciples. But it's only the first step on an escalator of challenge. We are to love one another (fellow members of God's kingdom), our 'neighbours' (anyone, anywhere, who needs our love and help) and our 'enemies'. On any appraisal of human nature, this last one asks the impossible.

What particular 'enemies' did Jesus have in mind? They could be personal enemies—people with whom we are in conflict, even in a family feud. Or he might have been referring to the most obvious enemies of the time—the Roman occupiers. In either case, his hearers would have been amazed at this command. Surely the ancient teaching of the scribes was preferable: 'Love your neighbour, hate your enemy'? That way, you knew where you were.

Jesus invokes the example of God himself to refute this argument. God's life-giving rain falls on the good and the bad, on enemies as well as friends. God loves all that he has made, not because it is lovable, but because he is love. If we are to be children of his kingdom, if we are to achieve moral perfection like his, then our love must be as indiscriminate as his.

The word used here for 'perfect' is used elsewhere in the New Testament for 'completeness' or 'wholeness', meaning a life lived perfectly in tune with the will of God. That sublime state should at the very least be our goal.

27 January

LOVE'S PERFUME

Six days before the Passover Jesus came to Bethany, the home of Lazarus, whom he had raised from the dead. There they gave a dinner for him. Martha served, and Lazarus was one of those at the table with him. Mary took a pound of costly perfume made of pure nard, anointed Jesus' feet, and wiped them with her hair. The house was filled with the fragrance of the perfume. But Judas Iscariot... said, 'Why was this perfume not sold for three hundred denarii and the money given to the poor?' ... Jesus said, 'Leave her alone. She bought it so that she might keep it for the day of my burial. You always have the poor with you, but you do not always have me.'

JOHN 12:1–5, 7–8 (abridged)

What a remarkable meal this must have been! Mary and Martha had given a dinner to celebrate the astonishing miracle by which their brother Lazarus had been brought back from the dead. In fact, Lazarus sat at table with them, a living demonstration of the power and love of Jesus. This home at Bethany was a favourite haunt of his, whenever he was in Jerusalem, and we are told that he 'loved' the family members who lived there. Now, in a highly dramatic way, one of them would show how much she loved him, too.

Typically (see Luke 10:38–42), Martha cooked the meal while Mary devised the most extravagant act of worship she could imagine. As they ate, she took a jar of costly perfume and poured it over Jesus' feet as he reclined at table. This was an act of pure, extravagant, glorious worship, with no thought of cost or propriety. No wonder some of those present, including (but not only) Judas (see Mark 14:4), complained of 'waste'. True worship doesn't count its cost. You can't keep a balance sheet on love.

Yet, as Jesus pointed out, the ointment would still fulfil its original purpose. It was not the body of her brother which it would anoint for burial, but that of her Lord.

'The house was filled with the fragrance': this is truly love's perfume.

28 January

PRACTICAL LOVE

Let no evil talk come out of your mouths, but only what is useful for building up, as there is need, so that your words may give grace to those who hear. And do not grieve the Holy Spirit of God, with which you were marked with a seal for the day of redemption. Put away from you all bitterness and wrath and anger and wrangling and slander, together with all malice, and be kind to one another, tender-hearted, forgiving one another, as God in Christ has forgiven you.

EPHESIANS 4:29–32

It's one thing talking about love, whether it's towards each other, neighbours, or enemies. It's quite another to put theory into practice. In this passage, love is defined in the most intensely practical way. It's much more than a warm feeling, it's something we actually have to do.

As a child I was taught, 'Sticks and stones can break your bones, but words can never hurt you.' I was hardly old enough for school when I knew that it was a lie. Broken bones heal, but the hurt from cruel words can fester for a lifetime. Just before this, Paul has urged his readers to 'speak the truth to our neighbours' (v. 25), but here he goes further. Sometimes the unadorned truth can be desperately destructive, so say 'only what is useful for building up'. To tell someone who already feels inadequate that they've always been a waste of space will only thrust them further into a pit of despair. Our words should 'give grace to those who hear'. 'Grace' is the Greek word *charis:* something of beauty or generosity, freely given.

Gracious speech and behaviour are inconsistent with the ugly (but all too common) human behaviours listed. Instead, we should seek positive values: a soft and forgiving heart, conscious that we ourselves are forgiven people.

The test applied by Paul is a spiritual one—unkind and angry words and actions 'grieve the Holy Spirit of God', whose mark Christians bear until the final day of their 'redemption'.

29 January

A NEW CREATION

So if anyone is in Christ, there is a new creation: everything old has passed away; see, everything has become new! All this is from God, who reconciled us to himself through Christ, and has given us the ministry of reconciliation; that is, in Christ God was reconciling the world to himself, not counting their trespasses against them, and entrusting the message of reconciliation to us. So we are ambassadors for Christ, since God is making his appeal through us; we entreat you on behalf of Christ, be reconciled to God.

2 CORINTHIANS 5:17–20

Most of us from time to time like to experience something new, whether it's the distinctive smell of a new car or the sights and sounds of a new place we have discovered. At the same time, we are at home with the familiar; 'new' in some way can imply risk. The scriptures are rooted in human experience, much of it familiar, but they constantly hold out the promise of something new until, in the very last book of the Bible, God says that he is making 'all things new' (Revelation 21:5).

Today's passage is not talking about the distant future, but now. Paul says that for anyone who is 'in Christ' there is a 'new creation'. When we are 'in Christ' the whole world changes, as if the original creation had been renewed by its Creator. It's not only that we are different, but that the world changes around us. People, objects and places take on a new dimension, because now we are seeing them from a different perspective.

To be 'in Christ' is Paul's shorthand for being part of God's new people, born anew into a new life—what he calls 'life in Christ'. In Christ we stand in solidarity with a new community, the 'kingdom people', those who march to the beat of a different drum—people with new goals, new ambitions, new hopes.

As members of this kingdom, we are its ambassadors. Through our lives and words, God calls the world to be reconciled to him.

30 January

FORGETTING THE PAST

For I am about to create new heavens and a new earth; the former things shall not be remembered or come to mind. But be glad and rejoice for ever in what I am creating; for I am about to create Jerusalem as a joy, and its people as a delight. I will rejoice in Jerusalem, and delight in my people; no more shall the sound of weeping be heard in it, or the cry of distress. No more shall there be in it an infant that lives but a few days, or an old person who does not live out a lifetime; for one who dies at a hundred years will be considered a youth… They shall build houses and inhabit them; they shall plant vineyards and eat their fruit.

ISAIAH 65:17–21 (abridged)

The prophet is sharing his vision of the 'new Jerusalem' that God would bring into being. The Jewish people had been through a time of desperate suffering, but here is a picture of a new world, in which the past, with all its pain, would be forgotten.

In this section of Isaiah the word 'create' is a recurrent one. The God who, by his word, brought the original creation into being has spoken. There will be new heavens and a new earth; the 'former things' are now forgotten. Those who had caused trouble, the people who had forsaken the Lord, will be destined to destruction, while those who have remained faithful will enter into this wonderful place of blessing.

And what a picture of bliss the prophet draws! No more weeping, no more cries of distress, no more premature deaths of infants, everyone living to a ripe and fulfilling old age. Old age was revered in the ancient world (where it was comparatively rare) as a sign of exceptional blessing from God. This passage is not about a future heaven on the other side of the grave, but of the promise of God's loving provision in the here and now for the needs of his people.

We can't put timetables to God's promises, but we can be sure of their fulfilment. For Christians, a similar vision of a new heaven and earth is the climax to the story of God's dealings with the human race.

31 January

ALL THINGS NEW

Then I saw a new heaven and a new earth; for the first heaven and the first earth had passed away... And I saw the holy city, the new Jerusalem, coming down out of heaven from God, prepared as a bride adorned for her husband. And I heard a loud voice from the throne saying, 'See, the home of God is among mortals. He will dwell with them; they will be his peoples, and God himself will be with them; he will wipe every tear from their eyes. Death will be no more; mourning and crying and pain will be no more, for the first things have passed away.' And the one who was seated on the throne said, 'See, I am making all things new.'

REVELATION 21:1–5a (abridged)

Here is the fulfilment of the prophet's vision. At last, with evil destroyed and God's triumph established in his whole creation, the man who recorded this series of visions sees 'a new heaven and a new earth'. The old order fades from sight, and he sees the new Jerusalem, coming down from God. The old Jerusalem was the city where the temple had been built, destroyed and rebuilt several times, until finally, after the Jewish rebellion against Rome in AD70, it was reduced to a pile of rubble. Jerusalem without the temple was not really 'the city of God', because the temple symbolized his presence among his people.

When these words were written, probably towards the end of the first century, the fate of Jerusalem and its temple would have been well known. Now, however, according to this vision, God has promised a new Jerusalem—but one without a temple (v. 22), because God would now be its 'temple' as he set up home 'among mortals' in a closer way than ever before. All the promises of Isaiah that we read yesterday would be fulfilled: no tears, no death, no pain. As the voice of God proclaimed from his throne, he would make 'all things new'.

The final purpose of God is to recreate his world and to make his home with his people. This is no remote, distant deity, but a God of love who will gather his children around him and dwell with them there.

February: The dark days

Here we are, in the Western hemisphere at least, in the 'dark days' of February. The Bible is a book of almost cruel honesty, and makes no attempt to suggest that the journey of life can be completed without ever passing through the dark and shadowy valleys of anxiety, suffering and fear. At the same time, it never sounds a hopeless note. Even in the darkness, there is light.

1 February

THE VALLEY OF TROUBLES

Therefore, I will now allure her, and bring her into the wilderness, and speak tenderly to her. From there I will give her her vineyards, and make the Valley of Achor a door of hope… On that day, says the Lord, you will call me, 'My husband', and no longer will you call me, 'My Baal'. For I will remove the names of the Baals from her mouth, and they shall be mentioned by name no more… I will abolish the bow, the sword, and war from the land; and I will make you lie down in safety. And I will take you for my wife for ever; I will take you for my wife in righteousness and in justice, in steadfast love, and in mercy.

HOSEA 2:14–19 (abridged)

The Valley of Achor was so named after Joshua punished with death Achan and his family, who had taken and hidden forbidden loot from a conquered Canaanite settlement (Joshua 7). The place was named 'Achor' because the word meant 'Trouble' and indeed the sins of Achan had brought great trouble on the Israelites. The story and name came to represent a place of failure and disobedience, with its inevitable consequence of trouble.

In this striking passage, the prophet Hosea depicts Israel as an unfaithful wife who has flirted with 'Baal', the heathen god of neighbouring nations. She, like Achan, had been seduced by jewellery, and in the process forgot the Lord her God.

But these words speak of hope, even in the valley of trouble. She will be led in from the wilderness of sin and failure and will hear words of tenderness. Her vineyards will be restored to her and God will 'make the Valley of Achor a door of hope'. Not only that, but he will create a new and intimate relationship with her—she will become his wife, he says, 'in righteousness and in justice, in steadfast love, and in mercy'.

When we go though times of failure and sin, together with the sad consequences that can follow them, it may be hard to believe that the 'Valley of Achor' can be a 'door of hope'—hard, but true to experience.

2 February

A CRY FOR HELP

Turn, O Lord, save my life; deliver me for the sake of your steadfast love. For in death there is no remembrance of you; in Sheol who can give you praise? I am weary with my moaning; every night I flood my bed with tears; I drench my couch with my weeping. My eyes waste away because of grief; they grow weak because of all my foes. Depart from me, all you workers of evil, for the Lord has heard the sound of my weeping. The Lord has heard my supplication; the Lord accepts my prayer.

PSALM 6:4–9

Like many of the psalms, this is a desperate cry for help. It would seem that the psalmist is, or has been, very ill, so much so that fear of death has overcome him. Note that he shows little or no notion of a meaningful life beyond death. The dead simply inhabited 'the pit', *Sheol*, a place where nothing much happened and even words of prayer or praise could not reach God's ears. The effect of this was to make recovery from illness a primary concern; the prayer is anguished, passionate and heartfelt.

The psalmist appeals to God's 'steadfast love'—*chesed*, one of the loveliest words in Hebrew and almost untranslatable into English. Probably 'steadfast love' is as near as we can get, although the King James Bible's 'loving-kindness' probably captures the feel of it best. The unchanging God is a God of kindness and love, who wants the best for his people, and so we can expect him to care about our aches, pains and fears. Because he is a God of loving-kindness, they are always his constant concern. We are not trying to persuade a reluctant despot to be kind for once. This ruler is kind by nature.

Although Sheol was a place of desolation, Psalm 139 makes a bold and surprising assertion that God is present in every part of his creation, including 'the pit'. 'If I make my bed in Sheol, you are there' (v. 8). Nowhere is beyond the reach and love of God.

3 February

THE DARK NIGHT OF THE SOUL

My God, my God, why have you forsaken me? Why are you so far from helping me, from the words of my groaning? O my God, I cry by day, but you do not answer; and by night, but find no rest. Yet you are holy, enthroned on the praises of Israel. In you our ancestors trusted; they trusted, and you delivered them. To you they cried, and were saved... You who fear the Lord, praise him! ... For he did not despise or abhor the affliction of the afflicted; he did not hide his face from me, but heard when I cried to him. From you comes my praise in the great congregation.
PSALM 22:1–5, 23–25a (abridged)

This is yet another psalm wrung from the depths of need. Indeed, its opening words were cried out by Jesus on the cross in a moment of deep anguish. It is testimony to one of the great qualities of the psalms: honesty to the point of naked emotion. The psalmist was not afraid to tell his God exactly how he felt about the Almighty.

I remember a woman in my parish whose husband had died unexpectedly during the night. I went to see her first thing in the morning, and she launched herself at me: 'I hate God!' she screamed. Months later, she asked to see me. She told me how appalled she was to think of what she had said to me. Could God ever forgive her? Really, she assured me, she didn't hate him. I knew that, of course, but I could also sense the emotion behind her outburst. I reminded her of the honesty of the psalmist, and suggested that if God could accept the death of his only Son for us (and even forgive, at his request, those who did it), then he could surely forgive her. In any case, God is not interested in fake devotion.

Inevitably, the psalmist, like my parishioner, finds calmer waters, remembers God's past mercies—and joins the crowd in the temple offering him praise.

Prayer is not a performance. It must come from the heart, however raw the emotions we find there.

4 February

SHOWERS OF BLESSING

'Come, let us return to the Lord; for it is he who has torn, and he will heal us; he has struck down, and he will bind us up. After two days he will revive us; on the third day he will raise us up, that we may live before him. Let us know, let us press on to know the Lord; his appearing is as sure as the dawn; he will come to us like the showers, like the spring rains that water the earth.' What shall I do with you, O Ephraim? … Your love is like a morning cloud, like the dew that goes away early. Therefore I have hewn them by the prophets, I have killed them by the words of my mouth, and my judgment goes forth as the light. For I desire steadfast love and not sacrifice, the knowledge of God rather than burnt-offerings.

HOSEA 6:1–6 (abridged)

The prophet Hosea wrote in the eighth century BC. He lived in the northern kingdom, Israel, and his message of warning and hope was addressed to a nation about to disappear from the scene. Conquered by the Assyrians, its citizens were taken into exile or deprived of land and status. Those were desperate days, and it seems that Hosea wasn't quite sure whether the carrot or the stick would best serve to alert the people to the danger they were in, or the fate that awaited them.

We see the carrot here in wonderful words of invitation: 'Let us return to the Lord; for it is he who has torn, and he will heal us.' Indeed, after a brief delay he will bring them back to true life and raise them up again. The subsequent blessing would come like the spring showers that brought life to the dry fields of winter.

But we also see the stick. Hosea was a realist. These people were stubborn and fickle, easily drawn away from God. 'Your love is like a morning cloud', soon burnt away by the heat of the sun. What God wanted, they had so far failed to give him: 'steadfast love' and a longing to be true to his will and purpose.

'Steadfast love'—an unwavering faith—is infinitely more valued by God than ritual offerings or empty worship.

5 February

THORN IN THE FLESH

Therefore, to keep me from being too elated, a thorn was given me in the flesh, a messenger of Satan to torment me, to keep me from being too elated. Three times I appealed to the Lord about this, that it would leave me, but he said to me, 'My grace is sufficient for you, for power is made perfect in weakness.' So, I will boast all the more gladly of my weaknesses, so that the power of Christ may dwell in me.

2 CORINTHIANS 12:7b–9

Paul has been 'boasting' (his own word) about the 'exceptional character of the revelations' he had been given by God, apparently in some kind of trance experience. He is aware of the danger of spiritual pride, and, as if to make sure he didn't fall into that trap, a 'thorn in the flesh' was given to him. The source of this 'thorn' is not entirely clear, because Paul calls it a 'messenger of Satan', which implies that God's 'adversary' was involved, yet he is clear that the Lord himself approved of it as a means by which God's power could be perfected in Paul's helplessness.

What was this 'thorn in the flesh'? We are not told, so scholars have expended much imagination as to its nature. Epilepsy and poor eyesight have been suggested, on the rather tenuous basis of evidence from Acts and other letters from the apostle. Whatever it was, it may represent to us some element in our lives that we see as a constant problem or weakness. Like Paul, we may have prayed often that the Lord would 'take it away'. However, in this case that would not be the best answer. Better for him, says the Lord, that he should carry the 'thorn', with all its nagging inconvenience, as a humbling witness to the great truth that God's power is perfected in human weakness.

There is no suggestion that God could not remove the 'thorn' from Paul, just the assertion that Paul's faith would be strengthened by bearing it day by day. Many Christians have had a similar experience, when in times of weakness they have experienced 'the power of Christ' dwelling in them.

6 February

YOUR WILL, NOT MINE

They went to a place called Gethsemane; and [Jesus] said to his disciples, 'Sit here while I pray.' He took with him Peter and James and John, and began to be distressed and agitated. And he said to them, 'I am deeply grieved, even to death; remain here, and keep awake.' And going a little farther, he threw himself on the ground and prayed that, if it were possible, the hour might pass from him. He said, 'Abba, Father, for you all things are possible; remove this cup from me; yet, not what I want, but what you want.'

MARK 14:32–36

Anyone who doubts that Jesus was fully human cannot have read these words of Mark. Here is a man who knows that the next day he will be treacherously delivered into the hands of his enemies and put to death by crucifixion, probably the cruellest form of execution ever devised. No human being, even one imbued with the divine nature, could have failed to be appalled at the prospect.

Jesus had with him his closest and most trusted friends. All he asked them to do was to stay there while he moved off a little farther, and to 'stay awake'. In the event, they observed the first request but failed in the second. Jesus then prayed a remarkably revealing prayer—revealing because it shows us that obedience to his Father's will was not lightly achieved, even for the Son of God. It seems as though Jesus was enquiring whether there wasn't some other way to win the world's salvation, a Plan B that did not involve a hideous death. The petition was followed, however, with the most crucial caveat: 'Yet not what I want, but what you want.'

As soon as Jesus had finished praying, Judas the betrayer and a party of guards arrived to arrest him. As he said, 'the hour has come' (v. 41).

Jesus did not address this prayer to a remote God but to 'Abba'—an affectionate name for 'father' in Aramaic. Even so, the Father knew there was no other way to achieve his loving purpose for the world.

7 February

THROUGH THE VALLEY

The Lord is my shepherd; I shall not want. He maketh me to lie down in green pastures; he leadeth me beside the still waters. He restoreth my soul: he leadeth me in the paths of righteousness for his name's sake. Yea, though I walk through the valley of the shadow of death, I will fear no evil: for thou art with me; thy rod and thy staff they comfort me. Thou preparest a table before me in the presence of mine enemies: thou anointest my head with oil; my cup runneth over. Surely goodness and mercy shall follow me all the days of my life: and I will dwell in the house of the Lord for ever.
PSALM 23 (KJV)

This best-known and best-loved of all the psalms is also a memorable and beautiful piece of poetry. Most of us have drawn strength from its imagery of the loving shepherd who guides and cares for his people, even when they walk through 'the valley of the dark shadow'.

Shepherds were familiar to everyone in biblical times. Eastern shepherds don't follow the sheep, as British ones do, but lead them, walking ahead to check for pitfalls and dangers and to search out pasture on the dry hillsides of summer. They spent all their days with the sheep, even sleeping with them at night. Such was their total commitment to the task that they were prepared to lay down their lives for their sheep, as Jesus pointed out (John 10:14–15). Although shepherds came very low in the social pecking order of ancient Israel (because their duties in the fields prevented their full participation in the practice of their religion), the shepherd became an image of the good monarch. The godly king cares for his people, protects them and guides them. It's not surprising, then, that the royal shepherd was also seen to epitomize the qualities of the anointed Messiah whom God would one day send to his people.

'Though I walk through the valley of the shadow of death, thou art with me…' For me, as for many others, those became words to treasure during dark days of bereavement.

8 February

WITH US IN THE BOAT

When evening had come, he said to them, 'Let us go across to the other side.' And leaving the crowd behind, they took him with them in the boat, just as he was. Other boats were with him. A great windstorm arose, and the waves beat into the boat, so that the boat was already being swamped. But he was in the stern, asleep on the cushion; and they woke him up and said to him, 'Teacher, do you not care that we are perishing?' He woke up and rebuked the wind, and said to the sea, 'Peace! Be still!' Then the wind ceased, and there was a dead calm. He said to them, 'Why are you afraid? Have you still no faith?' And they were filled with great awe and said to one another, 'Who then is this, that even the wind and the sea obey him?'
MARK 4:35–41

Much of Jesus' ministry took place around the lake of Galilee, and several of his first disciples were fishermen. It was a long way around the lake on foot, but boats provided a quicker route across.

Galilee has always had a reputation for sudden and violent storms, the water lashed by winds blowing through the natural tunnel provided by the Jordan valley. As the boats used on the lake were flat-bottomed, they provided little stability in high winds, and it was not unknown for them to sink. Such was the fate feared by the disciples as the storm broke. Meanwhile, Jesus, probably tired by his ministry around the north end of the lake, slept soundly on a cushion.

It may have been stark fear or even shock that their leader should presume to sleep through the storm, oblivious to their danger, which evoked an angry question as they woke him. 'Teacher, don't you care that we are perishing?' Of course he cared, yet he also saw their fear as a failure of faith. Now, as though to drive home the point, he stood and rebuked the storm. 'Peace! Be still!' The storm ceased, leading the disciples to conclude that 'even the wind and the sea obey him'.

This story is about faith, but it also reminds us of the presence of Christ with us in the 'boat' of life, even when we encounter stormy seas.

9 February

COMING TO US ACROSS THE WATERS

Immediately [Jesus] made the disciples get into the boat and go on ahead to the other side, while he dismissed the crowds. And after he had dismissed the crowds, he went up the mountain by himself to pray. When evening came, he was there alone, but by this time the boat, battered by the waves, was far from the land, for the wind was against them. And early in the morning he came walking towards them on the sea. But when the disciples saw him walking on the sea, they were terrified, saying, 'It is a ghost!' And they cried out in fear. But immediately Jesus spoke to them and said, 'Take heart, it is I; do not be afraid.'

MATTHEW 14:22–27

I recall preaching on this story a few years ago. It had just been read, very dramatically, as the Gospel for the day, and I began by conducting a quick congregational survey. 'How many of you were thinking, as you heard that story, "He didn't really, did he?"' After a slight hesitation, a lot of hands went up. I then said that when the first Christians heard that story I doubted if a single one of them thought 'He didn't really, did he?'—that's to say, querying whether it was factually true—but rather 'What does it mean?' For the people of the first century, stories had meanings, which were much more important than questions about whether they really happened. (And just for the record, I think he did.)

The 'meaning' of this story is wonderful and inspiring. In yesterday's reading we heard how Jesus was in the boat with his disciples when storms struck. To know that Jesus is with us in our troubles is a great encouragement. Here, he wasn't with them but was miles away, praying on a hillside. Yet when the storm struck and they were in peril from the waves, he came to them where they were. And how did he come? Why, actually walking across the very things that scared and threatened them!

It is when the storms of life threaten to overwhelm us that Jesus comes to us, 'walking on the waters' of our fears.

10 February

IN A DRY LAND

O God, you are my God, I seek you, my soul thirsts for you; my flesh faints for you, as in a dry and weary land where there is no water. So I have looked upon you in the sanctuary, beholding your power and glory. Because your steadfast love is better than life, my lips will praise you... My soul is satisfied as with a rich feast, and my mouth praises you with joyful lips when I think of you on my bed, and meditate on you in the watches of the night; for you have been my help, and in the shadow of your wings I sing for joy.

PSALM 63:1–3, 5–7

This longing of the soul for God's refreshment during periods of spiritual dryness is a common one in the psalms—as it is in everyday spiritual experience. It would be a remarkable Christian who could say that they had never known a day when the cup of faith and joy was not brimful! The power of the imagery in these psalms may derive from the experience of people who lived with the constant threat of drought, on the very borders of vast tracks of arid desert. They knew what it was to be dry, and they knew the blessings of rain.

The psalmist did not, in fact, satisfy this thirst at a spring of water, but in 'the sanctuary', the temple, where he could behold God's power and glory and reflect on his 'steadfast love'—that elusive quality of 'loving-kindness' that a holy and just God shows to his thirsty children. That steadfast love of the Lord is 'better than life', an astonishing claim, taken at face value. It is for this that his lips will sing praise.

There follow yet more evocative images of the refreshment that God brings to the seeking soul. It is like feasting richly, it is joyful, it lights up the dark hours of night. It offers a life lived under the shadow of God's wings, sheltered from the burning heat of noonday. No wonder the psalmist 'sings for joy'.

The answer to spiritual 'dryness' for the psalmist is not despair or self-analysis, but a fresh look at the beauty, grace and mercy of the Lord God.

11 February

THE SOUL'S LONGING

As a deer longs for flowing streams, so my soul longs for you, O God... My tears have been my food day and night, while people say to me continually, 'Where is your God?' These things I remember, as I pour out my soul: how I went with the throng, and led them in procession to the house of God, with glad shouts and songs of thanksgiving, a multitude keeping festival. Why are you cast down, O my soul...? Hope in God; for I shall again praise him, my help and my God. My soul is cast down within me; therefore I remember you from the land of Jordan and of Hermon, from Mount Mizar. Deep calls to deep at the thunder of your cataracts; all your waves and your billows have gone over me. By day the Lord commands his steadfast love, and at night his song is with me, a prayer to the God of my life.

PSALM 42:1, 3–8 (abridged)

This lovely psalm is a song of regret and faith. The regret is plain: the writer is living far away from Jerusalem, in the north of the country near Mount Hermon and the source of the Jordan (no one seems to know where 'Mount Mizar' was). For some reason—illness, perhaps, or family responsibilities—he was living among unfamiliar people, who found his religious attachment to Jerusalem quaint. 'Where is your God?' they asked mockingly. He longed to join the crowds again at the temple, to hear the singing, share in the processions and celebrations. It's a human situation that most of us can recognize. Regret was casting down his spirit, to the extent that he found himself constantly weeping at the thought of the life he had once lived.

Yet this is also a song of faith. His longing for God was real ('as a deer longs for flowing streams'), but that was because his God was real, too. He urged himself to 'hope in God', to believe that things would change, that he would share in the temple worship again. The Lord's 'waves and billows' have gone over him, yet he knows God's 'steadfast love' and consequently, alongside the tears, the song of praise is still with him.

In truth, the believer is never very far away from God.

12 February

THE WAY TO THE FATHER

'Do not let your hearts be troubled. Believe in God, believe also in me. In my Father's house there are many dwelling-places. If it were not so, would I have told you that I go to prepare a place for you? And if I go and prepare a place for you, I will come again and will take you to myself... And you know the way to the place where I am going.' Thomas said to him, 'Lord, we do not know where you are going. How can we know the way?' Jesus said to him, 'I am the way, and the truth, and the life. No one comes to the Father except through me.'

JOHN 14:1–6 (abridged)

These words are very familiar to many people, perhaps because this passage is often used at funerals. Jesus' invitation is wonderfully reassuring on such an occasion: 'Set your troubled hearts at rest' (v. 1, REB). And how can we, in such a situation? 'Believe in God, believe also in me'. The word translated as 'believe' could equally well be rendered 'trust', so Jesus was telling his disciples to trust their heavenly Father, and to trust him. Would he have misled them?

Sometimes, in moments of deep grief or emotion, rational argument is not what we need so much as someone to trust. Who is more trustworthy than God himself, and his anointed Son? Jesus assured them that beyond the present life there was more journeying to be done and more 'dwelling-places' to enjoy. More than that, he would go ahead to prepare the way, and then return to 'take them to himself'. Not that he needed to—they 'knew the way' already.

This prompted Thomas to interject that as they didn't know where Jesus was actually going, how could they possibly know how to get there? Jesus' reply is one of his great 'I am' sayings: 'I am the way, and the truth, and the life'. Jesus is the way to God (the path that leads to him); he is the truth about God, and he has in him the life of God.

There are many paths to God, but in some way we can't necessarily understand, they all lead to him through Jesus.

13 February

NOT LOSING HEART

So we do not lose heart. Even though our outer nature is wasting away, our inner nature is being renewed day by day. For this slight momentary affliction is preparing us for an eternal weight of glory beyond all measure, because we look not at what can be seen but at what cannot be seen; for what can be seen is temporary, but what cannot be seen is eternal. For we know that if the earthly tent we live in is destroyed, we have a building from God, a house not made with hands, eternal in the heavens.

2 CORINTHIANS 4:16—5:1

The 'we' who do not lose heart are the apostles. Paul has been describing the kind of lives they lived—afflicted, perplexed, persecuted, struck down, given up for death. And he wasn't exaggerating. So far as we can tell, only John escaped eventual execution, and they were all objects of open hostility from the various authorities of the times.

Yet today's passage breathes hope and faith rather than despair or defeat. They do not 'lose heart'—perhaps bearing in mind the words of Jesus from yesterday's reading. Whatever happens to their bodies, their 'real' identities are being constantly renewed. Paul seems to have had a particular and enviable ability to see things in perspective. He describes all this suffering as a 'slight momentary affliction'—simply a preparation for an 'eternal weight of glory' that lay ahead.

He sums up the position in words that might sound like escapism from anybody else, but coming from a man who knew what 'real life' was like, they become a profound statement of faith. The visible world and everything connected with it is temporary. But the 'invisible' world will never become the 'past' because it is, like God, eternal. Our earthly 'tent' (and Paul the tent-maker knew all about them!) will one day decay; but our 'house not made with hands', our heavenly home, is also, like God, eternal.

Paul's words of hope are a healthy corrective to a natural human tendency to be obsessed with the present and ignore the distant scene.

14 February

THE UPLIFTED EYES

I lift up my eyes to the hills—from where will my help come? My help comes from the Lord, who made heaven and earth. He will not let your foot be moved; he who keeps you will not slumber. He who keeps Israel will neither slumber nor sleep. The Lord is your keeper; the Lord is your shade at your right hand. The sun shall not strike you by day, nor the moon by night. The Lord will keep you from all evil; he will keep your life. The Lord will keep your going out and your coming in from this time on and for evermore.
PSALM 121

This is the second of the 'Songs of Ascent' (Psalms 120—134), sung by pilgrims as they made their way to Jerusalem to worship in the temple. Several of them were presumably sung at the start of the journey. Some, like this one, would be sung by those still on the way but within sight of the hills that are such a feature of Jerusalem.

As they journeyed, often for many days or even weeks, the pilgrims may have wondered where the strength they needed could be found. The nations around them tended to worship gods representing various aspects of creation—trees, sun, moon, hills and rivers. But in the pilgrim song, the traveller dismisses such an idea. Their help came from the One who created the hills, 'who made heaven and earth'.

They had a reliable guide for their journey, too. Unlike human escorts, this one never slept so he could watch over them night and day. The Lord would be their 'keeper', providing shade from the noonday sun and protection from the (supposed) dangers of the moon at night. On this journey, and by extension for the whole journey of life, he would keep them from evil, watching over their lives with meticulous care. So a song that begins with a question ('Where will my help come from?') continues with the answer: 'My help comes from the Lord'.

Our 'goings out and comings in' are such a part of everyday life that we may forget to place them into the hands of the one who will 'keep' us through them.

15 February

PEACE THAT THE WORLD CANNOT GIVE

'I have said these things to you while I am still with you. But the Advocate, the Holy Spirit, whom the Father will send in my name, will teach you everything, and remind you of all that I have said to you. Peace I leave with you; my peace I give to you. I do not give to you as the world gives. Do not let your hearts be troubled, and do not let them be afraid… If you loved me, you would rejoice that I am going to the Father, because the Father is greater than I.'

JOHN 14:25–28 (abridged)

I have always felt that 'don't worry' is the most useless piece of advice to give or to receive. After all, we don't choose to worry, and often there really is something to worry about, even if exaggerated by our emotional state. So why did both Jesus and Paul urge us not to worry (Philippians 4:6)?

The difference between the advice of Jesus and Paul and that given to us by well-meaning friends is that on each occasion the former give cogent reasons for it. The apostle offers an alternative therapy—thanksgiving and prayer. Jesus sets his invitation in the context of two wonderful gifts that he was leaving to his anxious disciples. The first was the Holy Spirit, the 'Advocate' who would plead their cause, the one who would teach them all they needed to know. The second was his own peace, *eirene* in Greek (the derivation of the name Irene).

Eirene is a lovely word for a beautiful idea. As well as 'peace', it also conveys ideas of tranquillity, concord, unity. It was 'in Jesus' that they would know real peace, because in that relationship they would be at one with the source of peace and tranquillity. This is what he calls 'the peace that the world cannot give', the kind of inward tranquillity and unity with the Father that marked the whole of Jesus' life.

Jesus never told his disciples that following him would be painless. What he did say is that whatever their circumstances, they could possess his priceless gift of inward peace and tranquillity.

16 February

HOW LONG, O LORD?

How long, O Lord? Will you forget me for ever? How long will you hide your face from me? How long must I bear pain in my soul, and have sorrow in my heart all day long? How long shall my enemy be exalted over me? Consider and answer me, O Lord my God! Give light to my eyes, or I will sleep the sleep of death, and my enemy will say, 'I have prevailed'... But I trusted in your steadfast love; my heart shall rejoice in your salvation. I will sing to the Lord, because he has dealt bountifully with me.
PSALM 13 (abridged)

If we are thinking about 'dark days', they wouldn't appear to get much darker than the psalmist was experiencing here. He was ill, it would appear—very ill, to the point of death, or so he felt, at least. As well as sickness, he felt sorrow and 'pain in [his] soul', and all to the extent that it was public knowledge and his 'enemy' was able to score one over him. It's a pitiful picture, but not remote from normal human experience. We feel rotten; life seems painful and hopeless—and where, we ask plaintively, is the God we've put our trust in? He seems to have forgotten us completely.

Then the voice of complaint becomes the voice of prayer, even if it does have a slightly querulous edge. While he was complaining about God's absence, it's quite possible that the psalmist had also given up praying. Complaint and despair are enemies of faith, and without faith prayer has a hollow ring. Now at last, even in these prickly terms, he is calling once again on God. Perhaps recovery is on the way!

And, of course, it is. These psalms of complaint invariably end with an assertion of trust in God. Here, it is a very strong one, based on God's 'steadfast love', his unchanging 'loving-kindness'. So reassuring is this confession of faith that the psalmist's heart begins to sing again.

This psalm begins with protest, moves into prayer and ends with praise. Honesty before God leads us to cry for his help and then to be thankful that he provides it.

17 February

THE SHARED BURDEN

'Come to me, all you that are weary and are carrying heavy burdens, and I will give you rest. Take my yoke upon you, and learn from me; for I am gentle and humble in heart, and you will find rest for your souls. For my yoke is easy, and my burden is light.'

MATTHEW 11:28–30

Many people know this saying of Jesus from the Anglican Communion service. More than that, it is a promise cherished by millions of Christians across the world, a wonderful invitation to those who 'labour and are heavy laden', as the King James Bible put it.

The crowd who first heard these words would have known all about being 'weary' and carrying heavy burdens. Life was hard, with survival as its bottom line. The men worked in the fields or vineyards, bearing 'the burden of the day and the scorching heat' (Matthew 20:12). The women worked in the home, not only caring for the children but grinding maize, building fires, cooking and serving and cleaning in small, airless homes. The sabbath must literally have been a Godsend, a break from toil and a chance to pause and reflect and enjoy family life together.

So an invitation by Jesus to bring burdens to him would have sounded almost too good to be true. The physical tiredness, and the burdens of responsibility and care for the very young and very old, were familiar elements of daily life. As they brought them to Jesus, the burden wouldn't vanish but would be shared. Like the second ox under a double yoke, their load would be halved. Indeed, the 'gentle and humble' beast to which Jesus likened himself would bear the weight in such a way that the burden would seem 'light' and the yoke 'easy'.

It's hard to think of another saying of Jesus that expresses so perfectly the ideal relationship between the believer and the Saviour.

'Come to me!' It sounds so simple. Why do we find it so difficult?

18 February

A WAY THROUGH THE WILDERNESS

Comfort, O comfort my people, says your God. Speak tenderly to Jerusalem, and cry to her that she has served her term, that her penalty is paid, that she has received from the Lord's hand double for all her sins. A voice cries out: 'In the wilderness prepare the way of the Lord, make straight in the desert a highway for our God. Every valley shall be lifted up, and every mountain and hill be made low; the uneven ground shall become level, and the rough places a plain. Then the glory of the Lord shall be revealed, and all people shall see it together, for the mouth of the Lord has spoken.'
ISAIAH 40:1–5

This reading is immediately recognizable by lovers of Handel's *Messiah*, one of the world's most cherished musical masterpieces. These are in fact the opening words of the second section of Isaiah, in which the returning exiles are given vision and hope for a future blessed by the reign of the Lord God. Historically, they had endured almost a hundred years of constant enemy threat and, finally, the occupation and ransacking of Jerusalem by the Babylonians. Now, however, a new voice sounds—with a new message. Instead of constant calls to repent before it's too late, these are words of comfort and reassurance.

There is a way through the wilderness, but only for those who prepare 'the way of the Lord'. Now that the penalty for past sins has been paid in full, their God will come to deliver them. Their part is to prepare a highway for his triumphant arrival, like the highways of glory prepared for conquering generals after their triumphs. They must make things 'straight', the hills of rebellion and disobedience must be brought low, the hollows of faithlessness and fear must be filled in. Then—but only then—they will see 'the glory of the Lord'.

It is a challenging thought that the Lord comes to us through the wilderness. This is the dusty, hot, oppressive way, but perhaps it is the only way for him to reach his captive people and set them free.

19 February

RIVERS IN THE DESERT

Do not remember the former things, or consider the things of old. I am about to do a new thing; now it springs forth, do you not perceive it? I will make a way in the wilderness and rivers in the desert. The wild animals will honour me, the jackals and the ostriches; for I give water in the wilderness, rivers in the desert, to give drink to my chosen people, the people whom I formed for myself so that they might declare my praise.

ISAIAH 43:18–21

We are still in the prophecies of the second section of Isaiah, the voice of hope after years of oppression and exile. Perhaps the people have been burdened with bad memories or even fears that the dark days will return. Well, they are not to 'remember' them, or 'consider the things of old', because God is about to do a new thing. Indeed, it is imminent, even instant. All they have to do is open their eyes and understand what is happening.

God will do the seemingly impossible: he will make a way in the wilderness and streams in the desert. The people lived in a land where heat, not cold, and drought, not wetness, were perennial problems. The epitome of that heat and dryness was the 'wilderness', the desert that surrounded most of Israel—great tracts where nothing grew, where the rocks were bleached by the beating sun and where mere survival was difficult and at times impossible.

That was how life had felt. For years, survival had been their only goal. The Babylonians had been both the scorching sun of oppression and the drought of spiritual exclusion. Now God calls them to forget the past and to have hope for the future, when even the desert animals, the jackals and ostriches, would honour the Lord and his people would 'declare his praise'.

It's not easy to put the disappointments and failures of the past behind us, but if we don't we may miss the 'new thing' that is about to happen in our lives.

20 February

YEARS THAT THE LOCUSTS HAVE EATEN

O children of Zion, be glad and rejoice in the Lord your God; for he has given the early rain for your vindication, he has poured down for you abundant rain, the early and the later rain, as before. The threshing-floors shall be full of grain, the vats shall overflow with wine and oil. I will repay you for the years that the swarming locust has eaten... my great army, which I sent against you. You shall eat in plenty and be satisfied, and praise the name of the Lord your God.

JOEL 2:23–26a (abridged)

Plagues of locusts are truly terrifying. We have eyewitness accounts of such a plague in Palestine in 1915, when locusts arrived and laid eggs by the thousand. Sixty thousand baby locusts could come from a patch of soil no bigger than a square metre. Once hatched, they crawled some 150m a day, devouring every scrap of vegetation.

Clearly there had recently been such a plague in Judah, which the prophet saw as a moment of judgment by God for the sins of the people. He called on them to repent, first the priests and then the people. They were to call a solemn assembly and then 'cry out to the Lord' (1:14). Then God might stay his hand, call off the locusts and restore peace and prosperity to the land.

It seems that the national act of repentance took place, because today's passage is preceded by the statement that the Lord 'had pity on his people' and would finally remove the 'northern army' (the locusts) from them (2:18, 20). Then, as we read, God promised gladness for the nation. The early and late rains would water the fields. The harvests would be good. The vats would overflow. And, best of all, 'I will repay you for the years that the swarming locust has eaten.' He would do all this so that they would know that he was their God.

'Locust years' are the wasted times, when God was far away and life was empty and meaningless. Yet the Lord can and will restore those years when we turn back to him.

21 February

SEEING CLEARLY

Then Job answered the Lord: 'I know that you can do all things, and that no purpose of yours can be thwarted. "Who is this that hides counsel without knowledge?" Therefore I have uttered what I did not understand, things too wonderful for me, which I did not know. "Hear, and I will speak; I will question you, and you declare to me." I had heard of you by the hearing of the ear, but now my eye sees you; therefore I despise myself, and repent in dust and ashes.'

JOB 42:1–6

The book of Job is a profound look at the problem of human suffering and our response to it, but it is also an extended essay on the futility of seeking knowledge or 'wisdom' without reference to God, who is its only source. At the end of the book, after Job has bombarded the Almighty with complaints and questions following the disasters that overtook him and his family, God answers him 'out of the whirlwind' (38:1). There is to be no more room for dialogue. Job may ask questions, but there must come a time when in humility he simply listens to the voice of his Creator. As this book several times asserts, 'The fear of the Lord is the beginning of wisdom.' Until we give him his true place, our understanding is distorted.

Today's reading is Job's final and humble response to this overwhelming revelation. He admits to God's charge. Yes, he had 'hidden counsel without knowledge'. He had spoken of things beyond him, even daring to question the wisdom of the one who is the source of all wisdom. He admits that he has 'uttered what he did not understand' (join the club, Job!). Because he has now seen God's glory in the wonder of the creation that the Lord has just spread before him, what he had previously only heard about makes sense. As we say, 'seeing is believing'.

To understand anything of the truth of God, we need a massive change of perspective. That's what had happened to Job.

22 February

WAITING PATIENTLY

I waited patiently for the Lord; he inclined to me and heard my cry. He drew me up from the desolate pit, out of the miry bog, and set my feet upon a rock, making my steps secure. He put a new song in my mouth, a song of praise to our God. Many will see and fear, and put their trust in the Lord. Happy are those who make the Lord their trust, who do not turn to the proud, to those who go astray after false gods.

PSALM 40:1–4

To wait patiently sounds so simple, yet for most of us it seems very, very difficult. We hate being kept waiting, whether it's in a post office queue, for a train, or for a friend who's a bad timekeeper. Impatience fuels road rage, inflames pointless anger at innocent officials and employees and raises our blood pressure to dangerous heights.

The psalmist had 'waited patiently for the Lord'. I assume he means that he had asked God for something or cried out to him in a time of trouble, and God 'kept him waiting'. That's true to experience. Monica, the mother of Augustine of Hippo, was impatient for her brilliant son to become a Christian. She had prayed for it ever since he was born, yet here he was, an adult man, public orator in Milan and far away—and still God had not answered her prayer. She went to the house of the local priest and started shouting outside his window, 'Why does God not hear my prayer for Augustine?' Eventually the priest appeared at the window. 'Go away, woman,' he said. 'It is not possible that God has not heard your prayer, and in his own time he will answer it.' And he did, too—as soon as Monica stopped nagging him!

The psalmist had prayed and waited, and now he found himself in a secure place, his heart singing a new song, full of praise and gratitude to God.

The grace of patience does not come easily, yet beyond doubt it is a priceless gift from a God who does not measure time as we do.

23 February

A CLEAN HEART

You desire truth in the inward being; therefore teach me wisdom in my secret heart. Purge me with hyssop, and I shall be clean; wash me, and I shall be whiter than snow. Let me hear joy and gladness; let the bones that you have crushed rejoice. Hide your face from my sins, and blot out all my iniquities. Create in me a clean heart, O God, and put a new and right spirit within me. Do not cast me away from your presence, and do not take your holy spirit from me. Restore to me the joy of your salvation, and sustain in me a willing spirit.

PSALM 51:6–12

By tradition, this poem of contrition is ascribed to King David, written after his adultery (and manslaughter) had been exposed and the judgment of God declared. The preceding verses set out in abject language David's bitter repentance: 'Have mercy on me, O God… blot out my transgressions. Wash me thoroughly from my iniquity and cleanse me from my sin… Against you, you alone, have I sinned, and done what is evil in your sight' (vv. 1–4).

Now he turns to consider how he can rebuild what would once have been called a 'godly lifestyle'—a life lived in the way God requires. For this, David and all of us need 'truth in the inward being' and, perhaps more fundamental than anything else, a 'clean heart', one where a 'new and right spirit' dwells. Outward behaviour, in other words, flows from inward motivation.

There is a lovely Welsh hymn, very popular with rugby crowds, as it happens, that celebrates this 'clean heart'. *Calon lan*—a pure heart—is what the hymn prays for, above anything else. It is the prayer that David uttered in the aftermath of the great moral failure of his life, but it is one that every Christian can make their own. It is the 'clean heart' that keeps the whole person, body, mind and spirit, pure.

'Restore to me the joy of your salvation,' prayed David. Sin does not deprive us of the hope of eventual salvation, but it does take the joy out of it.

24 February

EXPECTATION AND HOPE

It is my eager expectation and hope that I will not be put to shame in any way, but that by my speaking with all boldness, Christ will be exalted now as always in my body, whether by life or by death. For to me, living is Christ and dying is gain. If I am to live in the flesh, that means fruitful labour for me; and I do not know which I prefer. I am hard pressed between the two: my desire is to depart and be with Christ, for that is far better; but to remain in the flesh is more necessary for you.

PHILIPPIANS 1:20–24

When Paul wrote this letter, he was in prison or under house arrest. It might be expected that even the great apostle would have been feeling rather down in these circumstances. However, writing to what would seem to be his 'favourite' church at Philippi, he is positively upbeat.

Before this passage, Paul has assured them that what has happened to him 'has actually helped to spread the gospel, so that it has become known throughout the whole imperial guard and to everyone else that my imprisonment is for Christ' (vv. 12–13). He then goes even further. Death itself will not change anything because, so far as he is concerned, to die and 'be with Christ' is 'far better' even than continuing life. On the other hand, if he lives he will be able to continue to labour 'fruitfully' for them and for the other churches.

The heart of Paul's case is really quite simple: 'living is Christ and dying is gain'. He presumably means that as the centre of his life is his relationship with Christ, when he dies he will be closer to Christ than he could possibly be on earth—not just 'in Christ' (as he usually describes it) but with Christ for all eternity. That is the gain, but it might be a loss for the churches he had planted and the new Christians he cared for so deeply.

'For to me, living is Christ and dying is gain'—a bold statement of faith, but one that expresses the believer's certain hope of resurrection to eternal life.

25 February

THE PLACE OF PEACE

Jesus answered them, 'Do you now believe? The hour is coming, indeed it has come, when you will be scattered, each one to his home, and you will leave me alone. Yet I am not alone because the Father is with me. I have said this to you, so that in me you may have peace. In the world you face persecution. But take courage; I have conquered the world!'

JOHN 16:31–33

These are the final words of Jesus to his disciples in the upper room, where they had gathered on the evening of his betrayal. They had been edgy and nervous, but as he spoke of the promised coming of the Holy Spirit, and of his and the Father's continuing loving care of them in the future, they became less anxious. Finally, they said, 'Now… we believe that you came from God' (v. 30). Today's passage is the response of Jesus to their statement of faith.

At first he seems to throw cold water on it. He warns that the future will not be easy for them, starting with the coming night, when they will run away and leave him (see Mark 14:50). However, whatever troubles and persecutions lay ahead, they could know that in him they could have peace.

The phrase 'in me' speaks of the relationship of dependence between the disciple and the Lord. They 'belong' to Jesus, the good shepherd who defends his flock. While they remain 'in him' they will be safe and secure. That doesn't mean that life will be easy—far from it. However, there would now be a principle at work that would enable them to 'take courage'. The 'world'—the unbelieving, Christ-rejecting society in which the disciples would be called to bear witness—has been conquered. It may seem all-powerful but by his death and resurrection Christ has disarmed it. 'In him' they are victors.

For all of us there will be times when the pressures of the world around us and of events seemingly beyond our control may feel overwhelming. 'Take courage!' says Jesus. 'In me you may have peace… I have conquered the world!'

26 February

MOSES IN THE BULRUSHES

Now a man from the house of Levi went and married a Levite woman. The woman conceived and bore a son... When she could hide him no longer she got a papyrus basket... put the child in it and placed it among the reeds on the bank of the river. His sister stood at a distance, to see what would happen to him. The daughter of Pharaoh... saw the basket among the reeds and sent her maid to bring it. When she opened it, she saw the child. He was crying, and she took pity on him. 'This must be one of the Hebrews' children,' she said. Then his sister said to Pharaoh's daughter, 'Shall I go and get you a nurse from the Hebrew women...?' Pharaoh's daughter said to her, 'Yes.' So the girl went and called the child's mother.

EXODUS 2:1–8 (abridged)

The Hebrews had been welcomed in Egypt after Joseph had helped to save the nation during a time of famine, but now a Pharaoh had come to the throne who 'did not know Joseph' (1:8). For him, these aliens were simply a nuisance. In an attempt to limit their numbers, he ordered that all Hebrew male babies should be killed.

One desperate couple put their son in a makeshift boat and floated it in the reeds at the edge of the Nile. Perhaps they knew that women from the royal palace came to bathe there. At any rate, the Pharaoh's daughter found the baby, and the baby's sister offered to find a Hebrew woman to act as wet nurse for the child. In fact, the results from the family's point of view were even better. The baby was to be taken back to his home, nursed there through infancy, and then taken to the royal court, where the princess would bring him up as her own. She even gave the child a Hebrew name, 'Moses', which means 'I drew him out'.

So the one God had destined to be the human agent of the Hebrews' rescue from slavery was given the advantages of a royal upbringing. The child of Levite parents, the priestly tribe, he was being prepared for a task he did not expect and did not want.

As the hymn writer William Cowper put it, 'God moves in a mysterious way'!

27 February

UNDER THE SHADOW OF THE LORD

You who live in the shelter of the Most High, who abide in the shadow of the Almighty, will say to the Lord, 'My refuge and my fortress; my God, in whom I trust.' For he will deliver you from the snare of the fowler and from the deadly pestilence; he will cover you with his pinions, and under his wings you will find refuge; his faithfulness is a shield and buckler. You will not fear the terror of the night, or the arrow that flies by day, or the pestilence that stalks in darkness, or the destruction that wastes at noonday... Because you have made the Lord your refuge, the Most High your dwelling place, no evil shall befall you, no scourge come near your tent.

PSALM 91:1–6, 9–10

This is a glorious psalm of faith, addressed to those who live 'in the shelter of the Most High'. In a land where temperatures were often very high and the scorching sun was a constant hazard, how refreshing it was to find a place of shelter under a rocky outcrop or a shady olive tree! The 'Most High' is seen as one who offers just such shelter.

In a catalogue of potential hazards of life in those days, the psalmist goes on to celebrate God's ability to shield his people. The fowler's snare, the deadly pestilence, the 'terror of the night' (what could that be?), plague and destruction: each potential catastrophe will not strike terror into the believer's heart, because he knows that the Lord is his refuge and the Most High his dwelling-place.

The psalmist is not suggesting that such dangers don't exist, nor even that God's people will be immune from them. Plague and pestilence, arrows and bombs, night-time terrors and noon-day destruction are sadly part of life as we know it. What he is asserting is that God is not indifferent to our plight, but in the midst of such troubles spreads his shadow of security over us.

Timothy Dudley-Smith's modern-day version of this psalm makes a moving hymn of faith: 'Safe in the shadow of the Lord, Beneath his hand and power, I trust in him, I trust in him, My fortress and my tower.'

28 February

HELP IN THE DARK DAYS

Gracious is the Lord, and righteous; our God is merciful. The Lord protects the simple; when I was brought low, he saved me. Return, O my soul, to your rest, for the Lord has dealt bountifully with you. For you have delivered my soul from death, my eyes from tears, my feet from stumbling. I walk before the Lord in the land of the living. I kept my faith, even when I said, 'I am greatly afflicted'; I said in my consternation, 'Everyone is a liar.' What shall I return to the Lord for all his bounty to me? I will lift up the cup of salvation and call on the name of the Lord, I will pay my vows to the Lord in the presence of all his people.

PSALM 116:5–14

The psalmist has obviously experienced a period either of illness ('the snares of death encompassed me') or a hurtful personal experience ('I said in my consternation, "Everyone is a liar"'). Now he wants to tell everyone how the Lord has blessed him through that time of testing, and to express his gratitude to God for 'all his bounty' to him. His private experience will be an occasion of public testimony—'in the presence of all his people'.

For the writer, God is gracious, righteous and merciful—an interesting combination because it tells us that his grace and mercy are exercised without any dilution of his holiness. We also find here a touching picture of true humility—fancy describing oneself as 'simple' (and the Hebrew word leans towards 'stupid' rather than 'innocent')! He had been brought low by his experience but the Lord rescued him—help in time of darkness indeed. With that blessing behind him, he can rise above whatever clouds had shrouded his life: 'Return, O my soul, to your rest, for the Lord has dealt bountifully with you.' I love the New English Bible version: 'Be at rest once more, my heart!'

Most of us have gone through an experience that has cast a shadow over our lives. Perhaps only then can we know fully the grace of God, who lifts us up.

29 February

SHINING LIKE STARS

Therefore, my beloved... work out your own salvation with fear and trembling, for it is God who is at work in you, enabling you both to will and to work for his good pleasure. Do all things without murmuring and arguing, so that you may be blameless and innocent, children of God without blemish in the midst of a crooked and perverse generation, in which you shine like stars in the world. It is by your holding fast to the word of life that I can boast on the day of Christ that I did not run in vain.
PHILIPPIANS 2:12–16 (abridged)

This 'extra' reading for a leap year picks up the image of Christians as light-bearers in dark places, those who 'hold fast to the word of life' in the midst of a 'crooked and perverse generation'. Paul's language is stronger probably than most of us would use, partly because we have become used to living in a society where God is not very important to most people. Paul, on the other hand, lived in a god-saturated society, although the identity of the 'god' or gods' varied enormously. At the time of this letter, the apostle was under house arrest, probably in Ephesus, and acutely aware that the faith that he lived and preached (and the Philippian Christians bravely professed) was scorned by the dominant culture of the day. This society, in other words, was god-saturated in the sense that almost everyone believed in one god or another, but they rejected the God and Father of the Lord Jesus.

In such a culture, the primary requirement of God's people was to live a blameless life—to 'walk the walk' rather than just 'talk the talk'. So 'murmuring and arguing' are out. They are to live their lives in reverence for God (that's the meaning of 'fear and trembling'), 'working out' in their lives what God has by his grace already 'worked in'.

By doing this, they will 'shine like stars' on a dark night, 'holding fast to the word of life'—the life-giving message of salvation.

Stars don't create light, they reflect it. The light that shines from the life of faith is not its own, but Christ's.

March: Rescue

March is the season of the year when both Judaism and Christianity begin to reflect on the great theme of 'rescue'—deliverance from slavery and evil. For the Jews this is captured in the story of the Passover and exodus, when God brought their ancestors out of slavery in Egypt and set them on the road to the promised land. For Christians, it is the story of the suffering, death and resurrection of Jesus. Both the Passover and the cross were means to an end, and that end was the freedom of God's people.

1 March

A CRY FOR HELP

After a long time the king of Egypt died. The Israelites groaned under their slavery, and cried out. Out of the slavery their cry for help rose up to God. God heard their groaning, and God remembered his covenant with Abraham, Isaac, and Jacob. God looked upon the Israelites, and God took notice of them.

EXODUS 2:23–25

This short passage is full of profound insight into the nature of prayer. No doubt the Israelites had been praying for rescue all through the long years of slavery. As their families shared their evening meal at the end of another gruelling day, they must have called on the God of their fathers to deliver them. As so often, however, their prayers didn't seem to penetrate the roof. It must have felt as if God had forgotten them, stranded in an alien land with no hope of improvement. They were captives of the most powerful, ruthless nation on earth.

The death of a pharaoh must have sparked some hope, however. Perhaps now the God of Isaac, Abraham and Jacob would come and help them? So, while the people of Egypt mourned a royal death, the people of Israel raised their voices to the king of heaven. Part of their prayer consisted of groans—and Paul tells us that God hears 'sighs too deep for words' (Romans 8:26). But the major factor in their prayer was their *need*. It was 'out of their slavery' that their cry rose to God.

Some aspects of life in Egypt were not too bad. The land was fertile. There was food. The present was known, whereas any alternative was unknown and therefore frightening. But now their prayer has a touch of desperation. 'God heard their groaning'—not their eloquence!—and 'remembered his covenant' with their forefathers (not that he had ever forgotten it, of course). Perhaps they knew it, or perhaps they didn't, but their prayers had penetrated the ceiling at last!

We don't have to be desperate or enslaved to pray effectively, but we do need to recognize and admit that we need help from beyond ourselves.

2 March

THE GOD WHO HEARS OUR CRY

Then the Lord said, 'I have observed the misery of my people who are in Egypt; I have heard their cry on account of their taskmasters. Indeed, I know their sufferings, and I have come down to deliver them from the Egyptians, and to bring them up out of that land to a good and broad land, a land flowing with milk and honey... So come, I will send you to Pharaoh to bring my people, the Israelites, out of Egypt.'

EXODUS 3:7–8, 10

Unknown to most of the suffering Hebrews, one of their number was being secretly prepared in the eastern desert lands to be God's agent in answering their cries for help. They had not been forgotten but only the Lord knew the correct timing for their rescue. A certain young man had to grow up, learn the realities of life and face the challenge of the call of God. That man was Moses, the baby in the bulrushes.

Brought up in the royal court, Moses eventually fled to the desert of Midian to avoid being revealed as the killer of an Egyptian taskmaster. Now, living with the family of a Midianite priest, Jethro, he was keeping the family flock and had led it in search of pasture to the foothills of Mount Horeb. There he had an encounter with God that was to change his own life, the lives of his people and, indeed, the whole religious story of the world.

What Moses learned was that God was not deaf! He had heard the prayers of his people in Egypt and had now 'come down to deliver them'. More than that, he would bring them out of Egypt to a promised land 'flowing with milk and honey'. The news must have made Moses' heart beat faster with joy. At last their God was going to act to save them! However, the next words from the Lord must have brought him up short: 'I will send you to Pharaoh to bring my people out of Egypt.' Yes, God would act, but Moses would be his agent.

God's blessing comes through my hands, my lips, my feet. Faced with his call, we can't say, 'Lord, here am I. Send someone else!'

3 March

I AM WHO I AM

But Moses said to God, 'Who am I that I should go to Pharaoh, and bring the Israelites out of Egypt?' He said, 'I will be with you... when you have brought the people out of Egypt, you shall worship God on this mountain.' But Moses said to God, 'If I come to the Israelites and say to them, "The God of your ancestors has sent me to you," and they ask me, "What is his name?" what shall I say to them?' God said to Moses, 'I AM WHO I AM... This is my name for ever, and this my title for all generations.'
EXODUS 3:11–15 (abridged)

God had been preparing Moses for this moment but it seems to have taken Moses himself completely by surprise. 'Why me?' he asked. After all, he had settled in an alien land, Egypt seemed far away, and the land of his distant forefathers, Abraham, Isaac and Jacob, even further.

Yet he knew that it was God, the unseen, infinite deity, who was calling him to an apparently impossible task, to bring the enslaved Israelites out of Egypt to freedom in a new, promised land. Moses heard the words, but the rest of a long dialogue with God (3:13—4:3) consists of his objections and misgivings about the whole project.

We have the first of them here: 'Who am I?' God answered that one very directly: 'I will be with you.' This would be a joint enterprise, human and divine. He need have no hesitation on that score.

The second was more fundamental: 'Who are you?' The answer was a moment of supreme revelation, not just to Moses but in the whole unfolding panorama of faith. The God who was speaking was not some tribal god or mere symbol of deity, but the origin of all being. His name was Yahweh, 'I AM'. The name—used over six thousand times in the Old Testament—is probably based on the Hebrew verb 'to be'. God is permanently present tense. Mortals and tribal gods come and go, but he is 'from everlasting to everlasting' (Psalm 90:2). The one sending Moses was more than capable of enabling him to fulfil the task.

'The one who calls you is faithful, and he will do this' (1 Thessalonians 5:24).

4 March

THE RELUCTANT HERO

But Moses said to the Lord, 'O my Lord, I have never been eloquent... but I am slow of speech and slow of tongue.' Then the Lord said to him, 'Who gives speech to mortals? Who makes them mute or deaf, seeing or blind? Is it not I, the Lord? Now go, and I will be with your mouth and teach you what you are to speak.' But he said, 'O my Lord, please send someone else.'

EXODUS 4:10–13 (abridged)

This dialogue between God and Moses is a wonderful picture of human response to divine call—not an idealized picture, in which the godly subject instantly says 'Yes, Lord' and marches off to do his will, but a more realistic picture of the reluctant recruit dragged kicking and screaming into the place of blessing!

God had already been hard at work getting Moses to this point. First he needed rescuing from the hands of Pharaoh's killing squads as a child. Then his escape from Egypt to Midian had to happen. He had to be brought to Mount Horeb and the burning bush. Outwardly in events, and also inwardly in his own experience and character, Moses had been shaped by God for his purpose—yet when the call came, he wriggled and writhed and objected. 'Who am I?' (3:11). 'Who are you?' (v. 13). 'They won't believe me' (4:1). 'I haven't the eloquence to persuade anybody of anything' (v. 10). Finally, when every objection had been answered, the truth popped out. The real problem was within the man himself: 'O my Lord, please send someone else.'

Moses may have felt that he had finally wriggled off the hook. Far from it! Not only had God anticipated his response, but he had already taken steps to counter it. His brother Aaron, was 'even now' on his way to meet him (v. 14). Before the problem had arisen, God had provided an answer to it. The reluctant hero was trapped!

When we know that God wants us to do something, we may object, delay and even bluntly say 'no'. Yet the God who calls has an uncanny way of getting the answer he wants in the end.

5 March

A PRAYER IN A TIME OF TROUBLE

The Lord answer you in the day of trouble! ... May he send you help from the sanctuary, and give you support from Zion... May he grant you your heart's desire, and fulfil all your plans. May we shout for joy over your victory, and in the name of our God set up our banners. May the Lord fulfil all your petitions. Now I know that the Lord will help his anointed; he will answer him from his holy heaven with mighty victories by his right hand. Some take pride in chariots, and some in horses, but our pride is in the name of the Lord our God.

PSALM 20:1–2, 4–7 (abridged)

This is one of the so-called 'royal' psalms, sung on occasions such as coronations, weddings or, as here, on the eve of a battle. The king was about to lead his people into conflict and the congregation had gathered to pray for blessing on the enterprise. However much we may dislike the military theme, or the very idea of God blessing warriors in battle, the truth is that this was a prayer in a time of desperate need, and also a stirring expression of trust and confidence in God.

So it doesn't seem wrong to apply the hymn to the day-to-day conflicts of life. We all need help and protection in 'the day of trouble'. Our 'heart's desire' may be a restored relationship or healing from sickness, the happiness of a friend or the ending of an injustice. It is very reassuring to hear the prayers of others for us in such situations.

The last verse of our passage expresses a faith that runs throughout the Old Testament. The King James Bible gives the true flavour of it: 'Some trust in chariots, and some in horses: but we will remember the name of the Lord our God'. It was with similar words that David approached his duel with Goliath: 'You come to me with sword and spear and javelin; but I come to you in the name of the Lord of hosts' (1 Samuel 17:45). Perhaps it was for that same David, now king, that this psalm was sung on the eve of a similar conflict.

In 'the day of trouble', we realize how important to us is our trust in the Lord.

6 March

LED INTO THE LIGHT

O send out your light and your truth; let them lead me; let them bring me to your holy hill and to your dwelling. Then I will go to the altar of God, to God my exceeding joy; and I will praise you with the harp, O God, my God. Why are you cast down, O my soul, and why are you disquieted within me? Hope in God; for I shall again praise him, my help and my God.
PSALM 43:3–5

Last month we looked at part of Psalm 42, which seemed to spring from similar circumstances. The writer is far off, oppressed by an unnamed enemy, 'cast down' and 'disquieted'. In the psalmist's case, we may assume that this was a physical separation—exile, perhaps, or simply living in an alien environment—but everything he says could equally well apply to that inner 'far-offness' with which most of us have been familiar at some time. Sometimes spiritual or emotional 'exile' is worse than the physical kind.

In the verse before our passage the psalmist has spoken of a feeling that he has been 'cast off' by God, 'the God in whom I take refuge'. That in itself is a disabling experience. If we have put our trust in God, it is devastating to feel that he has abandoned us.

Here he turns his anxiety into prayer—and a kind of critical self-examination. The prayer is that God will send his light and truth to lead him to the 'holy hill and to your dwelling'—obviously a reference to Mount Zion and the temple in Jerusalem. Far away, he could only hope that one day the Lord would provide both a lantern and a map—'light' and 'truth'. Then he will be able to go to the altar of God, 'to God my exceeding joy'. In praise and thanksgiving the years of separation and pain would be forgotten—as they are, indeed, when friends or families are reunited after long separation. And then the final 'pick-me-up': 'Why are you cast down, O my soul? Hope in God.'

Physical distances cannot separate us from the God of eternity, however we feel. 'Why are you cast down?' Hope in God—who is always there.

7 March

THE TWO PILLARS

They set out from Succoth, and camped at Etham, on the edge of the wilderness. The Lord went in front of them in a pillar of cloud by day, to lead them along the way, and in a pillar of fire by night, to give them light, so that they might travel by day and by night. Neither the pillar of cloud by day nor the pillar of fire by night left its place in front of the people.
EXODUS 13:20–22

These pillars of fire and cloud accompanied the Israelites all through their long wilderness journey to Canaan. This is a description of their first appearance, as they left Egypt and made their way eastwards towards what is usually called the 'Red Sea'.

The whole experience must have been traumatic for the Hebrews. One day they were slaves; the next they were free, and sent on their way with gifts from the Egyptian people, who couldn't wait for them to leave and bring the dreadful plagues to an end. Freedom is one thing. Finding yourself on the edge of a wilderness, with no clear notion as to your destination or how you are going to get there, is another. There would have been babies, children, old people and the infirm, as well as animals. Perhaps there were carts or wheelbarrows, but for the most part it was a journey on foot with burdens to be carried on every back. At the head of the column was this strange new leader, Moses, striding alongside his brother Aaron. They must have hoped he knew what he was doing, because in coldly rational terms this was a crazy enterprise.

But there were the two pillars. Whatever explanation there might be for these phenomena, for the people these pillars were like sacraments —signs of the presence of God with his people. When they stopped, the Lord stopped with them. When they moved, he went with them. They were on a long journey, the two pillars told them, but on that journey they would never be alone.

Jesus promised, 'Remember, I am with you all ways, to the end of the age' (Matthew 28:20, literally).

8 March

CROSSING THE RED SEA

The Lord drove the sea back by a strong east wind all night, and turned the sea into dry land; and the waters were divided. The Israelites went into the sea on dry ground, the waters forming a wall for them on their right and on their left. The Egyptians pursued… Then the Lord said to Moses, 'Stretch out your hand over the sea, so that the water may come back upon the Egyptians…' So Moses stretched out his hand over the sea, and at dawn the sea returned to its normal depth. As the Egyptians fled before it, the Lord tossed the Egyptians into the sea.

EXODUS 14:21–23, 26–27 (abridged)

The crossing of the Red Sea is one of the defining moments in the history of Israel. The Israelites, fleeing from slavery in Egypt under Moses' leadership, were confronted by a watery barrier across their route. Modern-day scholars are fairly sure that it was not the 'Red Sea' as we know it, but the Sea of Reeds, a shallow, reed-filled lake more or less where the Suez Canal now makes its way down to the Red Sea.

As they waited on its shores, Pharaoh once again had a change of mind and sent his renowned charioteers to bring them back. The people could see ahead of them an impassable barrier, behind them an implacable enemy. As panic began to strike, they noticed that the pillar of cloud—the sign of God's presence—had moved from the front of their column to the rear, placing itself between them and the Egyptians.

That night the wind blew strongly from east to west, and in the morning it became clear that a miracle had occurred. The east wind had blown a dry corridor across the lake. 'Tell the Israelites to go forward,' God commanded Moses (v. 15)—and they did, people, carts and animals. The Egyptians, trying to follow, were less fortunate. As they ground to a halt, so the wind dropped—and as Moses stretched out his hand, the waters returned to trap the Egyptians in the lake.

For us, there are often similar though less visible barriers to places of blessing. In every case, the way through the barrier is the guide on the journey.

9 March

THE PROMISED RESCUER

When... Mary had been engaged to Joseph, but before they lived together, she was found to be with child from the Holy Spirit. Her husband Joseph, being a righteous man and unwilling to expose her to public disgrace, planned to dismiss her quietly. But just when he had resolved to do this, an angel of the Lord appeared to him in a dream and said, 'Joseph, son of David, do not be afraid to take Mary as your wife, for the child conceived in her is from the Holy Spirit. She will bear a son, and you are to name him Jesus, for he will save his people from their sins.'
MATTHEW 1:18–21

From the moment when things first went wrong for the human race, back in the garden of Eden, there has been an echo of a promise. God has not ceased to love his self-willed, disobedient children. Faintly at times, and sometimes with astonishing clarity, the voice of hope sounds throughout the Old Testament until, in the prophets like Isaiah and Ezekiel, it becomes a clear and shining promise. God will send a rescuer, a saviour, to bring his rebellious people back to himself.

Now, in the very first chapter of the New Testament, that hope is given a name. The time has come and the first person to learn of it is a village carpenter, Joseph. He is engaged to a girl (probably no more than 14 or 15 years old) named Mary, and she is pregnant. Joseph has been careful to respect her honour—they have not 'lived together'. Even in the face of this shocking discovery, he thinks of her reputation and determines to break off their engagement quietly. Yet now it is revealed that she has not been unfaithful to him. Her baby is none other than the long-promised 'rescuer'. He is to be named Jesus—*Yeshua* in Hebrew—because 'he will save his people from their sins'.

So when the mighty deliverer comes, he will not be an armed angelic warrior but a tiny baby born to a carpenter and his wife.

As a child I used to sing a chorus: 'He did not only come to seek—it was to save he came. And when we call him "Saviour" then we call him by his name.'

10 March

A MIGHTY SAVIOUR

'Blessed be the Lord God of Israel, for he has looked favourably on his people and redeemed them. He has raised up a mighty saviour for us in the house of his servant David, as he spoke through the mouth of his holy prophets from of old, that we would be saved from our enemies and from the hand of all who hate us. Thus he has shown the mercy promised to our ancestors, and has remembered his holy covenant, the oath that he swore to our ancestor Abraham, to grant us that we, being rescued from the hands of our enemies, might serve him without fear, in holiness and righteousness before him all our days.'

LUKE 1:68–75

We have already reflected on some later verses from this song of Zechariah, celebrating the birth of his son, who would become John the Baptist, herald and forerunner of the 'mighty saviour'. The language and thought patterns are very much those of the Hebrew psalmists and prophets, but the theme is strikingly, daringly new. What was now being seen was nothing less than the fulfilment of the promises God made to 'our ancestors'—specifically to Abraham, when God swore by an oath that through him all the nations of the earth would be blessed.

All the language of deliverance is here. God has moved to 'redeem' his people—buy them back from slavery and set them free. He has sent this 'mighty saviour' to do it—to 'rescue us from the hands of our enemies' and enable us to 'serve him without fear'. All of this is to fulfil his promises enshrined in his 'holy covenant', a binding agreement sealed with an oath. This is indeed the language of rescue, which is a large part of what 'salvation' means. We are not just plucked from danger, but set free for a new life of faith, without fear, holy and righteous.

Of these great promises one child, John, was to be the herald, and the other, Jesus, the fulfiller.

11 March

RESCUED FROM TROUBLE

O magnify the Lord with me, and let us exalt his name together. I sought the Lord, and he answered me, and delivered me from all my fears. Look to him, and be radiant; so your faces shall never be ashamed. This poor soul cried, and was heard by the Lord, and was saved from every trouble... O taste and see that the Lord is good; happy are those who take refuge in him.

PSALM 34:3–6, 8

This beautiful psalm takes us back to a foundational principle of the scriptures, that God alone is the protector and saviour of his people. When we read about 'salvation' in the New Testament, we should remember that this is where it started. When we are in trouble, whether brought about by human enemies, disease, danger, poverty or those nameless dreads that can haunt the imagination, the Lord God is our source of deliverance and security.

Clearly the psalmist has experienced this, and so deep is his gratitude that he can't keep it to himself: 'O magnify the Lord with me, and let us exalt his name together'. In a time of trouble he had 'sought the Lord', and God had answered him, delivering him from all his fears. The writer describes himself as a 'poor soul' (either the language of self-pity or a frank admission of the state he had been in), yet God had heard his prayer and saved him from 'every trouble'.

That is his witness to the goodness and graciousness of God. What is so infectious about this psalm, however, is the way he uses his own experience of grace to encourage others to seek the same blessing. People spend fortunes on things that they believe will make them look 'radiant' (it's one of the favourite words of advertisers!), yet this invitation seems so simple and is available to those who are 'poor' in spirit. 'Look to him'—look away from yourself, stop wallowing in it, let the light of God light up your face.

'Taste and see that the Lord is good.' Try him—you won't be disappointed.

12 March

FOR ALL THE PEOPLE

And there were in the same country shepherds abiding in the field, keeping watch over their flock by night. And, lo, the angel of the Lord came upon them, and the glory of the Lord shone round about them; and they were sore afraid. And the angel said unto them, Fear not: for behold, I bring you good tidings of great joy, which shall be to all people. For unto you is born this day in the city of David a Saviour, which is Christ the Lord… And suddenly there was with the angel a multitude of the heavenly host praising God, and saying, Glory to God in the highest, and on earth peace, good will toward men.

LUKE 2:8–11, 13–14 (KJV)

If we're thinking about rescuers, this account is an essential and unique part of the story. The Messiah ('Christ') has come, and from now on the world has a universal saviour, one 'for all the people'.

We're accustomed to hearing this passage read at carol services, often as part of that wonderful unfolding narrative recorded in the service of Nine Lessons and Carols. First the fall, then the prophecies of the promised Saviour, and now, on a hillside outside Bethlehem—'the city of David'—the first news of the birth of 'a Saviour, who is Christ the Lord'. The message came to a group of shepherds, the most humble members of society, disregarded very often because (as we saw in an earlier reading) their duties prevented them from fulfilling their religious obligations. Yet to them the wonderful news was broken.

This Saviour was both for them and for everybody. They received both a personal message and an astonishing piece of general news. Always the message of the Saviour has those two elements. That Jesus Christ was born is wonderful news, of historic significance for the human race, and true whether anyone believes it or not. But it is also life-changing news for each individual who receives it and believes it.

In Jesus, God shows his gracious favour towards humans. That is the literal meaning of the song: 'Peace on earth, for those on whom God's favour rests'.

13 March

NO ALTERNATIVE

Assemble yourselves and come together, draw near, you survivors of the nations! They have no knowledge—those who carry about their wooden idols, and keep on praying to a god that cannot save. Declare and present your case; let them take counsel together! Who told this long ago? Who declared it of old? Was it not I, the Lord? There is no other god besides me, a righteous God and a Saviour; there is no one besides me. Turn to me and be saved, all the ends of the earth! For I am God, and there is no other.

ISAIAH 45:20–22

Lady Thatcher had a catchphrase that she called TINA—'there is no alternative'. Whether that is a profound political truth or not, it is certainly a great theme of the Bible. There is no other god but Yahweh, the Eternal One, and consequently there is no other Saviour.

The argument goes like this. There is one Creator, the source of everything that exists. Of that creation he is the Wisdom—its meaning and purpose. Without him, the whole of existence is pointless. To live as though there is no Creator, and hence no meaning or purpose to the universe, or—even worse—to think that we know better than our Creator, is to live blinded to the truth about our condition. It is God who gives meaning and purpose to what he has made, and it is God who knows what is best for his creatures.

Thus, for creatures to create objects to worship and even call them 'gods' is a ludicrous exercise. There is a God—the invisible, eternal and almighty Creator. To him alone we owe reverence and worship, and through him alone we can be saved from the consequences of our own sins and failures. So, 'turn to me and be saved, all the ends of the earth!' 'There is no other god besides me, a righteous God and a Saviour; there is no one besides me.' There is no alternative!

This wonderful call of the prophet goes far beyond Israel, to 'the ends of the earth'. God longs for all of his creatures, made in his image, to turn to him and be saved.

14 March

RESCUED AND HONOURED

The glory of Lebanon shall come to you, the cypress, the plane, and the pine, to beautify the place of my sanctuary... The descendants of those who oppressed you shall come bending low to you, and all who despised you shall bow down at your feet; they shall call you the City of the Lord, the Zion of the Holy One of Israel. Whereas you have been forsaken and hated, with no one passing through, I will make you majestic forever, a joy from age to age. You shall suck the milk of nations, you shall suck the breasts of kings; and you shall know that I, the Lord, am your Saviour and your Redeemer, the Mighty One of Jacob.

ISAIAH 60:13–16 (abridged)

To appreciate passages like this, which have a strong whiff of national triumph about them, we have to understand the Israelites' situation. Originally chosen by the Lord God to be his representatives among the nations of the earth, they found themselves instead at the mercy of the surrounding powers, a defeated, occupied, enslaved people. It was hard for them to retain their faith in the God of their forefathers.

Even worse, the prophets claimed that they had brought all this upon themselves by their failure to honour God's commandments. Having flirted with the pagan practices of their neighbours, they were now their neighbours' subjects. They were a pathetic shadow of the people led by David and Solomon in their days of glory.

Yet here in Isaiah, there is a message of hope. They have paid for their sins. Their God will come to save them. And when he does, it will demonstrate to the unbelieving world that he is the only true Saviour. The proud nations who had conquered them would come 'bending low' before them and acknowledge that Israel itself is 'the city of the Lord'. The once-despised people will draw new strength from their former oppressors—'sucking their breasts', as the prophet puts it.

The promise of God to his people does not change, whatever their present circumstances. He destines them to be 'a joy from age to age'.

15 March

A SAVING TOUCH

She came up behind him and touched the fringe of his clothes, and immediately her haemorrhage stopped. Then Jesus asked, 'Who touched me? ... Someone touched me; for I noticed that power had gone out from me.' When the woman saw that she could not remain hidden, she came trembling; and falling down before him, she declared... why she had touched him, and how she had been immediately healed. He said to her, 'Daughter, your faith has made you well; go in peace.'

LUKE 8:44–48 (abridged)

This is the last part of a longer story—the healing of a desperate woman who had had a haemorrhage for twelve years. The Mosaic Law insisted that a woman with any 'issue of blood' was impure and therefore cut off from normal relations with her husband—and from attendance at the temple. Doctors had been unable to help her but she hoped that this healer from Nazareth might be the answer. Pushing through the surrounding crowd, she stretched out and simply touched the fringe of his garment. Instantly she felt herself to be healed.

Jesus knew that 'power had gone out' from him—the only indication in the Gospels that his healing ministry was costly and draining. He called her out, not for condemnation but to confirm that through her faith she had not only been cured but made 'whole' (the meaning of the Greek word used here). She had experienced 'salvation'—wholeness, true health of body, mind and spirit.

This story shows Jesus as the Saviour of the marginalized: this poor woman was a social outcast. It shows that he ignored religious taboos: according to the Law he should have gone straight to the temple for cleansing. Instead, he went on to the house of a synagogue official and healed his daughter. And it shows that when Jesus heals, he does the job thoroughly—making people 'whole'.

Jesus 'saves' everyone who turns to him. All we bring to him is our need, not our social or religious credentials.

16 March

THE APPLE OF HIS EYE

I call upon you, for you will answer me, O God; incline your ear to me, hear my words. Wondrously show your steadfast love, O saviour of those who seek refuge from their adversaries at your right hand. Guard me as the apple of the eye; hide me in the shadow of your wings, from the wicked who despoil me, my deadly enemies who surround me.

PSALM 17:6–9

The writer of this psalm seems torn between several conflicting emotions. Initially he is trying to persuade God that he should 'attend to his cry' because of his good behaviour: 'My steps have held fast to your paths' (v. 5). At the end his prayer becomes quite violent: 'Rise up, O Lord, confront them, overthrow them!' (v. 13). In between, there is this beautiful song celebrating God's steadfast love and expressing the psalmist's trust in his protection.

Before we write the psalmist off as someone who simply doesn't know his own mind, we might care to reflect on the range of emotions most of us are capable of encompassing in the space of a few minutes of prayer and reflection. Yes, we may at times feel good about ourselves, even smugly self-righteous. Yes, we may feel real anger at the way people treat us. And at the same time, we may in our heart of hearts recognize that God is our only security and refuge. As we have seen, the great thing about the psalms is their honesty, and that is the one thing above everything else that God looks for in our prayers.

Most important, though, is to recognize in all these situations that our hope is in the God who made us and loves us. We can be 'the apple of his eye'. That's a vivid phrase, suggesting that we are the 'pupil', the centre of his vision. The eye that sees the sparrow fall (Matthew 10:29) watches over his precious people, too.

When you look into someone's pupil you see a tiny reflection of yourself. The Hebrew word for 'pupil' can also mean 'little man'. God sees us as his little ones, right in the centre of his vision and of his love and concern.

17 March

FROM DEATH TO LIFE

And just as Moses lifted up the serpent in the wilderness, so must the Son of Man be lifted up, that whoever believes in him may have eternal life. For God so loved the world that he gave his only Son, so that everyone who believes in him may not perish but may have eternal life. Indeed, God did not send the Son into the world to condemn the world, but in order that the world might be saved through him.

JOHN 3:14–17

Some years ago I invited groups of people on various occasions to summarize the gospel in no more than 25 words. Some (not many) spotted that 25 is more or less the number of words in John 3:16, but almost every group's summary was close to a paraphrase of that verse. The distilled wisdom of over 2000 people drawn from every Christian tradition showed that Christians do agree about the heart of the faith.

And this is it! Using as an example the story of the Israelites in the wilderness faced with a plague of snakes (Numbers 21:6–9), it asserts that God loved our world in such a way that he gave his only Son to death on the cross to rescue us from the consequences of our disobedience and sin and give us eternal life. Like the brass serpent on a pole that Moses paraded through the camp, Jesus would be 'lifted up' on the cross to bring healing and life to those who trusted in him.

God's love doesn't come and go with his people's fickleness and failure. He remains faithful, even if we are faithless (2 Timothy 2:13), because it is his nature. So God demonstrates his love for us by giving his Son to death on the cross.

I sometimes wish verse 17 were as popular as verse 16! Many people think of Christianity as a religion of judgment and condemnation, when in fact it is a religion of forgiveness and salvation. God did not send his Son to condemn, but to save.

'Eternal life' is not simply life that goes on for ever but life 'in all its fullness' (John 10:10, REB).

18 March

COMING TO YOUR HELP

There is none like unto the God of Jeshurun, who rideth upon the heaven in thy help, and in his excellency on the sky. The eternal God is thy refuge, and underneath are the everlasting arms: and he shall thrust out the enemy from before thee; and shall say, Destroy them. Israel then shall dwell in safety alone: the fountain of Jacob shall be upon a land of corn and wine… Happy art thou, O Israel: who is like unto thee, O people saved by the Lord, the shield of thy help, and who is the sword of thy excellency!
DEUTERONOMY 33:26–29A (KJV, abridged)

It must be admitted that this text has proved a minefield for translators because the Hebrew text is unclear. This explains why the NRSV is so different from the King James Version printed above—and it's a pity, because this passage contains one of the best-loved phrases in scripture ('underneath are the everlasting arms'), which has provided comfort and security to countless people down the years.

I have chosen the traditional wording because it is as likely to be correct as any other translation, and it certainly encapsulates a great truth: when we are in danger or despair, the Lord comes to us across our sea of troubles. More than that, he provides 'refuge' until the storm blows itself out, and the reassurance that his 'arms' are upholding us.

Again, these encouraging words come to us in the heart of a passage of almost ferocious nationalism, in which the Lord God promises to drive out all of Israel's enemies. They were indeed a beleaguered nation, surrounded by foes, and it must have been wonderful to have this picture of God riding through the skies to their rescue, rather like the US Cavalry in those old movies! Because God was their deliverer, they could live in safety in a land rich with grain and wine. Because he was their Saviour, their shield (of defence) and their sword (of battle), they could be happy in the place he had provided for them.

The same God 'rides' to our rescue; the same God is our Saviour. The same God enables us to live by resting on the unseen 'everlasting arms'.

19 March

HEALING FOR THE BROKEN-HEARTED

The eyes of the Lord are on the righteous, and his ears are open to their cry. The face of the Lord is against evildoers, to cut off the remembrance of them from the earth. When the righteous cry for help, the Lord hears, and rescues them from all their troubles. The Lord is near to the broken-hearted, and saves the crushed in spirit. Many are the afflictions of the righteous, but the Lord rescues them from them all.

PSALM 34:15–19

These days, we don't really like the word 'righteous'. Probably the most common use of the word is hyphenated—'self-righteous'—and that's certainly not a compliment. Yet in the Bible 'righteous' is an important and valued word. God is righteous by his very nature: he does what is right. And his people are called to be righteous, which means, put simply, to do what God requires. The righteous, in the language of the psalmist, are not miserable, tight-lipped, self-righteous puritans, but those 'whose way is blameless, who walk in the law of the Lord' (Psalm 119:1).

The contrast is with the 'evildoers'. In both cases the emphasis is on behaviour, not belief or attitude. God's people show their allegiance to him by the lives they lead, by being 'righteous'. Those who oppose or reject God also show it by their actions: they do what is evil.

God is close to the righteous, so that when they cry for help he hears and answers them. Being righteous—doing right—is often costly, and 'many are their afflictions', but 'the Lord rescues them from them all'. In truth, God has a special concern for those who are down: 'the Lord is near to the broken-hearted'. The experience of many believers tells us that we often feel the presence of God most strongly when our hearts are broken (by bereavement, for example) or our spirits crushed by circumstances.

Jesus said, 'Blessed are the poor in spirit, for theirs is the kingdom of heaven' (Matthew 5:3). Sometimes, to see God clearly we need to go down, not up.

20 March

SENT BY THE FATHER

By this we know that we abide in him and he in us, because he has given us of his Spirit. And we have seen and do testify that the Father has sent his Son as the Saviour of the world. God abides in those who confess that Jesus is the Son of God, and they abide in God... God is love, and those who abide in love abide in God, and God abides in them.

1 JOHN 4:13–16 (abridged)

'The Father has sent his Son as the Saviour of the world': that is another succinct summary of the Christian gospel. The story of the Bible is of an unfolding divine purpose. It doesn't run according to a rigid road-map, because human beings, with all their faults and foibles, are involved, but it does wind like a thread through the unfolding history of Israel and then broadens into a cosmic answer to a cosmic problem. The world is off the rails and God's purpose is to get it back on again—indeed, to ensure that the final outcome is even better than the garden where the story began.

The vital link is the sending of Jesus, the Son of God, to save the human race from its folly. The essential motivation is simply the love of God, and the inner spark that moves rebellious hearts to respond to that love and that saving act is the Holy Spirit of God, given to those who believe. So salvation is truly a trinitarian concept. Father, Son and Spirit combine as one (which they are) to bring about salvation.

The other powerful truth here is hidden in the same verse. Jesus was sent as the Saviour of 'the world'. This repeats a belief expressed by John earlier in this letter: '[Jesus] is the atoning sacrifice for... the sins of the whole world' (2:2). When we say that Jesus Christ died for 'us', we don't just mean for Christians but for everyone. The blood of Jesus shed on the cross is more than adequate to cover the sins of every person who has ever lived. Whoever believes in him is forgiven.

We abide—'make our home'—in God, and he abides in us. We put our trust in him and he, amazingly, takes the risk of putting his trust in us.

21 March

UP TO MY NECK IN TROUBLES

Save me, O God, for the waters have come up to my neck. I sink in deep mire, where there is no foothold… My eyes grow dim with waiting for my God… But as for me, my prayer is to you, O Lord. At an acceptable time, O God, in the abundance of your steadfast love, answer me. With your faithful help rescue me from sinking in the mire; let me be delivered from my enemies and from the deep waters. Do not let the flood sweep over me, or the deep swallow me up, or the Pit close its mouth over me. Answer me, O Lord, for your steadfast love is good; according to your abundant mercy, turn to me.

PSALM 69:1–3, 13–16 (abridged)

This sounds like the prayer of a desperate man, out of his depth in deep waters and feeling very sorry for himself. It may be that he was ill, even on the verge of death. At any rate, the reference to 'the Pit' (the grave, *Sheol*) suggests that. On the other hand, he is troubled by enemies and all but submerged in a situation beyond his control.

This is a psalm for anyone who feels that life has got on top of them, or illness or the antagonism of others has sapped their spirits. It's not hard to identify with the poor man as he describes his condition. Perhaps significantly, he claims that it is 'zeal for God's house' that has consumed him (v. 9). There may well be occasions when our concern for the church or our personal responsibilities in it become a burden rather than a joy.

Where does he find an answer? Why, in the nature of the God on whom he is so desperately calling. Once again, in a phrase constantly on the lips of the psalmists, he appeals to God's 'steadfast love', which shows itself in 'abundant mercy' and 'faithful help'. When he feels weak and helpless, his strong tower supports him. When he is sinking, unseen hands deliver him from the watery depths.

The Psalms show life in every facet—joy, but also anxiety, fear and despair. And through it all shines the loving-kindness of the Lord.

22 March

COMPASSION FOR THE CROWD

Then Jesus went about... teaching in their synagogues, and proclaiming the good news of the kingdom, and curing every disease... When he saw the crowds, he had compassion for them, because they were harassed and helpless, like sheep without a shepherd. Then he said to his disciples, 'The harvest is plentiful, but the labourers are few; therefore ask the Lord of the harvest to send out labourers into his harvest.'

MATTHEW 9:35–38 (abridged)

This passage is like a brief video clip of the whole ministry of Jesus. We can see him moving from place to place, always taking the opportunity of slipping into the local synagogue and addressing the assembled congregation. We can hear his message—the 'good news' that the time had come, God was calling them, the gates of a new regime of love and justice were open. We can watch him bending over the sick and healing them, touching the lepers and making them whole, laying his hands on the blind to restore their sight.

And there were the crowds: hundreds of people who flocked to see and hear him, perhaps in hope of a miracle for themselves or a loved one. They were mostly ordinary, poor people, living under enemy occupation but probably more worried about daily survival—food for the table, water for the animals, rain for the fields. They were leaderless and confused—'harassed and helpless', in Matthew's vivid phrase, 'like sheep without a shepherd'. Yet here was the good shepherd himself, longing to draw them into the fold of his Father's love.

The phrase 'he had compassion' is weak compared with the word used by the Gospel writer. 'His stomach turned over at the sight' might be nearer its literal meaning. His response was to call his disciples to prayer for more 'labourers' to gather in this waiting harvest of hope.

In the next chapter, Jesus tells the disciples that they are the answer to their own prayer! They were to go and heal the sick, bring hope to the crowds and share the good news with them. So often, our prayers are also a call to action.

23 March

THE LAMB OF GOD

They asked him, 'Why then are you baptizing if you are neither the Messiah, nor Elijah, nor the prophet?' John answered them, 'I baptize with water. Among you stands one whom you do not know, the one who is coming after me; I am not worthy to untie the thong of his sandal.' ... The next day he saw Jesus coming towards him and declared, 'Here is the Lamb of God who takes away the sin of the world!'

JOHN 1:25–27, 29

John the Baptist was a notable figure who had made his base in the Jordan valley, where he preached powerfully, calling on people to repent of their sins and show that they intended to lead a new life in line with God's commandments by being baptized by him in the river. Vast numbers flocked to hear him and, not surprisingly many assumed that he was yet another claimant to the role of the promised Messiah, the servant of God sent to rescue his people and restore Israel.

John firmly rejected that notion, which led the scribes who had come from Jerusalem to 'investigate' him to enquire why he was acting like a Messiah if he wasn't one. Here is John's answer. He had already explained that he was simply the 'voice crying in the wilderness' (Isaiah 40:3), but now he spoke of one 'coming after me', a person who stood among them unrecognized, one whose sandals John was not worthy to untie. Doubtless John's followers took note of his words.

Their curiosity about this anonymous deliverer would have been heightened the very next day. John saw Jesus and told his disciples, 'Here is the Lamb of God who takes away the sin of the world'—words familiar to many from the Communion service. The disciples' minds would have gone to the Jerusalem temple, where lambs were sacrificed on the altar all day long for the sins of the people. However, John was telling them that the sacrifice of this 'lamb' would achieve more than that. It would be sufficient to take away the sin of the whole world.

'Lamb of God, who takes away the sin of the world, grant us peace.'

24 March

FREED FROM FEAR OF DEATH

Since, therefore, the children share flesh and blood, [Jesus] himself likewise shared the same things, so that through death he might destroy the one who has the power of death, that is, the devil, and free those who all their lives were held in slavery by the fear of death... Therefore he had to become like his brothers and sisters in every respect, so that he might be a merciful and faithful high priest in the service of God, to make a sacrifice of atonement for the sins of the people.

HEBREWS 2:14–15, 17

One of the issues much debated by the early Church was the nature of Christ. Was he a 'god' visiting this planet in human disguise? Or was he an extraordinarily holy and wise human being—a prophet, but not divine? Between those two positions the argument raged for at least three centuries—and it still does.

The apostles and their close associates (among whom we must number the writer of this anonymous letter to the Hebrews) were in no doubt. The Jesus of the apostolic eyewitnesses was both fully human and fully divine. Without being less than a normal first-century Jewish man, Jesus was much more than that. He was, and is, the Son of God. Sometimes the New Testament writers are more concerned to assert his divinity, sometimes his humanity, but both are seen as essential elements of the second person of the Trinity.

Here the writer emphasizes that Jesus was truly human. Otherwise, he could not have identified fully with God's human children in their exposure to sin and temptation and their experience of death. God's Son was one of us, so he experienced temptation and death itself, and conquered them. By identifying with us, he can offer as our 'high priest' a sacrifice for our sins and free us from slavery to the fear of death.

'He had to become like his brothers and sisters in every respect.' There is the heart of what is called the 'incarnation', the coming of the Son of God into our fearful and sinful world.

25 March

THE ONE MEDIATOR

I urge that supplications, prayers, intercessions, and thanksgivings should be made for everyone, for kings and all who are in high positions, so that we may lead a quiet and peaceable life in all godliness and dignity. This is right and is acceptable in the sight of God our Saviour, who desires everyone to be saved and to come to the knowledge of the truth. For there is one God; there is also one mediator between God and humankind, Christ Jesus, himself human, who gave himself a ransom for all.

1 TIMOTHY 2:1–6

There are earthly rulers, says Paul, and we should pray for them, so that our lives may be 'quiet and peaceable'. But there is one ruler who is over them all, whose purpose is nothing less than that everyone should come to know the truth and be saved.

Paul then summarizes the way in which this salvation is brought about. First, there is 'one God'. Christians do not believe in a multiplicity of deities, as did the Greeks and Romans of the time. That God is also utterly holy and pure, whereas we, his human creatures, are manifestly not. Second, 'there is one mediator between God and humankind'. A mediator is a go-between, a living bridge between two estranged positions. We are familiar with the word from reports of industrial disputes; the ideal mediator in those circumstances would be somebody with experience both of management and shopfloor employment, who could understand and represent both positions.

The mediator between God and us is now identified: 'Christ Jesus'. His qualifications are perfect, for he was 'himself human' but also the Son of God. He can represent us to the Father (as a human being) and the Father to us (as divine). This mediator goes even further, however. He not only bridges the gulf between sinful humanity and its holy Creator, but he himself paid the price to end the dispute.

The cross of Jesus, our mediator, bridges the vast gap between our fallen race and its Creator.

26 March

SAVED BY GRACE

But God, who is rich in mercy, out of the great love with which he loved us even when we were dead through our trespasses, made us alive together with Christ—by grace you have been saved—and raised us up with him and seated us with him in the heavenly places in Christ Jesus, so that in the ages to come he might show the immeasurable riches of his grace in kindness towards us in Christ Jesus. For by grace you have been saved through faith, and this is not your own doing; it is the gift of God—not the result of works, so that no one may boast.

EPHESIANS 2:4–9

Remember that there was no punctuation in the original manuscripts of Paul's letters, and you may get the feel of this passage. So excited is he by the whole idea of 'grace' that he becomes almost incoherent. Sentences get interrupted; lovely phrases are tossed in as parentheses ('by grace you have been saved') and the whole thing bubbles along to its climax, 'the gift of God—not the result of works, so that no one may boast'. Fully to appreciate it, we have to share fully Paul's delight at this rediscovery of a transforming truth. 'Salvation', being made whole, is not a DIY job. It is the most generous gift of a gracious God.

The key words are 'grace' and 'works', and they are often grievously misunderstood. To say that we are saved by the grace of God is not to say that we are inert tools in his hands. To say that 'works' cannot save us is not to say that it doesn't matter how we behave. By 'grace' Paul meant the motivation and drive of our salvation. It was God's idea, not ours, and he has carried it out in Christ. There is no more for humans to do than trust in the Saviour. At the same time, this salvation is a transforming event. Those thus saved are 'created in Christ Jesus for good works' (v. 10). What we are (in Christ) determines what we do, just as what we do reveals the extent of the work of God's grace in us.

God brought us to life in Christ out of his 'great love', even though we were 'dead through our trespasses'. Undeserved blessing is the meaning of grace.

27 March

GOD OUR REFUGE

God is our refuge and strength, a very present help in trouble. Therefore we will not fear, though the earth should change, though the mountains shake in the heart of the sea; though its waters roar and foam, though the mountains tremble with its tumult. There is a river whose streams make glad the city of God, the holy habitation of the Most High. God is in the midst of the city; it shall not be moved.

PSALM 46:1–5A

The other day, I was standing on a traffic island as cars, buses and lorries roared past me on both sides. Nevertheless, I felt safe—and it was then I remembered that traffic islands are also called 'refuges', places of security and safety. This psalm is a celebration of God who is our 'refuge and strength, a very present help in trouble'. Even if the earth changes, God does not change. The people of ancient Israel lived in fear of the sea, but even if it 'roars and foams' and the mountains 'tremble with its tumult' everything will be all right.

The psalmist also understands how this could be true. It is because God is in the midst of the city—in fact, a reference to the temple. In the city of God stands the 'holy habitation of the Most High'. The temple spoke to ancient Israel of the unfailing presence of the God of all the earth. He dwelt among them and watched over them. They were not so naïve as to think that the Creator of the universe actually lived in a building constructed by human hands—a point Solomon made clear at the dedication of the first temple (see 1 Kings 8:27). But the holy building was a symbol to them of the presence of their invisible and almighty God—an outward sign of an inward truth. That was why they should not fear. They could be safe within the refuge he provided.

In contrast to the dark waters of the deep, which may threaten to overwhelm us, 'there is a river whose streams make glad the city of God'. We can trace that same divine stream through scripture to Jesus himself (John 7:38) and finally to the new Jerusalem (Revelation 22:1).

28 March

REMEMBERING THE RESCUE

Moses said to the people, 'Remember this day on which you came out of Egypt, out of the house of slavery, because the Lord brought you out from there by strength of hand; no leavened bread shall be eaten... When the Lord brings you into the land of the Canaanites, the Hittites, the Amorites, the Hivites, and the Jebusites, which he swore to your ancestors to give you, a land flowing with milk and honey, you shall keep this observance in this month... You shall tell your child on that day, "It is because of what the Lord did for me when I came out of Egypt." ... You shall keep this ordinance at its proper time from year to year.'

EXODUS 13:3, 5, 8, 10

Remembering is an important part of being human. Our ability to remember not simply where food is to be found or the nearest watering hole or where to fly in the winter, but people, events and ideas, is one of the distinguishing marks of humanity. The tragedy of Alzheimer's disease is the loss of that precious attribute.

In the Bible there are things we are commanded by God to remember. We are to 'remember your creator in the days of your youth' (Ecclesiastes 12:1), and to 'remember the sabbath day, and keep it holy' (Exodus 20:8). We are to 'remember the Lord your God', and specifically by keeping his commandments (Deuteronomy 8:11–18). In today's reading, the Israelites are commanded to remember the day that God brought them out of slavery and set them on the path to the promised land. This the Jewish people have done for three millennia, by faithfully keeping the Passover festival, in which those events are thankfully remembered. They eat unleavened bread, like their forefathers, and drink a cup of remembrance. They eat bitter herbs and retell the story. It's safe to say that while they do so, they will never forget where they have come from and who brought them out.

Human beings have the gift of remembering but also the tendency to forget. When life feels cold and bleak, we can recall past blessings and take heart.

29 March

REMEMBERING THE SAVIOUR

For I received from the Lord what I also handed on to you, that the Lord Jesus on the night when he was betrayed took a loaf of bread, and when he had given thanks, he broke it and said, 'This is my body that is for you. Do this in remembrance of me.' In the same way he took the cup also, after supper, saying, 'This cup is the new covenant in my blood. Do this, as often as you drink it, in remembrance of me.' For as often as you eat this bread and drink the cup, you proclaim the Lord's death until he comes.

1 CORINTHIANS 11:23–26

This is an account of the institution of Holy Communion. It's significant that the event Paul recounts took place at a Passover meal, thus linking two acts of deliverance from slavery—the Israelites from Egypt, and those who trust in Christ from the bondage of sin. As the disciples joined in the meal, Jesus changed the traditional words, probably causing astonishment and shock to his hearers. Suddenly the unleavened bread became his body, given for them. The final cup of wine, traditionally kept for the coming Messiah, became his blood, shed for the forgiveness of sins. And the whole action was to be repeated by Christians down the ages, 'in remembrance of me'.

Like the Jewish people, we have a 'Passover' to celebrate: not our deliverance from a cruel Pharaoh but from the destructive power of our own rebellion and sin. We are to do this in remembrance of Jesus—and to do it often. As the bread is consumed and the wine drunk, what Jesus did once becomes part of us now. We are not passive spectators but participants. And the key to it is 'remembrance'. Yes, it happened long ago in a faraway land, but what Jesus did then shapes who and what we are now, and in remembering we are bringing that past event into our present lives.

It is a good idea, perhaps once a year, for Christians to share in a Passover meal. Like Israel, we are a liberated people and we owe it all to God. Like Israel, we are to remember who we are and how we come to be here.

30 March

THE PROMISE IS FOR YOU

Now when they heard this, they were cut to the heart and said to Peter and to the other apostles, 'Brothers, what should we do?' Peter said to them, 'Repent, and be baptized every one of you in the name of Jesus Christ so that your sins may be forgiven; and you will receive the gift of the Holy Spirit. For the promise is for you, for your children, and for all who are far away, everyone whom the Lord our God calls to him.' … So those who welcomed his message were baptized.

ACTS 2:37–39, 41A

This happened on the first day of Pentecost, when the apostles preached in Jerusalem about Jesus' resurrection. As that event had only happened a few weeks earlier, their words made a huge impression and a large crowd gathered, hanging on their words. Peter finished with a ringing challenge: 'God has made him both Lord and Messiah, this Jesus whom you crucified' (v. 36). The 'you' referred, he explained, to the 'entire house of Israel'—collective responsibility, indeed!

Shocked at this, the crowd had a simple question. What should they do? Peter's answer was also simple at one level. They should 'repent'—change their whole way of thinking—and 'be baptized in the name of Jesus Christ', so that their sins might be forgiven. When they did that, they would receive the gift of the Holy Spirit, a gift long promised. Centuries earlier, Joel had foretold a day when the Lord would 'pour out' his Spirit and his servants would 'prophesy' (Joel 2:28), which was just what the apostles had been doing.

Peter made the promise a personal one, however. 'The promise is for you and for your children,' he said, before widening it into a global invitation—'and for all… whom the Lord our God calls to him'. God's rescue operation for the human race, our 'salvation', is both for each one as an individual and for the whole race.

Every individual must make a personal response to the offer of salvation, yet God's purpose is that 'all should come to repentance' (2 Peter 3:9).

31 March

JESUS, REMEMBER ME!

One of the criminals who were hanged there kept deriding him and saying, 'Are you not the Messiah? Save yourself and us!' But the other rebuked him, saying, 'Do you not fear God, since you are under the same sentence of condemnation? And... we are getting what we deserve for our deeds, but this man has done nothing wrong.' Then he said, 'Jesus, remember me when you come into your kingdom.' He replied, 'Truly I tell you, today you will be with me in Paradise.'

LUKE 23:39–43 (abridged)

This little cameo from the story of the crucifixion is unique to Luke's Gospel and typical of his concern for the marginalized members of society. Jesus was crucified (as Lord McLeod of the Iona Community once pointed out) not between two vases of flowers and a couple of candles but between two thieves. One of them, in his death agony, screamed abuse at Jesus. The other, perhaps seeing something special about the man hanging between them, chided him. Jesus had done nothing wrong—a fact acknowledged even by Pilate, who condemned him. Nevertheless, because of the malice of his accusers, he was being crucified. Then the thief addressed the figure between them directly. 'Jesus,' he said, 'remember me when you come into your kingdom.'

Why should he think of Jesus as inheriting a kingdom, or coming in kingly power? And why should he be the only person in the whole of the Gospels to address Jesus by his personal name? Presumably Mary and Joseph called him 'Jesus', but that is never recorded. To everyone else he was 'Lord' or 'Rabbi' or 'Teacher'. But not to this poor criminal, on the verge of a terrible death. Perhaps, glancing up, he had read the inscription on the board above: 'Jesus of Nazareth, king of the Jews'. Taking it at face value, he called him by his name—Jesus (meaning 'saviour')—and cast himself on his royal mercy.

The thief asked only to be 'remembered', but he received much more. Today, not at some future date, he would be with Jesus in the garden of delights.

April: New life

April is in many places the time of spring, when after the rigours of winter the land begins to break once again into colour and fruitfulness. For Christians, it is also part of the season of Easter, the great celebration of life in all its fullness. That will be our theme for the month.

1 April

NOT HERE, BUT RISEN

When the sabbath was over, Mary Magdalene, and Mary the mother of James, and Salome bought spices, so that they might go and anoint him. And very early on the first day of the week, when the sun had risen, they went to the tomb. They had been saying to one another, 'Who will roll away the stone for us from the entrance to the tomb?' When they looked up, they saw that the stone, which was very large, had already been rolled back. As they entered the tomb, they saw a young man, dressed in a white robe, sitting on the right side; and they were alarmed. But he said to them, 'Do not be alarmed; you are looking for Jesus of Nazareth, who was crucified. He has been raised; he is not here. Look, there is the place they laid him.'

MARK 16:1–6

The three women have made their way to the tomb where Jesus had been laid on the Friday evening. The sabbath had intervened, but at the earliest possible moment ('when the sun had risen') they brought their spices to anoint his dead body. It was, they must have thought, the last loving service that they could offer to the man they had followed and admired so much. They wondered who would be around to help them roll back the heavy stone, but they needn't have worried—it had already been rolled back. They entered the tomb and saw a 'young man dressed in a white robe', identified by the other Gospels as an angel. He had a brief, clear but astonishing message for them. 'You're looking for Jesus, but he isn't here. He has been raised.' Not here—risen!

There, in three words, is the heart of the Easter message—indeed, the heart of the Christian gospel.

Not only over the tomb of Jesus but also over the grave of everyone who trusts in him could be written these words: 'Not here—risen!'

2 April

THE GARDEN OF RESURRECTION

But Mary stood weeping outside the tomb. As she wept, she bent over to look into the tomb; and she saw two angels in white… They said to her, 'Woman, why are you weeping?' … She turned round and saw Jesus standing there, but she did not know that it was Jesus. Jesus said to her, 'Woman, why are you weeping? For whom are you looking?' Supposing him to be the gardener, she said to him, 'Sir, if you have carried him away, tell me where you have laid him, and I will take him away.' Jesus said to her, 'Mary!' She turned and said to him in Hebrew, 'Rabbouni!' (which means Teacher). Jesus said to her, 'Do not hold on to me, because I have not yet ascended to the Father. But go to my brothers and say to them, "I am ascending to my Father and your Father, to my God and your God."'

JOHN 20:11–17 (abridged)

John tells us, 'There was a garden in the place where he was crucified' (19:41). In that garden they buried Jesus' body, but within a few hours the dead 'seed' had sprung into life, as Jesus himself had predicted. 'Unless a grain of wheat falls into the earth and dies, it remains just a single grain; but if it dies, it bears much fruit' (John 12:24).

This lovely story, retold every Easter and celebrated in art and literature, earths this theology in a deeply human encounter. Mary Magdalene was a woman whom Jesus had delivered from some awful mental or spiritual catastrophe (see Luke 8:2). Probably as a result, she was profoundly devoted to Jesus. Distraught at his death, she went to pay her last respects at his grave but found that the body was no longer there. First the two angels, then a man outside in the garden, asked her why she was weeping. She explained that she was looking for Jesus, at which the man simply called her by name: 'Miriam,' he said—using the affectionate (or 'pet') version of her name. At that, she realized that she was in the presence of the risen Lord. No wonder she ran to the disciples to tell them, 'I have seen the Lord!' (v. 18).

Jesus left her for heaven, but only so that one day she could join him there.

3 April

THE RISEN SON

Paul, a servant of Jesus Christ, called to be an apostle, set apart for the gospel of God... the gospel concerning his Son, who was descended from David according to the flesh and was declared to be Son of God with power according to the spirit of holiness by resurrection from the dead, Jesus Christ our Lord, through whom we have received grace and apostleship to bring about the obedience of faith among all the Gentiles for the sake of his name, including yourselves who are called to belong to Jesus Christ.

ROMANS 1:1, 3–6

Once again, we can catch Paul's breathless excitement as he dictates his greeting to the Christians in Rome, the very heart of the 'enemy empire'. He himself had been called to be an apostle, one of the special messengers of Jesus Christ, even though he had never met him in the flesh. Then he had been 'set apart' to proclaim the gospel of God. We notice that this time it is the gospel of God, whereas often Paul speaks of the gospel of Christ. God is its origin and source. The gospel is his good news for the human race, and is about his Son, Jesus Christ.

Jesus 'descended from David' in human terms but his resurrection, to which Paul bears constant witness, attests to the truth of his divinity. It was that mighty event which declared to all the world that Jesus of Nazareth, a distant descendant of the great king, was in fact the Son of God. It was not that Jesus was merely human until the resurrection. Whatever he was after that event, he had always been, and the resurrection is the demonstration of the fact. It was through that same Jesus, at once both human and divine, that the Roman Christians' lives had been transformed. They had been 'obedient' to the faith preached to them; they now 'belonged' to Jesus Christ.

Matthew's Gospel says there was an earthquake at the resurrection of Jesus. In that case, the shockwaves echoed far and wide. They had already reached the heart of the empire, in the lives of these believers in the imperial city.

4 April

THE SOURCE OF LIFE

The Father loves the Son and shows him all that he himself is doing; and he will show him greater works than these, so that you will be astonished. Indeed, just as the Father raises the dead and gives them life, so also the Son gives life to whomsoever he wishes... Anyone who does not honour the Son does not honour the Father who sent him. Very truly, I tell you, anyone who hears my word and believes him who sent me has eternal life, and does not come under judgment, but has passed from death to life
JOHN 5:20–21, 23–24

Life is a gift of God. That is a fundamental truth of the Bible, acknowledged from the opening chapter of Genesis to the last words of Revelation. By whatever process it comes about, life comes from its primary source, the Creator. Here, Jesus is arguing with a group who had objected to his healing of a man on the sabbath, to which Jesus responds with this assertion of his divine authority. What he does, he does because 'the Father' has authorized and empowered him to do it.

This will include 'greater works' than the one they have just witnessed, which will be the giving of life to the dead. The God who gives physical life is also the God who gives what Jesus calls 'eternal life'. This is a great theme of John's Gospel—the gift for those who hear the message of Jesus and believe that God sent him. Eternal life is not simply 'life that goes on for ever'. It is life on an eternal plane, a mode of being that is vastly superior to the life we have on earth. This is the 'abundant life' that Jesus came to provide for the members of his 'flock' (John 10:10)—'life in all its fullness'.

Those who put their trust in Jesus already have this life growing like a seed within them. They have 'passed from death into life', even though they still possess physical life. To God, they are already citizens of the kingdom of heaven, their status guaranteed, their future secure.

'Just as the Father raises the dead and gives them life, so also the Son gives life to whomsoever he wishes.'

5 April

LIFE AND HOPE

If there is no resurrection of the dead, then Christ has not been raised; and if Christ has not been raised, then our proclamation has been in vain and your faith has been in vain. We are even found to be misrepresenting God, because we testified of God that he raised Christ—whom he did not raise if it is true that the dead are not raised. For if the dead are not raised, then Christ has not been raised. If Christ has not been raised, your faith is futile and you are still in your sins. Then those also who have died in Christ have perished. If for this life only we have hoped in Christ, we are of all people most to be pitied.

1 CORINTHIANS 15:13–19

In this letter to the Corinthians, Paul is trying to reassure them about the resurrection of the dead. The first Christians expected Jesus to return during their lifetime, but over 20 years had passed and there was no sign of his appearing, so some began to worry about what would happen to them when they died and about their loved ones who had already died. In this brilliantly argued passage, Paul asserts the truth of the resurrection of Jesus as an incident in recorded history, and also the resurrection of those who trust in him.

Paul is certainly not one to pull punches! If their faith is so weak that they doubt Jesus' resurrection, then their faith is 'futile'. Sins have not been forgiven; the Christian dead have perished. If their hope in Christ is limited by the horizons of an earthly life, then their faith is pitiable. It is a stirring declaration of a resurrection faith, which Christianity has always been. The passage of time between the raising of Jesus from the dead and the final day of resurrection cannot weaken the fact of the empty tomb. Only God knows the dates on the calendar but the promise is certain. Those who share the life of the risen Christ will be raised to a new and glorious life with God for ever. That, not the grave, is their destiny.

While God lives, so will all those who have been raised to new life in his Son.

6 April

THE BREATH OF GOD

In the day that the Lord God made the earth and the heavens, when no plant of the field was yet in the earth and no herb of the field had yet sprung up—for the Lord God had not caused it to rain upon the earth, and there was no one to till the ground; but a stream would rise from the earth, and water the whole face of the ground—then the Lord God formed man from the dust of the ground, and breathed into his nostrils the breath of life; and the man became a living being.

GENESIS 2:4–7

This is part of the second creation story in Genesis. Chapter 1 gives an overview of the creative process, setting out the unfolding vista of sun and planets, light and dark, dry land and water, followed by life in all its forms. Finally, as the crowning act, God formed the first human beings, male and female, 'in his own image'. Now, in this second story, we have a graphic account of man's creation 'from the dust of the ground'. That phrase vividly places human beings in their context. They are not angelic beings, imported from the heavenly realms to populate the earth. Our origins, while divinely ordained, are rooted in the physical world we inhabit, part of that unfolding creation.

The story also gives a reason for our existence: 'there was no one to till the ground'. We are God's stewards, here to guard this part of his creation. We are not the lords of the earth but its carers. So the first man was a gardener, but in the most beautiful garden imaginable.

God formed man from the dust of the ground but transformed that dust with one magnificent action. He 'breathed into his nostrils the breath of life'. The word for 'breath' is *ruach*, the same word as 'spirit', including the Holy Spirit of God. God put spirit, breath, life into man and he became a 'living being'. That is the true dignity of humanity. The steward of the earth is also the image of its Creator.

The breath of God, his 'Spirit'—brought life to what had been inanimate material. The breath of the same Spirit gives us the new life of Christ.

7 April

THE VALLEY OF DRY BONES

The hand of the Lord came upon me, and he brought me out by the spirit of the Lord and set me down in the middle of a valley; it was full of bones. He led me all round them; there were very many lying in the valley, and they were very dry. He said to me, 'Mortal, can these bones live?' I answered, 'O Lord God, you know.' Then he said to me, 'Prophesy to these bones, and say to them: O dry bones, hear the word of the Lord… I will cause breath to enter you, and you shall live. I will lay sinews on you, and will cause flesh to come upon you, and cover you with skin, and put breath in you, and you shall live; and you shall know that I am the Lord.'

EZEKIEL 37:1–6 (abridged)

This vivid image of dry bones in a barren valley being connected together, dressed with muscle and sinews and coming to life again, is yet another expression of the biblical theme of new life. The dry bones, lying parched in the desert landscape, are 'the whole house of Israel' (v. 11)—a nation that had lost hope and now felt completely cut off from the Lord God, the source of life. Yet the prophet is told to 'prophesy to these bones', to tell them to 'hear the word of the Lord', to call upon the 'four winds' to 'breathe upon these slain, that they may live' (v. 9). Remembering the story of the creation of the first man, and that 'breath' and 'spirit' are the same word in Hebrew, what we see here is like a re-enactment of that first act of creation in Genesis.

The rest of the passage completes the picture. As Ezekiel prophesied to them, suddenly there was a rattling noise and the bones 'came together, bone to its bone… and flesh had come upon them, and skin had covered them' (vv. 7–8). It was, as the Lord told the prophet, as though graves were being opened and the dead brought back to new life. This would be the manner of Israel's restoration. God would 'put his spirit within them, and they would live' (v. 14).

The God who brings life back into 'dry bones' can also breathe new life into the heart that has shrivelled under the heat of sorrow, doubt or rejection.

8 April

BREATH AND SPIRIT

Thus says God, the Lord, who created the heavens and stretched them out, who spread out the earth and what comes from it, who gives breath to the people upon it and spirit to those who walk in it: I am the Lord, I have called you in righteousness, I have taken you by the hand and kept you; I have given you as a covenant to the people, a light to the nations, to open the eyes that are blind, to bring out the prisoners from the dungeon, from the prison those who sit in darkness. I am the Lord, that is my name; my glory I give to no other, nor my praise to idols.

ISAIAH 42:5–8

In the wonderful poetry of this section of Isaiah, the people of Jerusalem, so recently stricken and conquered by the Babylonians, are offered vistas of future blessing. Here the prophet reminds them that it is the Lord who created the heavens and the earth and, most significantly, 'gives breath to the people upon it and spirit [same word as 'breath'] to those who walk in it'. He also reminds them that the same God who is the source of life is the one who has called them, who has taken them by the hand and kept them, even through dark days. And they have been called and redeemed for a purpose: the ultimate blessing of the whole earth, just as the Lord promised to Abraham: 'in you all the families of the earth shall be blessed' (Genesis 12:3).

This amazing national manifesto, repeated and extended in Isaiah 61:1–3, was taken by Jesus at the start of his ministry as his messianic agenda (Luke 4:18). In other words, it had always been God's purpose that his servant nation, Israel, and his Servant Son, Jesus, were called to fulfil this promise of blessing. The first servant failed, but at least it brought to birth in its ranks the second Servant, who fulfilled it.

'Breath' and 'spirit' are gifts of God but, like all his gifts, they are given for a purpose, and that is the blessing of all humankind.

The Wisdom that brought the universe into being also gave it meaning and purpose—the blessing of its people through the agents he has chosen.

9 April

TURNING DESERTS INTO WELLS

How lovely is your dwelling-place, O Lord of hosts! My soul longs, indeed it faints for the courts of the Lord; my heart and my flesh sing for joy to the living God. Even the sparrow finds a home, and the swallow a nest for herself, where she may lay her young, at your altars... Happy are those whose strength is in you, in whose heart are the highways to Zion. As they go through the valley of Baca they make it a place of springs; the early rain also covers it with pools. They go from strength to strength; the God of gods will be seen in Zion.

PSALM 84:1–3, 5–7

This is a joyful pilgrim song. The writer is on the threshold of the holy city. Perhaps the temple is in sight. As his heart leaps at the prospect, he reflects on his journey there and his anticipation of what lies ahead. The journey wouldn't have been easy. Israel is hot for most of the year and, while distances aren't great, in those days they were covered on foot for the most part. Yet the prospect of Jerusalem and entering the 'house of the Lord' constantly lifted his spirits. God provided strength for the journey for those who carried in their hearts the thought of the destination. That turned even the dry and parched valley of Baca into a place of springs—perhaps literally, perhaps metaphorically. The word 'Baca', the name of a tree that grows in arid places, sounds like the Hebrew word for 'weeping', which may have struck a chord with the psalmist's poetic heart. The verse would then mean, 'The valley of weeping was turned into a place of refreshment and blessing'.

As for the joyful prospect ahead, the psalmist again conjures up a memorable image. The little sparrow finds a home near God's altar in the temple and the swallow raises her brood there. Just like them, for the pilgrim, getting there would be like coming home.

For the Christian, the pilgrimage is not across Samaria or down the Jordan valley, but through the hills and dry places of life. Yet we can find strength on the journey and the promise of a real 'home' with God at the end of it.

10 April

THE FLOOD

Noah was six hundred years old when the flood... came on the earth. And Noah with his sons and his wife and his sons' wives went into the ark... Of clean animals, and of animals that are not clean, and of birds, and of everything that creeps on the ground, two and two, male and female, went into the ark with Noah... And after seven days the waters of the flood came on the earth... The flood continued for forty days on the earth; and the waters increased, and bore up the ark, and it rose high above the earth... And... everything on dry land in whose nostrils was the breath of life died... Only Noah was left, and those that were with him in the ark. And the waters swelled on the earth for one hundred and fifty days.

GENESIS 7:6–10, 17, 21 (abridged)

The story of the flood, apart from being an enthralling narrative, sets out a few more key themes of the Old Testament and of our understanding of God. The story begins with Noah aged 600 years. The amazing ages of people in the early chapters of the Bible probably reflect the chronicler's desire to show that early death was not part of God's plan for his creation, or simply to honour advanced age. At any rate, Noah, a 'righteous man' (6:9), was warned of a vast flood—God's judgment on the corruption of the people. Noah and his family would avoid its consequences if they built a huge boat, in which they and representative animals, snakes and birds could survive. Preposterous as the idea sounded, Noah did 'all that God commanded' (6:22).

Many ancient civilizations have a similar flood story, but the Bible's account is the only one that makes obedience to God a condition of survival. The flood continued for 40 days (a timescale that would assume a symbolic role in the Bible) and then the waters remained for nearly six months. Somehow or other (the narrator omits such helpful details), the passengers had enough food and clean water to survive.

Jesus used the story of Noah and the flood to warn his hearers that it is folly to ignore both the warnings and the promises of God (Matthew 24:37–39).

11 April

SAVED FROM THE WATERS

Then God said to Noah, 'Go out of the ark, you and your wife, and your sons and your sons' wives with you. Bring out with you every living thing that is with you of all flesh—birds and animals and every creeping thing that creeps on the earth—so that they may abound on the earth, and be fruitful and multiply on the earth.' So Noah went out... And every animal, every creeping thing, and every bird, everything that moves on the earth, went out of the ark by families.

GENESIS 8:15–19 (abridged)

The story of the Bible is set against a background of deep water, from the 'face of the deep' in its first sentence to the prophetic promise that in the new Jerusalem 'the sea was no more' (Revelation 21:1). In between we have many references to the threat posed by uncontrolled waters—just think of the Red Sea, or Jonah, or the terrified disciples in a storm on Galilee.

The flood, this archetypal sign of judgment, stands as a picture of the ultimate threat—the deep waters that can overwhelm us, which can only be controlled by the one who created them and 'gathered them together into one place' (Genesis 1:9). Noah and his family became symbols of those called by God to salvation, carried through the time of judgment and eventually delivered back on dry land. Peter uses the experience of that family—eight people 'saved through water' —as a prefiguring of Christian baptism (1 Peter 3:20–21).

There is also a suggestion of stewardship. The original command to the first humans was to be 'fruitful and multiply, and fill the earth and subdue it; and have dominion... over every living thing' (Genesis 1:28). Noah has now learnt, through his rescue of the animals and his care of them in the ark, that 'subduing' and 'having dominion'—any kind of power—carry with them a powerful responsibility.

If God has given us power over parts of his creation, he has also given us the awesome responsibility of caring for them. That is what 'stewardship' means.

12 April

THE RAINBOW

The Lord said in his heart, 'I will never again curse the ground because of humankind, for the inclination of the human heart is evil from youth; nor will I ever again destroy every living creature as I have done. As long as the earth endures, seedtime and harvest, cold and heat, summer and winter, day and night, shall not cease… I establish my covenant with you, that never again shall all flesh be cut off by the waters of a flood, and never again shall there be a flood to destroy the earth… I have set my bow in the clouds, and it shall be a sign of the covenant between me and the earth.'
GENESIS 8:21–22; 9:11, 13

The Bible often speaks of 'covenants', agreements or promises made by God, sometimes with conditions, sometimes unconditional. This story speaks of the first such covenant, between God and the earth. In other words, the Creator promises—this time without condition—that he will not destroy the planet, whatever the provocation of its human tenants, but will maintain its rhythm of seasons, its life-giving pattern of rain and heat, day and night. Coming at the end of the story of the flood, it can be seen as a pledge of the Creator's constant concern for and involvement in his creation.

Like other covenants in the Bible, this one also has a 'sign', a visible or tangible pledge to remind the parties to the covenant of its existence and importance. In this case, it is the rainbow. Of course rainbows existed before the flood, just as bread and wine existed before the last supper, but by this action the Lord invested the rainbow with a new significance. Every time the people saw it in the sky, they could call to mind this solemn pledge that God has made.

It does not mean that extremes of weather or earthquakes or other natural phenomena won't ever happen. It does mean that they occur within the divinely ordered remit for the earth.

The rainbow, in all its splendour, occurs when sunshine follows rain. Both are necessary to make this covenant promise visible to human eyes.

13 April

SENT TO SAVE LIFE

Then Joseph said to his brothers, 'Come closer to me.' And they came closer. He said, 'I am your brother Joseph, whom you sold into Egypt. And now do not be distressed, or angry with yourselves, because you sold me here; for God sent me before you to preserve life. For the famine has been in the land these two years; and there are five more years in which there will be neither ploughing nor harvest. God sent me before you to preserve for you a remnant on earth, and to keep alive for you many survivors. So it was not you who sent me here, but God.'

GENESIS 45:4–8

This is the last part of the story of Joseph and his brothers. Joseph, the favourite son of Jacob, is sold by his envious brothers to slavery in Egypt, but he prospers there and saves the nation from famine. Now, with Joseph second only to Pharaoh in the land, his wretched brothers come looking for food because the famine has reached Canaan too. Eventually Joseph identifies himself to them in these words, which in the circumstances are remarkably generous and forgiving.

The key to Joseph's approach is his belief that all these events had been part of a divine plan. The brothers thought they had planned to get rid of their bumptious younger sibling. Yet, long before the famine, God was planning to rescue the descendants of Abraham, Isaac and Jacob from the famine and to bring them to Egypt. 'It was not you who sent me here, but God,' Joseph told them.

The brothers went back to their homeland and brought their families and Joseph's beloved father to live in Egypt, on land that Pharaoh ceded to them. There they grew in numbers and the whole story of slavery and rescue began to take shape—a story that forged a new nation and, to a large extent, a new religion. In those events they would be brought into a new relationship with the God of their fathers.

'You plotted evil… but God turned it into good' (Genesis 50:20, GNB). How often that's been true in human experience!

14 April

SALT AND LIGHT

'You are the salt of the earth; but if salt has lost its taste, how can its saltiness be restored? It is no longer good for anything, but is thrown out and trampled under foot. You are the light of the world. A city built on a hill cannot be hidden. No one after lighting a lamp puts it under the bushel basket, but on the lampstand, and it gives light to all in the house. In the same way, let your light shine before others, so that they may see your good works and give glory to your Father in heaven.'
MATTHEW 5:13–16

For the crowd gathered on the hillside listening to Jesus preaching, salt and light would have been familiar objects. Salt was used to prevent meat going bad, and to give added flavour to food. Light was essential in a land where darkness fell early all year round. No home would be complete without a barrel of salt and some lamps or candles.

The problem was (as they all knew) that salt could lose its 'saltiness' if it was stored away for too long. And once lost, that saltiness could never be restored. If his followers—the 'people of the kingdom'—were the 'salt of the earth', it was vital that they didn't keep the salt in the barrel too long! Salt is meant to be applied, and their lives should serve both to preserve the world from 'going bad' and to bring to people's lives an added 'flavour'. That is a high calling!

Jesus then offered a second picture of the disciple's calling. He or she is to be 'the light of the world', but again, the light has to be 'applied' to illuminate the whole room.

There is one small problem in this, however. Jesus also said, 'I am the light of the world' (John 8:12). How can we be what he is? Presumably the answer is that Jesus is the origin of this light and his followers reflect it. From the life of the Christian there should shine into the whole world the reflected light of the Saviour.

When Christians shine with the light of Christ, it is not so that other people say 'Oh, aren't they good!' but so that they give glory to God.

15 April

TREASURE IN HEAVEN

'Do not store up for yourselves treasures on earth, where moth and rust consume and where thieves break in and steal; but store up for yourselves treasures in heaven, where neither moth nor rust consumes and where thieves do not break in and steal. For where your treasure is, there your heart will be also.'

MATTHEW 6:19–21

Once again Jesus returns to the subject of priorities—ours and God's. This could be said to be the central theme of the Sermon on the Mount, of which these sayings are a part. There is a wrong priority to be rejected and a right priority to be pursued.

To take the wrong one first, we are wasting time if we simply put our efforts into accumulating possessions. Compared to consumers in today's developed world, most of Jesus' audience would have had a modest lifestyle. A small house, some mats to sleep on, a few cows, sheep and chickens and bits of basic furniture would have been the extent of their domestic luxuries. But human nature always seeks for more. Probably they were keen to have as fine a herd as Mr Joseph down the track, or as eyecatching a necklace as Mrs Levi in the next village. But the pursuit of possessions as a goal in life has an inbuilt flaw: they don't last. Thieves, rust and moths lie in wait. And, of course, we can't take them with us when we finally go.

This brings us to the right priority, which is to build for the future—for eternity, in fact. The people of the kingdom were to invest their energy in things of eternal value. Paul said that three things last for ever: faith, hope and love (1 Corinthians 13:13). Those who commit their lives to such things are building for the future. As so often, Jesus summed up the whole argument in one memorable saying: 'Where your treasure is, there your heart will be also.'

What we value most—the car, garden, pets, travel, wealth or 'success'—dictates our priorities. So Jesus asks us: 'What is your treasure?'

16 April

NEW WINE

When the steward tasted the water that had become wine, and did not know where it came from (though the servants who had drawn the water knew), the steward called the bridegroom and said to him, 'Everyone serves the good wine first, and then the inferior wine after the guests have become drunk. But you have kept the good wine until now.' Jesus did this, the first of his signs, in Cana of Galilee, and revealed his glory; and his disciples believed in him.

JOHN 2:9–11

This is the last part of John's account of the first miracle of Jesus, or 'sign', as he prefers to call it. It took place at a wedding in Cana, not far from Nazareth. Jesus, his mother and some of his disciples were guests—but the wine ran out! This was a double catastrophe. The wedding ceremony involved many blessings and many cups of wine; and the party, which often lasted for several days, would have been a disaster if there were nothing to drink but water. At Mary's instigation and apparently with some reluctance, Jesus got involved, ordering the servants to fill huge jars used for storing water for ritual purifications with ordinary water. He then told them to draw some off and take it to the master of ceremonies. By the time it reached him, the water had become wine of the very finest quality, as he was quick to recognize.

This is a strange 'sign', quite unlike most of Jesus' miracles. No one was healed, no famine averted. What was rescued was the most important event in the lives of two young people. What was demonstrated, as John observes, was the 'glory' of Jesus.

John's Gospel deserves to be read at many different levels. We can peel away layer after layer and still find hidden meaning. Here we have a parable of transformation—from dull, insipid water to rich red wine; from the 'old' religion of ritual to the 'new' way of joy and life. And all in the context of a wedding—a new start in a new relationship.

The new wine at the wedding at Cana models the rich new life of the kingdom.

17 April

ELISHA AND THE CHILD

When Elisha came into the house, he saw the child lying dead on his bed. So he went in and closed the door on the two of them, and prayed to the Lord. Then he got up on the bed and lay upon the child, putting his mouth upon his mouth, his eyes upon his eyes, and his hands upon his hands; and while he lay bent over him, the flesh of the child became warm. He got down, walked once to and fro in the room, then got up again and bent over him; the child sneezed seven times, and the child opened his eyes.
2 KINGS 4:32–35

We have no writings of the first two great prophets of Israel, Elijah and Elisha, but we do have many accounts of their courage, wisdom and miraculous deeds. This story concerns a wealthy Shunammite woman who had offered Elisha a 'penthouse' for his use whenever he came to her district. He offered to help her in any way he could to repay her kindness, but she declined. However, knowing that she was childless, he told her that she would one day embrace a son of her own.

In due time she did indeed have a son as Elisha had prophesied, but one day he collapsed in the field during harvesting and died on his mother's lap. At once, and without telling anyone of his death—not even her husband—she set off to find Elisha, threw herself to the ground and grasped his feet, crying out that she had never asked for a son but saying no more. The prophet despatched his 'assistant', Gehazi, to the house, telling him to lay the prophet's staff on the boy's face, but 'there was no sign of life' (v. 31).

The passage above takes up the story from that point. To a reader today, it sounds like a rather sophisticated version of mouth-to-mouth resuscitation—a technique not really known until recent times. But whether by the prophet's God-given intuition and wisdom, or by direct miraculous intervention, the boy was restored to life.

In a time of deep anguish, the woman knew where to turn; and when he needed wisdom, the prophet knew whom to ask.

18 April

LITTLE GIRL, GET UP!

When they came to the house of the leader of the synagogue, [Jesus] saw a commotion, people weeping and wailing loudly. When he had entered, he said to them, 'Why do you make a commotion and weep? The child is not dead but sleeping.' And they laughed at him. Then he put them all outside, and took the child's father and mother and those who were with him, and went in where the child was. He took her by the hand and said to her, 'Talitha cum', which means, 'Little girl, get up!' And immediately the girl got up and began to walk about (she was twelve years of age).

MARK 5:38–42

There are obvious parallels between this healing by Jesus and the one by Elisha: a child is apparently dead, one of the parents is desperate and tracks down the only person who can help, and the healing takes place behind closed doors. There is also a delay between the plea for help and the arrival on the scene of the healer (see vv. 24–35).

In this case, the parent is a 'leader of the synagogue'—perhaps something like a churchwarden. His name was Jairus and, like the Shunammite woman, he fell at the feet of the healer to plead for help. His request was full of faith: 'Come and lay your hands on her, so that she may be made well, and live' (v. 23).

Eventually, Jesus reached the house of Jairus, where the professional mourners were already in business. He turned them out, shut himself in the room with his closest disciples and the parents, and simply said to the girl, 'Get up'—the sort of call her mother probably made to her every morning. At his voice she stirred and got up, and began to walk about, to the amazement of everyone.

Had she been dead or 'sleeping'—in a coma, perhaps? All we know is that Jesus' voice broke through whatever was shutting down her mind and body and gloriously restored them to life 'in all its fullness'.

As soon as the girl woke up, Jesus told the family to give her 'something to eat' (v. 43). They, too, could share in the miracle of her life restored.

19 April

YOUNG MAN, RISE!

Soon afterwards [Jesus] went to a town called Nain, and his disciples and a large crowd went with him. As he approached the gate of the town, a man who had died was being carried out. He was his mother's only son, and she was a widow; and with her was a large crowd from the town. When the Lord saw her, he had compassion for her and said to her, 'Do not weep.' Then he came forward and touched the bier, and the bearers stood still. And he said, 'Young man, I say to you, rise!' The dead man sat up and began to speak, and Jesus gave him to his mother.

LUKE 7:11–15

This is another story of Jesus raising someone from what seems to have been death—indeed, in this case there's little doubt, if things had got as far as the funeral. This is a tragic and touching account. The young man who had died was his mother's only son, and she was a widow, which meant that her only means of support in life had gone. Not only that, but there is always something particularly distressing in a parent witnessing the death of their own child. It seems a contradiction of nature: we feel that we should die in some kind of 'order'. But there she is, in this sad picture, following her dear son's funeral bier.

Jesus entered Nain as the funeral crowd was leaving it, and saw the widow in tears. Not for the first or last time, he was moved with compassion for her—his feelings were deeply touched. His first words to her were of comfort: 'Do not weep.' His second words were directed to the body: 'Young man, I say to you, rise!' At once the young man sat up and, in a touching gesture, 'Jesus gave him to his mother'.

The crowd's reaction had two elements to it: fear (or 'reverence')—they knew they had witnessed a mighty act of power—and praise to God, whom they glorified for what they had seen him do (v. 16).

If Jesus is the Son of God, if the world was created through him, and if what came into being in him was life, it shouldn't surprise us that he is able to give life to the dead (see Romans 1:4; John 1:3–4).

20 April

WASH, AND BE CLEAN!

Naaman, commander of the army of the king of Aram... suffered from leprosy... Elisha sent a messenger to him, saying, 'Go, wash in the Jordan seven times, and your flesh shall be restored and you shall be clean.' But Naaman became angry and went away, saying, 'I thought that for me he would surely come out, and stand and call on the name of the Lord his God, and would wave his hand over the spot, and cure the leprosy! Are not Abana and Pharpar, the rivers of Damascus, better than all the waters of Israel? ... But his servants... said to him, 'Father, if the prophet had commanded you to do something difficult, would you not have done it? How much more, when all he said to you was, "Wash, and be clean"?'

2 KINGS 5:1, 10–13 (abridged)

This story concerns a Gentile, a general in the army of a nation not always friendly towards Israel—Aram, modern Syria. He was a mighty warrior, but also a sufferer from leprosy—probably not the disease known by that name today, but certainly a severe skin infection, which in its advanced stages destroyed flesh and muscles.

Naaman had a Hebrew slave, taken by him on an army expedition. This young woman told his wife about the prophet Elisha, so Naaman did what the protocol of the time required: he approached the king of Aram and asked him to negotiate with the king of Israel for a consultation. The latter thought that this approach was just troublemaking, and tore up his letter. When Elisha heard about it, however, he invited Naaman to come to him, so 'that he may learn that there is a prophet in Israel' (v. 8). Naaman turned up in his chariot, expecting a spectacular miraculous healing, but Elisha simply told him to go and wash seven times in the Jordan. The soldier was outraged—until his servants pointed out the obvious. He would have done something difficult to be healed, so what was wrong with doing something easy? Naaman was big enough to take the rebuke, bathed in the Jordan—and was healed.

The act of faith is simple. Its consequences, however, are enormous.

21 April

THE OPEN HAND

Your kingdom is an everlasting kingdom, and your dominion endures throughout all generations. The Lord is faithful in all his words, and gracious in all his deeds. The Lord upholds all who are falling, and raises up all who are bowed down. The eyes of all look to you, and you give them their food in due season. You open your hand, satisfying the desire of every living thing. The Lord is just in all his ways, and kind in all his doings. The Lord is near… to all who call on him in truth. He fulfils the desire of all who fear him; he also hears their cry, and saves them.

PSALM 145:13–19 (abridged)

The whole of this psalm (except for one brief reference to the psalmist's enemies) is a joyful song of praise. At times it is almost a list, in poetic language, of the wonderful attributes of the Lord. In our passage, for instance, we begin with a recognition of God's kingly rule over his people—a kingdom that will never end. Then his marvellous attributes follow in quick succession. He is faithful and gracious—that is, trustworthy and generous. He upholds those who fall and raises up those who are 'bowed down'—with sorrow, age or infirmity. All living creatures look to him for sustenance, and 'in due season' he feeds them. That is paralleled with a striking image of the open hand of God, 'satisfying the desire of every living thing'.

The following verse is a lovely illustration of the beauty of Hebrew poetry, where 'the Lord is just in all his ways' is balanced with 'and kind in all his doings'. To be kind but unjust is weakness; to be just but unkind is harsh. The Lord matches his justice with his kindness, especially attentive to those who 'call on him in truth'—genuinely and sincerely. The Lord is not distant but near enough to 'hear the cry' of those who reverence his name and to 'fulfil their desires'.

The promise that God fulfils our desires does not mean that he satisfies every whim of his people. Because he has 'dominion' over our lives, he takes responsibility for our well-being, which may not always match our desires.

22 April

WHAT I HAVE, I GIVE YOU

Peter and John were going up to the temple at the hour of prayer, at three o'clock in the afternoon. And a man lame from birth was being carried in... When he saw Peter and John about to go into the temple, he asked them for alms. Peter looked intently at him, as did John, and said, 'Look at us.' And he fixed his attention on them... But Peter said, 'I have no silver or gold, but what I have I give you; in the name of Jesus Christ of Nazareth, stand up and walk.' And he took him by the right hand and raised him up; and immediately his feet and ankles were made strong. Jumping up, he stood and began to walk, and he entered the temple with them, walking and leaping and praising God.

ACTS 3:1–8 (abridged)

This incident, from Luke's story of the early Church, tells of the first miracle performed by the disciples in Jesus' name. For whatever reason, such miracles seem to have become less frequent once the Church had survived its first encounters with both the Jewish and the Gentile world. They probably took place as visual evidence for the incredulous crowds of the truth of the gospel being preached.

Certainly this particular miracle, performed at the doors of the temple itself, made quite a stir. Peter and John were clear: it was in the name of the risen Lord Jesus that they had healed this man (v. 16). As a result of the ensuing furore, the apostles were arrested by the temple authorities. After an agonizing debate in the Council, they were ordered 'not to speak or teach at all in the name of Jesus' (4:18)—a command rejected by Peter and John, who were promptly released.

As usual in Luke's style, the story itself is graphically told. Little details stick in the memory—the apostles looked 'intently' on the lame man. He thought it was money he would get. In fact, it was something infinitely more worthwhile.

'What I have I give you'—what an offer! Especially when what Peter had to offer was perfect health—wholeness, salvation.

23 April

OUT OF DARKNESS INTO LIGHT

But you are a chosen race, a royal priesthood, a holy nation, God's own people, in order that you may proclaim the mighty acts of him who called you out of darkness into his marvellous light. Once you were not a people, but now you are God's people; once you had not received mercy, but now you have received mercy.

1 PETER 2:9–10

Peter was writing to Christians scattered across the Roman empire, probably just after the first wave of persecution in AD64 under Nero. He called them the 'exiles of the Dispersion' (1:1), using language traditionally applied to the Jewish people. Now the privilege of suffering was being borne by the new people of God, those who had been 'chosen and destined by God the Father and sanctified by the Spirit to be obedient to Jesus Christ' (1:2).

To these dispersed Christians, bewildered and anxious, Peter addresses majestic words of confidence. You are not runaways, refugees or exiles. You are 'a chosen race, a royal priesthood, a holy nation, God's own people'—again, phrases traditionally applied to the blood descendants of Abraham (see Exodus 19:6). The Church had inherited those promises. They, too, were chosen, a holy nation, even though their earthly nationality was diverse. Even more dramatically, they were a 'royal priesthood' in the succession of Aaron and David. Like the priests of Israel, they represented God to the people and the people to God. Like the kings of Israel, they cared for God's flock.

This priesthood was not exclusive to one particular caste or group within the Church. It is the Church itself that is a 'priesthood', and each part of it contributes to its ministry. And what is that ministry? To 'proclaim the mighty acts of him who called you' out of the darkness of unbelief into the light of his love.

Becoming the people of God was both a privilege and a responsibility, as Israel had discovered.

24 April

ALIVE TO GOD

For if we have been united with [Christ] in a death like his, we will certainly be united with him in a resurrection like his. We know that our old self was crucified with him so that the body of sin might be destroyed, and we might no longer be enslaved to sin. For whoever has died is freed from sin. But if we have died with Christ, we believe that we will also live with him. We know that Christ, being raised from the dead, will never die again; death no longer has dominion over him… So you also must consider yourselves dead to sin and alive to God in Christ Jesus.

ROMANS 6:5–9, 11

The imagery behind this powerful piece of writing by Paul is of baptism, which in those early days of the Church normally took place by total immersion in a pool. This portrayed the burial (or, I suppose, drowning) of the 'old' person, and then as the candidate came up out of the water the picture was of rising to new life in Christ. So the whole theme of this closely argued chapter is on death and life—a 'death' with Christ to sin and a new life in Christ to righteousness.

'Whoever has died is freed' echoes a common legal saying of the time, that death cancels all contracts (including marriage). But the thrust of Paul's thought goes deeper than that. Christ died for sin—not his own but ours. Having died, however, he was raised from the dead so that death and sin could no longer have any power over him.

This same process is at work in the Christian. In faith and baptism we identify ourselves with Jesus' death to take away sin. But we also identify ourselves with his risen life, in which the 'dominion' of sin is broken. This cannot mean that the Christian is incapable of sin, but to those who are 'united with Christ' (meaning something like 'fused together into one'), sin is a defeated enemy, even if a mopping-up operation has to continue until we finally enter heaven.

This process of death and resurrection has a wonderful goal: to make us 'alive to God in Christ Jesus'.

25 April

LISTEN, AND LIVE

Ho, everyone who thirsts, come to the waters; and you that have no money, come, buy and eat! Come, buy wine and milk without money and without price. Why do you spend your money for that which is not bread, and your labour for that which does not satisfy? Listen carefully to me, and eat what is good, and delight yourselves in rich food… I will make with you an everlasting covenant, my steadfast, sure love for David.
ISAIAH 55:1–3 (abridged)

My Bible headlines this passage 'An invitation to abundant life', and that is exactly what it is. The people of Israel have endured conquest, exile and slavery, but now they are home and the prophet is holding before them a vision of a bright and golden future. In their circumstances, there could not be much of greater appeal than free bread, wine and milk. This goodness cannot be earned; it will be a gift of God, the one with whom they are in a covenant relationship.

There are conditions, however. These good things are 'without price' but not without cost. The rich food in which they can delight is for those who 'listen carefully' to the word of God. The abundant life is for those whose ears are tuned to his will. Until now they have scratched around, desperate to know where the next meal is coming from, but they have found no satisfaction. Now there is a new offer. Turn to the Lord, listen to him, and the covenant he made long ago with their nation will be transformed into an everlasting one, a demonstration of his love for the descendants of David.

The following verses make it plain that this era of blessing will also include other nations (v. 5). But it is the obedience and trust of his chosen people that is the condition of blessing. If they fully trust him, he will fully supply their needs.

Christians will find in these verses what we might call 'pre-echoes' of the teaching of Jesus. He himself might well have said, 'Ho, everyone who thirsts, come to the waters'—the waters of eternal life (see John 4:10–14).

26 April

FOR GOD'S GLORY

Now a certain man was ill, Lazarus of Bethany, the village of Mary and her sister Martha. Mary was the one who anointed the Lord with perfume and wiped his feet with her hair; her brother Lazarus was ill. So the sisters sent a message to Jesus, 'Lord, he whom you love is ill.' But when Jesus heard it, he said, 'This illness does not lead to death; rather it is for God's glory...' Accordingly, though Jesus loved Martha and her sister and Lazarus... he stayed two days longer in the place where he was.

JOHN 11:1–6 (abridged)

Today we start three readings which tell the story of the raising of Lazarus by Jesus. This miracle, notably absent from the other Gospels, has a prominent place in John's—indeed, it is seen as the final straw that broke the back of the temple authorities and led to Jesus' arrest. The story offers a unique insight into the whole subject of death and resurrection, which will dominate the rest of John's Gospel.

Two sisters, Mary and Martha, and their brother Lazarus (an unusual household by first-century Jewish standards) were among a select handful of people described in this Gospel as being 'loved' by Jesus. Their home at Bethany on the outskirts of Jerusalem was a familiar resting place for him and the disciples on their visits to the city. So it's not surprising that when Lazarus fell ill his sisters immediately sent an urgent message to Jesus, presumably expecting that he would drop whatever he was doing and rush to their side.

In fact, he did nothing of the kind. He waited a couple more days, to the surprise of his disciples. After first hinting that things were not quite as straightforward as he had implied ('Lazarus has fallen asleep', v. 11) Jesus told his disciples bluntly that 'Lazarus is dead' (v. 14)—adding that he was glad he had not been there, 'so that you may believe' (v. 15). By then he and the Twelve had set out for Bethany.

Jesus loved his friends, but allowed them to go through a traumatic experience. They were not the last to discover that it is the 'end' that reveals the glory.

27 April

THE RESURRECTION AND THE LIFE

When Martha heard that Jesus was coming, she went and met him, while Mary stayed at home. Martha said to Jesus, 'Lord, if you had been here, my brother would not have died…' Jesus said to her, 'Your brother will rise again.' Martha said to him, 'I know that he will rise again in the resurrection on the last day.' Jesus said to her, 'I am the resurrection and the life. Those who believe in me, even though they die, will live, and everyone who lives and believes in me will never die. Do you believe this?' She said to him, 'Yes, Lord, I believe that you are the… Son of God.'

JOHN 11:20–21, 23–27 (abridged)

This is the heart of John's story of the raising of Lazarus. Martha hurried out to meet Jesus as he arrived, and her words sound like a rebuke. How often the first words of a bereaved person express this kind of disappointment, or even anger. 'If only he'd gone to the doctor sooner… If only the ambulance had come more quickly… If only I'd recognized how ill she was.' Jesus didn't attempt to explain his delay. He simply said, 'Your brother will rise again'—the common belief of most Jews at that time. 'Oh yes,' countered Martha, 'I know he'll rise again in the resurrection on the last day'—and you can almost hear her thinking, 'and a fat lot of good that is. It's now I want him, it's now I miss him'.

Again, Jesus picks up her remark, but in a marvellously positive way. 'I am the resurrection.' He wasn't talking about a distant event, hidden in the Father's foreknowledge. He was talking here and now. This is the last and greatest of the 'I am' sayings. 'I am the light of the world… the good shepherd… the way, the truth, and the life'… yes, but beyond all those, 'I am the resurrection'. Those who believe in Jesus have the resurrection life now. If they are dead, they will rise. If they are living, then (in the deepest sense of the words) they will never die.

Jesus asked, 'Do you believe this?' Martha's answer was deeply human. 'Yes, Lord, I believe—not all this theory and theology, which I don't understand, but you, and who you are to me.'

28 April

UNBIND HIM, AND LET HIM GO

So they took away the stone. And Jesus looked upwards and said, 'Father, I thank you for having heard me... I have said this for the sake of the crowd standing here, so that they may believe that you sent me.' When he had said this, he cried with a loud voice, 'Lazarus, come out!' The dead man came out, his hands and feet bound with strips of cloth, and his face wrapped in a cloth. Jesus said to them, 'Unbind him, and let him go.'

JOHN 11:41–44 (abridged)

After his conversation with Martha, Jesus had a similar one with her sister, Mary. This time, however, Jesus seems to have been rendered speechless by the sight of her tears and those of the crowd who had come to mourn Lazarus: he was 'greatly disturbed' and 'deeply moved' (v. 33). At the invitation to visit the tomb, Jesus also wept, evoking from the crowd strangely contrasting responses. Some said, 'See how he loved him!' while others wondered why, given such deep affection, he couldn't have kept Lazarus from dying.

When Jesus ordered the stone to be rolled away, Martha (ever practical) pointed out that there would be a dreadful stench, as Lazarus had been dead for four days. Jesus simply reminded them of his promise that if they believed, they would see 'the glory of God' (v. 40). So they removed the stone. Jesus offered a prayer of thanks to his Father, making it clear that what was to happen would be a sign that Jesus was sent by him. Then, turning to the tomb, he shouted, 'Lazarus, come out!' The dead man staggered out, still wrapped in his burial cloths. 'Unbind him,' Jesus ordered—from the stranglehold of death and from the 'sting' of death, which is sin (1 Corinthians 15:56). 'Let him go'—out into life and fresh air, back to family and friends, back to his old life, but a life that would never be the same again.

Lazarus was raised, but would one day experience death again. Jesus was raised, and death would 'no longer have dominion over him' (Romans 6:9). It is the resurrection of Christ that is the model for those who believe in him.

29 April

SINGING FOR JOY

It is good to give thanks to the Lord, to sing praises to your name, O Most High; to declare your steadfast love in the morning, and your faithfulness by night, to the music of the lute and the harp, to the melody of the lyre. For you, O Lord, have made me glad by your work; at the works of your hands I sing for joy. How great are your works, O Lord! Your thoughts are very deep!

PSALM 92:1–5

This is headed 'A psalm for the Sabbath day', which suggests that it was not so much a worship song for public occasions as an aid to personal devotion. It is certainly a psalm full of gratitude, by a writer who sees this attribute as shaping his approach to the whole sabbath day (and perhaps every day). In the morning he declares God's 'steadfast love'; in the evening, as night falls, he gets out his lute, harp or lyre and sings of God's faithfulness.

The motivation for this gratitude is simply put. 'You, O Lord, have made me glad by your work.' The second half of the verse echoes and expands the thought: 'at the works of your hands I sing for joy'. In other words, his gratitude is for what God has done—in all his 'work' day by day and in the creation itself. The psalmist recognizes that those great works are the fruit of God's wisdom, which gives meaning and purpose to the creation itself: 'Your thoughts are very deep.'

This is how the psalmist sees his Creator, as a God of awe and wonder but also as someone of infinite love. So, for him, God is not remote but personal and real, one on whom he can rely. It is this combination of thankfulness and joy that has shaped the character of the man who wrote these words: 'For you, O Lord, have made me glad.'

The middle part of this psalm is more sombre, as the psalmist reflects on those who fail to understand these things or experience this joy and gladness. He has little thought that God might have a purpose for them, too, nor any thought of sharing with them this wonderful vision of God's goodness.

30 April

ALWAYS FULL OF SAP

The righteous flourish like the palm tree, and grow like a cedar in Lebanon. They are planted in the house of the Lord; they flourish in the courts of our God. In old age they still produce fruit; they are always green and full of sap, showing that the Lord is upright; he is my rock, and there is no unrighteousness in him.

PSALM 92:12–15

These final verses of Psalm 92 pick up the positive note of the opening, but also seem to suggest that the writer is himself approaching, or is in, old age. If so, his earlier references to 'the dullard' and 'the stupid' (v. 6) perhaps suggest a temptation for those of 'riper years' to deplore the stupidity or dullness of the young without doing anything about it!

However, there is a different, and more charitable, interpretation of the psalmist's words. People have set themselves up against God, and sometimes they seem to flourish. Yet he is anxious to assert that the 'righteous' (by which he means the God-fearing) also flourish but in more rewarding ways. They may not have riches, wealth or power, but even in old age they still produce 'fruit', like the palm trees. They flourish 'in the courts of our God'—in the worship of the temple, where through happy familiarity they feel completely at home. Although physically old, they are spiritually full of life—living proof of the graciousness of God, who has been their rock all through life. Could that be said of those who had lived their lives as though God did not exist, or in selfish indulgence?

Probably all of us can think of people like those described by the psalmist—elderly men and women whose lives are full of the joy and freshness of faith.

Psalm 37:35 sees the wicked 'towering like a cedar of Lebanon', whereas our psalmist sees the righteous as growing 'like a cedar in Lebanon'. There's more than one way of flourishing, and the way of the God-fearing will in the end be seen as the truly satisfying one.

May: The Helper

Most of us at one time or another have been in desperate need of someone to help us, to stand beside us in a time of testing or to support us when we feel down. The whole concept of a 'helper' is a positive one, so it is wonderful to discover that God has provided us with a divine Helper, the Holy Spirit. It is the nature and work of the Spirit of God that provides our theme for May.

1 May

THE ADVOCATE

'If you love me, you will keep my commandments. And I will ask the Father, and he will give you another Advocate, to be with you forever. This is the Spirit of truth, whom the world cannot receive, because it neither sees him nor knows him. You know him, because he abides with you, and he will be in you. I will not leave you orphaned; I am coming to you.'
JOHN 14:15–18

We start our studies on the 'helper' in John's Gospel with Jesus' promise that he would ask the Father to give his followers a special 'Advocate'—the Holy Spirit, or 'Spirit of truth'. Of course the Spirit of God had been around as long as God had been around—eternally, without beginning or end. He was involved in the very act of creation, when the Spirit of God 'swept over the face of the waters' (Genesis 1:2) and the same 'breath' of God brought the first man to life (2:7).

Jesus' promise, however, was both more specific and more personal. The 'Advocate' (also translated 'Counsellor', 'Helper' or 'Comforter') catches the atmosphere of the law court (which may have been Jesus' intention). Your advocate is the lawyer who pleads your cause and gives you advice, support and help when you need it most. Each of those ideas contributes to our understanding of a rather strange Greek word, which literally means something like 'the alongside-helper'.

The Spirit of God had fulfilled that role for many people in ancient times, but always for a specific purpose or a limited duration. Now, with the return of Jesus to the Father, the children of the new covenant will not be left 'orphaned'. This special helper will come to them to plead their case, support their cause, strengthen them in time of need and provide wisdom when they call on him. The Holy Spirit was with them now, and would be 'in' them (or 'among' them) in the future.

God the Father is above us; God the Son is for us; God the Holy Spirit is within us. Yet the Trinity remains undivided—in the gift of the Spirit, the Father and the Son also come to us.

2 May

BORN OF THE SPIRIT

'Very truly, I tell you, no one can enter the kingdom of God without being born of water and Spirit. What is born of the flesh is flesh, and what is born of the Spirit is spirit. Do not be astonished that I said to you, "You must be born from above." The wind blows where it chooses, and you hear the sound of it, but you do not know where it comes from or where it goes. So it is with everyone who is born of the Spirit.'

JOHN 3:5–8

The description 'born-again Christian' has entered into the English language, usually meaning someone who has had a dramatic, life-changing conversion experience. In fact, as this passage makes clear, the term is saying the same thing twice: all Christians, by definition, are 'born again', or, more correctly, 'born from above'. To become a Christian is not an intellectual decision or a question of subscribing to a set of beliefs, but an encounter with the Holy Spirit, who alone can bring new spiritual life. That encounter may come in many different ways, some spectacular, some quiet and gradual, but the result is the same. A person who was 'born of the flesh' (in other words, had normal physical life) has been given a new life by the Holy Spirit.

This amazing process is likened by Jesus to the blowing of the wind. We can't actually see the wind; we can only see what it does—leaves blown across the garden, tree branches bending, waves being lashed high at sea. So is the work of the Holy Spirit. We can't see him at work, but we can see his work. 'Born of the Spirit' is a fascinating phrase, taking us back to Eden and the 'breathing' of life into the first man, and pointing forward to the gift of the Holy Spirit that would be given in the name of Jesus to all who believe in him. To be alive is wonderful. To be alive 'in the Spirit' is to be fully alive—alive to God.

There is a moment when the baby in the womb is 'quickened'—it begins to move and kick. There is also a moment when the human heart is touched by the Spirit of God in a divine 'quickening'.

3 May

THE SPIRIT OF THE LORD

Samuel said to Jesse, 'Are all your sons here?' And he said, 'There remains yet the youngest, but he is keeping the sheep.' And Samuel said to Jesse, 'Send and bring him; for we will not sit down until he comes here.' He sent and brought him in. Now he was ruddy, and had beautiful eyes, and was handsome. The Lord said, 'Rise and anoint him; for this is the one.' Then Samuel took the horn of oil, and anointed him... and the spirit of the Lord came mightily upon David from that day forward.

1 SAMUEL 16:11–13 (abridged)

This is the final part of the intriguing story of David's anointing to be the future king of Israel. God had directed the prophet Samuel to the home of David's father, Jesse, to meet his sons. One by one the seven oldest sons—tall, sturdy, attractive young men—passed before the prophet, only to be rejected. As God explained to a baffled Samuel, 'The Lord does not see as mortals see; they look on the outward appearance but the Lord looks on the heart' (v. 7). Finally, the prophet had to ask if these were all of Jesse's sons. He might well have replied, 'How many more do you want?' but in fact he simply admitted that there was still the youngest, out in the fields. David was duly sent for, and eventually appeared before Samuel. He was 'ruddy'—well tanned from the sun—and handsome, with 'beautiful eyes'.

The Lord indicated to his prophet that this was the one. He was to anoint David with the horn of oil he had brought with him. Although it was some time before David actually became king, his destiny was sealed. He had been chosen, called and anointed—and he would prove to be Israel's greatest king as well as the ancestor of an even greater descendant, the one the hymn calls 'Great David's greater Son', Jesus.

Throughout the Bible, anointing is a mark of being set aside for a specific calling, and also a sign of the gift of God's Spirit to enable that calling to be fulfilled. Jesus is known to us as 'Christ', which means 'anointed one'.

4 May

THE THIRSTY SOUL

I remember the days of old, I think about all your deeds, I meditate on the works of your hands. I stretch out my hands to you; my soul thirsts for you like a parched land. Answer me quickly, O Lord; my spirit fails. Do not hide your face from me, or I shall be like those who go down to the Pit. Let me hear of your steadfast love in the morning, for in you I put my trust. Teach me the way I should go, for to you I lift up my soul. Save me, O Lord, from my enemies; I have fled to you for refuge. Teach me to do your will, for you are my God. Let your good spirit lead me on a level path.
PSALM 143:5–10

One of the most reassuring things about the book of Psalms is the evidence it provides that human nature hasn't changed. Most of us can echo various prayers of the psalmist. His fears are our fears, his hopes and longings ours, too. Here he echoes a familiar phrase in the psalms: 'You are my God'. On the basis of that personal commitment, he can pour out his soul in a time of trouble. In the earlier verses we have hints of the nature of that distress. An enemy has 'pursued' him, crushing his life to the ground and making him 'sit in darkness like those long dead' (v. 3). His spirit faints within him; his heart is 'appalled' (v. 4). Nevertheless, he turns to God, first recalling past mercies and blessings. The Lord has already done wonderful things, and meditating on them brings him reassurance. Then he turns his thoughts into prayer: 'I stretch out my hands to you' (a lovely gesture of dependence); 'my soul thirsts for you' like a traveller in a desert land.

As he prays, a pattern of trust emerges. He prays for guidance: 'Teach me the way.' He prays for rescue from his troubles: 'Save me, O Lord, from my enemies.' He prays for inner obedience to God's purpose: 'Teach me to do your will.' And he prays for a renewed life: 'Lead me on a level path.'

Guidance, rescue, insight and renewal: that would make a very good pattern of prayer for anybody.

5 May

THE ROOT OF JESSE

A shoot shall come out from the stump of Jesse, and a branch shall grow out of his roots. The spirit of the Lord shall rest on him, the spirit of wisdom and understanding… counsel and might… knowledge and the fear of the Lord. His delight shall be in the fear of the Lord. He shall not judge by what his eyes see, or decide by what his ears hear; but with righteousness he shall judge the poor, and decide with equity for the meek of the earth; he shall strike the earth with the rod of his mouth, and with the breath of his lips he shall kill the wicked. Righteousness shall be the belt around his waist, and faithfulness the belt around his loins.

ISAIAH 11:1–5 (abridged)

These words of Isaiah the prophet come from a period in Israel's history when the future looked ominous. The nation had turned from God and was about to experience the terrible consequences: defeat by hated enemies and enslavement in a foreign land. Yet even in the darkness, the prophet sounds a note of hope. As we read two days ago, Jesse the Bethlehemite, the father of the most renowned king of Israel, has descendants, and one of those will be the promised saviour.

The description of that saviour, the anointed Servant of the Lord, has been seen by Christians since the earliest days of the Church as a prophetic picture of Jesus. He was born in Bethlehem, the birthplace also of David, son of Jesse. Through his legal father, Joseph, he was a descendant of Jesse—an ancestry traced by Matthew in the opening verses of his Gospel. Few would care to dispute that the 'spirit of the Lord' rested on Jesus, nor deny him those wonderful qualities of wisdom, understanding, counsel, might, knowledge and reverence of the Lord. Jesus himself defined his mission as to bring blessing to the poor and to the meek of the earth (Matthew 5:3, 5; Luke 4:18), and through him the world will one day be judged (see Romans 2:16).

The shepherd boy who became their greatest king was the hope of Israel. The 'good shepherd' who was crowned with thorns is now the hope of the world.

6 May

LIKE THE RISING SUN

Now these are the last words of David: The oracle of David, son of Jesse, the oracle of the man whom God exalted, the anointed of the God of Jacob, the favourite of the Strong One of Israel: The spirit of the Lord speaks through me, his word is upon my tongue. The God of Israel has spoken, the Rock of Israel has said to me: One who rules over people justly, ruling in the fear of God, is like the light of morning, like the sun rising on a cloudless morning, gleaming from the rain on the grassy land.

2 SAMUEL 23:1–4

There are a lot of 'last words' in the Bible—Moses, Jacob, Jesus in the upper room, and here King David. He was anointed king by Samuel, but David is clear that this anointing was actually by 'the God of Jacob', of whom Samuel was the agent. Kings and priests of Israel were anointed with oil as a sign that their role was beyond human achieving. Only with the spirit of the Lord upon them could they hope to fulfil it.

David speaks here of his 'oracle'—the prophetic utterance that God gave him. The last part of verse 1 could well be translated 'the singer of Israel's psalms', which makes good sense of the following amplifications—that the 'spirit of the Lord speaks through me, his word is upon my tongue'. He was seen as a prophetic figure by the people of Israel, during his lifetime and through the nation's history.

Three parallel expressions stress his status: first, his family ('son of Jesse'); second, his exaltation by God; and third, his position as an anointed monarch. This is why the Jews expected that one day 'another David', an anointed, kingly figure, the 'Messiah', would appear. Then there follows a beautiful picture of the good ruler. He rules justly and in the fear of God. Such a rule lights up the people, like 'the sun rising on a cloudless morning'. David, with all his human faults, was such a king, constantly aware of the reality and daily presence of God.

'The spirit of the Lord speaks through me.' That's a bold claim, but anyone who reads his psalms will feel that David had the right to make it.

7 May

THE INESCAPABLE PRESENCE

Where can I go from your spirit? Or where can I flee from your presence? If I ascend to heaven, you are there; if I make my bed in Sheol, you are there. If I take the wings of the morning and settle at the farthest limits of the sea, even there your hand shall lead me, and your right hand shall hold me fast. If I say, 'Surely the darkness shall cover me, and the light around me become night', even the darkness is not dark to you; the night is as bright as the day, for darkness is as light to you.

PSALM 139:7–12

This is an amazing piece of poetry, a perfect example of the characteristic 'parallelism' of Hebrew poetry—balancing one thought or picture with another, either in contrast or in amplification. More than that, it is a profound statement of truth about God. We refer to him as 'our Father in heaven', but it would be a serious mistake to think that he stays at home or is limited to some celestial realm. He is the God of the whole creation and fills every part of it with his presence, so that there is literally nowhere where God is not.

The psalmist puts it in a series of propositions. 'Just suppose' I could fly above the clouds, would you be there? Yes. Just suppose I went to the abode of the dead, *Sheol*—surely you wouldn't be there? Yes, I would. Suppose I flew with the dawning sun as it travels to the ends of the earth across the seas, would you be there? Yes. And suppose I lived permanently in the pitch dark of an Eastern night, could you find me there? Yes, easily—darkness and light are the same to me.

This notion of the omnipresence of God, inhabiting every corner of his creation and from whom nothing is hidden, is seen by the psalmist not as scary but as deeply reassuring. The hand of God will lead him, the light of God will find him, the presence of God will support him wherever he is, even in the grave.

The psalmist is not trying to escape from God but rejoices to know that wherever he is and whatever he does, he is never beyond the reach of God's love.

8 May

THE SPIRIT GAVE THEM REST

Then they remembered the days of old, of Moses his servant. Where is the one who brought them up out of the sea with the shepherds of his flock? Where is the one who put within them his holy spirit, who caused his glorious arm to march at the right hand of Moses, who divided the waters before them to make for himself an everlasting name, who led them through the depths? Like a horse in the desert, they did not stumble. Like cattle that go down into the valley, the spirit of the Lord gave them rest.
ISAIAH 63:11–14

It's interesting that these words of encouragement and faith are set in the context of complaint that the present generation has forgotten what God once did for them, or even—appalling thought—that God has turned his back on them. Of course, the prophet is writing in this way to remind them that God doesn't change and that the blessings their ancestors enjoyed are still available for those who trust him.

After all, previous generations also rebelled against God, forgot his faithful promises, strayed from his ways. But the turning point for them, as it could be for the present generation, was remembering—such a key word in the Bible. They remembered the days of Moses, the crossing of the Red Sea and the journey through the wilderness when, time and again, they learnt that however dire the situation, God was with them and his Spirit would put their hearts at rest.

These are words for times of spiritual depression or seeming defeat. Circumstances change—they certainly did for the people of Isaiah's time—but the God who cares for them does not. They needed to 'remember', and to trust that the unchanging God would not abandon his own. Like cattle coming down from the parched upper slopes of the hills to the cool pastures of the valley, they would find that there is still rest and refreshment for the weary pilgrim.

On the night of his betrayal, Jesus called his disciples to 'remember him', and gave them visible signs—bread and wine—to make that remembering easier.

9 May

THE SPIRIT FOR ALL

Then afterwards I will pour out my spirit on all flesh; your sons and your daughters shall prophesy, your old men shall dream dreams, and your young men shall see visions. Even on the male and female slaves… I will pour out my spirit. I will show portents in the heavens and on the earth, blood and fire and columns of smoke. The sun shall be turned to darkness, and the moon to blood, before the great and terrible day of the Lord comes. Then everyone who calls on the name of the Lord shall be saved.

JOEL 2:28–32A (abridged)

These words are, in a spiritual sense, revolutionary. Joel promises that after the Lord has delivered his people, following their repentance, his Spirit will be poured out upon 'all flesh'. This would have seemed an astonishing idea to his hearers, for surely God's Spirit was given to individuals for specific tasks (Gideon, Samson, David, Elisha and so on) and certainly not to Gentiles? Yet now the promise is for all—and it couldn't be more explicit. 'All flesh' simply means all human beings—men and women, young and old, even male and female slaves. Truly God has no favourites, as the apostle Peter learnt in dramatic circumstances (see Acts 10:34–35).

These words of Joel were quoted by Peter on the day of Pentecost, when the Holy Spirit was 'poured out' on the disciples and then on many of the crowd who heard them preach. He placed the promise as relating to 'the last days', which fits in with Joel's prediction that it would precede 'the great and terrible day of the Lord'. That was how the early Christians thought of the period of time between the ascension of Jesus to heaven and his promised return as the Judge of all. What they couldn't possibly have known was how long the 'last days' would be, as God in his mercy has provided more time for people to repent and believe.

This passage was not intended to terrify its hearers but to offer a wonderful promise of God. His Spirit is intended for all, for every human being.

10 May

FILLED WITH THE SPIRIT

But the angel said to him, 'Do not be afraid, Zechariah, for your prayer has been heard. Your wife Elizabeth will bear you a son, and you will name him John… Many will rejoice at his birth, for he will be great in the sight of the Lord. He must never drink wine or strong drink; even before his birth he will be filled with the Holy Spirit. He will turn many of the people of Israel to the Lord their God. With the spirit and power of Elijah he will go before him… to make ready a people prepared for the Lord.'
LUKE 1:13–17 (abridged)

This encounter took place in the temple, by the altar of incense, where Zechariah was officiating as a priest. He and his hitherto barren wife were to have a son—the promised 'Elijah' who would precede the Lord's anointed, the Messiah. In order to fulfil that task, the child would be 'filled with the Holy Spirit', even before his birth. In that power he would prepare people for the one who was to come.

In all of this, as in so much of John's ministry, there are constant echoes of the Old Testament. Like the heroes of the past, he would be filled with the Spirit of God for a particular task. Like many of them, he would be the unexpected son born to a mother who had assumed she was unable to have children. Like many of them, he would abstain from alcohol. It is almost as though John were the last of the Old Testament prophets. Jesus himself seemed to be implying this in one of his more teasing statements: 'Among those born of woman no one has arisen greater than John the Baptist; yet the least in the kingdom of heaven is greater than he' (Matthew 11:11). Presumably he was not belittling the ministry of John, his cousin, but pointing up the distinction between the last voice of the old covenant and those fortunate ones who were the first beneficiaries of the new one.

John was filled with the Spirit of God to do his work. At his baptism, Jesus was also filled with the Holy Spirit for his work. The difference was that Jesus would then baptize others, not with water but with the Holy Spirit.

11 May

HUMAN AND DIVINE

The angel said to her, 'Do not be afraid, Mary, for you have found favour with God. And now, you will conceive in your womb and bear a son, and you will name him Jesus. He will be great, and will be called the Son of the Most High, and the Lord God will give to him the throne of his ancestor David…' Mary said to the angel, 'How can this be, since I am a virgin?' The angel said to her, 'The Holy Spirit will come upon you, and the power of the Most High will overshadow you; therefore the child to be born will be holy; he will be called Son of God.'

LUKE 1:30–32, 34–35

This statement by the angel Gabriel represents one of the two most daring claims of the Bible. The first is that everything created has its source in one divine being, God. The second is that at a point in the history of that creation the divine being entered human life in the form of a baby. Neither statement is immediately credible or comprehensible to the human mind. Yet the Old Testament begins with the first, as a founding principle; and the New Testament begins with the second, upon which the whole succeeding story of Christianity depends.

To believe either is an act of faith—but it is not blind faith. We can observe God's creation and ask ourselves whether it appears to be shaped by design or by chance. There really is no other explanation on offer. And we can look at the life of Jesus as the Gospels record it and ask whether or not this looks like a life inhabited by the divine.

This story of the angel and Mary may help us. Whatever precise interpretation we may put on the words, the message is clear. A child will be born who will have God the Holy Spirit as his father and Mary of Nazareth as his mother. So the baby will be a perfect fusion of two beings, which means that he will be both human and divine. Not sometimes one and sometimes the other, but always both!

Son of Mary, Son of God: in this way Jesus in himself bridges the moral and spiritual gulf between God's holiness and our sinfulness.

12 May

A MESSAGE FOR AN OLD MAN

It had been revealed to [Simeon] by the Holy Spirit that he would not see death before he had seen the Lord's Messiah. Guided by the Spirit, Simeon came into the temple; and when the parents brought in the child Jesus, to do for him what was customary under the law, Simeon took him in his arms and praised God, saying, 'Master, now you are dismissing your servant in peace, according to your word; for my eyes have seen your salvation, which you have prepared in the presence of all peoples, a light for revelation to the Gentiles and for glory to your people Israel.'

LUKE 2:26–32

Simeon's song of praise is known by many Christians as the *Nunc Dimittis*, the Latin for 'Now dismiss'. It's still part of the Anglican service of Evening Prayer, and is by any estimation a lovely piece of poetry. Simeon, 'guided by the Spirit', is in the temple when Mary and Joseph bring the infant Jesus for his dedication to the Lord, as required by the law. This practice went back to the first Passover, when the firstborn sons of Egypt died in the plague but the Hebrew boys were spared through the sacrifice of a lamb. All firstborn males were to be 'offered' to the Lord, and then, as it were, 'bought back' by the making of a sacrifice—in this case a 'pair of turtledoves' (v. 24), which suggests that Jesus' parents were counted as poor people.

The song itself is a short but moving summary of various scriptural themes relating to God's promises being fulfilled in the coming of a saviour. Simeon is happy to die, secure in the knowledge that the future is in God's hands and that his old eyes have actually seen the anointed one, God's work of healing and restoration. Jesus was a tiny baby, but inherent in those few pounds of human flesh was the salvation of the world, for the promise was not only to 'your people Israel' but the light of Jesus would also shine in revelation to the Gentiles.

Jesus' parents were too poor to afford a better sacrifice than a pair of birds. In such a way, the one 'born king of the Jews' (Matthew 2:2) entered the world.

13 May

SPIRIT, WATER, FIRE

As the people were filled with expectation, and all were questioning in their hearts concerning John, whether he might be the Messiah, John answered all of them by saying, 'I baptize you with water; but one who is more powerful than I is coming; I am not worthy to untie the thong of his sandals. He will baptize you with the Holy Spirit and fire. His winnowing-fork is in his hand, to clear his threshing-floor and to gather the wheat into his granary; but the chaff he will burn with unquenchable fire.'
LUKE 3:15–17

John the Baptist was the 'voice in the wilderness' prophesied by Isaiah (40:3), 'preparing the way of the Lord'. He became a figure of enormous influence, huge crowds flocking to the Jordan valley to hear him preach and be baptized by him in the river. It was not surprising, then, that some wondered whether he was the promised Messiah.

John was at pains to dismiss such ideas. He was the forerunner of the Messiah, not the promised one himself. He baptized with water, washing away the outward marks of defilement as a sign of repentance; the coming one would baptize with (or 'in') the Holy Spirit, and with 'fire'. This baptism would be more than a ritual cleansing from defilement. Rather, it would represent a complete conversion of character, inward cleansing and the breath of a new life.

Not only that, but the true Messiah of God would be infinitely more powerful than John, who used a vivid metaphor to describe their relative positions: 'I am not worthy to untie the thong of his sandals'—the slave's duty in the household. There is no account of John performing miracles as Jesus did, and, when John was eventually cruelly killed by Herod, he was taken to his burial by his disciples and left there, while Jesus the Messiah was gloriously raised from death by his Father.

John had his task and he fulfilled it perfectly, with no thought of status or reputation or public acclaim. In many ways, he is the perfect example of the true witness to Christ, saying, 'Look, here is the Lamb of God!' (John 1:36).

14 May

TRULY BLESSED

The Lord spoke to Moses, saying: Speak to Aaron and his sons, saying, Thus you shall bless the Israelites: You shall say to them, The Lord bless you and keep you; the Lord make his face to shine upon you, and be gracious to you; the Lord lift up his countenance upon you, and give you peace. So they shall put my name on the Israelites, and I will bless them.
NUMBERS 6:22–27

This is known as the 'Aaronic blessing', because Aaron and his sons were the priests of Israel and this was the blessing that the Lord had commanded them to use. Needless to say, its use has spread more widely, so that today these are familiar words to people in many different circumstances, from weddings and great State occasions to the bedsides of the dying. There is a peculiar quality of comfort and assurance in the words of this prayer, possibly because it constantly invokes the Lord and especially because it is asking him to 'look' on us—in other words, to keep a watch over us.

It is also a prayer for peace—a peace which is a gift of God. There can be few of us who would not wish to be blessed and 'kept' by the Lord, to live under his care. We would love to feel that God's 'face' was 'shining on us'—that we were living under his approval. And all of us, without exception, need to live under his grace, to know that all that we have and are is a gift from our Creator. So comprehensive is this blessing that it seems to touch every fundamental need of the human heart: protection, peace, acceptance.

The smiling face of the Creator looks down on his troubled people and blesses them. The loving care of the Creator enfolds his children in his care and gives them peace.

15 May

THE HELPER OF THE NEEDY

Rise up, O Lord; O God, lift up your hand; do not forget the oppressed. Why do the wicked renounce God, and say in their hearts, 'You will not call us to account'? But you do see! Indeed you note trouble and grief, that you may take it into your hands; the helpless commit themselves to you; you have been the helper of the orphan… O Lord, you will hear the desire of the meek; you will strengthen their heart, you will incline your ear to do justice for the orphan and the oppressed, so that those from earth may strike terror no more.

PSALM 10:12–14, 17–18

The psalmist is very troubled by the arrogance and apparent immunity of those he calls 'the wicked' (v. 2). Why does God stand so 'far off'? Why doesn't he do something about them? The psalmist even has a suggestion or two, in verses which we've omitted: break their arms; cause them to perish from the land (vv. 15–16). It's a problem often posed, and not only by believers. If God is so good and mighty, why does he let these people get away with it? Not only that: they prosper (v. 5), they behave as though God didn't exist and no one will ever hold them to account. 'They think in their heart, "God has forgotten, he has hidden his face, he will never see it"' (v. 11).

This psalm is a call to God to 'rise up' and do something about it. However, the psalmist, being a man of faith, knows in his heart that the Lord does see all that the wicked are doing. God notes the trouble and grief that they are causing, and as the 'helpless' commit themselves into God's hands they find that he will 'strengthen their heart'. Justice will eventually be done and, until it is revealed, those who trust God must hold fast to his promises. The orphan and the oppressed will receive justice because God is a God of justice. Meanwhile, the consolation of the 'meek' is within themselves, in that strengthened heart, in that confident trust.

'Justice now!' we cry. 'Justice one day,' God replies. 'Until then—trust me.'

16 May

BE STILL, AND KNOW THAT I AM GOD

Come, behold the works of the Lord; see what desolations he has brought on the earth. He makes wars cease to the end of the earth; he breaks the bow, and shatters the spear; he burns the shields with fire. 'Be still, and know that I am God! I am exalted among the nations, I am exalted in the earth.' The Lord of hosts is with us; the God of Jacob is our refuge.
PSALM 46:8–11

This is the psalm that begins with the triumphant words, 'God is our refuge and strength, a very present help in trouble.' The same psalm ends with this vivid invitation to 'behold the works of the Lord'—to see with the eye of faith what it really means for God to be a 'refuge'.

First we are invited to view the 'desolations' he has brought on the earth—but this is not desolation as we usually understand it. God will end war by smashing the weapons that make it possible. He is a God who intervenes, who is actively on the side of peace and justice, who opposes those bent on war and terror by destroying them and their evil works. If that's desolation, perhaps we could do with a bit more of it.

His words were addressed to a people who lived in constant fear of war and invasion. If we think our own times are violent, we should reread some Old Testament history! Mostly it is an account of one battle after another, of conquest and defeat, of people carried off into exile, of towns and villages burnt to the ground and their residents put to the sword. There is nothing new about bloodshed and violence.

But this is not the will of the God who is our refuge and strength. He calls us to 'be still', to cease from our endless arguments and disputations and conflicts, and recognize that he is God. The earth has one ruler, and he is not an earthly king or emperor but the 'Lord of hosts', the God who has revealed himself to the descendants of Jacob.

No one is a greater 'peacemaker' than the God who 'makes wars cease to the end of the earth', but for that vision of peace to be realized his human creatures will need to 'be still and know' that he is God.

17 May

HELP IN WEAKNESS

We know that the whole creation has been groaning in labour pains until now; and not only the creation, but we ourselves, who have the first fruits of the Spirit, groan inwardly while we wait for adoption, the redemption of our bodies. For in hope we were saved… But if we hope for what we do not see, we wait for it with patience. Likewise the Spirit helps us in our weakness; for we do not know how to pray as we ought, but that very Spirit intercedes with sighs too deep for words. And God, who searches the heart, knows what is the mind of the Spirit, because the Spirit intercedes for the saints according to the will of God.

ROMANS 8:22–27 (abridged)

This is a passage about weakness—not only human weakness, which is a common theme of the Bible, but the weakness of what the apostle Paul calls 'the whole creation'. Its weakness, as he sees it, is its transitory nature: everything we know weakens and decays in time. Nothing, not even the hills, seas and skies, will last for ever.

And in that transitory scene, humans are exposed in all their mortal frailty. Yes, even those who 'have the first fruits of the Spirit', who are alive with the risen life of Christ, are in a transitory situation: we 'wait for… the redemption of our bodies'. That is the Christian hope, in which we were saved—the hope that finally our redemption will be complete and we shall stand as new people in the kingdom of God.

Meanwhile, we 'groan inwardly'—a lovely phrase! Happily, God hears and interprets our groans not as complaints or impatience but as longings, which the Spirit translates into wordless prayers. Our 'groans' may be occasioned by the weaknesses of our flesh, the weight of mortality. Or they may be the longing for the fulfilment of God's purpose—the 'freedom of the glory of the children of God' (v. 21).

The heart of prayer is not eloquence but the inward working of the Holy Spirit. Sometimes tears, sometimes laughter, sometimes sighs—the Spirit translates all of them into intercession that reaches the heart of God.

18 May

A SYMPATHETIC SAVIOUR

Since, then, we have a great high priest who has passed through the heavens, Jesus, the Son of God, let us hold fast to our confession. For we do not have a high priest who is unable to sympathize with our weaknesses, but we have one who in every respect has been tested as we are, yet without sin. Let us therefore approach the throne of grace with boldness, so that we may receive mercy and find grace to help in time of need.

HEBREWS 4:14–16

The high priest was a crucial figure in temple worship. He alone could enter the 'holy place' on the Day of Atonement, passing through the heavy curtain that excluded everyone else, bearing in a basin the blood of a newly slaughtered bull as a sacrifice. There, before the altar, he would 'make atonement' for the publicly confessed sins of the people.

A priest is called to represent God to the people, and the people to God. The high priest of Israel represented to the people the authority and holiness of God, but to God he represented the prayers of the people. In one sense the first of these was virtually impossible, because the high priest was himself human, not divine. The second function was more achievable, because the high priest also needed forgiveness, also had needs and fears and weaknesses. On the other hand, because of his particular role in the religion of Israel, he may have found it difficult to identify with many of the problems facing ordinary people.

However, as the writer of Hebrews argues, Jesus, the Son of God—whom the writer has already identified as our 'high priest' (3:1)—is perfectly qualified both to represent God to us, as his anointed Son, and us to God, as the 'Son of Man'. He knew the stresses and sorrows of human life. He was let down by friends, betrayed by a colleague, unjustly accused. That is why he can 'sympathize'—perhaps a better word would be 'identify'—with our failures, burdens and weakness.

The sacrifice Jesus offered for us was not the blood of a bull but his own blood. His 'sympathy' for us is not simply a generous attribute but a costly gift.

19 May

PHARAOH'S DREAM

It is as I told Pharaoh; God has shown to Pharaoh what he is about to do. There will come seven years of great plenty throughout all the land of Egypt. After them there will arise seven years of famine, and all the plenty will be forgotten in the land of Egypt; the famine will consume the land... And the doubling of Pharaoh's dream means that the thing is fixed by God, and God will shortly bring it about. Now therefore let Pharaoh select a man who is discerning and wise, and set him over the land of Egypt.
GENESIS 41:28–30, 32–33

The speaker here is, of course, Joseph, he of the 'amazing technicolor dreamcoat'. A prisoner in the royal jail, his reputation as an interpreter of dreams meant that when the king's soothsayers couldn't interpret his dream about the fat and thin cattle, Joseph was brought from the cells to help. He made it clear that it was God, not his own skill, that interpreted dreams, and then proceeded to tell Pharaoh what this very important dream meant. His interpretation was followed by some advice: to appoint a man with power to supervise the next seven years' harvests, so that enough was stored away to meet the need caused by the seven years of poor harvests that would follow.

Joseph was given the job, with consequences for himself, his family and the whole Hebrew people that were to shape their history and, indeed, the history of the world. Through Joseph and through his tangled relationships with his family, God was secretly working out his purpose. It was not only the people of Egypt who would be saved from famine, but also those precious descendants of Abraham, through whom God had promised that 'all the families of the earth' would be blessed (Genesis 12:3).

'God has shown to Pharaoh what he is about to do.' Yes, but, as so often, it took someone else to explain the uncomfortable truth to him. God speaks in many ways but sometimes we need help to understand what he is saying to us.

20 May

RECEIVE THE HOLY SPIRIT

When it was evening... and the doors of the house where the disciples had met were locked for fear of the Jews, Jesus came and stood among them and said, 'Peace be with you.' After he said this, he showed them his hands and his side... Jesus said to them again, 'Peace be with you. As the Father has sent me, so I send you.' When he had said this, he breathed on them and said to them, 'Receive the Holy Spirit. If you forgive the sins of any, they are forgiven them; if you retain the sins of any, they are retained.'
JOHN 20:19–23 (abridged)

This is John's account of the giving of the Holy Spirit to the disciples, not at Pentecost (some 50 days later) but on the very evening of the resurrection. They were gathered, full of fear and anxiety, in the upper room, with the doors locked for fear of the temple authorities, when Jesus 'came and stood among them'. Twice he greeted them with the word 'Peace!', recognizing the terrifying nature of his appearance among them just two days after they had seen him brutally killed on the cross. He then commissioned them for the task for which he had long been preparing them: 'As the Father has sent me, so I send you.'

They must have been staggered at the nature of the task. The Lord God Almighty had sent Jesus into the world as his representative, to live and die for his people. Now they—a bunch of former fishermen, tax collectors, farmers, political activists and other Galilean villagers—were being commissioned for the same task, to be carried out in the same way. So his simple but dramatic gesture of breathing on them must have seemed totally appropriate. To breathe on them was to share with them his 'spirit', who was none other than the Holy Spirit of God. By the Spirit's power they would proclaim both God's judgment of sin and the forgiveness made possible by the death of his Son.

The promised outpouring of the Spirit would come at Pentecost with wind and fire and shouts. This is an altogether quieter, more intimate blessing, the passing on of the Spirit from the Master to his anxious disciples.

21 May

WIND AND FIRE

When the day of Pentecost had come, they were all together in one place. And suddenly from heaven there came a sound like the rush of a violent wind, and it filled the entire house where they were sitting. Divided tongues, as of fire, appeared among them, and a tongue rested on each of them. All of them were filled with the Holy Spirit and began to speak in other languages, as the Spirit gave them ability.

ACTS 2:1–4

Here, at the beginning of the book of Acts, is the account of the events on the day of Pentecost, the Jewish festival which fell about 40 days after Jesus' resurrection. The disciples had been promised a mysterious 'Helper' or 'Advocate', the Holy Spirit, who would stand by them, inspire and guide their lives, give them words to speak and enable them to achieve great things. How much they understood of this, it's hard to tell. In any case, as they waited in the upper room that had been their base since the resurrection, there was a dramatic divine intervention. 'All of them,' says Luke, 'were filled with the Holy Spirit'.

The word 'all' is interesting, because we have already been told that there were about 120 of them (1:15), including a number of women, among them Mary the mother of Jesus. Traditional depictions of Pentecost often simply show the twelve apostles 'crowned' with tongues of fire, but the repetition by Luke of the word 'all' (1:14, 2:1, 3–4) implies that the larger group of disciples were the astonished recipients of the gift of the Spirit. They 'all' began to speak in other languages, thus enabling the multilingual crowd, already in Jerusalem for the festival, to understand their message.

Peter, already seen as the leader of the apostles, addressed the people who had gathered in amazement outside the house, explaining that this was the gift of the Spirit promised by the prophet Joel, and then proclaiming with a new boldness the message of the resurrection.

It is still the Holy Spirit who drives us out with the message of the gospel.

22 May

THE OIL THAT NEVER RUNS OUT

She said, 'As the Lord your God lives, I have nothing baked, only a handful of meal in a jar, and a little oil in a jug; I am now gathering a couple of sticks, so that I may go home and prepare it for myself and my son, that we may eat it, and die.' Elijah said to her, 'Do not be afraid; go and do as you have said; but first make me a little cake of it... and afterwards make something for yourself and your son. For thus says the Lord the God of Israel: The jar of meal will not be emptied and the jug of oil will not fail until the day that the Lord sends rain on the earth.' She went and did as Elijah said, so that she as well as he and her household ate for many days. The jar of meal was not emptied, neither did the jug of oil fail.

1 KINGS 17:12–16 (abridged)

This is the first of three stories we shall be reading about the prophet Elijah. He lived in the ninth century BC, between the early prophets, such as Samuel and Nathan, and the later prophets of Israel such as Isaiah and Jeremiah, a time when the Israelite religion was under constant pressure from the cults of the surrounding nations, especially the fertility cult of Baal. This first story is a typical example of one of his miracles, each of them significant in the contemporary setting.

There was a famine in the land and Elijah had come to a town called Zarephath, where the Lord had told him that a widow would feed him. When he got there, he saw a woman gathering sticks, and first asked her for water. He then added 'and a morsel of bread' (v. 11). She explained that she had nothing left to eat beyond a handful of meal and a little oil in a jug. After that was consumed, she and her son would die of hunger. Elijah nevertheless insisted that she first made him a little cake, and coupled it with a promise that if she did this, she and her son would not go short of food. In the event, the prophet stayed with her 'many days' and the supplies never ran out.

'First make me...' It seems selfish of Elijah, but in fact he was inviting the widow to put God first and thus to discover that those who do so lack nothing.

23 May

REST AND FOOD

[Elijah] sat down under a solitary broom tree. He asked that he might die: 'It is enough; now, O Lord, take away my life, for I am no better than my ancestors.' Then he lay down under the broom tree and fell asleep. Suddenly an angel touched him and said to him, 'Get up and eat.' He looked, and there at his head was a cake baked on hot stones, and a jar of water… The angel of the Lord came a second time, touched him, and said, 'Get up and eat, otherwise the journey will be too much for you.' He got up, and ate and drank; then he went in the strength of that food for forty days and forty nights to Horeb the mount of God.

1 KINGS 19:4–8 (abridged)

Elijah is in a fit of depression. Ahab's wife, Jezebel, had opposed his work and killed many of the Lord's prophets. Now she was hunting Elijah himself. Defeated and isolated, he fled to the desert and sheltered under a broom tree, pleading with God to end his life there and then.

The divine strategy was rather more positive than that, but before it could be put into motion, there were a couple of ways in which Elijah needed practical help. He needed rest, food and drink, and miraculously, there in the desert, all three were provided. Cakes were baking on some hot stones nearby, and alongside them was a jug of water. Elijah rested for a while and was awakened for a second helping. Then he was able to go 'in the strength of that food' on a 40-day journey on foot to Horeb. When he got there, he found a cave and spent the night in it (v. 9).

The scene was now set for a historic encounter between the Lord and his prophet—an encounter that would lead to enormous changes. Elijah would have known that he had been brought to this place at this moment for a purpose. The rest, the food and the drink were not incidentals but crucial elements in the drama to follow.

Sometimes a problem seems so overwhelming that we can't see beyond it. Like Elijah, we need rest and refreshment before we can be shown the way ahead.

24 May

THE SOUND OF SHEER SILENCE

[God] said, 'Go out and stand on the mountain before the Lord, for the Lord is about to pass by.' Now there was a great wind, so strong that it was splitting mountains and breaking rocks in pieces before the Lord, but the Lord was not in the wind; and after the wind an earthquake, but the Lord was not in the earthquake; and after the earthquake a fire, but the Lord was not in the fire; and after the fire a sound of sheer silence... Then there came a voice to him that said, 'What are you doing here, Elijah?'

1 KINGS 19:11–13 (abridged)

This wonderful story, echoed in the words of the hymn 'Dear Lord and Father of mankind', is a powerful reminder that God does not necessarily come to us in power and might. As Elijah, at God's command, stood outside the cave, he saw a succession of displays of power: wind, earthquake, fire. Surely, he must have thought, the Almighty God is going to speak his message to me in these phenomena, making what he has to say unavoidable and unmistakable. When humans want attention, they generally shout. Would not God do the same? After all, on Mount Sinai, at the giving of the law to Moses, such displays of power convinced Moses and his companions that they were encountering the living God, Yahweh (Exodus 19:16–19).

God did not speak through the earthquake, wind or fire—though of course he might have done! As Elijah stood there, surprised and disappointed, perhaps, not to have caught the voice of God in the elements, there was something just as dramatic and possibly more rare. It was, as our translation correctly renders it, 'the sound of sheer silence'. That is, of course, a paradox: silence, by definition, has no sound. Yet total silence is as elemental as an earthquake and equally disturbing. No sound of wind or birds, no human voice, no movement of foot, yet in the very absence God spoke.

When words have failed, time and again people have found that silence has spoken. Sometimes it's only when we shut up that God opens up.

25 May

THE OIL OF ANOINTING

You shall make of these a sacred anointing-oil blended as by the perfumer... With it you shall anoint the tent of meeting and the ark of the covenant, and the table and all its utensils, and the lampstand and its utensils, and the altar of incense, and the altar of burnt-offering with all its utensils, and the basin with its stand; you shall consecrate them, so that they may be most holy; whatever touches them will become holy. You shall anoint Aaron and his sons, and consecrate them, in order that they may serve me as priests. You shall say to the Israelites, 'This shall be my holy anointing-oil throughout your generations.'

EXODUS 30:25–31 (abridged)

In the midst of the complicated directions recorded in Exodus by which the rituals of Israel's religion were to be ordered, there come these instructions about the holy anointing oil. Blended from myrrh, cinnamon, aromatic cane, cassia and olive oil, it would become a vital element in the consecration of objects of worship and of the priests who led worship. The kings of Israel were also anointed with it, but so were the altars of the temple, the ark of the covenant, the lampstand and other utensils. It was the anointing that set them apart for holy use.

For centuries the kings and queens of England have been anointed with oil at their coronation, and increasingly candidates for baptism are anointed—the ancient practice of 'chrism'. In every case, the purpose is to seal with the holy oil a significant change of status or purpose. This anointing is a sign of the Spirit of God, because it is the Holy Spirit who 'separates' people for a divine calling (see, for instance, Acts 13:2). The supreme example in scripture is, of course, the Messiah, 'Anointed One' in Hebrew. The sweet-smelling perfume must have lingered long after the actual ceremony, reminding the one anointed of the beauty and attractiveness of the life surrendered to God's will.

We can't anoint ourselves—we have to be anointed by another. The Holy Spirit is a gift, not a prize to be earned.

26 May

ANOINTED TO DO GOOD

Then Peter began to speak to them: 'I truly understand that God shows no partiality, but in every nation anyone who fears him and does what is right is acceptable to him. You know the message he sent to the people of Israel, preaching peace by Jesus Christ—he is Lord of all. That message spread throughout Judea... how God anointed Jesus of Nazareth with the Holy Spirit and with power; how he went about doing good and healing all who were oppressed by the devil, for God was with him.

ACTS 10:34–38 (abridged)

The apostle Peter was surprised to find himself addressing an entirely Gentile audience in Caesarea, a Roman military headquarters on the coast of Judea. His audience was the household of a Roman centurion, Cornelius, and Peter was there because both he and Cornelius had had visions in which this unexpected meeting was arranged. This Gentile household ('unlawful' for a Jew to enter, v. 28), clearly wanted to hear 'all that the Lord had commanded him to say to them' (v. 33).

This is the first part of Peter's speech in reply, in which he introduces the subject of Jesus—the 'anointed' representative of God, who went about 'doing good and healing all who were oppressed'. He is able to assume that these Gentiles would already know some of this story, though it's unclear whether they knew of the belief in Jesus' resurrection. There must have been a freshness about this picture of a man who was dedicated to doing good, 'for God was with him'.

The effect of Peter's words was amazing. While he was still speaking, the Holy Spirit 'fell upon all who heard' him (v. 44), so that Peter was compelled to say that he could see no reason why these Gentiles should not be baptized on the spot. He was able to return to Jerusalem and convince the church leaders that Gentiles, every bit as much as Jews, were now to be recognized as part of God's chosen people.

The God who in Jesus went about 'doing good', healing people and setting the oppressed free, is also a God who has no favourites.

27 May

THE FRUIT OF THE SPIRIT

By contrast, the fruit of the Spirit is love, joy, peace, patience, kindness, generosity, faithfulness, gentleness, and self-control. There is no law against such things. And those who belong to Christ Jesus have crucified the flesh with its passions and desires. If we live by the Spirit, let us also be guided by the Spirit.
GALATIANS 5:22–25

The 'contrast' that Paul mentions is with 'the works of the flesh' (v. 19)—the inevitable product of a life driven by our own fallen natures. The life driven by the Spirit of God also produces results. He calls it 'fruit', which picks up a saying of Jesus: 'you will know them by their fruits' (Matthew 7:20). The distinguishing marks of the people of the kingdom, in other words, were not what they said or even the precise things they professed to believe, but whether what they said and believed had any product. And the product is this list of qualities, which anyone would recognize as praiseworthy. Love, joy, peace, patience, kindness, generosity, faithfulness, gentleness and self-control are exactly the qualities that Jesus himself showed. Now the Holy Spirit, sent by the Father at his request, will plant the seed of these virtues in the hearts of those who follow him.

A plant doesn't have to struggle to produce its fruit; fruit is the inevitable consequence of its nature. As Jesus also said, you get grapes from vines and figs from fig trees (Matthew 7:16). These beautiful attributes will begin to emerge from the life in which the Holy Spirit is at work—and if they don't, we should begin to ask ourselves why not. These are the 'cardinal virtues' of Catholic spirituality, in contrast to the 'deadly sins'. The world is entitled to look at those who profess to follow Christ and expect to see at least signs of their emergence.

I can't force fruit to grow in my life, but I can work to remove whatever might be hindering its appearance, and I can also consciously open myself to the Holy Spirit, who plants the seeds and nurtures them to maturity.

28 May

THE GIFTS OF THE SPIRIT

No one can say 'Jesus is Lord' except by the Holy Spirit... To each is given the manifestation of the Spirit for the common good. To one is given through the Spirit the utterance of wisdom, and to another the utterance of knowledge according to the same Spirit, to another faith by the same Spirit, to another gifts of healing by the one Spirit, to another the working of miracles, to another prophecy, to another the discernment of spirits, to another various kinds of tongues, to another the interpretation of tongues. All these are activated by one and the same Spirit, who allots to each one individually just as the Spirit chooses.

1 CORINTHIANS 12:3B, 7–11

The church at Corinth had been on something of a rollercoaster ride. On the one hand, it had tolerated sexual immorality in its midst; it was riven with quarrelling, jealousy and a tendency to split into factions. All in all, Paul felt that they were immature Christians, who still needed spiritual 'milk' rather than solid food (see 1 Corinthians 3:1–4; 5:1–2).

On the other hand, this was a church overflowing with spiritual gifts: the Greek word is *charismata*. They practised prophecy, healing and speaking in tongues. They were clearly very proud of these gifts, and Paul doesn't condemn them for it. But he does want to teach them that gifts of this kind are not the only ones that are valuable to Christians, nor in many ways the most important.

In this passage, he tries to put the question of spiritual gifts into a balanced context. For instance, every Christian who confesses Christ has already exhibited the most fundamental spiritual gift: 'No one can say "Jesus is Lord" except by the Holy Spirit.' Beyond that, God has given many and varied gifts of the Spirit to the Church. Some are dramatic and miraculous. Some are quieter, but equally to be valued: wisdom, knowledge, faith. Each gift is for the blessing and benefit of the whole Christian community.

These are 'gifts', so we can't choose them. The giver, the Holy Spirit, decides.

29 May

THE GREATEST GIFT

If I speak in the tongues of mortals and of angels, but do not have love, I am a noisy gong or a clanging cymbal. And if I have prophetic powers, and understand all mysteries and all knowledge, and if I have all faith, so as to remove mountains, but do not have love, I am nothing. If I give away all my possessions, and if I hand over my body so that I may boast, but do not have love, I gain nothing. Love is patient; love is kind; love is not envious or boastful or arrogant or rude. It does not insist on its own way; it is not irritable or resentful; it does not rejoice in wrongdoing, but rejoices in the truth.

1 CORINTHIANS 13:1–6

The previous chapter about spiritual gifts ends with a tantalizing promise: 'And I will show you a still more excellent way' (12:31). This 'more excellent' gift is not spectacular or even, in the normal sense of the word, miraculous. It is love. However, as Paul's hearers would immediately have recognized, it is a very special kind of love. The Greeks had several words for love, but the noblest of all kinds was *agape*, which is sacrificial, self-giving love. The early Christians took this Greek word and applied it to what we might call 'Christian love', the sort of love Christ showed for us on the cross, the sort of love we show when we give ourselves unreservedly to him and to others. *Agape* became by use an almost exclusively Christian concept, sacrificial love being at the heart of the faith and of true Christian discipleship.

This passage is one of the few occasions when Paul's language rises to poetic heights as he struggles to convey the central place of love in the life of the Church and the Christian. Love exceeds every other gift because it should be the motivation and goal of all the spiritual gifts. Tongues—even 'angelic' ones!—prophetic powers, insight and knowledge, mountain-moving faith and even the offering of my body itself are nothing without love.

Love changes things and changes people—but only if it is agape-*love.*

30 May

LOVE NEVER ENDS

Love never ends. But as for prophecies, they will come to an end; as for tongues, they will cease; as for knowledge, it will come to an end. For we know only in part, and we prophesy only in part; but when the complete comes, the partial will come to an end. When I was a child, I spoke like a child, I thought like a child, I reasoned like a child; when I became an adult, I put an end to childish ways. For now we see in a mirror, dimly, but then we will see face to face. Now I know only in part; then I will know fully, even as I have been fully known. And now faith, hope, and love abide, these three; and the greatest of these is love.

1 CORINTHIANS 13:8–13

In just three words (four, in the original Greek) Paul sums up this memorable hymn to love: *agape* never ends. Even the highest gifts eventually come to an end. Tongues will be redundant when our relationship with God is transparent. Prophecy comes to an end when all has been fulfilled. 'Knowledge', in the sense of a special spiritual insight, will come to an end because we shall know all the truth in its fullness—no longer seeing it through a distorting mirror, but 'face to face'. In the most profound way, we shall have 'grown up', and the things we needed as children will be surplus to requirements.

What will remain are the fundamentals: faith, hope, love. Paul was the great apostle of faith, arguing that it is faith alone that enables us to grasp the grace of God. Yet faith, though it abides for ever, is not as great a gift as love. Hope is a sublime gift for the believer, celebrated by Paul as an essential element in our salvation (Romans 8:24). But though it too abides for ever, it is not as glorious a gift as love. In the end, love will be triumphant. We shall stand in the very presence of God, and God is love.

If true, deep and self-giving love survives everything, and is as eternal as God himself, then the love experienced in our earthly relationships will surely also never end.

31 May

THE WATER OF LIFE

Then the angel showed me the river of the water of life, bright as crystal, flowing from the throne of God and of the Lamb through the middle of the street of the city. On either side of the river is the tree of life with its twelve kinds of fruit, producing its fruit each month; and the leaves of the tree are for the healing of the nations... Let everyone who is thirsty come. Let anyone who wishes take the water of life as a gift.

REVELATION 22:1–2, 17

The last section of Revelation provides a dramatic contrast to the mayhem of the preceding chapters. Now, with the final conquest of evil accomplished, the heavenly city, 'new Jerusalem', descends like a bride from heaven. There are many beautiful features within its walls, but none more likely to appeal to people in a dry land than its promise of water. The 'river of the water of life' flows through the main street of the city, nourishing the trees that line its banks. Unlike earthly fruit trees, these are not restricted to one or two seasonal crops of fruit, but yield a monthly harvest. The trees are collectively described as 'the tree of life', which takes us right back to the beginning, where just such a tree grew in Eden (Genesis 2:9). The leaves of these trees are 'for the healing of the *ethnoi*', the various peoples and tribes of the earth. The God-given 'water of life' will be for all, and from it all will be made whole.

Jesus told the Samaritan woman that if she had realized his identity she could have asked him for 'living water'—a slightly ambiguous statement, as 'living water' could simply mean spring water as opposed to the flat water which she was drawing from the deep well. However, later in the same conversation he expanded the point: those who drink his living water will never thirst again (see John 4:7–15). Water slakes our thirst and gives us strength and energy. Without it, we perish. Here, right at the end of the Bible, in this wonderful vision of the heavenly future, there is water for all, and therefore life for all.

'Sir, give me this water, so that I may never be thirsty' (John 4:15).

June: The good life

The Bible has much to say about the 'good life', which it generally sees as a life lived in fellowship with God. In the Old Testament, it is usually seen in terms of keeping his commandments, walking in the way of his statutes, whereas in the New Testament it is more often defined as life 'in Christ'—in fellowship with him and with all his people. In practice, the two are closer than they sound: both call us to 'walk with God'.

1 June

THE ROAD TO HAPPINESS

Happy are those who do not follow the advice of the wicked, or take the path that sinners tread, or sit in the seat of scoffers; but their delight is in the law of the Lord, and on his law they meditate day and night. They are like trees planted by streams of water, which yield their fruit in its season, and their leaves do not wither... The wicked are not so, but are like chaff that the wind drives away. Therefore the wicked will not stand in the judgment, nor sinners in the congregation of the righteous; for the Lord watches over the way of the righteous, but the way of the wicked will perish.
PSALM 1 (abridged)

The first psalm sets the style and tone of the rest. It starts with the word 'happy'—'blessed'—and it defines this happiness in terms that recur all through the book. Those who are happy 'delight in the law of the Lord'. This is much more than saying that those who keep the commandments will be blessed, because for the psalmist, as for all Jews, the law is not seen as a set of rules, a tiresome burden imposed on unwilling humans, but a way of life. Those made in his image will know the fulfilled life only by walking in God's way.

The psalm balances the positive—the way of the righteous—with the negative, the way of the wicked. Indeed, the first clue to the happy life is to avoid the wrong path. Treading where sinners tread, or 'sitting in the seat of scoffers'—being a cynic—is to take that wrong path. The truly happy person delights in the law of the Lord, reflects on it, draws strength and sustenance from it like a tree sucking up moisture from the nearby river. In contrast, we have the fate of the wicked. They are lightweight, mere chaff blown in the wind. They have no permanence, no roots, and by their lifestyle they exclude themselves from God's people. Their destiny is to perish, whereas the righteous will find that the Lord watches over their journey through life.

All the other psalms are like an extended commentary on this one. Happiness is determined by our choices, especially about the company we keep.

2 June

THE GOOD PATH

My child, if you accept my words and treasure up my commandments within you, making your ear attentive to wisdom and inclining your heart to understanding; if you indeed cry out for insight, and raise your voice for understanding; if you seek it like silver, and search for it as for hidden treasures—then you will understand the fear of the Lord and find the knowledge of God. For the Lord gives wisdom; from his mouth come knowledge and understanding; he stores up sound wisdom for the upright; he is a shield to those who walk blamelessly, guarding the paths of justice and preserving the way of his faithful ones. Then you will understand righteousness and justice and equity, every good path.

PROVERBS 2:1–9

We shall continue this month with a selection of readings from Proverbs, the longest and most important part of the 'Wisdom literature' of the Old Testament. This passage sets the tone for the whole book: wisdom is much more than cleverness or intelligence. Rather, it is a God-like characteristic, a gift of God ('the Lord gives wisdom'), and includes such qualities as understanding, insight, righteousness, justice, equity and prudence.

Perhaps the key word is 'understanding', in the sense of a mind and will tuned to God's, alert to his prompting. It can be 'sought' (the wise person will pray for wisdom and insight) and, for those who receive the gift, wonderful doors of understanding are opened. Wisdom is associated with right living but also helps to shape a life lived blamelessly and justly. As the writer constantly asserts, it is closely associated with 'the fear of the Lord', which doesn't mean a servile terror but a healthy respect. Wisdom, in Hebrew thought, is meaning and purpose. It is more than facts, more even than truth. It is, in the most profound sense, access to the mind of God.

Some of the wisest people are not necessarily university educated, but have learnt how to tune their minds to the purpose of God.

3 June

THE FATHER'S CHILDREN

The Lord by wisdom founded the earth; by understanding he established the heavens; by his knowledge the deeps broke open, and the clouds drop down the dew. My child... keep sound wisdom and prudence, and they will be life for your soul and adornment for your neck. Then you will walk on your way securely and your foot will not stumble. If you sit down, you will not be afraid; when you lie down, your sleep will be sweet. Do not be afraid of sudden panic, or of the storm that strikes the wicked; for the Lord will be your confidence and will keep your foot from being caught.
PROVERBS 3:19–26 (abridged)

The morality of Proverbs is not simply a practical secular morality. It is rooted and grounded in the nature of God. By his role as Creator, he has established the principles by which his creatures can live in peace, security and contentment, even when danger and difficulty arise. His law reflects his wisdom, and it is the wisdom of the Creator—what we might call the 'maker's instructions'. Observe them and everything functions properly. Ignore them and you're in trouble!

Here we have a picture of the godly man or woman. They can walk without stumbling, following safe paths. They can lie down to sleep without fear or panic. The reason lies in their understanding of God's care of his children. Apparently, storms only hit the 'wicked'!

But behind this apparently simple picture of confidence lies a deep principle, which underscores all of the Wisdom literature. God has not abandoned his creation or his children. Even though troubles come—think of poor Job!—God is still 'on the throne of the universe'. He has charge both of the created order and of his people living within it. Our confidence is not that everything will be all right in the end, but that God will be there. His wisdom will chart the path of history; his hand will guide us through dark times towards the light.

Inwardly and outwardly, it is trust in the wisdom of God that shapes the life of his children.

4 June

THE GOOD NEIGHBOUR

Do not withhold good from those to whom it is due, when it is in your power to do it. Do not say to your neighbour, 'Go, and come again, tomorrow I will give it'—when you have it with you. Do not plan harm against your neighbour... Do not quarrel with anyone without cause, when no harm has been done to you. Do not envy the violent and do not choose any of their ways; for the perverse are an abomination to the Lord, but the upright are in his confidence. The Lord's curse is on the house of the wicked, but he blesses the abode of the righteous. Toward the scorners he is scornful, but to the humble he shows favour.

PROVERBS 3:27–34A (abridged)

Once again, Proverbs offers its homely advice in the form of moral contrasts, well suited to the style of Hebrew poetry. On the one hand there is the good neighbour, who is generous to the limit of his resources, 'upright' and reliable, humble and—of course—wise. On the other hand there is the bad neighbour, who makes promises he has no intention of keeping ('I'll ring you back' would be today's equivalent). He plans harm against his neighbour, quarrels with him needlessly, envies him and is 'perverse'—the sort of person who says one thing and does another. He is scornful (Proverbs has no time for that), and he is stubborn, unwilling to compromise on anything.

The writer invites his readers to choose between these two ways. Those who make the right choice, to follow the way of the 'upright', are in God's confidence, which would mean that he trusts them because they trust him. The perverse are simply an 'abomination'—the strongest term of condemnation in the Old Testament. Their homes are 'cursed' because they have perverted as well as disobeyed God's law. On the other hand, those who walk God's way will know his favour and his blessing.

Loving our neighbour, for the writer of Proverbs, is an essentially practical thing: generosity, kindness, the gentle word.

5 June

LEARN FROM THE ANTS

Go to the ant, you lazybones; consider its ways, and be wise. Without having any chief or officer or ruler, it prepares its food in summer, and gathers its sustenance in harvest. How long will you lie there, O lazybones? When will you rise from your sleep? A little sleep, a little slumber, a little folding of the hands to rest, and poverty will come upon you like a robber, and want, like an armed warrior... There are six things that the Lord hates, seven that are an abomination to him: haughty eyes, a lying tongue, and hands that shed innocent blood, a heart that devises wicked plans, feet that hurry to run to evil, a lying witness who testifies falsely, and one who sows discord in a family.

PROVERBS 6:6–11, 16–19

The first part of this reading has a bit of the flavour of an Aesop's fable. The 'lazybones' (I like the 'sluggard' of the King James Version) is advised to take a lesson from the ants, who are always hard at work, scurrying to and fro about their endless business. You will get nowhere by lying on your back, snoozing in the shade. The consequence of that will be land not tilled, seed not sown and harvest not reaped. The inevitable result is poverty, not only for the sluggard but for his family as well.

The second extract from the same chapter sets out six things that the Lord hates—or seven, as it turns out, to complete the balance of the first verse. They vary from 'sowing discord in a family' to murder. They are offences of the tongue, of the will, of the eyes, of the feet (hurrying to run to evil), of the hands and heart. The list covers both public crimes and private sins, offences of action and of attitude. Reading the list is likely to evoke in most people a start of recognition as we see our small personal faults as what they are—things the Lord hates.

One practical use of these proverbs for the reader is to use them as a checklist, a kind of divine assessment of moral performance. Few can read passages like these and emerge feeling completely exonerated.

6 June

WISDOM'S GIFTS

And now, my children, listen to me: happy are those who keep my ways. Hear instruction and be wise, and do not neglect it. Happy is the one who listens to me, watching daily at my gates, waiting beside my doors. For whoever finds me finds life and obtains favour from the Lord; but those who miss me injure themselves; all who hate me love death.

PROVERBS 8:32–36

Who, you might ask, is the 'me'? Is it the writer of Proverbs? Is it God ('whoever finds me finds life')? Or—and this is almost certainly the correct answer—is it this strange 'Wisdom', who emerges from the pages with almost God-like characteristics? Wisdom, as we've already seen, is much more than intelligence or cleverness. Ultimately it is the mind of God, and human wisdom is acquired only by those who tune their minds to God's. So it's not surprising, perhaps, that the idea of Wisdom becomes god-like. 'Immortal, invisible, God only wise'—the words of the hymn fooled me as a choirboy, until I realized that you had to move the adjective: 'the only wise God'. God's wisdom is unique because it is the wisdom of the Creator. Of the whole universe he is the 'wisdom'—the meaning and the purpose. God is what it's all about.

It follows that the path to 'life' is to open ourselves to the gifts of his wisdom. This is not a matter of intellectual study and you don't have to qualify for Mensa to obtain it. The path to wisdom is to seek it with all our hearts, to pray daily to know the mind of God. Jesus became for us 'wisdom from God' (1 Corinthians 1:30), so through him we can have access to this wonderful gift. It won't come as a package—we have to 'learn wisdom'—and we may need patience as we seek it, as we 'wait beside its doors'. But those who are open to this gift will have a quality that sometimes eludes the most brilliant minds.

To seek true wisdom is to seek God; as Proverbs frequently asserts, this reverent search eventually yields its riches: 'the fear of the Lord is the beginning of wisdom'.

7 June

THE BLESSING OF AN HONEST FRIEND

Do not boast about tomorrow, for you do not know what a day may bring. Let another praise you, and not your own mouth… Better is open rebuke than hidden love. Well meant are the wounds a friend inflicts, but profuse are the kisses of an enemy… Do not forsake your friend… do not go to the house of your kindred on the day of your calamity. Better is a neighbour who is nearby than kindred who are far away.

PROVERBS 27:1–2, 5–6, 10 (abridged)

Jesus said that the second great commandment was to 'love your neighbour as yourself' (Luke 10:27), and opened out this concept in the story of the good Samaritan (vv. 30–37). Here, in these ancient Wisdom writings, the same theme is explored: who is my neighbour, and what place should friendship have in the life of true wisdom?

First, there is a word about the transitory nature of human life. All that we do and decide is against the backdrop of our mortality. We can't even predict the events of the next day. Then, there is a reminder of the virtue of humility. Self-praise, as we say, is no praise at all.

Then the teacher turns to the question of human relationships. If it's pleasant to hear another praising us, how should we react when a friend finds it necessary to rebuke us openly? It's surely true that 'open rebuke is better than hidden love'—it certainly costs more, both for the one rebuking and the one receiving it. If the rebuker is a close friend, however, we may assume that though the experience is painful, their words are well meant, intended not to wound but to heal. That is a profound truth, whether we are doing the rebuking or the receiving. The intention determines whether the action is malicious or loving.

Finally we have a tribute to the value of friendship. The friend is also the neighbour—he or she is near. Many of us know that at on the 'day of calamity' friends have been a precious lifeline, a gift of God.

'You are my friends,' Jesus said to his disciples (John 15:14). What a privilege to be friends of the Son of God!

8 June

NEITHER POVERTY NOR RICHES

Every word of God proves true; he is a shield to those who take refuge in him... Two things I ask of you; do not deny them to me before I die: Remove far from me falsehood and lying; give me neither poverty nor riches; feed me with the food that I need, or I shall be full, and deny you, and say, 'Who is the Lord?' or I shall be poor, and steal, and profane the name of my God.

PROVERBS 30:5, 7–9

That God is a 'shield' is a frequent claim of the Old Testament, especially the Psalms. The shield was the soldier's primary defensive weapon. God 'shields' his people as their protector, warding off the evil that would otherwise invade their lives. The believer is only required to 'take refuge' in him—to trust that the shield is adequate for the task.

We are then led into a piece of lyrical poetry. These sayings are described as 'The words of Agur son of Jakeh. An oracle', but no one seems to have much idea who Agur was. His name is not Hebrew, and the word translated 'oracle' could also refer to a place in Arabia, Massa. So we may have here a contribution to the scriptures by a Gentile.

The ideas, however, are consistent with the rest of Proverbs. The writer uses a lot of numerical sayings, where his requests or prayers are numbered, as though he were saying to God (or Wisdom), 'I've got a couple of things I'd like to ask for.' Here, one request is slightly surprising. To pray neither for poverty nor riches runs counter to the usual Hebrew concept that God rewards with prosperity those who do his will. The writer is keenly aware of the dangers of both poverty and wealth. The former might drive him to desperation, even to the extent of theft. The latter might lure him away from God, under the impression that as he has everything, he doesn't need God.

Living with poverty demands a deep inner contentment. Living with wealth requires a profound sense of spiritual priorities. As Jesus said, the second is probably the more difficult (Mark 10:25).

9 June

GOOD AND GRACIOUS

Praise the Lord! Happy are those who fear the Lord, who greatly delight in his commandments. Their descendants will be mighty in the land; the generation of the upright will be blessed. Wealth and riches are in their houses, and their righteousness endures forever. They rise in the darkness as a light for the upright; they are gracious, merciful, and righteous. It is well with those who deal generously and lend, who conduct their affairs with justice. For the righteous… are not afraid of evil tidings; their hearts are firm, secure in the Lord… In the end they will look in triumph on their foes. They have distributed freely, they have given to the poor; their righteousness endures forever; their horn is exalted in honour.

PSALM 112:1–9 (abridged)

This is another psalm about the ingredients of the 'good life', variously described here as 'happy', 'blessed', 'exalted'. The key to it all, not surprisingly, is to 'delight in [God's] commandments'. The fruit of that delight is a life of righteousness, that key concept of the Bible—living in the way that God requires and blesses.

Obedience to God's law shows itself in intensely practical ways. The people get up early to help others; they are gracious, merciful and righteous. They deal generously and 'lend'—money, presumably—without charging interest. They conduct their business with justice. Although one of the rewards of such a life is typically seen as 'wealth and riches', these good people have 'distributed freely' to the poor.

As well as the practical benefits (mostly, we may note, for other people), their characters and lifestyle are shaped by the same principles. Bad news doesn't worry them unduly because their hearts are firm and steady, 'secure in the Lord'. Their lives are unshaken by external events and they will eventually see the conquest of evil.

'Happy are those who fear the Lord' sounds like a self-contradicting statement. How can those who are fearful be happy? Yet to reverence or deeply respect God creates in the heart not terror but a strong sense of peace.

10 June

THE ONE WHO IS ON MY SIDE

'O that my words were written down! O that they were inscribed in a book! O that with an iron pen and with lead they were engraved on a rock forever! For I know that my Redeemer lives, and that at the last he will stand upon the earth; and after my skin has been thus destroyed, then in my flesh I shall see God, whom I shall see on my side, and my eyes shall behold, and not another.'

JOB 19:23–27

Job is not a happy man, and with reason. In one fell swoop, he lost his wife, his home, his servants, his land and his flocks. Humanly speaking, he was ruined, yet he never 'cursed God', as his wife advised him to do (2:9–10). Sitting amid the ruins of what had been, 'comforted' by three unhelpful friends, he held fast to his faith that somehow, somewhere and sometime, his God would come to his aid.

In this passage, the well-known words about knowing that his Redeemer 'lives' follow a long passage of self-loathing. Job feels that God has put him 'in the wrong' (v. 6) and closed his net around him, and that God counts him as his 'adversary' (v. 11). His friends have turned against him: 'Even young children despise me,' he complains (v. 18). Job, in other words, is in a state of deep depression, but he holds on to one sustaining conviction, which he wishes were 'engraved on a rock for ever'. That is that his 'redeemer' (literally, his 'vindicator') will stand alongside him one day. There will be someone to plead his cause before God, and so successfully that God himself will end up 'on my side'. This passionate piece of pleading is notoriously difficult to interpret but one thing is clear. In all his anger, doubt, depression and confusion, Job clings to the belief that eventually, perhaps only after death, his 'redeemer' will argue his case and he will be accepted by God.

For the Christian, the 'Redeemer' is, of course, Jesus. God's own Son 'pleads our cause', stands beside us and brings us to the Father.

11 June

CHOOSING LIFE

See, I have set before you today life and prosperity, death and adversity. If you obey the commandments of the Lord your God that I am commanding you today… the Lord your God will bless you in the land that you are entering to possess. But if your heart turns away and you do not hear, but are led astray to bow down to other gods and serve them, I declare to you today that you shall perish; you shall not live long in the land that you are crossing the Jordan to enter and possess. I call heaven and earth to witness against you today that I have set before you life and death, blessings and curses. Choose life so that you and your descendants may live, loving the Lord your God, obeying him, and holding fast to him.

DEUTERONOMY 30:15–20 (abridged)

Life is all about choices. We don't choose to be born or into which family, but from then on choices—ours and our parents'—shape our lives. Most of us have sometimes made bad choices over relatively small things—colour of carpets, make of car, that sort of thing. In the end, they can usually be put right fairly easily. But there are some choices which are so crucial that to get them wrong can cause years of pain—the choice of a marriage partner, for instance, or of vocation. Foremost among those major choices is this fundamental one: will I live my life to please myself or seek to please God? Will I obey my instincts and desires or will I obey the moral law of my Creator?

'Choose!' says Moses. Choose life or death. Choose to worship God or idols. Choose blessing or curses. He put the issue to the people of Israel on the verge of entering the promised land, and begged them to choose 'life', to love God, obey him and hold fast to him. If they did, they would know blessing and prosperity. If they didn't, they would 'perish'. The choice was not expressed in terms of servile obedience to a tyrant, but as glad and willing obedience to a God they loved.

The same choice is before us today. It's the narrow road or the broad one (Matthew 7:13–14). It's still spiritual life or spiritual death.

12 June

GAINS AND LOSSES

Yet whatever gains I had, these I have come to regard as loss because of Christ... I regard everything as loss because of the surpassing value of knowing Christ Jesus my Lord. For his sake I have suffered the loss of all things, and I regard them as rubbish, in order that I may gain Christ and be found in him, not having a righteousness of my own that comes from the law, but one that comes through faith in Christ, the righteousness from God based on faith. I want to know Christ and the power of his resurrection and the sharing of his sufferings by becoming like him in his death, if somehow I may attain the resurrection from the dead. Not that I have already obtained this or have already reached the goal; but I press on to make it my own, because Christ Jesus has made me his own.

PHILIPPIANS 3:7–12 (abridged)

The apostle Paul came from a good and devout Jewish family. In this letter he enumerates all the things that gave him status and confidence among his own people: circumcised, with an impeccable background, a zealous Pharisee who kept the law 'blamelessly'. But he doesn't list these qualities in order to boast about them—quite the contrary. Here, in this passage, which immediately follows the enumeration of his advantages, he values these 'gains' as in fact 'losses'—indeed, 'rubbish'—when compared to the incalculable gain he had found through 'knowing Christ'.

That knowledge had 'surpassing value', more than compensating for the loss of the benefits that his background would have brought him. He was prepared to lose them all in order to gain Christ and be found 'in him'. Now his overwhelming ambition in life was to 'know Christ', including his cross and his risen life. With touching honesty Paul doesn't claim to have got there yet, but he presses on towards it, confident that as Christ Jesus has already claimed him as his own, he will one day achieve the goal of knowing Christ fully and completely.

Sometimes we need to remember the past; sometimes we need to forget!

13 June

THE SPRINGTIME OF THE HEART

The voice of my beloved! Look, he comes, leaping upon the mountains, bounding over the hills... My beloved speaks and says to me: 'Arise, my love, my fair one, and come away; for now the winter is past, the rain is over and gone. The flowers appear on the earth; the time of singing has come, and the voice of the turtle-dove is heard in our land. The fig tree puts forth its figs, and the vines are in blossom; they give forth fragrance. Arise, my love, my fair one, and come away. O my dove, in the clefts of the rock, in the covert of the cliff, let me see your face, let me hear your voice; for your voice is sweet, and your face is lovely.

SONG OF SOLOMON 2:8, 10–14

The Song of Solomon provides a total and compelling answer to anyone who claims that the Judeo-Christian religion is anti-sex. It is a hymn in praise of human love, a dialogue in memorable poetry between a young man and a young woman who are head over heels in love and can't wait to consummate it. The language suggests that it takes place on their wedding night. Much of it is frankly erotic, a quality sometimes lost on readers today through the vagaries of translation and the mysteries of poetic imagery.

At times in the history of the Church, this book has proved somewhat of a problem because of its enthusiastic endorsement of sexual love. That led some commentators to find a picture here of the relationship between Christ and the believer, but it is doubtful if the original author would have felt any need for such delicacy. Sexual love is a gift of God, and when it is based on the deep and touching devotion of two people, it is surely something for which we can praise God. 'My beloved is mine and I am his'—that sentence (v. 16) probably captures the heart of any deep relationship of love—including the love God has for us and the love we have for him.

The picture is of love bursting out with all the growth and new life of spring. Wherever and whenever life is renewed by love, it is springtime.

14 June

UNQUENCHABLE LOVE

I adjure you, O daughters of Jerusalem, do not stir up or awaken love until it is ready! ... Set me as a seal upon your heart, as a seal upon your arm; for love is strong as death, passion fierce as the grave. Its flashes are flashes of fire, a raging flame. Many waters cannot quench love, neither can floods drown it. If one offered for love all the wealth of one's house, it would be utterly scorned.

SONG OF SOLOMON 8:4, 6–7

The temptation to spiritualize this lovely piece of Hebrew poetry is irresistible! The Christian reader can't help thinking of 'God so loved that he gave...' (John 3:16) or 'No one has greater love than this, to lay down one's life for one's friends' (John 15:13). At least we can recognize that what is true of the love of a woman and a man cannot be less pure, less powerful or less eternal than the love of God for us.

Having said that, this is a wonderful tribute to the beauty and power of human love. Indeed, so powerful is that love that it should not be 'stirred up until it is ready'—a reminder that it is dangerous and irresponsible to kindle the fires of sexual desire unless and until those involved are able to cope with them properly. Easier said than done, as youth workers and counsellors know too well! Nevertheless there is wisdom in these words, and perhaps the picture of fulfilled love here, with two people committed to each other for life, would be more persuasive than reams of cool advice.

There is also an important truth here about love. Love, of the self-giving, sacrificial kind, 'never ends' (1 Corinthians 13:8), perhaps because God is love and God is eternal. The gift of love binds two people together—making of two people 'one flesh' (Genesis 2:24)—and the love they share has a gloriously eternal quality about it.

'God is love, and those who abide in love abide in God, and God abides in them' (1 John 4:16)—often the opening words of the Marriage Service. What a promise!

15 June

WRITTEN ON THE HEART

The days are surely coming, says the Lord, when I will make a new covenant with the house of Israel and the house of Judah. It will not be like the covenant that I made with their ancestors... a covenant that they broke, though I was their husband, says the Lord... I will put my law within them, and I will write it on their hearts... No longer shall they teach one another, or say to each other, 'Know the Lord', for they shall all know me... for I will forgive their iniquity, and remember their sin no more.

JEREMIAH 31:31–34 (abridged)

Most of Jeremiah's ministry was taken up with warning the people of Israel and Judah that without repentance their fate was sealed. However, there was always a carrot as well as a stick. If they repented, if they forsook other gods, if they sought the Lord with all their hearts and kept his commandments, then the future was bright.

Here Jeremiah speaks of the 'covenant' relationship that the Lord has with his people. First recognized after Abraham's willingness to sacrifice his son Isaac, it was confirmed and sealed with blood at Sinai, after the giving of the Law. From that latter event, a condition was attached. If the people would follow his Law, he would be their God. The story of the people of Israel from that time on was one of constant failure to keep their part of the covenant, although God remained faithful to his promise.

But now there is a new promise. The law having failed—human frailty apparently incapable of consistent obedience—there would be a new covenant. Under this one, the law would not be written on stone, as a kind of external code to be followed, but on their 'hearts'. This would be an internal, spiritual conversion, by which the will of God and his loving purpose would be implanted in their lives. Instead of simply being required to know the law, now they would know the lawgiver, as he revealed himself to them in a new way.

Jesus spoke of the 'new covenant in my blood', a covenant of grace and mercy.

16 June

ON STRONG FOUNDATIONS

Those who trust in the Lord are like Mount Zion, which cannot be moved, but abides forever. As the mountains surround Jerusalem, so the Lord surrounds his people, from this time on and forevermore. For the sceptre of wickedness shall not rest on the land allotted to the righteous, so that the righteous may not stretch out their hands to do wrong. Do good, O Lord, to those who are good, and to those who are upright in their hearts. But those who turn aside to their own crooked ways the Lord will lead away with evildoers. Peace be upon Israel!

PSALM 125

This psalm begins with two memorable images, especially for anyone who has visited Jerusalem. The city stood (still stands) on a hill—Mount Zion—which served as a kind of foundation for all its walls, buildings and the temple. But Jerusalem was surrounded by hills, which the psalmist sees as sentinels guarding it from infiltration by the enemy. Its residents could take a double comfort: the city was built on immovable foundations and was surrounded by silent but conspicuous sentinels.

The rest of the psalm picks up a common theme: the contrast between the righteous and the wicked. On the one hand, there are those who please the Lord, who dwell in the land he has 'allotted' to them. On the other, there is the 'sceptre of wickedness', the power of the enemy and of those who oppose the Lord. The latter, however, are banned from the holy city, so that the righteous are not tempted by their evil ways. Again, we have the contrast in the last two verses. The Lord does good to those who are 'upright in their hearts', meaning not simply a show of piety but the true, inner obedience of the faithful heart. On the other hand, the Lord 'leads away' those who turn aside from him, condemning them to the company of the 'evildoers'.

It is not the mountain on which the city is built that keeps his people secure, nor the surrounding hills, but the Lord himself.

17 June

THE BLAMELESS LIFE

O Lord, who may abide in your tent? Who may dwell on your holy hill? Those who walk blamelessly, and do what is right, and speak the truth from their heart; who do not slander with their tongue, and do no evil to their friends, nor take up a reproach against their neighbours; in whose eyes the wicked are despised, but who honour those who fear the Lord; who stand by their oath even to their hurt; who do not lend money at interest, and do not take a bribe against the innocent. Those who do these things shall never be moved.

PSALM 15

Who is 'fit' to walk with God? One answer, of course, is 'nobody', because however hard we try, we cannot exclude the possibility of sin and failure from our lives. That is why the whole principle of God's mercy and forgiveness is etched so deeply into the story of the Bible.

On the other hand, we do not need to abandon ourselves to a kind of fatalistic acceptance of moral failure. Here the psalmist describes a 'blameless walk', the life of those who seek to 'do what is right'. At least we can hold before us the ambition to live in this way, grateful that when we fail we can fall back on the forgiveness of God.

The blameless life is driven by our inner convictions: it comes 'from the heart'. It shows itself, however, in our external behaviour. We guard our tongues; we treat our neighbours with respect and speak truthfully and generously about them. Inevitably, the corollary of that is that we 'despise' the wicked, having no desire to mimic their ways. Money, inevitably, comes into it. The blameless person does not lend money at interest: debt leading to destitution arising from such greedy lending was a feature of life in ancient Israel. Bribery is out of the question.

Those who live in this way are unshakeable, built on firm foundations. And, of course, they feel at home in the presence of the Lord.

Many of these themes are picked up in the teaching of Jesus, together with the promise of the Holy Spirit's help in living the life of faith and truth.

18 June

TRUE HAPPINESS

'Blessed are the poor in spirit, for theirs is the kingdom of heaven. Blessed are those who mourn, for they will be comforted. Blessed are the meek, for they will inherit the earth. Blessed are those who hunger and thirst for righteousness, for they will be filled. Blessed are the merciful, for they will receive mercy. Blessed are the pure in heart, for they will see God. Blessed are the peacemakers, for they will be called children of God.'
MATTHEW 5:3–9

For the next four days we have readings from the Sermon on the Mount, which draws together the heart of the teaching of Jesus as he brought it to the people of Galilee. It clearly took place on a hillside, and the audience are described as 'his disciples'—those who had committed themselves to following him and his teaching. In the Jewish tradition, he sat down to preach, and began with the sayings known to us as the 'Beatitudes'—literally, the 'blessings'.

Each saying offers a kind of contradiction, because it says in effect that a circumstance of life or a characteristic attitude will bring blessing or happiness, whereas in several cases it would seem to the average person to bring exactly the opposite. How can those who mourn be happy? Or those who are 'poor in spirit', or 'meek'?

Reversing the sayings can help us understand: 'Those who mourn will be comforted; therefore they are blessed'; 'the meek will inherit the earth; therefore they are blessed'. The blessing or happiness comes from the hand of God in response to our human frailty. In the case of what seems to be the key promise, the emphasis is slightly different, although, again, reversing the order may help: 'Those who are pure in heart will see God; therefore they are blessed'. Meek, merciful, peacemakers, mourners, those who long for right and justice to prevail—perhaps it's not hard to see that they are blessed by God.

The Greek word for 'blessed', makarios, *literally means 'happy'. Are these clues, then, to the truly happy life?*

19 June

STAYING TRUE

'Blessed are those who are persecuted for righteousness' sake, for theirs is the kingdom of heaven. Blessed are you when people revile you and persecute you and utter all kinds of evil against you falsely on my account. Rejoice and be glad, for your reward is great in heaven, for in the same way they persecuted the prophets who were before you.'

MATTHEW 5:10–12

If the first seven Beatitudes offer a puzzling contrast with a popular conception of 'blessing or 'happiness', then here the contradiction becomes obvious and extreme. How can being persecuted, reviled and falsely accused be described as a happy experience, let alone a blessing? In these instances, even reversing the order of the words doesn't help very much, once we are past the first promise. The kingdom of heaven (already promised to the 'pure in heart') is to belong to those who are persecuted 'for righteousness' sake'. The next two verses simply expand on that idea, detailing the various ugly forms that this persecution may take.

The key phrase seems to be 'for righteousness' sake'. The New English Bible translates the phrase as 'for the cause of right'. In biblical language, 'righteousness' means 'doing what God requires', and what he requires is right and just. So those who struggle and fight for truth and justice are undoubtedly taking up 'the cause of right'—and if, as often happens, it brings upon them insults, false accusations and physical persecution, then this Beatitude is for them.

They are, Jesus says, to 'rejoice and be glad'. Why? Because their 'reward is great in heaven'. Reviled and insulted in the world, they will be numbered with the prophets of God in his coming kingdom.

Jesus didn't want the listening crowds—or us, who come after them—to be under any illusions. To follow him is to follow one who gave up his life for others in a costly act of love. It is the way of the cross but it is also the way of blessing.

20 June

WHY WORRY?

'Therefore I tell you, do not worry about your life, what you will eat or what you will drink, or about your body, what you will wear. Is not life more than food, and the body more than clothing? Look at the birds of the air; they neither sow nor reap nor gather into barns, and yet your heavenly Father feeds them. Are you not of more value than they? And can any of you by worrying add a single hour to your span of life? And why do you worry about clothing? Consider the lilies of the field, how they grow; they neither toil nor spin, yet I tell you, even Solomon in all his glory was not clothed like one of these. But if God so clothes the grass of the field... will he not much more clothe you—you of little faith?'

MATTHEW 6:25–30 (abridged)

As I've mentioned before, 'Don't worry' is an unhelpful piece of advice. Supposing there is something really worth worrying about? Are we just to pretend it's not there? Yet here is Jesus telling a crowd of mostly poor countryfolk not to worry about the very things that concerned them day by day. What if the harvest fails? What if there's nothing in the larder? Supposing there's no money to buy clothes? With so much disease around, what if I fall ill? Jesus, who was himself from the same rural, poor background, could not be accused of ignorance. He knew what life was like for these hardworking sons of the soil. Yet all he seems to say is, 'Don't worry'.

His argument is a simple one, yet profound. If God finds food for the birds and God clothes the flowers, won't he also feed and clothe his human children? There is a secondary argument too: worrying does nothing to solve the problem.

When Jesus says that they are of 'little faith', is he being scathing or encouraging? After all, he taught that faith 'the size of a mustard seed' is adequate if it is true faith in his heavenly Father (Matthew 17:20). The question is not 'How much faith?' but 'In whom?'

It's a good idea to be sure, if our faith is small, that it's in a great God.

21 June

A QUESTION OF PRIORITIES

'Therefore do not worry, saying, "What will we eat?" or "What will we drink?" or "What will we wear?" For it is the Gentiles who strive for all these things; and indeed your heavenly Father knows that you need all these things. But strive first for the kingdom of God and his righteousness, and all these things will be given to you as well. So do not worry about tomorrow, for tomorrow will bring worries of its own.'

MATTHEW 6:31–34

Much of the teaching of Jesus to the crowds was about priorities. What should come first in our lives and what can take a secondary position? Some of his parables make the same point—such as the businessman who thinks that filling his barns is the most important thing in the world, for instance (Luke 12:19). God knows what we need, and will provide for our needs, if not our wants. Yet this provision comes with a condition. Those who 'strive' for his kingdom and his righteousness will find that 'all these things' will be given to them as well.

'These things' are clearly the very wants that Jesus has been talking about: food, drink, clothes, health. They are God's gift to his children, the children of the kingdom. But the children have a responsibility to live the 'kingdom way'. If they do, they will no longer be worrying about what there will be to eat or drink or wear, because they will know that God is aware of their needs and is taking care of them.

So again it comes down to a question about meaning. What does it mean to strive for 'the kingdom of God' and his 'righteousness'? The kingdom, by definition, is where the king reigns, where his writ runs. The people of the kingdom are those who have freely put themselves under his just and gentle rule. The kingdom of God is a society of those who are 'striving' to live by a different rule than the world around them. God's righteousness, as we have seen, is perfect love and justice. The people of the kingdom seek to live by those standards.

An absolute provision for an absolute priority: that is the offer of Jesus.

22 June

CLOTHED WITH LOVE

As God's chosen ones, holy and beloved, clothe yourselves with compassion, kindness, humility, meekness, and patience. Bear with one another and, if anyone has a complaint against another, forgive each other… Above all, clothe yourselves with love, which binds everything together in perfect harmony. And let the peace of Christ rule in your hearts, to which indeed you were called in the one body. And be thankful.
COLOSSIANS 3:12–15 (abridged)

This letter from Paul was probably written about AD64 and sent to the church at Colosse (in present-day western Turkey) with instructions that after it had been read it should be forwarded to the church in Laodicea. Paul is clearly worried that the Christians in these churches will be led astray by false teachers, peddling what he calls 'philosophy and empty deceit' (2:8). What he sets out for them is a wonderful picture of the fullness of what God has done for us in Christ. In the light of that, they have no need to submit themselves to rules and regulations that are simply 'human commands and teachings' (2:22).

However, he obviously has a warm spot for this little church, and sets out in the most attractive terms what life in the Christian community should be like. All the virtues are there: compassion, kindness, humility, meekness and patience. The believers are not to admire these qualities from a distance but to 'clothe' themselves with them—to allow them to enfold every aspect of their lives. There is an even more fundamental item of clothing, however: *agape*, the noblest form of love, sacrificial and self-giving. 'Above all' they should 'clothe' themselves with that. When these virtues are being practised, when they are respecting each other and forgiving each other, then the peace that Christ gives will 'rule' or arbitrate in their hearts. In that way the different members of the church will become 'one body'. That indeed would be cause for gratitude, as Paul reminds them: 'And be thankful'.

Where Christ's peace rules, there is unity and love.

23 June

SHARING THE WORD OF CHRIST

Let the word of Christ dwell in you richly; teach and admonish one another in all wisdom; and with gratitude in your hearts sing psalms, hymns, and spiritual songs to God. And whatever you do, in word or deed, do everything in the name of the Lord Jesus, giving thanks to God the Father through him. Wives, be subject to your husbands, as is fitting in the Lord. Husbands, love your wives and never treat them harshly. Children, obey your parents in everything, for this is your acceptable duty in the Lord. Fathers, do not provoke your children, or they may lose heart.
COLOSSIANS 3:16–21

The first part of this passage probably describes what went on in the first-century equivalent of a home group. On Sundays the Christians met early, before the working day had begun, for the Eucharist. This was for all of the church in the area and included an *agape*, or 'love-feast' together. Then it was off to work, at home or elsewhere. In the evening they would gather again, but in homes, in small groups, informally. There they would share the 'word of Christ'—presumably stories and sayings of Jesus, at this time recited by heart. Soon there would be the first of the written Gospels for them to study together. As well as soaking in the word of Christ (letting it 'dwell in them richly'), they taught and corrected each other with God-given wisdom, and worshipped by singing together. It sounds very warm and welcoming!

The second part introduces a passage about Christian attitudes in the home—wives to husbands, husbands to wives, children to parents and so on. Today's readers may find the notion of women being 'subject' to their husbands rather difficult to take, but the almost identical passage in Ephesians (5:21–33) puts it in a different context: 'be subject to one another out of reverence for Christ'. In any case, we can't really read 21st-century ideas back into the first century!

The key to the Christian life as Paul sees it is gratitude (vv. 15–17). Cultivate an 'attitude of gratitude'!

24 June

ASKING AND RECEIVING

'So I say to you, Ask, and it will be given to you; search, and you will find; knock, and the door will be opened for you. For everyone who asks receives, and everyone who searches finds, and for everyone who knocks, the door will be opened. Is there anyone among you who, if your child asks for a fish, will give a snake instead of a fish? Or if the child asks for an egg, will give a scorpion? If you then, who are evil, know how to give good gifts to your children, how much more will the heavenly Father give the Holy Spirit to those who ask him!'

LUKE 11:9–13

These words of Jesus echo an idea from the Old Testament: 'If you seek me with all your heart, I will let you find me, says the Lord' (Jeremiah 29:13–14). To seek God, or his good gifts, is to find him, because he isn't playing hide-and-seek with us. He actually wants to be found; he wants to bless us. But the secret is in the asking and the seeking.

It all sounds so simple! Yet sometimes asking is the very last thing we want to do, because it involves admitting our own inadequacy. Human beings don't like to feel dependent, even on God. Yet the very heart of our relationship with him is one of dependence. He made us, he loves us, and he knows what's best for us. He is the heavenly Father, who wants his children to trust him and look to him for help and strength, rather than struggling on their own. So added here is the comparison of an earthly father's concern for his child's welfare. Using a familiar oratorical device—one that he often employed—Jesus asks the question, 'If you would do it, even though you are sinful, how much more will your heavenly Father meet his children's needs when they ask him?' In Luke, the 'gift' offered is the Holy Spirit. In a similar passage in Matthew (7:11), it says simply 'good things'—though we know that the very best of those things is the Spirit of God.

'But you never asked!' What a terrible epitaph that would be for someone who felt that they had somehow missed out on God's good gifts for his children.

25 June

WHEN I NEEDED A NEIGHBOUR

'A man was going down from Jerusalem to Jericho, and fell into the hands of robbers, who stripped him, beat him, and went away, leaving him half dead. Now by chance a priest was going down that road; and when he saw him, he passed by on the other side. So likewise a Levite, when he came to the place and saw him, passed by on the other side. But a Samaritan while travelling came near him; and when he saw him, he was moved with pity. He went to him and bandaged his wounds, having poured oil and wine on them. Then he put him on his own animal, brought him to an inn, and took care of him... Which of these three, do you think, was a neighbour to the man who fell into the hands of the robbers?' He said, 'The one who showed him mercy.' Jesus said to him, 'Go and do likewise.'

LUKE 10:34, 36–37

This is, of course, the famous story of the good Samaritan, the member of a despised tribe who nevertheless acted as a good neighbour to a man in need when highly respected members of the religious community had signally failed to do so. This story wouldn't have gone down well with its Jewish hearers, because the Samaritans were regarded as corrupters of the pure religion of Israel and were looked down on by their more orthodox neighbours. Yet again, Jesus uses a Samaritan as an example of a true God-fearer (it was a Samaritan who turned back to give thanks after being healed of leprosy while his Jewish companions rushed off to get their healing certified: Luke 17:16). It's unlikely that Jesus was suggesting that Samaritans were better or more godly than the Jews; rather, that neighbourliness is not defined by race or even religion, but by loving action.

'Who was neighbour to the man who fell among robbers?' asked Jesus. 'The one who showed him mercy,' replied the lawyer, who couldn't bring himself to say 'the Samaritan'!

Perhaps the priest and Levite feared being ritually defiled, thus missing their temple duties. If so, what a comment on the distortion of religious priorities!

26 June

GOOD NEWS FOR THE CHILD-LIKE

At that same hour Jesus rejoiced in the Holy Spirit and said, 'I thank you, Father, Lord of heaven and earth, because you have hidden these things from the wise and the intelligent and have revealed them to infants; yes, Father, for such was your gracious will...' Then turning to the disciples, Jesus said to them privately, 'Blessed are the eyes that see what you see! For I tell you that many prophets and kings desired to see what you see, but did not see it, and to hear what you hear, but did not hear it.'

LUKE 10:21, 23–24

This passage shows that Jesus was not always the rabbi telling stories or uttering wise sayings. Sometimes—perhaps only privately to his disciples—he spoke of his unique relationship to the Father.

The heart of this passage is on the nature of the revelation of God which we have in Jesus. Sometimes it seems that only those with degrees in theology can ever expect to understand his meaning and significance. Yet here Jesus—'rejoicing in the Holy Spirit'—thanks God that these things have been hidden from the intellectuals and revealed to 'infants'. No one needs a university degree to grasp the essential truth of the good news about Jesus. Indeed, as he several times affirmed, it is those of child-like faith and trust who hold the key to the kingdom of heaven. God loves us and sent his Son to show us what he is like, to save us from our sins and to bring us to eternal life. All the rest, in a sense, is decoration.

The disciples, he tells them, are uniquely blessed. Kings and prophets of Israel had longed for centuries to see the day when the Lord's Messiah would walk on earth, the time of salvation. The disciples had seen with their eyes what Isaiah and others could only perceive dimly in visions—blind eyes opened, the lame healed, lepers cleansed and the poor having good news preached to them.

Sometimes it's right to pray for wisdom, and sometimes it's right to pray for the simple faith of a child.

27 June

THE BLESSING OF GOD

May God be gracious to us and bless us and make his face to shine upon us, that your way may be known upon earth, your saving power among all nations. Let the peoples praise you, O God; let all the peoples praise you. Let the nations be glad and sing for joy, for you judge the peoples with equity and guide the nations upon earth... The earth has yielded its increase; God, our God, has blessed us. May God continue to bless us; let all the ends of the earth revere him.

PSALM 67:1–4, 6–7

I remember this song of praise being sung a lot at weddings. It's certainly appropriate for any occasion of joy and gratitude, but it also combines some prayers which would be appropriate for a couple setting out on a new relationship, or anyone seeking God's continuing blessing on their life.

Most of all, however, this psalm is a prayer that God will fulfil his loving purpose for the whole world. It is universal in its scope, going far beyond the usual prayer that God will bless his people Israel. His salvation, his saving health and power, is intended to be a blessing to 'all nations'—which mirrors the original promise to Abraham that through his 'seed' all the nations of the earth would be blessed.

Indeed, the 'nations'—which certainly includes the Gentile ones—are to be glad and sing for joy. And why? Because God judges justly and offers his guidance to all without discrimination. This is quite a radical psalm! There are more reasons to bless God: he provides 'increase', the growth by which seeds become harvests. The fields of corn and the hillsides covered with vines and olive trees are marks and evidences of his bounty. No wonder, then, that the final petition is that this rich blessing of justice, peace and prosperity should continue for ever, so that the 'ends of the earth' would revere his name.

Even if the 'heathen' don't realize it, God loves them and is working for their good.

28 June

THE LOVE THAT WILL NOT LET ME GO

Who will separate us from the love of Christ? Will hardship, or distress, or persecution, or famine, or nakedness, or peril, or sword? As it is written, 'For your sake we are being killed all day long; we are accounted as sheep to be slaughtered.' No, in all these things we are more than conquerors through him who loved us. For I am convinced that neither death, nor life, nor angels, nor rulers, nor things present, nor things to come, nor powers, nor height, nor depth, nor anything else in all creation, will be able to separate us from the love of God in Christ Jesus our Lord.
ROMANS 8:35–39

If the last reading has often been associated with weddings, this one, the climax of the first part of Paul's letter to the church at Rome, is even more closely associated with funerals. It's hard to think of more triumphant language in such a setting. Absolutely nothing, declares the apostle, in heaven above or earth beneath, can achieve the impossible, which is to separate the Christian believer from God's love expressed in Jesus. The words seem to tumble from his lips—angels, powers, earthly rulers, things we know and even things we don't yet know… even death itself, none will be able to cut us off from his love.

Many years ago I had a friend and colleague who was dying of liver cancer. One night in hospital, he told me, he had a moment of despair. He had a young wife and three children under ten, and he couldn't bear the thought of leaving them. A paralysing fear gripped him—the 'horror of great darkness'. And then, he said, all of a sudden, it was as though he heard God speaking to him. 'Call yourself a Christian, and a priest? Can't you trust me, even in this? I will be with you, and them, every step of the way.' A great calm and peace came on him, and all through the awful final months of his illness, although he went through many experiences—anger, disappointment, confusion—he never felt abandoned. Nothing separated him from that eternal love.

God's really is the 'love that will not let us go'.

29 June

A NEW WAY OF LIVING

In days to come the mountain of the Lord's house shall be established as the highest of the mountains, and shall be raised up above the hills. Peoples shall stream to it, and many nations shall come and say: 'Come, let us go up to the mountain of the Lord, to the house of the God of Jacob; that he may teach us his ways and that we may walk in his paths.' For out of Zion shall go forth instruction, and the word of the Lord from Jerusalem.

MICAH 4:1–2

The prophets of Israel looked forward to the Day of the Lord, a time of universal judgment and blessing, when finally the rule of our Creator would hold sway throughout the world. This day was for all, for the 'chosen people' of Israel and for the people of the 'nations'. On that day, as Micah sees it in his vision, a tremendous stream of blessing will flow from a renewed Jerusalem. The true 'word of the Lord' will go forth, and so attractive will its message be that people will rush to the city to hear and receive it. Those who previously, perhaps, despised the religion of Israel will suddenly have a new respect for it. Figuratively speaking, the hill on which the temple is built grows, so that it is higher than the other mountains. In other words, all other messages, all other wisdom and spiritual understanding, will finally acknowledge that the truth that heals and saves flowed from the Lord.

It is worth noting how this blessing would manifest itself. God would 'teach them his ways' and they would 'walk in his paths'. That just about sums up the Old Testament understanding of spirituality: it is about observing God's ways and walking in the path he has chosen. The Law, in other words, is not a heavy-handed burden to be reluctantly accepted, but a whole way of life, revealed by God as the way of blessing for his human creatures. It is not so much to be slavishly 'obeyed' as joyfully 'followed'.

To 'walk in God's paths' is the high point of blessing. They are a narrow road, it is true, but one that leads to 'life'.

30 June

TRUE AND LASTING PEACE

He shall judge between many peoples… they shall beat their swords into ploughshares, and their spears into pruning-hooks; nation shall not lift up sword against nation, neither shall they learn war any more; but they shall all sit under their own vines and under their own fig trees, and no one shall make them afraid; for the mouth of the Lord of hosts has spoken. For all the peoples walk, each in the name of its god, but we will walk in the name of the Lord our God forever and ever.

MICAH 4:3–5 (abridged)

It is hard to think of a more splendid vision of hope for suffering humanity than this. On the day of God's blessing, when truth and holiness stream out from a renewed Jerusalem, a glorious peace will extend over the whole world. This is not just a matter of wars stopping: the nations will not 'learn war' any more. It simply won't be on the syllabus. Weapons of war will be finally decommissioned, transformed into instruments of life and blessing—ploughshares and pruning hooks. This will be peace as God knows it: not the absence of conflict, but the presence of the divine *shalom*—peace, wholeness, health.

When true peace reigns, there will be further blessings, because now at last people can live in simplicity and security. For the people of the ancient world, that would mean exactly what is pictured here: men, women and children sitting under their own vines and fig trees, with no one to 'make them afraid'. Their peace will be secured not by the blue helmets of United Nations troops but by the explicit command of God. This is his peace, long promised and now fulfilled.

The final picture is one of a God-fearing world enjoying the blessings of peace. The Gentiles walk in 'the name of their gods', but 'we', says the prophet triumphantly, 'we will walk in the name of the Lord our God for ever and ever'.

When we pray 'Your kingdom come, your will be done on earth as in heaven', this is exactly what we are praying for: the peace of God on earth.

July: Refreshment

The Bible sees life as a journey with a destination—God himself. On this journey we need sustenance, like the sandwiches I used to take as a boy when we were going on a long railway journey. This refreshment for the traveller is a constant theme of the scriptures, whether it's manna in the wilderness or the bread and wine of Communion for the new Christian Church. God our Father doesn't leave us hungry and helpless!

1 July

A MEAL AND A PROMISE

Abraham hastened into the tent to Sarah, and said, 'Make ready quickly three measures of choice flour, knead it, and make cakes.' Abraham ran to the herd, and took a calf, tender and good, and gave it to the servant, who hastened to prepare it. Then he took curds and milk and the calf that he had prepared, and set it before them; and he stood by them under the tree while they ate. They said to him, 'Where is your wife Sarah?' And he said, 'There, in the tent.' Then one said, 'I will surely return to you in due season, and your wife Sarah shall have a son.' And Sarah was listening at the tent entrance behind him… So Sarah laughed to herself, saying, 'After I have grown old, and my husband is old, shall I have pleasure?' The Lord said to Abraham, 'Why did Sarah laugh, and say, "Shall I indeed bear a child, now that I am old?" Is anything too wonderful for the Lord?'

GENESIS 18:6–10, 12–14A

This story concerns three unexpected visitors to Abraham's tent. Clearly they were more than just 'men'—angels, perhaps—because the Lord himself echoes their promise about Sarah having a son.

The setting is the nomadic life of a wealthy man, Abraham, who had travelled from his home in Ur in obedience to a prompting from God. He was rewarded for his obedience and faith with one of the greatest promises of the Old Testament, that he would be the father of a nation. So far, however, the elderly Abraham and his wife have not produced a single child, let alone a nation! Accordingly, the words of these mysterious visitors (welcomed with traditional hospitality) might have seemed either teasing or incredible. Clearly that was Sarah's reaction, as she heard the conversation inside the tent. She laughed—and was sternly rebuked for it. Nothing, she and her husband were reminded, is impossible for God—words repeated by the angel to Mary when he announced the future birth of Jesus to a virgin.

'Is anything too wonderful for the Lord?' To ask the question of the Creator of the universe is to answer it!

2 July

DECEIVED WITH A MEAL

Rebekah said to her son Jacob, 'I heard your father say to your brother Esau, "Bring me game, and prepare for me savoury food to eat, that I may bless you before the Lord before I die." … Go to the flock, and get me two choice kids, so that I may prepare from them savoury food for your father… and you shall take it to your father to eat, so that he may bless you before he dies.' But Jacob said to his mother Rebekah, 'Look, my brother Esau is a hairy man, and I am a man of smooth skin. Perhaps my father will feel me, and I shall seem to be mocking him, and bring a curse on myself and not a blessing.' His mother said to him, 'Let your curse be on me, my son; only obey my word…' So he went and got them and brought them to his mother… Then Rebekah took the best garments of her elder son Esau… and put them on her younger son Jacob; and she put the skins of the kids on his hands and on the smooth part of his neck. Then she handed the savoury food… to her son Jacob.

GENESIS 27:6–7, 9–17 (abridged)

The food may have been savoury but the behaviour of Rebekah and Jacob, her favourite son, certainly wasn't. This story, part of the saga of the descendants of Abraham, is at least a reminder that the Bible paints its heroes 'warts and all'. To have the father's blessing was to become his heir apparent. Esau was the older son and emerges later as a man of considerable generosity and forgiveness, accepting a reconciliation with Jacob after the latter had begun to see the error of his ways.

The trick worked, of course. The old man Isaac had failing eyesight, and relied on touch to identify his older son, the 'hairy man' Esau. Deceived by the animal hair on Jacob's neck, he gave the younger man his blessing. Wisely, perhaps, Jacob fled before his deceit was detected.

It was this miscreant who became the father of twelve sons, one of whom, Joseph, achieved honour from the king of Egypt and brought the whole tribe of Israel to dwell in that land.

It is a wicked thing to abuse the sacred unity of breaking bread together.

3 July

BREAKING BREAD IN MIDIAN

Moses fled from Pharaoh. He settled in the land of Midian, and sat down by a well. The priest of Midian had seven daughters. They came to draw water, and filled the troughs to water their father's flock. But some shepherds came and drove them away. Moses got up and came to their defence and watered their flock. When they returned to their father Reuel, he said, 'How is it that you have come back so soon today?' They said, 'An Egyptian helped us against the shepherds…' He said to his daughters, 'Where is he? Why did you leave the man? Invite him to break bread.' Moses agreed to stay with the man, and he gave Moses his daughter Zipporah in marriage. She bore a son, and he named him Gershom; for he said, 'I have been an alien residing in a foreign land.'

EXODUS 2:15–22 (abridged)

These events precede Moses' experience at the burning bush (Exodus 3:1–6) and his call by God to lead the Hebrews out of slavery in Egypt. The young man, in fear for his life should Pharaoh apprehend him for the murder of a taskmaster, has fled to the mountainous area of Midian, and here meets the daughters of Jethro, 'the priest of Midian'.

The hospitality of the East required that the man who had helped the girls should at least be rewarded with a meal, so Moses—to all intents and purposes an 'Egyptian'—found himself breaking bread with the family and later marrying Jethro's daughter Zipporah. The name given to their son summarizes his father's position at that moment. Born of Hebrew parents and taught the worship of the God of Abraham, Isaac and Jacob, brought up as an Egyptian prince and now an asylum seeker in a Gentile society, he called the child 'Gershon': *ger* is the Hebrew for 'alien'. Moses must have wondered what he himself was at that point in his life: Jew, Egyptian, Midianite? Of course, the issue was soon to be resolved, but he wasn't to know that.

Jethro, this 'pagan' priest, has an unfolding role in the story of Moses—always wise, always principled and generous, a true 'God-fearer'.

4 July

THE PASSOVER MEAL

On the tenth of this month they are to take a lamb for each family... without blemish, a year-old male... You shall keep it until the fourteenth day of this month; then the whole assembled congregation of Israel shall slaughter it at twilight. They shall take some of the blood and put it on the two doorposts and the lintel of the houses in which they eat it. They shall eat the lamb that same night... roasted over the fire with unleavened bread and bitter herbs... This is how you shall eat it: your loins girded, your sandals on your feet, and your staff in your hand; and you shall eat it hurriedly. It is the passover of the Lord. For I will pass through the land of Egypt that night, and I will strike down every firstborn in the land of Egypt, both human beings and animals... when I see the blood, I will pass over you, and no plague shall destroy you when I strike the land of Egypt.

EXODUS 12:3, 5–8, 11–13 (abridged)

There is no meal, no ritual observance, in the whole of the Old Testament to equal this one in importance. Down the centuries, Jews worldwide have celebrated the Passover as they were commanded to do as a yearly remembrance of this divine act of deliverance for their people. The original Passover event was highly dramatic, as we can see. The last of the ten plagues of Egypt was about to strike the land with devastating effect. The eldest sons of every household would die. But if the Israelites obeyed God's command, sacrificed a lamb and daubed its blood on their doorposts, the angel of the Lord, on his fatal mission, would 'pass over' them and their sons would not be harmed.

The meal was to be eaten in haste, 'loins girded' (robes hitched up) ready for a rapid exit. What God required of his people was an act of faith in his promise, because they would not only have looked ridiculous in the eyes of the ordinary Egyptians but helpless in the hands of Pharaoh, if it all came to nothing.

In the event, the Israelites obeyed, God acted, and his people set out the next morning on the long walk to freedom and the promised land.

5 July

THE FLESHPOTS OF EGYPT

Israel came to the wilderness of Sin, which is between Elim and Sinai, on the fifteenth day of the second month after they had departed from the land of Egypt. The whole congregation of the Israelites complained against Moses and Aaron in the wilderness. The Israelites said to them, 'If only we had died by the hand of the Lord in the land of Egypt, when we sat by the fleshpots and ate our fill of bread; for you have brought us out into this wilderness to kill this whole assembly with hunger.' Then the Lord said to Moses, 'I am going to rain bread from heaven for you, and each day the people shall go out and gather enough for that day. In that way I will test them, whether they will follow my instruction or not.'

EXODUS 16:1–4

The chronicler is pretty hard on the poor old Israelites! He pictures them as a fairly spineless bunch of whingers and moaners—some of them were at it even before they'd crossed the Red Sea. This, however, was the first major confrontation between a frightened people and their charismatic but somewhat remote leader. Entering the desert area of Sin, they realized that they had no reliable source of food or drink.

They brought their complaints to Moses, but it was the particular argument they used that must have tried his patience. 'If only we'd died in Egypt in the plague! At least we would have died with our stomachs full of food!' They were seeing the past through rose-tinted spectacles—after all, they were slaves in Egypt, not aristocrats.

It was the Lord, rather than Moses, who dealt with their complaints, using them as a testing ground of their obedience and faith. He would 'rain bread from heaven' on them, but with strict instructions attached. In fact, the significance of the meal was almost instantly expanded. When the Lord gave them food, Moses warned them, it would be because 'the Lord has heard your complaining', which is 'not against us [Moses and Aaron] but against the Lord' (v. 8).

When we cry out, 'Oh God, why?' the challenge is to wait for the answer.

6 July

GOD'S RESPONSE TO OUR COMPLAINING

Then Moses said to Aaron, 'Say to the whole congregation of the Israelites, "Draw near to the Lord, for he has heard your complaining."' And as Aaron spoke to the whole congregation of the Israelites… the glory of the Lord appeared in the cloud. The Lord spoke to Moses and said, 'I have heard the complaining of the Israelites; say to them, "At twilight you shall eat meat, and in the morning you shall have your fill of bread; then you shall know that I am the Lord your God."'

EXODUS 16:9–12 (abridged)

Here we find Moses using his brother Aaron (as God had told him to do) as his spokesman. First he commands the people to 'draw near'—presumably so that they can all hear what is said. The unique nature of this 'drawing near', however, is that they are gathering not to hear the words of Moses and Aaron but of the Lord—because he has heard their complaining. This is something of a reassurance: God doesn't just hear our 'nice', respectable prayers, but also our complaints, doubts and even downright rebellion—yet without cutting us off.

Nevertheless, there is also a strong note of warning. They will get the food they wanted, mountains of it, but its arrival will be proof positive that 'the Lord' is their God. They had not simply been moaning at their human leaders but at the God of the whole earth. As if to confirm these words, the people saw 'the glory of the Lord… in the cloud'. Several times in the Old Testament this visible 'glory' appears, always at moments of great significance (such as the consecration of Solomon's temple: 1 Kings 8:11). It is always associated with a cloud—the sign of fruitfulness in a dry land. We can't guess exactly what the Israelites saw that day but they must have recognized it as a confirmation of Aaron's words. Presumably they meekly dispersed to their homes, to see what the rest of the day would bring.

Honesty in prayer is the first requisite. The second is faith that our God hears and responds to that honesty.

7 July

FOOD FOR THE JOURNEY

In the evening quails came up and covered the camp; and in the morning there was a layer of dew around the camp. When the layer of dew lifted, there on the surface of the wilderness was a fine flaky substance… When the Israelites saw it, they said to one another, 'What is it?' … Moses said to them, 'It is the bread that the Lord has given you to eat. This is what the Lord has commanded: "Gather as much of it as each of you needs, an omer to a person… all providing for those in their own tents."' The Israelites did so, some gathering more, some less. But when they measured it with an omer, those who gathered much had nothing over, and those who gathered little had no shortage… And Moses said to them, 'Let no one leave any of it over until morning.' But they did not listen to Moses; some left part of it until morning, and it bred worms and became foul.

EXODUS 16:13–20 (abridged)

By evening, the people began to see the answer to their cry for food. A passing flock of quail were unwise enough to descend on the Israelites' encampment. You can imagine the enthusiasm with which this supply of fresh poultry would have been seized! For probably the first time since leaving Egypt, they were able to eat fresh meat. The morning brought a further surprise—a layer of flaky substance on the ground. 'What is it?' the Israelites asked—*man hu* in Hebrew, which became its name, 'manna'. This remarkable gift of God was dubbed 'what's-its-name' by its original recipients! They gathered it eagerly, a ration of an omer—probably the capacity of an average cooking bowl—per person. All had the same but, we are told, all had enough, all were satisfied.

They were told not to gather more and try to store it, but inevitably some saw this as a pedantic prohibition and decided to disobey it. In the morning, they found that the manna had gone rotten. However, the people were allowed to gather double the quantity on Fridays, so that they would not be collecting it on the sabbath.

This was food for the journey, provided by the God who accompanied them.

8 July

HARVEST THANKSGIVING

[God said] When you enter the land that I am giving you and you reap its harvest, you shall bring the sheaf of the first fruits of your harvest to the priest. He shall raise the sheaf before the Lord, so that you may find acceptance... On the day when you raise the sheaf, you shall offer a lamb a year old, without blemish, as a burnt-offering to the Lord... On that same day you shall... hold a holy convocation; you shall not work at your occupations... When you reap the harvest of your land, you shall not reap to the very edges of your field, or gather the gleanings of your harvest; you shall leave them for the poor and for the alien: I am the Lord your God.

LEVITICUS 23:10–12, 21–22 (abridged)

Here is the biblical origin of our modern-day harvest thanksgiving. It takes us back to the early days of the settlement of Canaan, when the ritual offerings of the tabernacle, and later the temple, were at the heart of Jewish worship. What these rules establish is a principle: what we grow is not 'ours'. We are simply stewards of the land and its produce.

'All things come of you, O Lord, and of your own do we give you,' we pray. The principle of harvest thanksgiving is a recognition of that. In ancient Israel, the harvest was to be celebrated: in fact, everything culminated in a wonderful party lasting several days (vv. 39–43). But before that could be done, two priorities had to be observed. First, the heavenly giver must be recognized, so the very first of everything—sheaves of corn, grapes or olives from the trees, the first lamb from the herd—was to be solemnly offered to the Lord. In this way, the people would be visually reminded of the giver rather than the gift. The second priority was to recognize the needs of the 'poor' and the 'alien' by leaving the edges of the fields unharvested, so that they could glean corn for themselves. The Lord of the harvest takes care of them, too.

No gifts have we to offer for all Thy love imparts; but what Thou most desirest, our humble, thankful hearts.

MATTHIAS CLAUDIUS (1740–1815), TR. JANE M. CAMPBELL (1817–78)

9 July

EVERYDAY BLESSINGS

If you will only obey the Lord your God, by diligently observing all his commandments that I am commanding you today, the Lord your God will set you high above all the nations of the earth; all these blessings shall come upon you and overtake you, if you obey the Lord your God: Blessed shall you be in the city, and blessed shall you be in the field. Blessed shall be the fruit of your womb, the fruit of your ground, and the fruit of your livestock, both the increase of your cattle and the issue of your flock. Blessed shall be your basket and your kneading-bowl. Blessed shall you be when you come in, and blessed shall you be when you go out.

DEUTERONOMY 28:1–6

What are the rewards of the 'good life', the life lived in harmony with the will and purpose of God? Here, in this catalogue of blessings from the book of Deuteronomy, is the answer: multiple joy. The setting is a lifestyle far removed from our own hectic technological world, yet here are the building blocks of daily life, ancient or modern, each one chosen for a blessing. There will be blessing for the urban dwellers as they pursue their trade among the hustle and bustle of the markets. There will be blessing, too, in the fields, where the sickle reaps the crops. The people will be fertile, blessed with large families, and the ground will be fertile too, producing wonderful harvests. Even the cattle and flocks will be blessed, multiplying in numbers. The basket in which the fruit and grain are gathered will be blessed, and so will the bowl in which the meals are prepared. All will be fruitfulness. There will be blessing as people leave their house for their daily work, and blessing when the traveller returns. It's not very difficult to find parallels for today. Life lived God's way is good: that's the message.

'Only obey'—the problem is that little word 'only'! It sounds easy, but the human race has struggled all through its history to live in harmony with its Creator.

10 July

HATE EVIL AND LOVE GOOD

Therefore, because you trample on the poor and take from them levies of grain, you have built houses of hewn stone, but you shall not live in them; you have planted pleasant vineyards, but you shall not drink their wine. For I know how many are your transgressions, and how great are your sins—you who afflict the righteous, who take a bribe, and push aside the needy in the gate. Therefore the prudent will keep silent in such a time; for it is an evil time. Seek good and not evil, that you may live; and so the Lord, the God of hosts, will be with you, just as you have said. Hate evil and love good, and establish justice in the gate; it may be that the Lord, the God of hosts, will be gracious to the remnant of Joseph.

AMOS 5:11–15

Here the prophet Amos paints a picture of the dark side of the blessings promised in Deuteronomy. They are for those who live their lives in harmony with the will and purpose of God—but what about those who wilfully or negligently do not? For them, even the luxury they have acquired, the 'pleasant vineyards' and good wines, will bring them no lasting joy. They have trampled on the poor to get them, they have offered and taken bribes, they have ignored—'pushed aside'—the needy. In consequence, they will experience not the fruits of successful labour but the judgment of what the prophet calls 'an evil time'.

The good life, we may say, is essentially just that—a good life. It doesn't consist of property and land, riches and indulgence, luxury and power. That is how the 'good life' is often depicted but it is a lie. Only a life lived responsibly, unselfishly and generously can truly be called good.

To 'seek good and not evil', to 'hate evil and love good': these are the secrets of the genuinely good life.

11 July

CELEBRATING WITH JOY

On the fourteenth day of the first month the returned exiles kept the passover… It was eaten by the people of Israel who had returned from exile, and also by all who had joined them and separated themselves from the pollutions of the nations of the land to worship the Lord, the God of Israel. With joy they celebrated the festival of unleavened bread for seven days; for the Lord had made them joyful, and had turned the heart of the king of Assyria to them, so that he aided them in the work on the house of God.

EZRA 6:19, 21–22

These happy events followed the return of the exiled Jews from Assyria, whose king had promised them help with the task of rebuilding the temple in Jerusalem. Having returned, they tried to reinstitute the practice of their religion, which had largely lapsed during their years of captivity in a Gentile land. In this task they were urged on by two notable leaders, Ezra the priest and Nehemiah the 'governor', who dedicated themselves to the re-education of a people who had become ignorant of even the most basic elements of their faith. The Passover had been almost totally neglected during the exile—so when the account of its institution was read to the people, they heard it as something novel and exciting. Similarly, Ezra and Nehemiah arranged for the entire Law of Moses to be read aloud to the people and explained to them by the Levites (Nehemiah 8:7). As the crowds heard it, there were acts of penitence but also scenes of celebration, because they realized that this was their religious heritage, what distinguished them from the nations around.

Here we have the account of the first Passover under the new regime. They celebrated with joy, because 'the Lord… had turned the heart of the king of Assyria to them, so that he aided them'. Joy and gratitude went hand in hand, as they always should.

All of this celebration came about because 'the Lord had turned the Assyrian king's heart'. Hearts and minds can *be touched and transformed!*

12 July

THE RIVER OF DELIGHT

Your steadfast love, O Lord, extends to the heavens, your faithfulness to the clouds. Your righteousness is like the mighty mountains, your judgments are like the great deep; you save humans and animals alike, O Lord. How precious is your steadfast love, O God! All people may take refuge in the shadow of your wings. They feast on the abundance of your house, and you give them drink from the river of your delights. For with you is the fountain of life; in your light we see light.

PSALM 36:5–9

This lovely passage of joy and satisfaction—gifts of a generous God—is set amid a sombre picture of the dire effects of disobedience and sin. As so often, the psalmist sets his bright picture of blessing against a dark backdrop of moral rebellion, as though to invite his readers to choose. Which will it be? The river of delight or the bitter waters of sin?

Our chosen passage, however, is about the unchanging reliability and trustworthiness of the Creator. This 'steadfast love' is universal in its scope. It is like the 'mighty mountains' or the 'great deep'—images of awesome vastness. 'All people' can find refuge under the shadow of his wings and can 'feast on the abundance of his house'. In an inspired metaphor, they can also drink from 'the river of your delights'—the fresh cool water representing the rich pleasures God provides for his children. The reference to a 'fountain of life' is, of course, picked up by Jesus and applied to himself (John 4:10), as is the image of 'light' (John 8:12). Here, it is in God's light that we can 'see light': until he illuminates the human heart, the spiritual eyes of our understanding are struggling with the darkness.

All of this is encompassed in the phrase 'the steadfast love of the Lord'—a love that is infinitely precious.

To feast at God's table and drink from his river of delights are gifts of a generous God to those who love him. So is the light which he gives to open our eyes, so that we can find our way to the table and the river.

13 July

A TABLE OF LOVE

A soft answer turns away wrath, but a harsh word stirs up anger… The eyes of the Lord are in every place, keeping watch on the evil and the good. A gentle tongue is a tree of life, but perverseness in it breaks the spirit… All the days of the poor are hard, but a cheerful heart has a continual feast. Better is a little with the fear of the Lord than great treasure and trouble with it. Better is a dinner of vegetables where love is than a fatted ox and hatred with it.

PROVERBS 15:1, 3–4, 15–17

The book of Proverbs specializes in this kind of homespun wisdom, yet behind its apparently simple façade there is a depth of insight. For instance, we all know that a 'soft answer' turns away wrath and that a 'harsh word' stirs up anger. The added value here lies in the next verse. Everything we do goes on before 'the eyes of the Lord', who 'keeps watch on the evil and the good'. It isn't just a matter of self-control, but of recognition that we shall answer to God for every idle (or angry) word we speak. There is also a positive side to it: 'a gentle tongue is a tree of life'. A kind or thoughtful word can light up a situation, lift someone's spirits, be a blessing to their hearts.

The next verses pursue the same theme but examine its motivation. It all comes back to wisdom, and wisdom comes from God. We then have three striking contrasts—again, at one level obvious but at a deeper level challenging. The poor have a hard life but (without minimizing their plight) we can see that a 'cheerful heart' feasts on good things. It is true in many a developing world village today: no luxuries but much laughter and singing. The next contrast shows that those who have little except a reverence of the Lord are better off than those who have 'treasure' without it. Finally there is a contrast from the dinner table. A meal of vegetables (the food of the poor) is 'better' than a fatted ox served to a company who hate each other.

The fatted ox, treasure and riches have no value without 'the fear of the Lord'.

14 July

A FEAST OF WORD AND WINE

So they read from the book, from the law of God, with interpretation. They gave the sense, so that the people understood the reading. And Nehemiah, who was the governor, and Ezra the priest and scribe, and the Levites who taught the people said to all the people, 'This day is holy to the Lord your God; do not mourn or weep.' For all the people wept when they heard the words of the law. Then he said to them, 'Go your way, eat the fat and drink sweet wine and send portions of them to those for whom nothing is prepared, for this day is holy to our Lord; and do not be grieved, for the joy of the Lord is your strength.'

NEHEMIAH 8:8–10

After the people of Jerusalem had returned from many years of exile, Ezra the priest and Nehemiah the governor made arrangements for the law of God to be read to the people. During their time in Gentile lands, they had become unfamiliar with the teachings of their religion but this mass public reading, with scribes explaining the meaning of the words, was a shocking revelation. If this was what God required of his people, how sadly had they drifted away from it! Consequently, the listening crowd became distressed. There were tears and cries of dismay.

It was with these words that Ezra and Nehemiah pleaded with the people not to mourn or weep. This was a day of rejoicing, a day when the truth of God was once again being accepted as the way of holy living. Far from weeping, they should be celebrating—the best food, wine in abundance—and not just for themselves but also sharing with those who might have little.

There is a profound truth here for all of us. Repentance is costly but when we have seen what God requires and done what we can to amend our lives, he does not expect us to wear permanent sackcloth and ashes. Repentance leads to renewal, and forgiveness sets us free.

To hear God's word and respond to it, even if that involves painful repentance, is a path to fulfilment and joy.

15 July

OBEDIENCE REWARDED

The palace master said to Daniel, 'I am afraid of my lord the king; he has appointed your food and your drink. If he should see you in poorer condition than the other young men of your own age, you would endanger my head with the king.' Then Daniel asked... 'Please test your servants for ten days. Let us be given vegetables to eat and water to drink. You can then compare our appearance with the appearance of the young men who eat the royal rations...' At the end of ten days it was observed that they appeared better and fatter than all the young men who had been eating the royal rations. So the guard continued to withdraw their royal rations and the wine they were to drink, and gave them vegetables. To these four young men God gave knowledge and skill in every aspect of literature and wisdom; Daniel also had insight into all visions and dreams. At the end of the time that the king had set for them to be brought in... no one was found to compare with Daniel, Hananiah, Mishael, and Azariah.

DANIEL 1:10–13, 15–19 (abridged)

The book of Daniel relates events during the exile in Babylon of a group of Jewish men, one of whom, Daniel, had the gift of interpreting dreams and also of prophecy. The first part of the book tells how he became a noted and respected figure in a Gentile society; the later chapters mostly contain prophecies, in apocalyptic language, concerning the future. There is much scholarly argument about its date but, whenever it was actually written, it is clearly intended to encourage the Jewish people to be faithful to God whatever the circumstances.

Here, Daniel and his friends refuse to eat the rich but ritually unclean food from the king's table, but flourish on a diet of vegetables, which would have met the requirements of the Jewish food laws. As a reward, Daniel was given by God gifts of interpretation and insight which quickly earned him honour in the royal household.

To remain faithful to what we know to be right is an essential part of the life God requires of us—and in the end brings his blessing.

16 July

THE RELUCTANT DINERS

'The kingdom of heaven may be compared to a king who gave a wedding banquet for his son. He sent his slaves to call those who had been invited to the wedding banquet, but they would not come… They made light of it and went away, one to his farm, another to his business, while the rest seized his slaves, mistreated them, and killed them. The king was enraged. He sent his troops, destroyed those murderers, and burned their city. Then he said to his slaves, "The wedding is ready, but those invited were not worthy. Go therefore into the main streets, and invite everyone you find to the wedding banquet." Those slaves went out into the streets and gathered all whom they found, both good and bad; so the wedding hall was filled.'

MATTHEW 22:2–3, 5–10

This is one of Jesus' 'kingdom parables'. Several are quite difficult to interpret but it's important to stress that Jesus expected his audience to think about and apply these stories. He was not going to spoonfeed them. He also recognized that some would misunderstand his words, and saw that such ignorance could be wilful (Matthew 13:9, 14).

In this parable, the kingdom of heaven is compared to a king giving a wedding banquet for his son. Strangely, all of those invited—the great and the good—decline to attend. His servants are sent to explain that the banquet is of the finest food. Still they won't come—they 'made light of it', putting their farms or businesses first. Some go further, abusing and even killing his servants. Outraged, the king sends his servants out again, this time to the streets, to invite everyone they find there to the banquet. Finally the wedding hall is full of guests.

Clearly there is some reference here to the Jewish people, who were in danger of rejecting the banquet of the kingdom of heaven that had been prepared for them. Clearly there is also a wider principle at stake. Saying 'no' to God has consequences.

People still 'make light' of God's invitation, giving priority to business or pleasure.

17 July

FOOD IN THE DESERT

The disciples came to him and said, 'This is a deserted place, and the hour is now late; send the crowds away so that they may go into the villages and buy food for themselves.' Jesus said to them, '... you give them something to eat.' They replied, 'We have nothing here but five loaves and two fish.' And he said, 'Bring them here to me.' Then he ordered the crowds to sit down on the grass. Taking the five loaves and the two fish, he looked up to heaven, and blessed and broke the loaves... and the disciples gave them to the crowds. And all ate and were filled; and they took up what was left over of the broken pieces, twelve baskets full. And those who ate were about five thousand men, besides women and children.

MATTHEW 14:15–21 (abridged)

A few days ago we read the story of the manna in the wilderness—God's provision for his people as they began the journey to the promised land. Now we have a similar kind of story from the Gospels. As Moses, the servant of God, brought food to meet their daily needs, so that all had more than enough to eat, so now Jesus, the Son of God, brings food for the people of the new covenant.

A huge crowd had been listening to Jesus preaching in a 'deserted place'—not a literal desert, but near enough to provide the parallel that the writer surely wished to draw. Nightfall was coming and the people had had nothing to eat all day. The disciples pointed out that they only had two fish and five loaves (John tells us that they had been provided by a boy from the crowd). 'Bring them to me,' said Jesus. He then took the bread, gave thanks, blessed and broke it, and gave the pieces to the disciples to distribute. The miracle of the manna was repeated: everyone had enough to eat. In fact, they gathered up more fragments of the food than they had started with.

This is the only miracle of Jesus recorded in all four Gospels—evidence of its importance to the early Church. Perhaps they saw this done every Sunday: bread blessed, broken and shared, and the people of God spiritually fed.

18 July

A DAY OF GOOD NEWS

When these leprous men had come to the edge of the camp, they went into a tent, ate and drank, carried off silver, gold, and clothing, and went and hid them... Then they said to one another, 'What we are doing is wrong. This is a day of good news; if we are silent and wait until the morning light, we will be found guilty; therefore let us go and tell the king's household.' So they came and called to the gatekeepers of the city, and told them, 'We went to the Aramean camp, but there was no one to be seen or heard there, nothing but the horses tied, the donkeys tied, and the tents as they were.'

2 KINGS 8:7–11 (abridged)

This is the turning point in an amazing story. The city of Samaria had been under siege by the Arameans for so long that the people were at starvation point: 'a donkey's head was sold for eighty shekels of silver' (6:25). However, the prophet Elisha had told the king's messengers that 'tomorrow about this time' (7:1) two measures of barley would be sold for a single shekel in the gate of Samaria—a prophecy that they found incredible. The four 'leprous men' in our passage had decided that there was little to choose between dying in the city of hunger and throwing themselves on the mercy of the Arameans, so they secretly left the city and crossed over to the enemy camp. To their astonishment there was no one there: the Arameans had heard 'the sound of chariots and of horses' (7:6) in the twilight and had decided to flee, leaving everything behind. The four men ate and drank their fill and were engaged in looting what they could carry when their consciences were touched. They were keeping the good news to themselves. Think of the joy and relief it would bring to the starving people of Samaria! Good news is always to be shared.

We are generally quick to tell others our problems but we should be equally quick to share with them our blessings.

19 July

THE BREAD OF HEAVEN

'I am the bread of life. Your ancestors ate the manna in the wilderness, and they died... I am the living bread that came down from heaven. Whoever eats of this bread will live forever; and the bread that I will give for the life of the world is my flesh.' The Jews then disputed among themselves, saying, 'How can this man give us his flesh to eat?' So Jesus said to them, 'Very truly, I tell you, unless you eat the flesh of the Son of Man and drink his blood, you have no life in you. Those who eat my flesh and drink my blood have eternal life, and I will raise them up on the last day; for my flesh is true food and my blood is true drink. Those who eat my flesh and drink my blood abide in me, and I in them.'

JOHN 6:48, 50–56

These words of Jesus sound shocking to us, so it's not difficult to see why the 'Jews', even Jesus' disciples, found them unacceptable (see v. 60). After all, they had been taught that to drink blood was an abomination and here was Jesus sounding as though he was encouraging cannibalism. We probably all know friends and relatives today who feel much the same about the language Christians use to describe the elements in Holy Communion—the 'body' and 'blood' of Christ.

Yet the words of Jesus, powerful and direct, don't allow us to dodge the issue. He is the life-giving bread, which achieves so much more than the manna that fed the Israelites in the wilderness. They received their daily food but in the end, of course, they died. Those who eat 'this bread' and drink from the cup of Christ's blood will live for ever.

What could he mean? The disciples pressed him. His answer to them was to reject any idea of literally eating his flesh and blood. He was talking in spiritual terms: 'it is the spirit that gives life; the flesh is useless' (v. 63). They may not at that point in time have understood fully what he meant, but the Twelve, at least, continued to follow him.

'Lord, to whom can we go?' the disciples said. 'You have the words of eternal life' (v. 68). There it is—the word of life and the bread of heaven.

20 July

A MEMORABLE BREAKFAST

When they had gone ashore, they saw a charcoal fire there, with fish on it, and bread. Jesus said to them, 'Bring some of the fish that you have just caught.' So Simon Peter... hauled the net ashore, full of large fish, 153 of them; and though there were so many, the net was not torn. Jesus said to them, 'Come and have breakfast.' Now none of the disciples dared to ask him, 'Who are you?' because they knew it was the Lord. Jesus came and took the bread and gave it to them, and did the same with the fish.

JOHN 21:9–13 (abridged)

After his resurrection Jesus appeared on many occasions to his disciples, but surely this one is the most down to earth—not in or near Jerusalem, where he had been crucified, but 50 miles away, by the Sea of Galilee. Mark 16:7 tells us that, on the morning of the resurrection, Jesus said he would 'go ahead of them to Galilee' (their native territory). So here they were, waiting in Galilee for the promised meeting.

Peter, typically, didn't want to sit idly waiting. 'I'm going fishing,' he announced. Six of the other disciples set out with him as night was falling, fished all night and caught precisely nothing.

Just after daybreak, they saw a figure on the shore, but in the dawn light they could not recognize him. 'You haven't caught anything, then?' the man asked, and we can imagine that their reply was quite curt. What followed was extraordinary, for the 'stranger' suggested that they cast the net on the other side of the boat. Perhaps they thought he could see a shoal to that side of the boat. At any rate, they did as he suggested and caught such a haul that they could barely manhandle it into the boat. John said, 'It's the Lord!' at which Simon Peter, again typically, jumped into the lake and swam ashore. The others dragged the net of fishes in and, like true fishermen, counted them—153.

Jesus had prepared a fire; the fish was fresh from the lake; the hands of Jesus, still bearing the marks of the nails, broke the bread and gave thanks for it. No wonder 'they knew it was the Lord'!

21 July

A LUNCHTIME VISION

About noon the next day... Peter... became hungry and wanted something to eat; and while it was being prepared, he fell into a trance. He saw the heaven opened and something like a large sheet coming down, being lowered to the ground by its four corners. In it were all kinds of four-footed creatures and reptiles and birds of the air. Then he heard a voice saying, 'Get up, Peter; kill and eat.' But Peter said, 'By no means, Lord; for I have never eaten anything that is profane or unclean.' The voice said to him... 'What God has made clean, you must not call profane.' ... While Peter was still thinking about the vision, the Spirit said to him, 'Look, three men are searching for you. Now get up, go down, and go with them without hesitation; for I have sent them.'

ACTS 10:9–15, 19–20 (abridged)

This story marks an important turning point in the whole story of the Bible. Until now, the promises of God were focused almost exclusively on the Jewish people, the descendants of Abraham. It was to a Jewish crowd that the message of the resurrection was preached on the day of Pentecost, and it was Jews who received the gifts of the Spirit that day. Jesus had commanded his apostles to be his witnesses to the ends of the earth (Acts 1:8) but so far they hadn't got beyond Judea.

Earlier the same day, a God-fearing Roman centurion in Caesarea called Cornelius had received a vision telling him that his prayers were to be answered and that he was to contact a man called Peter, who was lodging with Simon the tanner in Joppa, near the seaside. He sent three of his attendants to find Peter in Joppa. While they were on the journey, Peter himself had this lunchtime vision, telling him that with God nothing and nobody was 'unclean'. Thus prepared, he was open to the prompting of the Spirit of God to welcome these Gentile visitors into the house and then agree to accompany them to Caesarea.

When Cornelius and his friends heard from Peter about Jesus, they believed—and in an amazing way the Holy Spirit 'fell' on them (10:44).

22 July

THE SHARED BLESSING

We must not put Christ to the test, as some of them did, and were destroyed by serpents. And do not complain as some of them did, and were destroyed by the destroyer. These things happened to them to serve as an example, and they were written down to instruct us, on whom the ends of the ages have come. So if you think you are standing, watch out that you do not fall... Therefore, my dear friends, flee from the worship of idols... The cup of blessing that we bless, is it not a sharing in the blood of Christ? The bread that we break, is it not a sharing in the body of Christ? Because there is one bread, we who are many are one body, for we all partake of the one bread.

1 CORINTHIANS 10:9–12, 14, 16–17

This is a plea to the Christians at Corinth to stop their pointless squabbling and start to live in true harmony. We have already picked up hints of party spirit there (some for Paul, others for Peter or Apollos and some—rather arrogantly!—for 'Christ', as though the others were not true Christians like themselves). In the next chapter Paul speaks of factions and divisions even at the Lord's table. So it is not surprising that his warnings to them are couched in pretty strong terms.

He uses the example of the Israelites on their wilderness journey, who, despite all that God had done for them, kept on complaining, and even turned at one stage to building an idol to worship, and engaged in a sexual orgy. God's 'new' people must avoid the same moral dangers, yet here were the Corinthians condoning these very things. They lived in a city that was a hotbed of immorality and idol worship, but they must separate themselves from it completely.

The apostle reminds them that week by week they share the 'cup of blessing' and the bread of life. The imagery was powerful: they shared one 'loaf' because in Christ they were one body. They drank from one cup because they were 'sharing' in the blood of Christ.

To eat and drink together is to share a common life—and our life is Christ's.

23 July

ABUSING THE BLESSING

When you come together as a church, I hear that there are divisions among you… When you come together, it is not really to eat the Lord's supper. For when the time comes to eat, each of you goes ahead with your own supper, and one goes hungry and another becomes drunk. What! Do you not have homes to eat and drink in? Or do you show contempt for the church of God and humiliate those who have nothing? What should I say to you? Should I commend you? In this matter I do not commend you!

1 CORINTHIANS 11:18, 20–22

This is a rare glimpse into the daily life and worship of the early Church. We would be hard pressed to think of a present-day Communion service as an occasion for indulgent eating and drinking! In fact, though, there are two events here, and obviously at Corinth one followed the other, presumably almost at once.

The first event was the 'love-feast', the *agape*. This was a proper meal together for the whole church—rich and poor, old and young, merchants, aristocracy, slaves, men and women. The idea was that they should truly share this meal, although obviously some would be able to contribute more than others. After the *agape*, they would move into the Eucharist, which was much as we know it today, with thanksgiving for the saving actions of Jesus and a recital of the words with which he instituted the event. Then the 'cup of blessing' was shared and the broken bread consumed.

At Corinth, however, the *agape* meal had become an excuse for indulgence. Clearly, some simply grabbed the best food and went ahead with their supper even if others were left hungry. They may have felt that because they had brought it, they could eat it—which left those who had nothing 'humiliated'. Some even got themselves drunk. No wonder Paul said they he 'did not commend' them!

'Fellowship' means 'sharing' and sharing means putting the needs of others at least on a level with our own. Selfishness abuses the blessing.

24 July

EATING WITH 'SINNERS'

After this [Jesus] went out and saw a tax-collector named Levi, sitting at the tax booth; and he said to him, 'Follow me.' And he got up, left everything, and followed him. Then Levi gave a great banquet for him in his house; and there was a large crowd of tax-collectors and others sitting at the table with them. The Pharisees and their scribes were complaining to his disciples, saying, 'Why do you eat and drink with tax-collectors and sinners?' Jesus answered, 'Those who are well have no need of a physician, but those who are sick; I have come to call not the righteous but sinners to repentance.'

LUKE 5:27–32

'Tax collectors' were nothing like the respectable and honest members of the Inland Revenue we know and love today! They were Jews who, for personal gain, had collaborated with the occupying Roman power by acting as local tax collectors. They worked on a commission basis, from little booths on the roads out of towns and cities, each attended by an armed Roman soldier. There was a tax level set by the authorities but the collectors were able to add something to that for themselves—and many of them, like Levi in this story, had done very well out of it.

Yet Jesus called tax collectors, among others, to follow him, and when they did so he accepted their hospitality. Indeed, he seemed to go out of his way to consort with those whom respectable society would regard as moral outcasts: the 'sinners' referred to here were probably prostitutes. He 'welcomed' them because God loved them, too, and he wanted to draw them into the kingdom of heaven.

The answer given by Jesus here could be a summary of his whole ministry—the purpose of his coming into the world—not for the 'righteous' (we might read that as 'self-righteous') but for sinners. Healing is for the sick, and it was for those who had fallen that Jesus came. just as much as for the upstanding members of the community.

'The Son of Man came to seek out and to save the lost' (Luke 19:10).

25 July

HONOURED GUESTS

When [Jesus] noticed how the guests chose the places of honour, he told them a parable. 'When you are invited... to a wedding banquet, do not sit down at the place of honour, in case someone more distinguished than you has been invited by your host; and the host who invited both of you may come and say to you, "Give this person your place," and then in disgrace you would start to take the lowest place. But when you are invited, go and sit down at the lowest place, so that when your host comes, he may say to you, "Friend, move up higher"; then you will be honoured in the presence of all who sit at the table with you. For all who exalt themselves will be humbled, and those who humble themselves will be exalted... When you give a luncheon or a dinner, do not invite your friends or... rich neighbours, in case they may invite you in return, and you would be repaid. But... invite the poor, the crippled, the lame, and the blind. And you will be blessed, because they cannot repay you.'

LUKE 14:7–14 (abridged)

This story has wonderful touches of irony and human interest: the pushy person who makes for the best seats, the modest guest who sits at the bottom of the table, and the host who has to deal with both of them. The whole story is, of course, a commentary on the summary at the end: 'Those who humble themselves will be exalted.' This appears throughout Jesus' teaching and was, after all, the pattern of his own life ('the Son of Man came not to be served but to serve': Matthew 20:28).

The second part of the story takes the idea further. Now it is not the guests who must act generously and humbly, but the host himself. If he favours his rich friends, then he and his family will get a return invitation and generosity has gone out of the window. True giving, Jesus says, expects nothing in return. Hence the best recipients of the wealthy man's generosity would be the 'poor, crippled, lame and blind'—the sort of people who could really do with a square meal.

This is the meaning of grace: the undeserved gift of a generous giver.

26 July

INVITING THE OUTSIDERS

'Someone gave a great dinner and invited many. At the time for the dinner… they all alike began to make excuses. The first said to him, "I have bought a piece of land, and I must go out and see it…" Another said, "I have bought five yoke of oxen, and I am going to try them out…" Another said, "I have just been married, and therefore I cannot come."… Then the owner of the house became angry and said to his slave, "Go out at once into the streets and lanes of the town and bring in the poor, the crippled, the blind, and the lame." And the slave said, "Sir, what you ordered has been done, and there is still room." Then the master said to the slave, "Go out into the roads and lanes, and compel people to come in… For I tell you, none of those who were invited will taste my dinner."'

LUKE 14:16–24 (abridged)

Again, we have a story of a banquet—the third one we have read. In this one, many were invited but, when everything was ready, they simply made spurious excuses: checking on a land purchase, giving some new oxen a road test, staying at home with their new wife. The last was in obedience to a command to a newly wed man (Deuteronomy 24:5). The host knew, though, that they were only excuses, and became angry. He told his slave to do exactly what Jesus had advised the host in the previous two narratives: invite the poor, crippled, lame and blind. Then the slave was given an even wider remit: invite everybody—except those who had spurned the original invitation. Luke, the Gentile, likes to emphasize the universal appeal of the gospel; Matthew, as we saw, highlights the Jewish rejection of it.

This is a parable about the way people respond to Jesus' invitation to enter the kingdom of heaven. The 'chosen' race had largely rejected it so the invitation to the banquet was to be extended, first to the rejects of that 'chosen' society (the 'tax-collectors and sinners') and then to everyone, from every nation and tribe.

The heavenly banquet is for all who are open to God's generous invitation.

27 July

FILLED WITH GOOD THINGS

O give thanks to the Lord, for he is good; for his steadfast love endures forever. Let the redeemed of the Lord say so… Some wandered in desert wastes, finding no way to an inhabited town; hungry and thirsty, their soul fainted within them. Then they cried to the Lord in their trouble, and he delivered them from their distress; he led them by a straight way, until they reached an inhabited town. Let them thank the Lord for his steadfast love… For he satisfies the thirsty, and the hungry he fills with good things. Some sat in darkness and in gloom, prisoners in misery and in irons, for they had rebelled against the words of God, and spurned the counsel of the Most High. Their hearts were bowed down with hard labour; they fell down, with no one to help. Then they cried to the Lord in their trouble, and he saved them from their distress.

PSALM 107:1–2, 4–13 (abridged)

The key phrase in this psalm is 'Then they cried to the Lord'. In distress, hunger or homelessness, despair, captivity or even spiritual rebellion, eventually they recognized their plight and called to him for help. Because his love is steadfast, he not only heard their cry but came to their rescue. Just as he feeds the animals and nourishes the grain, so he shows his love even to those who have disobeyed and failed him. Even those who rebel against the words of the Lord are rescued and restored when they cry to him. Prisoners in chains are released as he breaks their bonds. The thirsty and hungry are 'filled with good things'. Those who are trapped in the desert, wandering helplessly without food or water and far from any help, cry to the Lord—and he rescues them, guiding them along safe paths to the nearest dwellings where they can find help.

And what should be our reaction? 'Let the redeemed of the Lord say so'—don't keep the gratitude to yourself! Praise him for his generosity and faithfulness—and tell the world how good is our God.

God doesn't love us because we are lovely, but because he is love.

28 July

EATING AND DRINKING

You make springs gush forth in the valleys; they flow between the hills, giving drink to every wild animal; the wild asses quench their thirst. By the streams the birds of the air have their habitation; they sing among the branches. From your lofty abode you water the mountains; the earth is satisfied with the fruit of your work. You cause the grass to grow for the cattle, and plants for people to use, to bring forth food from the earth, and wine to gladden the human heart, oil to make the face shine, and bread to strengthen the human heart.

PSALM 104:10–15

People today sometimes talk as though they invented the environmental movement, or as if until the advent of TV natural history programmes no one marvelled at the beauty and intricacy of the world around us. Here is evidence to the contrary!

God is the Creator and provider for the whole earth. He feeds the soil, gives water to birds and wild animals, and nourishes the grass for cattle and the plants that people cultivate. This may seem a simplistic view to the cynic, who will point out that drought and famine have always been a part of human experience. That objection misses the point of the poem completely. Of course the psalmist knew about drought and famine. They were part of the pattern of life in the Middle East, as they still are in many parts of the world. His point is that what we have comes from the hand of God, and for that we are grateful. It is a hymn to the generous earth and the one who made it so.

Not only that, but God wants both animals and humans to enjoy his bounty. The gifts he gives are not to enable mere survival. Bread strengthens the heart as well as the body (we feel good on a full stomach). Oil makes the face shine, and wine from the grapes of the vineyard 'gladdens the human heart'.

Those of us who benefit most from the good gifts of the Creator are duty-bound to share that bounty with those who are at present deprived of it.

29 July

A PRACTICAL FAITH

So speak and so act as those who are to be judged by the law of liberty. For judgment will be without mercy to anyone who has shown no mercy; mercy triumphs over judgment. What good is it, my brothers and sisters, if you say you have faith but do not have works? Can faith save you? If a brother or sister is naked and lacks daily food, and one of you says to them, 'Go in peace; keep warm and eat your fill', and yet you do not supply their bodily needs, what is the good of that? So faith by itself, if it has no works, is dead.

JAMES 2:12–17

The letter of James sits slightly awkwardly in the canon of the New Testament, with its emphasis on good works. In fact, though, it has distinct echoes of the teaching of Jesus, especially Matthew 5—7. This is a sternly practical application of that teaching, probably for the benefit of Jewish Christians, who may well have wondered how the Christian gospel connected with the moral law they had been taught from childhood. Like Jesus, James answers that question trenchantly: it is the same, but even more so.

He seems also to worry that some of the believers might have got the idea that if they had 'faith' in Jesus, they no longer had any moral obligations, which could well have been a distorted version of Paul's teaching about faith and works. Don't be fooled, says James. True faith makes a difference: it enables us to live better, more moral, more responsible lives. Faith requires us to love our neighbour, to be merciful, generous, just. As we saw yesterday, to be grateful for what we have from God is to be generous to those who as yet do not have it. Dead 'faith' ignores the naked and hungry. True faith feeds and clothes them. If we claim to believe in Jesus, it follows that we should obey his words and try to follow his example—and he was the one who 'went about doing good' (Acts 10:38).

By its very nature, faith can never be self-centred.

30 July

NOT BY BREAD ALONE

Remember the long way that the Lord your God has led you these forty years in the wilderness, in order to humble you, testing you to know what was in your heart, whether or not you would keep his commandments. He humbled you by letting you hunger, then by feeding you with manna… in order to make you understand that one does not live by bread alone, but by every word that comes from the mouth of the Lord. The clothes on your back did not wear out and your feet did not swell these forty years… As a parent disciplines a child so the Lord your God disciplines you.
DEUTERONOMY 8:2–5 (abridged)

These are described by the chronicler as the words of Moses, spoken to the people of Israel as they prepared for the final stage of their journey to Canaan—a land that Moses himself would never enter. It is a long discourse, full of both warnings and promises. The people must remember the Lord their God, and especially what he had done for them by delivering them from slavery in Egypt and during the 40-year journey in the deserts of Sinai. They must be mindful to keep his commandments, which Moses was given on Sinai. Above all, they are to get their priorities right, to recognize that when their lands yield abundant crops and they feel rich, they will need God just as much as they did when they were hungry, thirsty and footsore in the desert.

In this passage, these warnings and promises are summed up in one sentence. All that God had done was for one overriding purpose: to demonstrate that 'one does not live by bread alone'. Of course we need the essentials for survival; that's why Jesus taught us to pray for our 'daily bread'. But it will not suffice on its own. A full stomach isn't a full life. What they needed just as much as 'bread' was 'every word that comes from the mouth of the Lord'. That word would help them to live what Jesus called 'life in all its fullness' (John 10:10, NEB).

Jesus quoted these words during his 'testing' by Satan in the wilderness (Luke 4:4). He was hungry but, more than food, he needed to do his Father's will.

31 July

THE GREAT BANQUET OF HEAVEN

Then I heard what seemed to be the voice of a great multitude... crying out, 'Hallelujah! For the Lord our God the Almighty reigns. Let us rejoice and exult and give him the glory, for the marriage of the Lamb has come, and his bride has made herself ready; to her it has been granted to be clothed with fine linen, bright and pure'—for the fine linen is the righteous deeds of the saints. And the angel said to me, 'Write this: Blessed are those who are invited to the marriage supper of the Lamb.'

REVELATION 19:6–9 (abridged)

The final chapters of Revelation offer a series of visions of the 'last days', the time when sin and its servants have been removed from the scene. The seer is told by an angel about the coming 'banquet' of heaven, at which God himself would be the host. It will be a wedding banquet to celebrate the marriage of the Lamb to his bride.

The Lamb, of course, is Jesus, with the marks of slaughter still upon him (Revelation 5:6) but seated alongside his Father on the throne of heaven. He is the one who had died but is now glorified, and around his throne, in a vast multitude that no one can count, stand all those who have been forgiven and saved through his death (7:9).

But who is the 'bride'? In Ephesians 5:23–32, Paul speaks about the relationship of husbands to wives in Christian marriage, and uses the relationship of Christ to the Church as a model of it. Christ is the 'head' of the Church, just as the husband is the 'head' of the family. Christ loves the Church and gave himself for it, just as husbands should love their wives 'as they do their own bodies'. Husbands should care for their wives, just as Christ 'nourishes and tenderly cares' for the Church. This is all a 'great mystery', but just as husband and wife become one flesh, so Christ and his Church are united in a bond of perfect love. So the bridegroom is Jesus and the bride is the Church, and their marriage will be celebrated with feasting in heaven.

No wonder John says that those invited to this great feast are 'happy'!

August: True love

'Where is love?' sang young Oliver in Lionel Bart's musical. It's a question that has haunted the human race. Where can true love be found? The Bible offers its own magnificent answer: in the very character and nature of our Creator. The God who made us loves us because he is Love. That love, supremely shown to us in Jesus, is the theme of this month's readings.

1 August

THE REWARDS OF LOVE

So Boaz took Ruth and she became his wife. When they came together, the Lord made her conceive, and she bore a son. Then the women said to Naomi, 'Blessed be the Lord, who has not left you this day without next-of-kin; and may his name be renowned in Israel! He shall be to you a restorer of life and a nourisher of your old age; for your daughter-in-law who loves you, who is more to you than seven sons, has borne him.' Then Naomi took the child and laid him in her bosom, and became his nurse. The women of the neighbourhood gave him a name, saying, 'A son has been born to Naomi.' They named him Obed; he became the father of Jesse, the father of David.

RUTH 4:13–17

The story of Ruth is one of loyalty and love, probably in that order. When Naomi lost her two sons—one of them the husband of Ruth, a Moabitess—she did not expect Ruth to insist on accompanying her back to Bethlehem. Out of that act of loyalty a bond of love was struck between the widow and her young daughter-in-law, and now, at the end of the story, that love is rewarded with the birth of a baby boy to Ruth and her new husband, Boaz. Boaz had also been loyal to his family responsibilities and that loyalty, too, had blossomed into love.

These last scenes of the book show Naomi's joy at the birth of her grandchild—a joy she thought had been lost for ever when both her sons died. As the women of the village tell her, Ruth, 'who loves you', has been more to her than seven sons. The picture of love is completed with Naomi holding the child in her bosom, but the story is truly completed only when the child himself becomes a grandparent. The great-grandson of Ruth, the loyal immigrant, was to be David, Israel's greatest king.

The Bible often speaks of God's 'faithful love'. Love and loyalty are twins, the one embellishing the other.

2 August

THE FAITHFUL ONE

I will sing of your steadfast love, O Lord, forever; with my mouth I will proclaim your faithfulness to all generations. I declare that your steadfast love is established forever; your faithfulness is as firm as the heavens. You said, 'I have made a covenant with my chosen one, I have sworn to my servant David: "I will establish your descendants forever, and build your throne for all generations."' … Righteousness and justice are the foundation of your throne; steadfast love and faithfulness go before you.

PSALM 89:1–4, 14

This psalm is a hymn to a love which is steadfast, trustworthy and reliable. Human experience confirms that the kind of person who professes love for us and yet in practice is unreliable, fickle and even unfaithful is extremely difficult to accept. Most of us would willingly exchange a little passion for a lot of faithfulness.

The refrain of the whole psalm is built around the words 'steadfast love' and 'faithfulness'. 'Steadfast love', as we have seen already, is one word in Hebrew, *chesed*, and it is the central property of the God of Israel. *Chesed* is what has marked his relationship with them from the start. He is faithful even when they are faithless.

This steadfast love is built into a covenant, a binding agreement into which God has freely entered. If they will be his people, he will be their God. He will never abandon his own, even if they wander away from him, disobey his commandments and flout his will. 'God is faithful' is an absolutely fundamental claim of the Bible, in both Old and New Testaments. In this psalm it is specifically applied to the throne of David and his successors. What God has promised, he will do—although in the event the promise was fulfilled in a way the people of David's day could not have envisaged.

Righteousness, justice, faithfulness and steadfast love are the marks of the psalmist's God. Three thousand years later, the world has changed but God hasn't.

3 August

LOVE AT FIRST SIGHT

Isaac went out in the evening to walk in the field; and looking up, he saw camels coming. And Rebekah looked up, and when she saw Isaac, she slipped quickly from the camel, and said to the servant, 'Who is the man over there, walking… to meet us?' The servant said, 'It is my master.' So she took her veil and covered herself. And the servant told Isaac all the things that he had done. Then Isaac… took Rebekah, and she became his wife; and he loved her. So Isaac was comforted after his mother's death.
GENESIS 24:63–67 (abridged)

The marriage of Isaac and Rebekah is one of the most memorable love stories of the Bible. It was an 'arranged' affair because Abraham felt, after his own wife had died, that his son should have a wife from his own people rather than a Canaanite one. A faithful servant was sent to choose a suitable candidate and, through a series of events, came across Rebekah. She agreed to travel to Isaac's encampment for Abraham to approve or disapprove the servant's choice.

Our passage relates the moment of their first meeting, with Rebekah seeing Isaac in the distance, walking towards the camels—perhaps impatient to see the young woman who was being proposed as his wife. She was obviously also impatient because she got down from her camel, modestly veiled herself and prepared for the meeting.

The servant explained all the circumstances through which he had chosen this young woman. He had prayed for God's guidance, set certain conditions and found that Rebekah met them all. He had gone to her house and negotiated with her father, who was happy for her to become Isaac's wife—the wife of a wealthy man. The final touch, however, is here. When Isaac saw her, 'he loved her'—and their marriage helped him to be comforted after his mother Sarah's death.

Abraham's servant is one of the anonymous heroes of the Old Testament, a devout man who knew that only with God's guiding hand could he hope to find the right wife for Isaac. Their love was the Lord's gift, in answer to prayer.

4 August

A SMALL PRICE FOR LOVE

When Laban heard the news about his sister's son Jacob, he... brought him to his house... Then Laban said to Jacob, 'Because you are my kinsman, should you therefore serve me for nothing? Tell me, what shall your wages be?' Now Laban had two daughters; the name of the elder was Leah, and the name of the younger was Rachel. Leah's eyes were lovely, and Rachel was graceful and beautiful. Jacob loved Rachel; so he said, 'I will serve you seven years for your younger daughter Rachel.' Laban said, 'It is better that I give her to you than that I should give her to any other man; stay with me.' So Jacob served seven years for Rachel, and they seemed to him but a few days because of the love he had for her.

GENESIS 29:13, 15–20

'They seemed but a few days because of the love he had for her': that in itself is a testimony to the reality of Jacob's feelings for this young woman. To wait seven years would sound preposterous to most men in his position, but in fact, because Laban subsequently insisted that he must first marry the older daughter, Leah, in accordance with local custom, it was not seven but fourteen.

Like his father Isaac, there could be no doubt, then, that Jacob's love for his wife was genuine, and it subsequently survived the crushing disappointment of Rachel's inability to conceive. Leah, the elder daughter of Laban, had ten sons, but eventually, to great joy, Rachel produced two, Benjamin and Joseph. Inevitably, they became their father's favourites, with consequences both for them and for the long-term future of the nation of Israel.

Romantic love is often thought of as a recent invention but these stories from patriarchal times demonstrate that it is always possible if the chemistry is right.

Many marriages in Bible times were little more than business arrangements, but this one shows that when God is at work in the circumstances of life he turns what could be formal and joyless into something life-enhancing.

5 August

BROTHERLY LOVE

And Jacob said, 'O God of my father Abraham and God of my father Isaac... I am not worthy of the least of all the steadfast love and all the faithfulness that you have shown to your servant, for with only my staff I crossed this Jordan; and now I have become two companies. Deliver me, please, from the hand of my brother, from the hand of Esau, for I am afraid of him; he may come and kill us all... Yet you have said, "I will surely do you good, and make your offspring as the sand of the sea."'

GENESIS 32:9–12 (abridged)

This prayer of Jacob, the younger son of Isaac, is spoken out of real fear about what will happen as he returns to meet his older brother Esau. He knows that he ought to go to him and seek reconciliation, but he is also desperately aware that the rift between them is entirely of his own making. He had stolen the birthrights of the elder son by trickery. Now, having gone away, as he says, with just a staff, he returns with a huge retinue of family, servants and herds, but is uncertain how his brother will react. He prays that God will deliver him from Esau but also (if we read on a bit further) prepares generous peace-offerings with which he hopes to assuage his brother's justifiable anger.

Before their encounter, Jacob meets a mysterious stranger, possibly an angel, as he crosses the ford of the Jabbok. In the course of a physical struggle between them, the stranger renames him 'Israel', which means 'one who strives with God'. From that title came, of course, the name 'Israelite' for his descendants and 'Israel' for the nation they would eventually found. From the ford he limps towards his meeting with Esau, having been injured in the night-time struggle.

In the event, blood proves thicker than water. Esau, with enormous generosity of spirit, welcomes him. Both brothers shed tears—of joy on Esau's part, and, we suspect, also of relief on Jacob's.

Jacob didn't deserve to be welcomed by Esau. It was, in the purest sense of the word, an act of sheer grace.

6 August

NOT LOVELY, BUT LOVED

It was not because you were more numerous than any other people that the Lord set his heart on you and chose you—for you were the fewest of all peoples. It was because the Lord loved you and kept the oath that he swore to your ancestors, that the Lord has… redeemed you from the house of slavery… Know therefore that the Lord your God is God, the faithful God who maintains covenant loyalty with those who love him and keep his commandments… If you heed these ordinances, by diligently observing them, the Lord your God will maintain with you the covenant loyalty that he swore to your ancestors; he will love you, bless you, and multiply you; he will bless the fruit of your womb and the fruit of your ground, your grain and your wine and your oil, the increase of your cattle and the issue of your flock, in the land that he swore to your ancestors to give you.

DEUTERONOMY 7:7–9, 12–13 (abridged)

This part of Moses' final address to the people of Israel as they prepare to approach the promised land sets their relationship with the Lord firmly in the context of love. The Hebrew notion of 'love' includes the idea of loyalty and faithfulness. Here Moses stresses the faithful love of God and calls on the people to love him faithfully.

God's love is not determined by the loveliness of its object. It can't be earned. It doesn't stem from admiration or attraction. It comes entirely from within himself. So his love for Israel wasn't based on some inherent characteristic of goodness in them, or on their power or strength, but simply on his own will. He kept the oath that he had made to Abraham. This is what is called here 'covenant loyalty'.

So it always is with the love of God. We can't earn it or deserve it, and he certainly doesn't love us because we are attractive, winsome or good. He loves because he is love (1 John 4:8). As water is wet and stone is hard, so God is love. It is his nature.

'God so loved the world that he gave his only Son' (John 3:16), not because the world was good or pure or lovely, but because he is.

7 August

DAVID AND JONATHAN

When David had finished speaking to Saul, the soul of Jonathan was bound to the soul of David, and Jonathan loved him as his own soul... Then Jonathan made a covenant with David... Jonathan stripped himself of the robe that he was wearing, and gave it to David, and his armour, and even his sword and his bow and his belt. David went out and was successful wherever Saul sent him; as a result, Saul set him over the army. And all the people, even the servants of Saul, approved.

1 SAMUEL 18:1, 3–5 (abridged)

In case this friendship sounds one-sided (Jonathan loved David 'as his own soul'), we might add the moving words of David's lament after Jonathan's death in battle: 'Greatly beloved were you to me; your love to me was wonderful, passing the love of women' (2 Samuel 1:26). Such language has led some people, in the current climate, to suggest that there was a homosexual element to their relationship, but in view of the general picture of David's love life, that seems highly unlikely!

Far more likely is that here is an example of a true and deep friendship, which is one of God's greatest gifts to human beings. From the moment they met, they seemed to click. Jonathan risked his father's wrath for backing David when the king was becoming deeply jealous of the young man. They shared interests, concerns, personal courage. Even when circumstances separated them, the bond of friendship remained.

In New Testament Greek, there was a word for this kind of friendship: *philadelphia*. It literally means 'brotherly love', and the early Christians used it to describe love for their fellow believers. In the story of the widow who lost a coin (Luke 15:9), it is used in the female form for her friends. Friendship is a gift of God, intended for our blessing, which is why we should always cherish our friends.

Jesus called his disciples his 'friends' (John 15:14). As the hymn says, 'What a Friend we have in Jesus!'

8 August

THE BELOVED PHYSICIAN

Do your best to come… soon, for Demas, in love with this present world, has deserted me and gone to Thessalonica; Crescens has gone to Galatia, Titus to Dalmatia. Only Luke is with me. Get Mark and bring him with you, for he is useful in my ministry. I have sent Tychicus to Ephesus. When you come, bring the cloak that I left with Carpus… Greet Prisca and Aquila, and the household of Onesiphorus. Erastus remained in Corinth; Trophimus I left ill in Miletus. Do your best to come before winter.

2 TIMOTHY 4:9–13, 19–21A (abridged)

This sounds like the apostle Paul at a low ebb. Under house arrest and with winter fast approaching, he seems to have been deserted by most of his companions, although some have been sent off by him and poor Trophimus is unwell in Miletus. He is clearly keen to have Timothy's company and he asks him to bring Mark along—significant because Paul and Mark had fallen out some years earlier, when the apostle felt the young man had let him down on a preaching mission. Obviously the relationship has been healed.

'Only Luke is with me.' Luke, almost certainly the author of the Gospel and of Acts, and Paul's companion on some of his journeys, was the faithful friend who was there in his moment of need. In an earlier letter, Paul described him as 'the beloved physician' (Colossians 4:14). There was a genuine bond between the two men, one a former Pharisee and Jewish to his roots, the other a Gentile intellectual.

Here again is a picture of true friendship—not, perhaps, as intense as that between Jonathan and David, but deep and faithful. If we had to face what Paul faced—house arrest, several trials and the almost certain prospect of martyrdom—who could be better to have alongside us than a faithful Christian friend who was a doctor?

Paul is sometimes caricatured as a bit of a misogynist and a loner. His letters show us a man who has friends—men and women—in plenty, and shares a warm relationship with them.

9 August

A FATHER'S LOVE

The Cushite said, 'Good tidings for my lord the king! For the Lord has vindicated you this day, delivering you from the power of all who rose up against you.' The king said to the Cushite, 'Is it well with the young man Absalom?' The Cushite answered, 'May... all who rise up to do you harm be like that young man.' The king... went up to the chamber over the gate, and wept; and as he went, he said, 'O my son Absalom, my son, my son Absalom! Would that I had died instead of you, O Absalom, my son, my son!' It was told Joab, 'The king is weeping... for Absalom.' So the victory... was turned into mourning for all the troops; for the troops heard that day, 'The king is grieving for his son.' The troops stole into the city that day as soldiers steal in who are ashamed when they flee in battle.
2 SAMUEL 18:31—19:3 (abridged)

David's son, Absalom, had led a rebellion against his father's regime. David's military chief of staff, Joab, took steps to quell the uprising and in the ensuing conflict Absalom was killed: his long hair got caught in a tree and he became an easy target (2 Samuel 18:9).

Here, the news of Absalom's death is brought to David, in terms which imply that its bearer expected the king to be delighted. In fact, he was appalled, weeping and wailing in grief. He even expressed the wish that he had died instead of Absalom—which would have made the rebellion successful. Unsurprisingly, this reaction did not play well with Joab and his army, who were deprived of the usual public celebrations of victory. Joab (always one to speak his mind) later told the king in no uncertain terms what he thought of his reaction (19:5–7).

In human terms it is completely understandable, however. The love of a parent for a child is not ruled by reason but by strong emotion. As we know, David was a man of passionate feelings, and here we see them expressed in terms of a father's love.

David loved his rebellious son, Absalom. Our heavenly Father loves his rebellious children. That is our ground of hope.

10 August

STEADFAST LOVE

O how abundant is your goodness that you have... accomplished for those who take refuge in you, in the sight of everyone! In the shelter of your presence you hide them from human plots; you hold them safe under your shelter from contentious tongues. Blessed be the Lord, for he has wondrously shown his steadfast love to me when I was beset as a city under siege. I had said in my alarm, 'I am driven far from your sight.' But you heard my supplications when I cried out to you for help... The Lord preserves the faithful, but abundantly repays the one who acts haughtily. Be strong, and let your heart take courage, all you who wait for the Lord.

PSALM 31:19–24 (abridged)

This sounds like a song of relief on the part of someone who has been through a very bad experience. It would seem that he had felt himself the victim of someone's plots. The emotional assault also included what the psalmist calls 'contentious tongues'—presumably, people spreading snide and untrue stories. So bad were these attacks, or so severe was their result, that he felt like a city under siege, hemmed in and cut off. Many people will be able to identify with his feelings. Office gossip, church strife, neighbours who have a grudge—these are, sadly, part and parcel of life. They happen to those who have 'asked for it' and equally to those who have done nothing to deserve it.

At least the psalmist knew where to turn when he was under attack—to the Lord. It was to him that he fled for shelter: the 'shelter of your presence'. In him he found a refuge. It is, he says, the Lord who preserves those who trust him. There is a quiet confidence in these words and a ring of authenticity about his faith in the 'steadfast love'—that phrase again!—of the God in whom he trusted.

Most of us at one time or another will experience the devastating loneliness of feeling 'besieged'. We may even feel that God, too, has turned his back on us. This psalm reminds us that when we need him most, God draws us under the 'shelter of his presence'.

11 August

LOVE IN A TIME OF TROUBLE

Incline your ear, O Lord, and answer me, for I am poor and needy. Preserve my life, for I am devoted to you; save your servant who trusts in you. You are my God; be gracious to me, O Lord, for to you do I cry all day long. Gladden the soul of your servant, for to you, O Lord, I lift up my soul. For you, O Lord, are good and forgiving, abounding in steadfast love to all who call on you. Give ear, O Lord, to my prayer; listen to my cry of supplication. In the day of my trouble I call on you, for you will answer me. There is none like you among the gods, O Lord, nor are there any works like yours. All the nations you have made shall come and bow down before you, O Lord, and shall glorify your name. For you are great and do wondrous things; you alone are God. Teach me your way, O Lord, that I may walk in your truth; give me an undivided heart to revere your name.
PSALM 86:1–11

This is another psalm 'in a day of trouble', but the exact nature of the trouble isn't revealed. It might well have been sickness—later on, the psalmist thanks God for delivering him from *Sheol* (the grave) (v. 13). It might possibly have been poverty. However, the tone of the poem suggests that it was probably a sin that the psalmist had committed and for which he needed forgiveness. 'You, O Lord, are good and forgiving': that was the sole ground of his hope.

His prayer is based on his faith in God ('save your servant who trusts in you') and on the graciousness of the Lord. He is confident that as he calls on God, so God will answer him. But he is also aware of his own failure and need. He asks to be taught God's way rather than his own, so that he may walk in God's truth. He prays for an 'undivided' heart—a fascinating petition! Presumably a divided heart is constantly torn between doing what God requires and doing what the individual prefers. So, an undivided heart would be wholly and without reservation set on doing the will of God, 'walking in his way'.

The undivided heart knows where its true loyalty lies.

12 August

HIGHER THAN THE HEAVENS

My heart is steadfast, O God, my heart is steadfast; I will sing and make melody. Awake, my soul! Awake, O harp and lyre! I will awake the dawn. I will give thanks to you, O Lord, among the peoples, and I will sing praises to you among the nations. For your steadfast love is higher than the heavens, and your faithfulness reaches to the clouds. Be exalted, O God, above the heavens, and let your glory be over all the earth. Give victory with your right hand, and answer me, so that those whom you love may be rescued… O grant us help against the foe, for human help is worthless. With God we shall do valiantly; it is he who will tread down our foes.

PSALM 108:1–6, 12–13

In this selection of psalms on the theme of God's love and faithfulness, this one begins in the most confident and rhapsodic way. The psalmist is in some kind of early morning ecstasy! His heart is bursting with faithful love for the Lord. He can't wait to get up, grab his harp and lyre and start the hymns of praise—whatever the neighbours may think. He's going to wake the dawn, no less. The reason for this ecstasy is once again the 'steadfast love' and faithfulness of God. They are, he sings, 'higher than the heavens'—stratospheric, we might say—and reach to the very clouds with their life-bearing cargo of rain.

He has another reason, which emerges as the psalm develops. Israel is on the verge of some kind of armed conflict. In this clash between God's people and the Gentile nations around, he sees God's 'glory' as being at stake. He pleads with him that in answer to his prayers and praises God will 'give victory'. There is at least a hint in this psalm that, lately, the armies of Israel have not been enjoying unqualified success (see v. 11: 'you do not go out, O God, with our armies'). Human help is 'worthless', but if God is with them, they will conquer their foes.

Christians today are very cautious about praying for success in battle but in general terms we know that we are in a spiritual war of some kind. In that situation, human help is worthless but 'with God we shall do valiantly'.

13 August

GIVING GOD PLEASURE

Praise the Lord! How good it is to sing praises to our God; for he is gracious, and a song of praise is fitting. The Lord builds up Jerusalem; he gathers the outcasts of Israel. He heals the broken-hearted, and binds up their wounds. He determines the number of the stars; he gives to all of them their names. Great is our Lord, and abundant in power; his understanding is beyond measure. The Lord lifts up the downtrodden; he casts the wicked to the ground... He covers the heavens with clouds, prepares rain for the earth, makes grass grow on the hills. He gives to the animals their food, and to the young ravens when they cry. His delight is not in the strength of the horse, nor his pleasure in the speed of a runner; but the Lord takes pleasure in those who fear him, in those who hope in his steadfast love.
PSALM 147:1–6, 8–11

This is yet another psalm extolling the 'steadfast love' of the Lord. Here, however, the context is different. The psalmist has no secondary agenda (victory in battle or rescue from his enemies). It is purely and simply a song of praise, and in the course of it he registers, one by one, the reasons for believing that the Lord constantly and demonstrably exercises his love in the world. That is why a 'song of praise is fitting'—not because God needs to be praised, like a difficult child or a touchy performer. The need comes from within us: the evidences of his love are so numerous that we are simply bound to 'sing praises'.

The list is almost endless. God draws in the outcasts and builds up a home for them in Jerusalem. He heals the broken-hearted, binding up their wounds. He is the creator of the starry heights. His power and wisdom are infinite, yet he cares for the downtrodden and judges the wicked. He sends rain and waters the crops. He feeds the animals and birds. Above all, God rejoices in those who 'fear' or reverence him. His pleasure is in those who 'hope in his steadfast love'.

In the Lord's Prayer we pray that God's name will be 'hallowed', treated with respect, regarded as holy. When we do this, we fill him with delight.

14 August

FAITHFUL SHEPHERDS

'And now I know that none of you, among whom I have gone about proclaiming the kingdom, will ever see my face again. Therefore I declare to you this day that I am not responsible for the blood of any of you, for I did not shrink from declaring to you the whole purpose of God. Keep watch over yourselves and over all the flock, of which the Holy Spirit has made you overseers, to shepherd the church of God that he obtained with the blood of his own Son… Therefore be alert, remembering that for three years I did not cease night or day to warn everyone with tears.'

ACTS 20:25–28, 31

This is part of the apostle Paul's farewell to the elders of the church at Ephesus. He was going up to Jerusalem and knew that it was unlikely that he would escape unscathed from that city. In the event, he didn't, being arrested and eventually taken under escort to Rome, where he had opted to be tried by Caesar—his right as a Roman citizen.

These words give the lie to the popular misconception that Paul was a tight-lipped, cold and ruthless man. He cared deeply for the churches he had planted, and he cared especially for the people he had appointed as ministers to them. He knew the fearful responsibility, the daily burden of caring for the churches. He wanted them to watch over their flocks like shepherds but, at the same time, he wanted them to watch over themselves: as people frequently say nowadays, 'Take care!' They were valuable and so were their congregations, because they had been bought with the blood of God's Son.

In one sense, we are all shepherds because we all 'watch over' someone—a dear friend, an elderly neighbour, a grandchild or niece or godchild. The shepherd watches and the shepherd cares.

15 August

PITY, LOVE AND GRACE

I will recount the gracious deeds of the Lord, the praiseworthy acts of the Lord, because of all that the Lord has done for us, and the great favour to the house of Israel that he has shown them according to his mercy, according to the abundance of his steadfast love. For he said, 'Surely they are my people, children who will not deal falsely'; and he became their saviour in all their distress. It was no messenger or angel but his presence that saved them; in his love and in his pity he redeemed them; he lifted them up and carried them all the days of old.

ISAIAH 63:7–9

This catalogue of God's gracious dealings with Israel precedes—in typical prophetic style—a robust warning about their present condition. Still, it's always good to be reminded of past blessings, just in case we are in one of those very human phases in which we are more caught up in our present problems.

Those blessings were gifts of love. They were signs of the reliable, faithful generosity that marked the relationship of the Lord God to his people. He had showed them mercy, forgiven their faults and failures, saved them from slavery, hunger and enemy tribes. And he hadn't done this through some 'messenger' or even angel, but by his own 'presence', by being with them through their journeying.

For the Christian, all of this is equally true. Our salvation may not be from physical slavery, human enemies or starvation, but our problems might be considered at least equally daunting—the pressure of secularism, the constant lure of materialism, the temptation to go with the prevailing flow of sexual licence. For us, too, under the new covenant of grace, it is not a messenger or angel whom God has sent to save us, but what John Henry Newman called 'his Presence and his very Self'—Jesus, his Son.

Just as the Israelites so easily forgot who had brought them through their troubles, we can forget that the God who blessed us in the past is still at hand.

16 August

THE FRUITS OF LOVE

Thus says the Lord: The people who survived the sword found grace in the wilderness... I have loved you with an everlasting love; therefore I have continued my faithfulness to you... Again you shall take your tambourines, and go forth in the dance of the merrymakers. Again you shall plant vineyards... the planters shall plant, and shall enjoy the fruit... See, I am going to bring them from the land of the north, and gather them from the farthest parts of the earth, among them the blind and the lame, those with child and those in labour, together... With weeping they shall come, and with consolations I will lead them back, I will let them walk by brooks of water, in a straight path in which they shall not stumble; for I have become a father to Israel, and Ephraim is my firstborn.

JEREMIAH 31:2–5, 8–9 (abridged)

'Hopeless' is probably the coldest word in the English language. 'I'm afraid further treatment would be hopeless... We've searched and searched, but it's beginning to look hopeless.' We say, 'Where there's life, there's hope', but the Bible would probably want to substitute the word 'God' for 'life'. No situation or person is 'hopeless' with him.

That is what Jeremiah wanted to tell the people of his time. Yes, there would be judgment for their sins, especially their disloyalty to the God who had loved and kept them. But in the end, when repentance had done its work, the same God who had judged their sins would heal and restore. So we have several visions like this one, of a future age full of joy and hope, where the 'fruits of love' are bursting through on every hillside and in every home. Jeremiah reminds them that the Israelites who sinned in the wilderness were nevertheless brought to the promised land of rest. The reason lay not in their genuine acts of repentance but in the nature of God himself. 'I have loved you with an everlasting love; therefore I have continued my faithfulness to you.'

The love of a human father may be inconsistent or even abusive but the love of the heavenly Father is utterly consistent and reliable.

17 August

THIS IS LOVE

Love has been perfected among us in this: that we may have boldness on the day of judgment... There is no fear in love, but perfect love casts out fear; for fear has to do with punishment, and whoever fears has not reached perfection in love. We love because he first loved us. Those who say, 'I love God,' and hate their brothers or sisters, are liars; for those who do not love a brother or sister whom they have seen, cannot love God whom they have not seen... Those who love God must love their brothers and sisters also... By this we know that we love the children of God, when we love God and obey his commandments. For the love of God is this, that we obey his commandments. And his commandments are not burdensome.

1 JOHN 4:17–21; 5:2–3 (abridged)

The apostle John (for whoever wrote the fourth Gospel certainly wrote this letter as well) has a profound insight into the love of God. This isn't, perhaps, surprising coming from the 'beloved disciple' and friend of Jesus. For him, as he has already said in this letter, 'God is love' (4:8), and the consequence of that is that those who belong to his Son can have 'boldness' even in the face of the day of judgment. The word implies confidence rather than a sort of cocky presumption. We shall answer to one who loves us. What more could we ask?

'Perfect love casts out fear.' Of course it does. We feel 'at home' with those we love and who we know love us. The writer wants to assure his readers that their relationship with God is built on the same kind of confidence, because 'we love because he first loved us'. In other words, the love a Christian shows (or should show) to others is simply a reflection of the love God has already shown us. It's also true that when we truly love someone, we want to please them, to do what they would wish us to do. So it is with God. We show our love for him by 'obeying his commandments'—commandments that are not 'burdensome'.

'Those who love God must love their brothers and sisters also.'

18 August

THE GREATER BLESSING

'And now I commend you to God and to the message of his grace, a message that is able to build you up and to give you the inheritance among all who are sanctified. I coveted no one's silver or gold or clothing. You know for yourselves that I worked with my own hands to support myself and my companions. In all this I have given you an example that by such work we must support the weak, remembering the words of the Lord Jesus, for he himself said, "It is more blessed to give than to receive."'
ACTS 20:32–35

This is the last part of Paul's farewell to the Ephesian elders (we read the first part a few days ago). Again, there is an undercurrent of deep emotion and affection as he commends them to God. They are the bearers of the 'message of his grace', and the message they bear will not only build up their hearers in faith and love but will also give them 'the inheritance among all who are sanctified'. It is a 'saintly' task.

Paul then offers his own ministry as an example to them. He had no ambitions for himself. He wasn't in it for silver, gold or fancy clothes. In fact, he worked (as a tent-maker) to support himself so that he wouldn't be a burden on the churches, few of whose members were wealthy (compare 1 Corinthians 1:26). He hoped that his example would encourage them to earn wages in order to support those who were in no position to do so—the ones he calls 'the weak'. He then quotes a saying of Jesus—not one to be found anywhere in the Gospels but, as he was speaking these words ten years before the first Gospel saw the light of day, we may assume it is utterly authentic: 'It is more blessed to give than to receive.' The miser is miserable; the generous heart sings.

The recipient is blessed by the one who gives. The giver is blessed by the one who has given us everything.

19 August

THE LOVE OF THE FORGIVEN

[Jesus] said to Simon, 'Do you see this woman? I entered your house; you gave me no water for my feet, but she has bathed my feet with her tears and dried them with her hair. You gave me no kiss, but from the time I came in she has not stopped kissing my feet. You did not anoint my head with oil, but she has anointed my feet with ointment. Therefore, I tell you, her sins, which were many, have been forgiven; hence she has shown great love. But the one to whom little is forgiven, loves little.' Then he said to her, 'Your sins are forgiven.' But those who were at the table with him began to say among themselves, 'Who is this who even forgives sins?' And he said to the woman, 'Your faith has saved you; go in peace.'

LUKE 7:44–50

Jesus had been invited to supper at the house of a Pharisee, Simon. Perhaps because the host was unsure about Jesus, or even intended to snub him, the normal formalities had been ignored: no water for his feet, no kiss of greeting, no oil for his face. However, once the meal had started, a woman—identified only as a 'sinner'—knelt at the feet of Jesus as he reclined at table. She wept over them and wiped them with her hair. She kissed them. She anointed them with oil—all the gestures of love and appreciation that Simon had so manifestly failed to offer.

This was all too much for the Pharisee. Simon began to think that a true prophet would not allow such a woman to touch him. Our passage is Jesus' reaction to Simon's unexpressed judgment. First, in Jewish style, he tells a story—about two men who were forgiven debts, one ten times greater than the other. Which would love their generous creditor more? Simon knew the answer, of course: the one who was forgiven the most. Quite so, said Jesus. And this woman, who has committed many sins, all of which have been forgiven, has shown great love for Jesus: 'But the one to whom little is forgiven, loves little'.

The bystanders were critical of Jesus for acting like God and forgiving her sins, but it was the woman's faith in him that had 'saved' her.

20 August

LOVE SPURNED

My beloved had a vineyard on a very fertile hill. He dug it and cleared it of stones, and planted it with choice vines; he built a watch-tower in the midst of it, and hewed out a wine vat in it; he expected it to yield grapes, but it yielded wild grapes. And now, inhabitants of Jerusalem and people of Judah, judge between me and my vineyard. What more was there to do for my vineyard that I have not done in it? When I expected it to yield grapes, why did it yield wild grapes? … I will remove its hedge, and… I will make it a waste; it shall not be pruned or hoed, and it shall be overgrown with briers and thorns… For the vineyard of the Lord of hosts is the house of Israel, and the people of Judah are his pleasant planting; he expected justice, but saw bloodshed; righteousness, but heard a cry!

ISAIAH 5:1–7 (abridged)

It would be unbalanced not to include in a selection of Bible readings on the subject of love the painful topic of love spurned. It is a recurring theme of many of the Old Testament writers because they saw the history of Israel as one in which God's faithful love was constantly rejected. Elijah and Elisha saw the people accepting the pagan practices of their neighbours. The later prophets, like Isaiah, were concerned with the widespread failure to observe, in spirit as well as letter, the requirements of God's law. It was this disobedience that led to their punishment at the hands of enemy powers, and eventual exile.

Here the principle is dramatically illustrated in a parable, applied specifically to the people of Judah. The story is of a man who planted a vineyard, dug it, fertilized it, installed a wine vat and did all that was necessary for it to produce the finest grapes. But when the crop grew, to his anger it consisted entirely of wild grapes—useless for making wine. His response was to take away his protection and leave the land to rot. They were his 'beloved', but they had rejected his love.

There is nothing sadder than love rejected. There is nothing more utterly tragic than the love of God spurned. Surely this is the greatest sin of all?

21 August

THE GIVER, NOT THE GIFTS

Though the fig tree does not blossom, and no fruit is on the vines; though the produce of the olive fails and the fields yield no food; though the flock is cut off from the fold and there is no herd in the stalls, yet I will rejoice in the Lord; I will exult in the God of my salvation. God, the Lord, is my strength; he makes my feet like the feet of a deer, and makes me tread upon the heights.

HABAKKUK 3:17–19

This is both a beautiful piece of poetry and an amazing insight into the nature of true faith. I remember, long ago, a member of our church youth group saying to me after a service that she was 'off God', the reason being that he hadn't answered a particular prayer and she felt let down. Well, most of us can mirror that experience, yet it is actually a sign of an immature faith to judge our relationship with God in this one-sided kind of way, as if he gives and we get.

The prophet Habakkuk offers an entire catalogue of disappointments. The fig trees haven't blossomed, the vines have produced no grapes, the olive bushes are barren and the fields are yielding no crops. Not only that, but there is 'no herd in the stalls'. This is economic recession with a vengeance! In a society and culture where God was seen as the ultimate cause of every event, it would have been understandable to complain bitterly that he had abandoned this poor family—and there are plenty of examples in the Psalms and elsewhere of exactly that kind of accusation. Yet the prophet retains a sublime and confident faith in God: 'yet I will rejoice in the Lord; I will exult in the God of my salvation'. For him, it is the giver, not the gifts, that defines the relationship.

It is very easy to base our love for God entirely on what he has given us rather than on what he is.

22 August

LOVE RESTORED

Return, O Israel, to the Lord your God, for you have stumbled because of your iniquity. Take words with you and return to the Lord; say to him, 'Take away all guilt; accept that which is good, and we will offer the fruit of our lips. Assyria shall not save us; we will not ride upon horses; we will say no more, "Our God", to the work of our hands...' I will heal their disloyalty; I will love them freely, for my anger has turned from them. I will be like the dew to Israel; he shall blossom like the lily, he shall strike root like the forests of Lebanon. His... beauty shall be like the olive tree, and his fragrance like that of Lebanon. They shall again live beneath my shadow, they shall flourish as a garden; they shall blossom like the vine, their fragrance shall be like the wine of Lebanon.

HOSEA 14:1–7 (abridged)

This is a wonderful picture of the effects of true repentance in restoring a relationship, not just to how it was, but to how it could be. They are to 'take words' to God—words of sorrow for sin and confession of guilt—but they are also to disown attitudes and practices they have long relied on. Alliances with foreign lands won't help, nor will 'horses' (cavalry?) and nor will the 'work of their hands', their own efforts at self-help. They are to return to God without condition or reservation.

If they do so, then the promises come tumbling from the prophet's lips. The Lord will love them 'freely', he will be like the refreshing dew of morning, he will make their land blossom and its forest grow. The land will again be beautiful and fragrant. More than that, they shall live 'beneath his shadow' and flourish there, protected and blessed. It sounds like Eden restored, which is probably exactly the image that Hosea had in mind.

A relationship restored after damage is often stronger, more loving, more accepting and more beautiful than the same one before things went wrong. This certainly seems true for the repentant sinner—the thief on the cross was told he would be in 'paradise' that very day (Luke 23:43).

23 August

LOVE, TRUTH AND PEACE

These are the things that you shall do: Speak the truth to one another, render in your gates judgments that are true and make for peace, do not devise evil in your hearts against one another, and love no false oath; for all these are things that I hate, says the Lord. The word of the Lord of hosts came to me, saying: Thus says the Lord of hosts: The fast of the fourth month, and the fast of the fifth, and the fast of the seventh, and the fast of the tenth, shall be seasons of joy and gladness, and cheerful festivals for the house of Judah: therefore love truth and peace.
ZECHARIAH 8:16–19

Right living involves right thinking. If we are to love God and our neighbour, then we shall find that we also love certain principles, certain ways of thinking, which reflect the mind of God. High among those principles are love, truth and peace. God, we are told, 'is love' (1 John 4:8). It is his very nature. And God is truth. That is to say, he speaks the truth because he is the truth. The Son of God on earth also said that he was not only the 'way' and the 'life', but also the 'truth' (John 14:6). God is also the 'God of peace' (1 Thessalonians 5:23)—the God who brings peace, who longs for his people to live in peace with each other and with him. Those who belong to God, who have put their trust in him, should therefore model and practise these godly attributes. They will be people of love, truth and peace.

Here, in this powerful passage from Zechariah, his hearers are commanded what not to love ('love no false oath') and what they should love ('truth and peace'). This truthfulness is to be utterly genuine and practical, affecting our words, our judgments and our secret inward attitudes. From love and truth, real peace can spring.

Love, in this sense, is not sentimental but practical. Truth, in this sense, is not an abstract concept but a way of life. And from such love and such truth, lasting peace will be born.

24 August

PRACTICAL LOVE

You shall not defraud your neighbour; you shall not steal; and you shall not keep for yourself the wages of a labourer until morning. You shall not revile the deaf or put a stumbling-block before the blind; you shall fear your God: I am the Lord. You shall not render an unjust judgment; you shall not be partial to the poor or defer to the great... You shall not go around as a slanderer... I am the Lord. You shall not hate in your heart anyone of your kin... You shall not take vengeance or bear a grudge against any of your people, but you shall love your neighbour as yourself: I am the Lord... You shall rise before the aged, and defer to the old; and you shall fear your God: I am the Lord. When an alien resides with you in your land, you shall not oppress the alien. The alien who resides with you shall be to you as the citizen among you; you shall love the alien as yourself, for you were aliens in the land of Egypt: I am the Lord your God.
LEVITICUS 19:13–18, 32–34 (abridged)

These very practical commandments seem to act as a commentary on the key verse: 'you shall love your neighbour as yourself' (v. 18), known as the second great commandment. Each is concluded with a terse but highly significant comment: 'I am the Lord' (Yahweh). So they are rooted in the very nature of God himself.

They are certainly practical—and very demanding. They ring in most cases as truly today as they did 3000 years ago. Theft, fraud, exploitation of workers and immigrants, injustice, slander and hateful thoughts are still all too common, and vengeance, especially on a tribal or national scale, is sadly still with us. The Lord God, the eternal I AM, still sees the abuse and anger and lies, and still opposes them.

Respect is also a theme. 'You shall rise before the aged, and defer to the old'—quite a word to a society that worships youth! And the resident alien is to be treated as a citizen, with full rights. The people must never forget that they, too, were 'aliens' in the land of Egypt.

Love that is not practical is not really love at all.

25 August

GENTLE AND COURTEOUS

Remind them to be subject to rulers and authorities, to be obedient, to be ready for every good work, to speak evil of no one, to avoid quarrelling, to be gentle, and to show every courtesy to everyone. For we ourselves were once foolish, disobedient, led astray, slaves to various passions and pleasures, passing our days in malice and envy, despicable, hating one another. But when the goodness and loving-kindness of God our Saviour appeared, he saved us, not because of any works of righteousness that we had done, but according to his mercy, through the water of rebirth and renewal by the Holy Spirit.

TITUS 3:1–5

These are instructions to Titus, one of Paul's assistants—people he trusted to watch over the growing churches he had planted. Although, in a few places, active persecution of Christians had already begun by the civil authorities, the Church's leaders were anxious to give them no pretext for such harassment. Christians were expected to be loyal citizens, law-abiding and peaceful. Yet here the instructions go further, to give us a valuable insight into the way in which the apostles would like their converts to be seen by the general public.

As well as being law-abiding and 'obedient' (which presumably applies to public life), in their private lives they are to be courteous, not to spread slander about people, to avoid getting involved in arguments and quarrels, and to be 'gentle'. On top of that, they are to be 'ready for every good work', which probably means being willing to help those in any kind of need. If all this sounds like a course in middle-class respectability, it can only be said that Paul wouldn't have known what that was! For him, this was a life that reflected the strong gentleness, the principled truthfulness and the Christ-like courtesy that would be a witness to their faith in a generally sceptical world.

It is, we may note, the 'goodness and loving-kindness of God our Saviour' that is the true model for Christians in their daily lives.

26 August

THE GRACE OF GIVING

Now as you excel in everything—in faith, in speech, in knowledge, in utmost eagerness, and in our love for you—so we want you to excel also in this generous undertaking. I do not say this as a command, but I am testing the genuineness of your love against the earnestness of others. For you know the generous act of our Lord Jesus Christ, that though he was rich, yet for your sakes he became poor, so that by his poverty you might become rich… It is appropriate for you who began last year not only to do something but even to desire to do something—now finish doing it, so that your eagerness may be matched by completing it… The gift is acceptable according to what one has—not according to what one does not have.

2 CORINTHIANS 8:7–12 (abridged)

We're all familiar with the posters and thermometer charts setting out how much is needed for repairs to the roof or the tower or the bells. Yet here is Paul, in the first century, urging the Christians at Corinth to give money—not, of course, to repair a roof or rehang the bells, but to relieve the hunger of their fellow Christians in Jerusalem. For him, giving was not to be done reluctantly or out of a sense of duty, but cheerfully (2 Corinthians 9:7) and as a test of the 'genuineness of their love'. It's no good wishing people well or even saying a prayer for them, if we have the means to help but withhold it.

Paul doesn't want the Corinthians to bankrupt themselves to bail out the Christians in Jerusalem. A little further on he puts it starkly: 'I do not mean that there should be relief for others and pressure on you' (v. 13). What he seeks is a fair balance, with giving according to their means. For him it would be a denial of Christian love for believers in one place to live in comfort while their fellow Christians were starving. This is still true today, and it's fair to say that Christian congregations are in the forefront of giving for those in need anywhere in the world.

Paul doesn't urge Christians to give in response to his command, but in response to the overwhelming generosity of our Lord Jesus Christ.

27 August

GENUINE MUTUAL LOVE

Now that you have purified your souls by your obedience to the truth so that you have genuine mutual love, love one another deeply from the heart. You have been born anew, not of perishable but of imperishable seed, through the living and enduring word of God. For 'All flesh is like grass and all its glory like the flower of grass. The grass withers, and the flower falls, but the word of the Lord endures forever.' That word is the good news that was announced to you.

1 PETER 1:22–25

The meaning of the phrase 'I love you' has been somewhat diluted by today's usage, where performers tell audiences 'I love you' and people appear to fall into and out of love with quite disturbing ease. To love someone is in fact to make an enormous emotional commitment. The vow at the exchanging of rings in the Marriage Service puts love in its proper context: 'All that I have I give to you.' That is why the measure of God's love is not words or even feelings, but actions: 'God so loved... that he gave...' (John 3:16).

In this passage the apostle Peter calls Christians scattered across the Middle East to exercise 'genuine mutual love'. The King James Version translates the phrase as 'unfeigned love of the brethren'. This is not a 'pretend' affection, not a matter of words or gestures. Then, to drive the point home, Peter calls the Christians to 'love one another deeply from the heart'. Again, the old translation seems to add warmth to the command: 'see that ye love one another with a pure heart, fervently'. The 'genuine mutual love' of Christians is probably a more powerful argument for the gospel than any number of eloquent sermons. I have seen people brought to faith almost entirely because they have been caught up in the pure and fervent love that ought to characterize the Christian community. Where words fail, love conquers!

Jesus called his followers to love their neighbours, to love each other and to love their enemies. I wonder which is the easiest and which the most difficult?

28 August

THE LOVE THAT NEVER FAILS

Sing for joy, O heavens, and exult, O earth; break forth, O mountains, into singing! For the Lord has comforted his people, and will have compassion on his suffering ones. But Zion said, 'The Lord has forsaken me, my Lord has forgotten me.' Can a woman forget her nursing-child, or show no compassion for the child of her womb? Even these may forget, yet I will not forget you. See, I have inscribed you on the palms of my hands; your walls are continually before me. Your builders outdo your destroyers, and those who laid you waste go away from you.

ISAIAH 49:13–17

The prophecies of this part of the book of Isaiah are marked by an impressive confidence in the God who keeps his promises. The people of Israel had been punished, defeated, conquered and taken away into exile. But now their sins were pardoned, they were back in Jerusalem, and the time had come to rebuild not just the towers and walls but also their faith in the Lord.

The prophet's theme in this famous passage is the utter reliability and faithfulness of God's love. Human feelings change, shift, alter. We fall in love and we fall out of love. But not God. The Israelites were his people and he would love them whatever happened and however much circumstances changed. That love might well include chastising and correcting them, but always within that rock-firm relationship.

As an indicator of the steadfastness of God's love, the prophet calls on the most powerful image of human love that we can imagine—that of a mother for her child. Can she forget the little one she bore in her womb? Well, yes, in some circumstances it might be possible to imagine even a mother's love being tested to breaking point. But not God's. Their names were 'engraved' on the palms of his hands—permanent reminders of the covenant into which he had freely entered.

As with the old covenant, so with the new: those who have put their trust in Jesus are also loved with an everlasting love.

29 August

GENUINE LOVE

Let love be genuine; hate what is evil, hold fast to what is good; love one another with mutual affection; outdo one another in showing honour. Do not lag in zeal, be ardent in spirit, serve the Lord. Rejoice in hope, be patient in suffering, persevere in prayer. Contribute to the needs of the saints; extend hospitality to strangers. Bless those who persecute you; bless and do not curse them. Rejoice with those who rejoice, weep with those who weep. Live in harmony with one another; do not be haughty, but associate with the lowly; do not claim to be wiser than you are. Do not repay anyone evil for evil, but take thought for what is noble in the sight of all. If it is possible, so far as it depends on you, live peaceably with all. Beloved, never avenge yourselves… 'Vengeance is mine, I will repay, says the Lord.'

ROMANS 12:9–19 (abridged)

I preached on this passage at a funeral because the family of the man who had died felt that it said everything they wanted to say about him. I thought that was as perfect a tribute as anyone could wish, because what Paul is writing about is, in fact, true love. So much that passes for 'love' is disguised self-interest or superficial affection. This is love at street level, love where it counts, at the cutting edge of life.

This passage is full of down-to-earth advice. Revenge is not a dish 'best served cold', but best dumped in the bin. Patience is difficult, yet such a wonderful remedy for stress. If we need to be competitive, let's compete to honour each other! Be generous to the needy, hospitable to those who lack company or even a bed for the night. Keep in tune with others, laughing with those who are happy and weeping with those who are not. The apostle is realistic, too. It's praiseworthy to try to live in peace with everyone, but there are some people with whom it is impossible to co-exist. So, 'as far as it depends on you', live in peace with all. The advice is as practical and genuine as the love it commends.

This passage is worth rereading until we have absorbed the truth that real love is love that works, that changes me and changes situations.

30 August

DO YOU LOVE ME?

Jesus said to Simon Peter, 'Simon son of John, do you love me more than these?' He said to him, 'Yes, Lord; you know that I love you.' Jesus said to him, 'Feed my lambs.' A second time he said to him, 'Simon son of John, do you love me?' He said to him, 'Yes, Lord; you know that I love you.' Jesus said to him, 'Tend my sheep.' He said to him the third time, 'Simon son of John, do you love me?' Peter felt hurt because he said to him the third time, 'Do you love me?' And he said to him, 'Lord, you know everything; you know that I love you.' Jesus said to him, 'Feed my sheep.'
JOHN 21:15–17

This encounter took place after Jesus' resurrection, when he appeared to some of the disciples who had been fishing on Lake Galilee. Among them was Peter, whose feelings at that moment must have been a bit mixed. He was obviously delighted to see his master risen from the dead—indeed, he jumped from the boat into the water to rush ashore to greet him—but he must also have known that sooner or later the matter of his ignominious denial that he even knew Jesus would come up. After all, he had sworn that if all the others deserted Jesus, he never would (Mark 14:29), yet faced with some banter from a servant girl, he had sworn with an oath that he did not know 'this man' (v. 71).

In fact, it was not Peter but Jesus who raised the sensitive matter, although not directly. He simply asked Peter whether in fact he loved the Master 'more than these [others] do?' Peter replied that Jesus knew that he loved him. The same question was asked three times (the same number of times as Peter had denied knowing Jesus), with the disciple getting more upset at each question and finally responding, 'Lord, you know everything; you know that I love you.' At each answer, Jesus recommissioned Peter to care for his 'sheep'.

Jesus actually used two different Greek verbs for 'love' in this conversation—to love sacrificially, and to be a friend. Perhaps we can ask ourselves, Do I love Jesus Christ with a self-giving love, and am I his 'friend'?

31 August

THE LOVE THAT SERVES

During supper Jesus, knowing that the Father had given all things into his hands, and that he had come from God and was going to God, got up from the table, took off his outer robe, and tied a towel around himself. Then he poured water into a basin and began to wash the disciples' feet and to wipe them with the towel that was tied around him... After he had washed their feet, had put on his robe, and had returned to the table, he said to them, 'Do you know what I have done to you? You call me Teacher and Lord—and you are right, for that is what I am. So if I, your Lord and Teacher, have washed your feet, you also ought to wash one another's feet. For I have set you an example, that you also should do as I have done to you.

JOHN 13:2–5, 12–15

The disciples have gathered at an 'upper room' in Jerusalem, which Jesus had acquired so that they could eat the Passover meal together. He knew that it would be the last meal they would share together before his crucifixion, but John sees all of this in cosmic terms. Jesus knew that the Father had 'given all things into his hands, and that he had come from God and was going to God'. The scene was set for their final evening together, a night of destiny indeed.

Yet, in an act of dramatic irony, it begins with the banal, everyday business of foot-washing—the normal courtesy extended to Eastern guests before a meal. The basin was there by the door, with a towel, but all the disciples had walked straight past it. To wash feet was a slave's task and they were not slaves. As they took their places at table, perhaps having removed their sandals ready for the foot-washing, someone picked up the basin and the towel. It wasn't a slave, or a Gentile, or a woman, but their 'Lord and Teacher', Jesus. He washed their feet and then, in words they would never forget, drove home the lesson. To lead is to serve. To follow Christ is to wash feet.

To love truly is also to serve truly. Even the Son of Man did not come to be served but to 'serve, and to give his life a ransom for many' (Mark 10:45).

September: The life watched over

Some people think of God as a kind of policeman in the sky, waiting to catch us out and punish us. Actually, the picture the Bible offers is rather different. Yes, we can keep (if we wish) the image of the police officer, but now he is not trying to catch us out but to protect us. He hovers near at hand to watch over our lives. The God of the Bible cares for his people, day and night. That is our theme for September.

1 September

THERE ARE NO 'ACCIDENTS'

Do two walk together unless they have made an appointment? Does a lion roar in the forest, when it has no prey? Does a young lion cry out from its den, if it has caught nothing? Does a bird fall into a snare on the earth, when there is no trap for it? Does a snare spring up from the ground, when it has taken nothing? Is a trumpet blown in a city, and the people are not afraid? Does disaster befall a city, unless the Lord has done it? Surely the Lord God does nothing, without revealing his secret to his servants the prophets. The lion has roared; who will not fear? The Lord God has spoken; who can but prophesy?

AMOS 3:3–8

The point the prophet Amos is making is a profound one, which he chooses to express in a series of poetic images. Each tells the same tale: we do not live in a random world. We could say, 'There are no accidents!' Of course, things happen that we could not possibly have expected or predicted. None of us knows what will happen 30 seconds from now, let alone 30 years! Yet part of the way the Hebrew prophets saw the world was to recognize that nothing is unknown to the all-knowing God. That was why God could reveal things to the prophets: 'Surely the Lord God does nothing, without revealing his secret to his servants the prophets.'

People today, including those who believe in God, sometimes find this concept disturbing. If God knows in advance, why doesn't he stop bad things happening? There is, however, a world of difference between saying that 'God knows' and insisting that God acts in a particular way. It is in fact deeply reassuring that the Creator who loves us is aware of every detail of our lives, and is with us in the dark valley as well as on the sunlit uplands.

God knows, God loves, God cares: whatever befalls us in life, those three statements remain true.

2 September

THIS IS THE WAY

Therefore the Lord waits to be gracious to you; therefore he will rise up to show mercy to you. For the Lord is a God of justice; blessed are all those who wait for him. Truly, O people in Zion, inhabitants of Jerusalem, you shall weep no more. He will surely be gracious to you at the sound of your cry; when he hears it, he will answer you. Though the Lord may give you the bread of adversity and the water of affliction, yet your Teacher will not hide himself any more, but your eyes shall see your Teacher. And when you turn to the right or when you turn to the left, your ears shall hear a word behind you, saying, 'This is the way; walk in it.'

ISAIAH 30:18–21

Here is a message of hope for a people who are heading for a time of suffering and exile. The prophet wants them to know that the Lord 'waits' to be gracious to them, and one day—as they in turn 'wait' for him—they will experience not only his justice but his mercy.

Here that mercy is seen as the gift of a 'Teacher'. This 'Teacher'—and the capital 'T' is significant—will be revealed to them and at last they will have reliable guidance in their lives. No more hit-and-miss decisions, no more mistaking the right way or wandering off the path: now, when they don't know which way to turn, their ears will hear a word behind them. A voice will say, 'This is the way; walk in it.'

It's not clear when this particular blessing will be bestowed, nor indeed whether the people of Israel and Judah ever reached the point at which the voice of their Teacher was able to guide them through the moral maze of life. From the point of view of history, it would seem that they went on making the same mistakes and reaching the wrong decisions—just like the rest of us. However, Christians will take heart from the promise of Jesus that the Holy Spirit whom he would send to his people would 'guide them into all the truth' (John 16:13).

It is one thing to hear the 'voice of the Teacher' behind us, telling us which way to go. It is quite another to listen and then to act on what we hear.

3 September

TO FOLLOW THE WAY

They came to Jericho. As he and his disciples and a large crowd were leaving Jericho, Bartimaeus son of Timaeus, a blind beggar, was sitting by the roadside. When he heard that it was Jesus of Nazareth, he began to shout out and say, 'Jesus, Son of David, have mercy on me!' Many sternly ordered him to be quiet, but he cried out even more loudly, 'Son of David, have mercy on me!' Jesus stood still and said, 'Call him here.' And they called the blind man, saying to him, 'Take heart; get up, he is calling you.' So throwing off his cloak, he sprang up and came to Jesus. Then Jesus said to him, 'What do you want me to do for you?' The blind man said to him, 'My teacher, let me see again.' Jesus said to him, 'Go; your faith has made you well.' Immediately he regained his sight and followed him on the way.
MARK 10:46–52

There is more to this narrative than meets the eye. Just previously, Jesus had asked James and John, 'What do you want me to do for you?' and they had asked for the places of honour at his side when he achieved kingly power (v. 37). Their reply was entirely to do with their own status and glory, which was not quite what Jesus had in mind. Now, confronted by a blind beggar shouting for 'mercy', he asks exactly the same question: 'What do you want me to do for you?' The beggar doesn't have to think twice: 'My teacher, let me see again.'

Jesus responded by telling him that his faith had 'made him well', which meant more than simply a 'cure'. Bartimaeus had been restored to 'wholeness', which is the same word as 'salvation'. That wholeness included but was not limited to the recovery of his sight. Immediately, we are told, two things happened. Bartimaeus could see again and 'he followed Jesus on the way'. 'The Way' was the first name used to describe the company of Christ's followers, so there is some significance in this statement about the former beggar. He became a disciple of Jesus; he followed him, joining the company of the people of the kingdom.

If Jesus said to me, 'What do you want me to do for you?' what would I reply?

4 September

WHENEVER I AM AFRAID

O Most High, when I am afraid, I put my trust in you… All day long they seek to injure my cause… They stir up strife, they lurk, they watch my steps. As they hoped to have my life, so repay them for their crime; in wrath cast down the peoples, O God! You have kept count of my tossings; put my tears in your bottle… Then my enemies will retreat on the day when I call… In God I trust; I am not afraid. What can a mere mortal do to me? My vows to you I must perform, O God; I will render thank-offerings to you. For you have delivered my soul from death, and my feet from falling, so that I may walk before God in the light of life.

PSALM 56:2–3, 5–9, 11–13 (abridged)

This is an example of the sheer honesty of the Psalms! Sometimes the trouble we get from other people is too much for us. We'd love to tell God what we really think of them, but somehow it would seem, well, unChristian. So we cover up our hurt and anger in weasel words, not wanting to sound hurt or angry or spiteful. Yet God knows everything about us, including our secret thoughts, and he would rather we told him exactly how we feel than try to dress it up in 'suitable' language.

The psalmist feels under siege from some unidentified enemies who are stirring up trouble for him, watching his steps—even, it would seem, prepared to threaten his life. He admits to being afraid, but 'when I am afraid, I put my trust in you, O Most High'. That doesn't mean that he enjoys a good night's sleep: he invites God to 'count his tossings' and record the volume of his tears.

The situation seems to have ended well, judging by the last few verses. Whatever the danger was, it appears to have passed, and it is time for the psalmist to render 'thank-offerings' in the temple for his deliverance. Once again, he will 'walk before God in the light of life'.

Here is the classic conflict between faith and fear. It is hard to put those wretched enemies out of his mind, yet the psalmist knows that with trust in God he should not be afraid. After all, what can a mere mortal do to him?

5 September

THE GOD WHO GOES BEFORE

'The Lord your God, who goes before you, is the one who will fight for you, just as he did for you in Egypt before your very eyes, and in the wilderness, where you saw how the Lord your God carried you, just as one carries a child, all the way that you travelled until you reached this place. But in spite of this, you have no trust in the Lord your God, who goes before you on the way to seek out a place for you to camp, in fire by night, and in the cloud by day, to show you the route you should take.'

DEUTERONOMY 1:30–33

This is part of the final message of Moses, as the chronicler records it, addressed to the people of Israel on the borders of the promised land—a land Moses would never enter. He is anxious that they should learn at last the lessons of the wilderness journey, during which they had moaned and rebelled and signally failed to trust the Lord who was leading them, or Moses his servant.

They had received abundant evidence of God's care for them during those long years. He had released them from slavery to the greatest human empire of the time, Egypt, and then fed them with manna every day, led them to water, protected them from enemy tribes and finally brought them to the Jordan. 'But in spite of this, you have no trust in the Lord your God.' What an indictment!

This, after all, was the God of the pillar of fire and cloud, which led them by day through the wilderness and protected them at night as they struck camp. They could look up and see that God was with them, that he was 'carrying' them every step of the way. Day by day, he 'showed them the route they should take'. Now that they were about to enter the promised land, under a new leader, Joshua, Moses wanted them at last to learn the lesson. Past blessings are the evidence of future care. God does not play games with us.

Trust is built on experience, but we are often quick to forget the evidence of God's past dealings with us when faced with a new problem.

6 September

HE KNOWS MY WAY

'Today also my complaint is bitter; his hand is heavy despite my groaning. O, that I knew where I might find him, that I might come even to his dwelling! I would lay my case before him, and fill my mouth with arguments... If I go forward, he is not there; or backward, I cannot perceive him; on the left he hides, and I cannot behold him; I turn to the right, but I cannot see him. But he knows the way that I take; when he has tested me, I shall come out like gold. My foot has held fast to his steps; I have kept his way and have not turned aside.

JOB 23:2–4, 8–11

Poor Job, deprived in a single day of his family, herds and riches, and then plagued with boils—no wonder his faith (which is certainly strong) has at times a bitter edge to it. Here, in response to one of his 'comforters', Eliphaz, Job describes in vivid language how someone can feel who is going through what the mystics call 'the dark night of the soul'. Just when Job needs him most, God appears to hide himself. Just when he most needs a word of encouragement or guidance, eternity is silent. Where has God gone? Has he switched off Job's prayers, gone into hiding somewhere and left him to cope on his own? Many people since Job have surely felt like that.

This sense of abandonment is most hurtful when it comes to decision making. If he edges forward, he doesn't find God. If he slides backwards, God isn't there either. He is to be found neither to the right nor to the left. What has happened to the Lord's omnipresence?

As it happens, Job has his own answer, and it's one in which he seems to find reassurance. While he doesn't know which way to go, his God knows the way he takes. In other words, although God seems distant from him, he is not distant from God. Although he struggles to find God, the Lord has got him in his sights all the while.

When we cannot pray and cannot sense the presence of God, he 'knows the way that we take'—and we shall come out of the testing refined 'like gold'.

7 September

THE HIGHWAY OF GOD

Then the eyes of the blind shall be opened, and the ears of the deaf unstopped; then the lame shall leap like a deer, and the tongue of the speechless sing for joy. For waters shall break forth in the wilderness, and streams in the desert; the burning sand shall become a pool, and the thirsty ground springs of water... A highway shall be there, and it shall be called the Holy Way; the unclean shall not travel on it, but it shall be for God's people; no traveller, not even fools, shall go astray. No lion shall be there, nor shall any ravenous beast come up on it... And the ransomed of the Lord shall return, and come to Zion with singing; everlasting joy shall be upon their heads... and sorrow and sighing shall flee away.

ISAIAH 35:5–10 (abridged)

All the Hebrew prophets offer visions of a future rich with promise—a time when evil, pain and sickness will be no more, when weapons will be turned to pastoral use and people will live peacefully and happily in the new kingdom. This would be the golden age, the Day of the Lord, the coming of the new Jerusalem (Zion). Such blessings are seen as the gift of God at a time he has appointed, but a time preceded, in most visions, by a period of suffering and repentance.

This picture by Isaiah is one of the most beautiful of such visions. One by one, the fears, irritations and problems of life in a parched land, where water was precious and survival a precarious business, are listed and then countered with blessings. The blind will see, the deaf hear, the dumb speak. There will be streams in the desert, pools in sandy places. Reeds will replace the dry grass of summer. And there will be a 'highway', a path towards holiness. It will be clearly marked, a safe road—no lions or ravenous beasts!—and even those of us who simply can't read maps won't get lost on it. Along it God's people will come, singing and rejoicing, as they stream into 'Zion'. What a picture!

The first Christians were called 'saints' by Paul, not because they were yet perfect but because they were on this very highway to holiness.

8 September

FINDING A HOME

Sing to God, sing praises to his name; lift up a song to him who rides upon the clouds—his name is the Lord—be exultant before him. Father of orphans and protector of widows is God in his holy habitation. God gives the desolate a home to live in; he leads out the prisoners to prosperity, but the rebellious live in a parched land. O God, when you went out before your people... the earth quaked, the heavens poured down rain at the presence of God, the God of Sinai, at the presence of God, the God of Israel. Rain in abundance, O God, you showered abroad; you restored your heritage when it languished; your flock found a dwelling in it.

PSALM 68:4–10 (abridged)

This is a joyful song indeed—a song celebrating the generosity of God. With the story of the exodus journey clearly in the background, the psalmist is confident that the God who met the needs of his people then would also do it now. Once again we can glean a vivid picture of life in biblical Israel. Rain is the clue to everything—rain in abundance, to slake the thirst of families and flocks. Even in the wilderness the people were provided with water by God, the 'God of Sinai'.

But there is a gentler, very compassionate theme to this psalm as well. Not only does God provide rain, he also provides for equally essential human and spiritual needs. This same God—the Lord, Yahweh—is the 'Father of orphans and protector of widows'. He gives the 'desolate'—the lonely, the abandoned, the miserable—a 'home to live in'. He releases prisoners and leads them to 'prosperity'.

There is a dramatic contrast at the heart of these verses. The God they reveal is both enormously powerful and genuinely gentle. He is awesome in might and matchless in mercy. No wonder the psalmist calls his people to 'sing praises to his name' and 'be exultant before him'.

Graham Kendrick may well have had this psalm in mind when he wrote the hymn 'Meekness and majesty', for in the deepest sense 'this is our God'.

9 September

ON THE UNKNOWN PATH

Early in the morning Joshua rose and set out from Shittim with all the Israelites, and they came to the Jordan. They camped there before crossing over. At the end of three days the officers went through the camp and commanded the people, 'When you see the ark of the covenant of the Lord your God being carried by the levitical priests, then you shall set out from your place. Follow it, so that you may know the way you should go, for you have not passed this way before. Yet there shall be a space between you and it, a distance of about two thousand cubits; do not come any nearer to it.' Then Joshua said to the people, 'Sanctify yourselves; for tomorrow the Lord will do wonders among you.'

JOSHUA 3:1–5

The Israelites had reached the end of their 40-year trek around the wilderness—a journey which, but for their disobedience, would have been completed in a matter of months. Now the only barrier between them and their promised land was the river Jordan, in spate at 'the time of harvest' (see v. 15).

Joshua gave explicit orders for the crossing. It would be a divinely ordered affair, and all the arrangements would underline that. The ark of the covenant—the sign of the presence of the Lord—would be borne by the priests into the middle of the river. Then, and only then, the people would make their way across the river, as the 'waters of the Jordan flowing from above' were cut off (v. 13).

The people would follow the ark of the covenant (though not too closely—respect was due to it), so that they might know the way to go, 'for you have not passed this way before'. Only the Lord, who had led them all those years with the pillar of cloud, could now lead them to their final destination.

Christians have always seen in this story a picture of our journey across the waters of death into the kingdom of heaven. None of us has 'passed this way before'—all the more reason to keep close to the Lord of the earth.

10 September

ON EAGLE'S WINGS

Have you not known? Have you not heard? The Lord is the everlasting God, the Creator of the ends of the earth. He does not faint or grow weary; his understanding is unsearchable. He gives power to the faint, and strengthens the powerless. Even youths will faint and be weary, and the young will fall exhausted; but those who wait for the Lord shall renew their strength, they shall mount up with wings like eagles, they shall run and not be weary, they shall walk and not faint.

ISAIAH 40:28–31

This is one of the best-known and most memorable passages from the book of Isaiah, a splendid piece of rhetoric addressed to those who have doubted the Lord's care for them. Far from turning from them or 'disregarding their rights' (v. 27), he is the untiring and inexhaustible source of strength and support for his people. The argument is expressed in a series of rhetorical questions: 'Have you not known? Have you not heard?' Of course they had, but in their fear or self-pity they had forgotten.

As so often, the whole is based on a single premise: 'The Lord is the everlasting God, the Creator of the ends of the earth.' They, and we, forget that at our peril. He is the Creator; we are his creatures. How could the one who brought the universe into existence tire or faint? The question is ludicrous. He is the source of strength and power, even for the faint and the powerless.

The prophet then offers his readers a contrast between the 'youths', with their seemingly inexhaustible energy, who nevertheless eventually grow weary and fall exhausted, and 'those who wait for the Lord'. The latter—no matter how old and feeble—will 'renew their strength', walk and run without tiring and even, in a stirring metaphor, soar with the eagle over the mountains.

'Waiting for the Lord' does not mean sitting idly by. Neither is it an empty optimism, but a patient trust in the God who knows our needs before we ask.

11 September

IN YOUR MIDST

Sing aloud, O daughter Zion; shout, O Israel! Rejoice and exult with all your heart, O daughter Jerusalem! The Lord has taken away the judgments against you, he has turned away your enemies. The king of Israel, the Lord, is in your midst; you shall fear disaster no more. On that day it shall be said to Jerusalem: Do not fear, O Zion; do not let your hands grow weak. The Lord, your God, is in your midst, a warrior who gives victory; he will rejoice over you with gladness, he will renew you in his love; he will exult over you with loud singing as on a day of festival.

ZEPHANIAH 3:14–18A

Most of the book of Zephaniah is given over to a fierce denunciation of the sins of Israel and Jerusalem. 'Ah, soiled, defiled, oppressing city' is how the prophet describes the nation's capital (3:1). Yet in the end he offers a vision of a time when the God of judgment and wrath will become the God of mercy and unfailing love. This will come about when the 'proudly exultant ones' have been removed from their midst, and a people 'humble and lowly' will have taken their place (3:11–12). Then the Lord will take away the 'judgments' against them and they will once again be able to 'rejoice and exult with all their heart'.

Probably the key phrase in this passage is 'in your midst'. 'The king of Israel, the Lord, is in your midst,' they are told. 'The Lord, your God, is in your midst, a warrior who gives victory.' They were familiar with the idea of the Lord God reigning in heaven, far above all earthly concerns, but they had lost the equally biblical picture of God among his people—a concept enshrined in the tabernacle of the great temple. But now they should not fear, because the God of all the earth was not just above but also among them, a king and a warrior, more than capable of watching over his people.

Of course, God is above us, our Creator and Lord, but the wonderful truth is that he is also among us. Jesus told the crowds, 'The kingdom of God is among you' (Luke 17:21).

12 September

THE PRESENCE OF GOD

Moses said to the Lord, 'See, you have said to me, "Bring up this people"; but you have not let me know whom you will send with me. Yet you have said, "I know you by name, and you have also found favour in my sight." Now if I have found favour in your sight, show me your ways... Consider too that this nation is your people.' [God] said, 'My presence will go with you, and I will give you rest.' And [Moses] said to him, 'If your presence will not go, do not carry us up... For how shall it be known that I have found favour in your sight, I and your people, unless you go with us? In this way, we shall be distinct... from every people on the face of the earth.'

EXODUS 33:12–16 (abridged)

The book of Exodus treats us to a number of these dialogues between Moses and God. They are used as a way of explaining the relationship between the chosen and anointed leader, Moses, and Yahweh, the Lord, who has called him. In conversational form we can see how both 'parties' viewed that relationship. For Moses, as he says here several times, God's 'favour' (our word 'grace') is the key. God has given Moses grace to fulfil his will and lead the Israelites out of Egypt towards the promised land. Without that grace he simply couldn't do it. What Moses seems to want is some evidence that he still retains God's 'favour', even after the disastrous episode at Sinai, when the people made and worshipped a golden calf (32:1–6).

So Moses asks God to show him his 'ways', to reveal himself more fully, so that he can be absolutely sure that the Lord is with him and the people—'your people', as he reminds God. God then promises that his 'presence' will go with them on the remainder of their journey and that they will find their place of 'rest'. The response of Moses sounds almost cheeky: 'If your presence will not go, do not carry us up from here.'

What was really distinctive about Israel's religion was not its rituals and rules, but God's presence among his people. For the Church, the same is true.

13 September

FOLLOW ME!

As Jesus passed along the Sea of Galilee, he saw Simon and his brother Andrew casting a net into the sea—for they were fishermen. And Jesus said to them, 'Follow me and I will make you fish for people.' And immediately they left their nets and followed him. As he went a little farther, he saw James son of Zebedee and his brother John, who were in their boat mending the nets. Immediately he called them; and they left their father Zebedee in the boat with the hired men, and followed him.

MARK 1:16–20

This is the story of the calling of the first apostles, two sets of brothers, all fishermen working on Lake Galilee. The words of Jesus' call are probably more familiar to many of us as 'Follow me and I will make you fishers of men'. However, Jesus did not use the Greek word for 'males' but the word for 'people' (*anthropoi*). Men and women would be 'caught' for the kingdom by the apostles' ministry down the years.

Surely the most surprising thing about this short narrative is the abruptness of the disciples' response. It sounds downright thoughtless to abandon their boats—and even poor Zebedee, suddenly deprived of his senior staff and heirs of the business—at such a brief invitation. We know from John's Gospel, though, that the four already knew about Jesus, and Andrew and Simon had met him and been told that they should eventually follow him (see John 1:35–42).

'Follow me' is such a basic invitation, yet it is at the heart of what it means to be a Christian. Once we have stripped away the theology and theories, a Christian is someone who 'follows Jesus'. Indeed, while the invitation is basic, it is also comprehensive, for those who follow must do so from first to last: you can't 'follow' someone in fits and starts or you will lose sight of them. To 'follow Jesus', then, is to keep close to him, follow his example, listen to his words and do as he says.

'Follow me, and I will transform your life'—that's really what Jesus said to the fishermen long ago. He also says it now to those who hear his call.

14 September

WATCHING OVER THE CITY

Unless the Lord builds the house, those who build it labour in vain. Unless the Lord guards the city, the guard keeps watch in vain. It is in vain that you rise up early and go late to rest, eating the bread of anxious toil; for he gives sleep to his beloved… Like arrows in the hand of a warrior are the sons of one's youth. Happy is the man who has his quiver full of them. He shall not be put to shame when he speaks with his enemies in the gate.
PSALM 127:1–2, 4–5

This psalm enshrines one of the most profound of all truths—as relevant in today's hectic world as it was in the streets of Jerusalem three thousand years ago. We can work night and day, travel the length of the land, worry and fret about bills and mortgages and security and education, but 'unless the Lord builds the house' it's so much wasted effort. We can get up early or stay up late working, engaging in 'anxious toil', but only God can give rest to the restless spirit.

It's almost as though the psalmist could look into our world of commuting and commerce, street crime and terrorism, credit cards and debt, double income families and children driven to succeed—and he tells us that we've got our priorities wrong. We can't guard the city; we can't find rest or happiness through struggle and effort. These are gifts of God to his children—as are the very children we bear.

The ancient world also worried about security. There were robbers and brigands and the thief who came secretly by night (see Matthew 24:43). The city shut its gates to keep out enemies, but some 'enemies' were already in its houses: 'Unless the Lord guards the city, the guard keeps watch in vain.' This is not a promise that those who trust in God will never experience burglary, but that they will know in their hearts a security that comes from him.

'He gives sleep to his beloved'—the sleep of the clear conscience, the forgiven heart, the trusting spirit. In the frantic bustle of life, which many of us cannot possibly avoid, these are priceless gifts.

15 September

THE TWO ROADS

'Do to others as you would have them do to you; for this is the law and the prophets. Enter through the narrow gate; for the gate is wide and the road is easy that leads to destruction, and there are many who take it. For the gate is narrow and the road is hard that leads to life, and there are few who find it. Beware of false prophets, who come to you in sheep's clothing but inwardly are ravenous wolves. You will know them by their fruits.'

MATTHEW 7:12–16A

This well-known passage from the Sermon on the Mount begins with the 'Golden Rule': 'Do to others as you would have them do to you.' That is not an exclusively Christian piece of teaching, but here it is given the endorsement of Jesus himself. Indeed, he says that 'this is the law and the prophets'—the very heart of God's moral law.

Close examination will show us that this is no easy option. Truly and honestly to treat others as we would wish to be treated is very, very demanding—a point underlined by the saying that follows it, about the two roads through life. One is narrow, unpopular, even lonely, but it leads to 'life' (meaning 'eternal life'). The other is broad, popular, thronged with company. Its only drawback is its destination: disaster. Few choose the first road, while many opt for the second.

It's doubtful that Jesus was making a numerical prediction about the future size of the Church. Instead, he was underlining the demands of the Golden Rule. It's easy to say, 'Do to others as you would be done by', but in practice hard to carry it out. The narrow road is the choice of those who can see that life is not something we can drift through, and that doing what is right is seldom easy, and is often costly. The broad road is for those who have realized that there is a price to pay for the good life, and are not prepared to pay it. You can tell the difference between the two groups, says Jesus. Just look at the results!

G.K. Chesterton once remarked that it was not that Christianity had been tried and found wanting, but that it had been found difficult and not tried!

16 September

THE PEACE OF GOD

Rejoice in the Lord always; again I will say, Rejoice. Let your gentleness be known to everyone. The Lord is near. Do not worry about anything, but in everything by prayer and supplication with thanksgiving let your requests be made known to God. And the peace of God, which surpasses all understanding, will guard your hearts and your minds in Christ Jesus.
PHILIPPIANS 4:4–7

The church at Philippi seems to have been one of Paul's favourites. It was begun at a riverside prayer-gathering of Jews and would-be converts to Judaism and supplemented by the conversion of the local gaoler and his family following an earthquake (Acts 16:25–34). It was a church where women took quite a lead, and where the apostle could feel that they were entirely with him in both sharing and defending the gospel. It was to them, in this very letter, that he wrote of the humility of Christ and his self-emptying for our salvation, and of the positive and beautiful things on which their minds should be focused. Now, in this passage, he shares with them the secret of the truly peaceful life.

First they must 'rejoice'. This rejoicing does not depend on circumstances or feelings, but on faith. The Lord is 'near'. Paul probably meant that the return of Jesus was close (the widespread belief of the early Church), or he may have meant that in every circumstance of life, and in line with his promise (Matthew 28:20), Jesus would be with them 'to the end of the age'. Either way, it was good reason to 'rejoice'.

Then, they must abandon worry—easier said than done! But he gives them precise instructions about the way to counter it. 'In everything... let your requests be known to God': let him in on those nagging secret doubts and fears. If that is done with 'thanksgiving' and faithful prayer, the God we trust will 'guard'—literally, throw a garrison around—our hearts and minds, our emotions and our thoughts.

We worry when we try to carry the burdens of life ourselves. We 'rejoice' when we let the God who loves and cares for us in on our problems.

17 September

ENCOURAGING THOSE WHO GRIEVE

But we do not want you to be uninformed, brothers and sisters, about those who have died, so that you may not grieve as others do who have no hope. For since we believe that Jesus died and rose again, even so, through Jesus, God will bring with him those who have died. For this we declare to you by the word of the Lord, that we who are alive, who are left until the coming of the Lord, will by no means precede those who have died. For the Lord himself… will descend from heaven, and the dead in Christ will rise first. Then we who are alive, who are left, will be caught up in the clouds together with them to meet the Lord in the air; and so we will be with the Lord forever. Therefore encourage one another with these words.

1 THESSALONIANS 4:13–18 (abridged)

Christians do grieve over the loss of loved ones, but not without hope. That's Paul's message to the church at Thessalonica. Expecting an imminent return of the Lord Jesus, some of the Christians were anxious about those who had died. Would they miss out on the blessings of Christ's new reign in glory? Not at all, says Paul. Those who are alive at the moment of the Lord's return will 'by no means precede' those who have died. All will be raised: the dead 'in Christ' will rise first, and then those Christians who are alive at his coming will be 'caught up in the clouds together with them'—a wonderful picture of reunion with those they have loved. Some of us are awaiting the Lord's return, but many, many more are awaiting the resurrection. It's wonderfully reassuring to know that all of us who are 'in Christ', whether alive or what the Bible calls 'asleep in Christ' (1 Corinthians 15:18, KJV), will one day 'meet him together'.

The apostle says that we should 'encourage one another with these words'—especially, of course, those who are grieving the loss of someone dear to them.

18 September

THE LORD IS MY HELPER

Let mutual love continue. Do not neglect to show hospitality to strangers, for by doing that some have entertained angels without knowing it. Remember those who are in prison, as though you were in prison with them; those who are being tortured, as though you yourselves were being tortured. Let marriage be held in honour by all, and let the marriage bed be kept undefiled; for God will judge fornicators and adulterers. Keep your lives free from the love of money, and be content with what you have; for he has said, 'I will never leave you or forsake you.' So we can say with confidence, 'The Lord is my helper; I will not be afraid.'

HEBREWS 13:1–6

It's interesting that a passage which deals principally with human behaviour, and especially with ways in which Christians can help each other, has as its climax the ringing words, 'The Lord is my helper'. But that sets its tone. We aren't just being nice to each other, assuming that 'one good turn deserves another' or that 'honesty is the best policy'. Rather, Christians are called to live in the constant presence of God, profoundly aware of the principle of grace. Out of an overflowing gratitude for the constant help of God, we offer our help to others.

Given that principle, the actual guidance here is both practical and specific. Based on 'mutual love', we are to show hospitality to strangers (with the bonus that we may unwittingly be entertaining angels) and to remember those in prison 'as though you were in prison with them'. We are also to remember those being tortured, which would have included many Christians in those days of state persecution. We are to honour marriage and not to love money. Instead, we are to cultivate contentment. In case this seems a burdensome agenda, we can come back to the guiding principle: 'The Lord is my helper'. What cannot be done in my own strength may well be done in his.

'Mutual love' is philadelphia, *usually translated as 'brotherly love'—the love that the children of the heavenly Father have for each other.*

19 September

STILL WITH YOU

For it was you who formed my inward parts; you knit me together in my mother's womb. I praise you, for I am fearfully and wonderfully made. Wonderful are your works; that I know very well. My frame was not hidden from you, when I was being made in secret, intricately woven in the depths of the earth. Your eyes beheld my unformed substance. In your book were written all the days that were formed for me, when none of them as yet existed. How weighty to me are your thoughts, O God! How vast is the sum of them! I try to count them—they are more than the sand; I come to the end—I am still with you.

PSALM 139:13–18

We have already read verses from the first part of this amazing psalm, in which the writer reflects on the constant presence of the Lord. Now he turns his thoughts to the beginnings of life—from conception through the development of the foetus to the moment of birth. What a mystery and what a miracle! I remember a young father saying to me that he had doubted the existence of God until he was present at the birth of his first child. 'How could you not believe?' he asked.

The psalmist is awestruck at the process: God was the one who had 'knitted him together' in his mother's womb, the one who even now knows the whole story of his life, even those parts that have not yet happened ! As he thinks of all this, he is overwhelmed by the wisdom and complexity of God's thoughts—and of course the more we learn about the processes of creation, the more awesome that wisdom appears. So the poor psalmist wracks his brain to comprehend—but fails. When he comes to the end of his questioning, what remains is the towering presence of his God.

When we reflect on the complexity of the universe, we may feel it is so vast and incomprehensible that it threatens our rather limited vision of God. Or we may realize with the psalmist that the more complex it is, the more wise and wonderful must be the divine mind that brought it into being.

20 September

LEARNING CONTENTMENT

I rejoice in the Lord greatly that now at last you have revived your concern for me; indeed, you were concerned for me, but had no opportunity to show it. Not that I am referring to being in need; for I have learned to be content with whatever I have. I know what it is to have little, and I know what it is to have plenty. In any and all circumstances I have learned the secret of being well-fed and of going hungry, of having plenty and of being in need. I can do all things through him who strengthens me.
PHILIPPIANS 4:10–13

Here is Paul writing to the church at Philippi, with gratitude for a gift of money, which had arrived when he needed it most—always the best kind of gift. Their concern had touched him deeply. He was under some kind of house arrest, knowing that his life was under threat. It's at moments like those that the thoughtfulness of friends counts most.

This generous gesture leads him to a reflection on contentment. He didn't want them to think that he was in desperate need, because the kind of life he had lived had inured him to hardship. He walked enormous distances on his missionary journeys. He found a place to sleep wherever he could. From time to time he aroused the wrath of the authorities and ended up in a prison cell or being flogged.

On other occasions—such as when he accepted hospitality in the home of the prosperous businesswoman Lydia—he lived quite comfortably. So he knew both sides of life: he could be 'rich' without letting it go to his head, and he could be 'poor' without it bringing him down. He had learned contentment—not an easy lesson for most of us, because one of the driving forces of ambition and progress is discontent. Yet no one could accuse Paul of lacking 'drive'!

The key to it all, in the apostle's thinking, is surely in that last sentence: 'I can do all things through him who strengthens me.'

Contentment—priceless and rare gift—is not something we can create artificially, but it is, says Paul, something we can 'learn'.

21 September

GOD'S PURPOSE FOR MY LIFE

I give you thanks, O Lord, with my whole heart… I bow down towards your holy temple and give thanks to your name for your steadfast love and your faithfulness; for you have exalted your name and your word above everything… All the kings of the earth shall praise you, O Lord… For though the Lord is high, he regards the lowly; but the haughty he perceives from far away. Though I walk in the midst of trouble, you preserve me against the wrath of my enemies; you stretch out your hand, and your right hand delivers me. The Lord will fulfil his purpose for me; your steadfast love, O Lord, endures forever. Do not forsake the work of your hands.

PSALM 138:1–2, 4, 6–8 (abridged)

'Purpose' is a strange and important word. Its negative ('purposelessness') tells us as much about it as its positive—to be without purpose is to drift, to end up unsatisfied. Some people say that God has a 'plan' for our lives, but that seems to suggest a kind of road map which must and will be followed, whatever we do about it. 'Purpose' is different. The Oxford English Dictionary defines it as 'the reason for which something is done or for which something exists'. Without purpose our lives are without 'reason', going nowhere. So to know that God will 'fulfil his purpose' for us is tremendously reassuring. We are not thrashing around in the dark or drifting through life, but living with 'purpose'.

The psalmist sees this 'purpose' in terms of the superiority of God's power and wisdom over all rivals, whether they be earthly kings or 'other gods'. From his throne he cares for the 'lowly'; in his power he dismisses the 'haughty'—those who think they can live without regard for him. With his 'right hand' (the strong and skilful one) he delivers and blesses his people. That 'steadfast love' which is so constant a theme of the psalms is the bedrock of the writer's confidence. It is because we can trust our faithful God that we can be confident in his purpose for our lives.

I am not going nowhere, but somewhere. With God, my life has purpose.

22 September

PROTECTION FROM EVIL

'And now I am no longer in the world, but they are in the world, and I am coming to you. Holy Father, protect them in your name that you have given me, so that they may be one, as we are one. While I was with them, I protected them in your name... I guarded them, and not one of them was lost except the one destined to be lost, so that the scripture might be fulfilled. But now I am coming to you, and I speak these things in the world so that they may have my joy made complete in themselves. I have given them your word, and the world has hated them because they do not belong to the world, just as I do not belong to the world. I am not asking you to take them out of the world, but I ask you to protect them from the evil one... Sanctify them in the truth; your word is truth.

JOHN 17:11–15, 17 (abridged)

This is part of what is known as the 'high priestly prayer' of Jesus for his disciples. Like the high priest in the temple, he took time to commend into his Father's care those who had been 'given' to him. As he later says in this prayer, he was also praying for all those 'who will believe in me through their word' (v. 20)—so in a true sense this prayer is for us, too. Jesus himself was leaving this world to return to the Father, and he knew that those who followed him would have a difficult and sometimes very dangerous time. He also knew that they would be exposed to many pressures from what he calls 'the world'—society organized as though God did not exist.

So he prayed that they may be protected. He had protected them while he was on earth. Only Judas the betrayer had slipped away, by his own deliberate decision. Now Jesus prayed that his Father would protect them in the future, holding them faithful to his teaching and guarding their steps through the uncharted territory they were about to enter. They would continue to live in 'the world', but they would not 'belong' to it. They were his, and he was his Father's.

Jesus prayed for me—indeed, he still does (Hebrews 7:25).

23 September

THE LORD'S PRAYER

'Pray then in this way: Our Father in heaven, hallowed be your name. Your kingdom come. Your will be done, on earth as it is in heaven. Give us this day our daily bread. And forgive us our debts, as we also have forgiven our debtors. And do not bring us to the time of trial, but rescue us from the evil one.'
MATTHEW 6:9–13

These are probably the best-known words in the New Testament, recited every day, in many languages, by millions of people. In fact, it's doubtful if Jesus intended to construct a piece of permanent 'liturgy' for his followers. He was simply giving them a pattern for all of their prayers: 'pray in this way', not necessarily in these words.

The prayer brings together all our main concerns and sets them in a clear order of priority: God first, others second and ourselves last. Most of us know it in its 'liturgical' form, but it's helpful to go back and read it in its two biblical forms—this one, and the parallel passage in Luke 11:2–4. The well-known and appropriate ending ('For thine is the kingdom…') is not present in the best biblical manuscripts. Matthew and Luke differ over the word usually translated 'trespasses'. Matthew's word ('debts') stresses the indebtedness into which sin puts us. Luke's 'sins' emphasizes moral failure. Probably Jesus gave various versions of this 'pattern prayer', which might account for the differences.

God does not actually 'lead' anyone into temptation (James 1:13), but he does 'put us to the test'. Jesus urges his followers to pray that they may be spared the 'time of trial' and so be delivered from the 'evil one'. The prayer moves seamlessly from the honour of God and the blessings of his kingdom to the principle of forgiving others and our own physical and spiritual needs—'daily bread' and deliverance from evil. It hinges on the phrase 'Your will be done'. Prayer is not getting God to do what I want, but working with God in what he wants.

When we have said 'Your will be done', we have really said it all!

24 September

IN THE DAY OF TROUBLE

The Lord is my light and my salvation; whom shall I fear? The Lord is the stronghold of my life; of whom shall I be afraid? When evildoers assail me to devour my flesh… they shall stumble and fall. Though an army encamp against me, my heart shall not fear; though war rise up against me, yet I will be confident. One thing I asked of the Lord, that will I seek after: to live in the house of the Lord all the days of my life, to behold the beauty of the Lord, and to inquire in his temple. For he will hide me in his shelter in the day of trouble; he will conceal me under the cover of his tent; he will set me high on a rock… I will sing and make melody to the Lord.

PSALM 27:1–6 (abridged)

This psalm can be valued at many levels. It is a superb example of Hebrew poetry, the parallel phrases falling into place one after another: 'Though an army encamp against me, my heart shall not fear; though war rise up against me, yet I will be confident.' Perhaps this one is a composition by King David himself: it might take a ruler to know what it feels like to have armies encamped around, and declarations of war in the air.

It can also be valued for its inspiring optimism—or should we say 'faith'? The writer is quietly confident that his God will 'hide him in his shelter in the day of trouble' and set him 'high on a rock'. Perhaps best of all is the deep spirituality of the psalm, embodied in its sense of priorities. 'One thing I asked of the Lord, that I will seek after.' Would that be victory in battle, long life, or riches? No—it is to 'live in the house of the Lord all the days of my life' (literally, to spend my days in the sanctuary of God's temple) and 'to behold the beauty of the Lord, and to inquire in his temple'. Today we might use different words but the cry of the heart is of a universal spiritual longing: to dwell close to God and discover how beautiful are his nature and his purposes.

'The Lord is my light and my salvation; whom shall I fear?' To ask the question is to answer it.

25 September

NOT TESTED TO BREAKING

These things happened to them to serve as an example, and they were written down to instruct us, on whom the ends of the ages have come. So if you think you are standing, watch out that you do not fall. No testing has overtaken you that is not common to everyone. God is faithful, and he will not let you be tested beyond your strength, but with the testing he will also provide the way out so that you may be able to endure it.
1 CORINTHIANS 10:11–13

Paul has just been relating the failures of faith and the disobedience of the Israelites on their wilderness journey. Having seen so many blessings and miracles—including the crossing of the Red Sea—they nevertheless failed God. If it could happen to them, he warns, it could happen to you!

His main point, however, is not so much warning as encouragement. Yes, God put the Israelites to the test in the wilderness and they failed, time and again. But God does not test anyone to breaking point. That is the story of the book of Job. He doesn't box us in with problems (though it may sometimes feel like it), but in the very act of testing he provides what we might call an escape route. In practice, this may be a special gift of faith—a kind of adrenalin rush of the Holy Spirit. It may be the support and love of a friend or partner. It may be something we can do that will free the logjam of pressure and emotion.

Whatever it is, it is promised to those who are being 'put to the test' (we may recall the phrase from our reading two days ago). 'God is faithful'—he keeps faith with us—and although it may at times be hard to see through the darkness and the tears, he is still beside us. What has happened to us is not unique: troubles are, unfortunately, the common lot of humankind. But our experience of God in the time of trouble will be unique, just for us.

Peter writes that the 'genuineness of our faith' will be 'tested by fire', but also that it will emerge as 'gold'—more glorious than it was before (1 Peter 1:7).

26 September

THE PATHS OF LOVE

Make me to know your ways, O Lord; teach me your paths. Lead me in your truth, and teach me, for you are the God of my salvation; for you I wait all day long. Be mindful of your mercy, O Lord, and of your steadfast love, for they have been from of old. Do not remember the sins of my youth or my transgressions; according to your steadfast love remember me, for your goodness' sake, O Lord! Good and upright is the Lord; therefore he instructs sinners in the way. He leads the humble in what is right, and teaches the humble his way. All the paths of the Lord are steadfast love and faithfulness, for those who keep his covenant and his decrees.
PSALM 25:4–10

For the devout Jew the law of the Lord is not a burden; it is a whole way of life. What Jesus and then Paul condemned was not the holy law of God but the multitudinous 'case law' and petty regulations that had been added over the centuries by the 'teachers of the law'—the ones known as 'the scribes' in the Gospels. In this psalm, the law of God is not mentioned directly but it is, of course, the 'truth' referred to in verse 5 and the 'path' in verses 4 and 10.

The 'other side' of the law is the 'steadfast love' of God. Constantly the psalmists ask God to 'remember' the love he has promised to show to his people. It combines the ideas of mercy and faithfulness, and extends to all those who 'keep his covenant and his decrees'.

The psalmist prays to be led into this truth—a truth he is ready and anxious to be taught. He readily admits that in the past he has 'transgressed' (flouted the law of God), but he asks the Lord to put that aside and teach him the truth. When he has done that, he will be on 'the way', walking the paths of righteousness and truth, which are built on 'steadfast love and faithfulness', the bedrock and foundation of all that God is.

For the psalmist, God's law was not a burden but a delight—an expression of his steadfast love.

27 September

BOUND TO THE TRUTH

Hear, O Israel: The Lord is our God, the Lord alone. You shall love the Lord your God with all your heart, and with all your soul, and with all your might. Keep these words that I am commanding you today in your heart. Recite them to your children and talk about them when you are at home and when you are away, when you lie down and when you rise. Bind them as a sign on your hand, fix them as an emblem on your forehead, and write them on the doorposts of your house and on your gates.
DEUTERONOMY 6:4–9

The opening words of this passage are known as the *shema*, the foundational creed of Judaism. They are learnt by heart and repeated endlessly. In this way, the Jewish religion established its uniqueness in the ancient world, a faith that believed passionately in one God who is to be loved with every part of our being—heart, soul, mind, strength. Jesus himself reasserted this divine precept (Mark 12:30).

The *shema* is much more than words. It is a whole way of seeing God and the world. Therefore, this profound truth was to be a part of everything the Jewish people did. It was to be recited to children, talked about and meditated on, attached to their foreheads and hands and fixed to their doorposts. These last commands have been taken literally: many orthodox Jews still wear 'phylacteries', little boxes containing tiny pieces of paper with the words of the *shema* on them. They are sometimes bound to their foreheads and hands, and they can also be seen fixed to doorposts in many Jewish homes.

More important (I'm sure they would agree) than wearing the phylactery is observing the truth it contains. The world looks different to those who believe that it has one almighty Creator and that he calls us to love him totally. Even more revolutionary is the idea that the same eternal God also loves his people with an everlasting love (Isaiah 54:8).

We may not feel the need literally to wear verses 4–5 on our person, but we would do well to write them on our hearts.

28 September

SUPPER AT EMMAUS

As they came near the village to which they were going, [Jesus] walked ahead as if he were going on. But they urged him strongly, saying, 'Stay with us, because it is almost evening and the day is now nearly over.' So he went in to stay with them. When he was at the table with them, he took bread, blessed and broke it, and gave it to them. Then their eyes were opened, and they recognized him; and he vanished from their sight. They said to each other, 'Were not our hearts burning within us while he was talking to us on the road, while he was opening the scriptures to us?'
LUKE 24:28–32

This beautiful post-resurrection episode is told by Luke with the skill of a master storyteller. Two disciples, one named Cleopas and the other, surely, his wife, were making a sad journey home to Emmaus from Jerusalem on the Sunday after the crucifixion. As they trudged along, reflecting on the depressing end of their hopes that Jesus would prove to be the promised Messiah, 'Jesus himself came near and went with them' (v. 15), but they didn't recognize him. He asked why they looked so troubled and they poured out the story to him. Jesus then began to expound the scriptures to them, demonstrating how the Messiah must suffer 'and then enter into his glory' (v. 26). Night was falling and they urged him to stay with them—and, at the simple meal that they shared, Jesus revealed himself to them 'in the breaking of the bread' (v. 35).

This couple had felt bereft, crushed, desperately disappointed. Yet with them, on that lonely walk, the Saviour of the world made a private rendezvous to set their troubled hearts at rest. He had appeared to Mary of Magdala in her sorrow. He later appeared to Simon Peter in his guilt. To Cleopas and his partner he appeared as the voice and vision of hope. Thus are the lives of those who love him watched over.

'Stay with us… it is almost evening and the day is now nearly over.' That might be a prayer for all of us who are approaching the evening of our days.

29 September

I AM WITH YOU ALWAYS

Now the eleven disciples went to Galilee, to the mountain to which Jesus had directed them. When they saw him, they worshipped him; but some doubted. And Jesus came and said to them, 'All authority in heaven and on earth has been given to me. Go therefore and make disciples of all nations, baptizing them in the name of the Father and of the Son and of the Holy Spirit, and teaching them to obey everything that I have commanded you. And remember, I am with you always, to the end of the age.'

MATTHEW 28:16–20

Very early in his Gospel, Matthew quotes Isaiah's prophecy of a great deliverer named 'Emmanuel, which means, "God is with us"' (1:23), and applies it to Mary's son. So far as we know, Jesus was never called 'Emmanuel', but Matthew clearly saw this prophecy as setting the agenda for the coming Messiah-Saviour. God would be 'with us' in a new kind of way in Jesus, and the Gospel story reveals the outworking of this truth. In Jesus of Nazareth, God was at work in a unique way.

That is the opening 'bookend' of Matthew's Gospel. Today's reading gives us the closing one. Jesus met his closest associates, the eleven remaining apostles, on a mountain after his resurrection. There, he commissioned them to their future ministry—to make disciples, to baptize and to teach 'everything that I have commanded you'. This was an awesome task but the closing words of the Gospel offer them the ultimate resource. Wherever they went and whatever they did, Jesus would be with them, right to the 'end of the age'.

This last great commission of Jesus was built around the Greek word for 'all'. All authority had been given to Jesus, in heaven and on earth. They were 'therefore' to go and make disciples of all nations, including the previously excluded Gentiles. They were to teach them all that he had commanded them. And he would be with them on all roads, all ways, however daunting the path.

All authority, all nations, all the truth—and Jesus with us all the way.

30 September

THE AWAKENED SPIRIT

O God, be merciful to me, for in you my soul takes refuge; in the shadow of your wings I will take refuge, until the destroying storms pass by. I cry to God Most High, to God who fulfils his purpose for me. He will send from heaven and save me, he will put to shame those who trample on me. God will send forth his steadfast love and his faithfulness... My heart is steadfast, O God, my heart is steadfast. I will sing and make melody. Awake, my soul! Awake, O harp and lyre! I will awake the dawn. I will give thanks to you, O Lord, among the peoples... For your steadfast love is as high as the heavens; your faithfulness extends to the clouds.

PSALM 57:1–3, 7–10 (abridged)

The psalmist seems to have been experiencing what he calls 'destroying storms' in his life. Even as he calls on God's mercy, he determines to 'take refuge in the shadow of your wings' until it has blown itself out. Faith is sometimes ridiculed as a crutch for the feeble, but the truth is that if you've broken your ankle you need a crutch, and it's a peculiarly stupid person who refuses to use one! At times we all go though stormy times in life, and it would be stupidly obstinate to refuse to seek refuge in the God who has offered to hide us under his wings, like a mother bird sheltering her young.

On the other hand, like our psalmist, we can retain a quiet confidence in God's purpose for us, which he will fulfil. Eventually, we shall be able to put the crutch away and find that once again our heart is 'steadfast' (notice how the statement is repeated, as though to emphasize the point). Our 'steadfast heart' is tied to the 'steadfast love' of God, which is 'as high as the heavens'. In fact, the writer is awakened, renewed, by gratitude for the saving help of God that he has experienced. He can't even wait for morning to come: his praises will 'awake the dawn'.

Sometimes it is only an experience of God's love and faithfulness in a time of desperate need that can awaken in us this overwhelming sense of gratitude.

October: Forgiveness and hope

Forgiveness and hope go together, because without the former we could not have the latter! Our hope (which in biblical language means 'confidence') is that God forgives those who truly turn to him. That was as true for people like David in the Old Testament as it is for us today. God's love is 'steadfast' and his mercy 'endures for ever'. In Jesus, he proved it.

1 October

TRUE PENITENCE

Have mercy on me, O God, according to your steadfast love; according to your abundant mercy blot out my transgressions. Wash me thoroughly from my iniquity, and cleanse me from my sin. For I know my transgressions, and my sin is ever before me. Against you, you alone, have I sinned, and done what is evil in your sight, so that you are justified in your sentence and blameless when you pass judgment. Indeed, I was born guilty, a sinner when my mother conceived me... The sacrifice acceptable to God is a broken spirit; a broken and contrite heart, O God, you will not despise.
PSALM 51:1–5, 17

This is certainly the most abject psalm of repentance in the Bible. Traditionally it has been described as 'a psalm of David, when the prophet Nathan came to him, after he had gone in to Bathsheba' (see the heading to the psalm). It surely sounds like the cry of a wounded, sad and guilty man—and with reason. King David, a 'man after God's own heart' (1 Samuel 13:14), had not only committed adultery with one of his subjects but had arranged the murder of her husband to cover up his sin. The prophet Nathan told David a story about a rich man who stole the prize lamb of a poor man. Such a man should die, David decreed. 'You are the man!' said Nathan (2 Samuel 12:7)—you, the king, who could have taken any woman in the land as your wife, had to steal the wife of one of your junior officers and then arrange his death in battle. Sadly, the baby born to Bathsheba died, while David, chastened profoundly, went on serving as king.

His sin was, of course, against Uriah, Bathsheba's husband, but he recognized in this psalm that at heart it was against God himself: 'Against you, you alone, have I sinned.' However, there is a sacrifice acceptable to God even for such sin, and it is 'a broken spirit; a broken and contrite heart'. And David, for all his guilt, had such a heart.

It is hard and costly to pray for a broken and contrite heart, but it is often the key to forgiveness and hope.

2 October

IF WE CONFESS

If we say that we have no sin, we deceive ourselves, and the truth is not in us. If we confess our sins, he who is faithful and just will forgive us our sins and cleanse us from all unrighteousness. If we say that we have not sinned, we make him a liar, and his word is not in us. My little children, I am writing these things to you so that you may not sin. But if anyone does sin, we have an advocate with the Father, Jesus Christ the righteous; and he is the atoning sacrifice for our sins, and not for ours only but also for the sins of the whole world.

1 JOHN 1:8—2:2

This passage will be familiar to many Anglicans from the preface to Morning and Evening Prayer, as it includes some of the words used to call worshippers to repentance (vv. 8–9). In these sonorous words we are reminded of a fundamental truth: 'All have sinned and fall short of the glory of God' (Romans 3:23). All need to acknowledge their failure, all need forgiveness. In this, at least, there is a solidarity about the human race.

'If we confess...'—that's the rub! Generally speaking, even privately, we try to justify ourselves. 'Perhaps I shouldn't have got so upset, but I was provoked.' 'I'd gladly forgive her, but she's got to forgive me first.' While we are intent on self-justification, the whole principle of divine forgiveness is suspended. Grace abounds for sinners, not for those pleading a spurious innocence! This letter is addressed to members of one of the churches associated with John, and his primary concern is that they shouldn't sin, yet he knows the human heart. 'If anyone does sin...' this is the remedy: confession, repentance, forgiveness and cleansing. And it comes about through the 'atoning sacrifice' of Jesus, who has paid the price of our sin and acts as our 'advocate with the Father'—pleading our cause like a barrister in court.

This forgiveness is not only available to 'us'—some little in-group of the godly—but 'for the sins of the whole world'.

3 October

FORGIVEN AND ACCEPTED

The Lord passed before him, and proclaimed, 'The Lord, the Lord, a God merciful and gracious, slow to anger, and abounding in steadfast love and faithfulness, keeping steadfast love for the thousandth generation, forgiving iniquity and transgression and sin, yet by no means clearing the guilty, but visiting the iniquity of the parents upon the children and the children's children, to the third and the fourth generation.' And Moses quickly bowed his head toward the earth, and worshipped. He said, '... Although this is a stiff-necked people, pardon our iniquity and our sin, and take us for your inheritance.'

EXODUS 34:6–9 (abridged)

The Israelites, with Aaron's connivance, had made and worshipped an idolatrous image of a calf while Moses was up Mount Sinai receiving laws which, among other things, strictly forbade such practices. They knew it was wrong—the worship of the one true invisible God was the distinguishing mark of the Hebrew nation—yet they did it, and consequently incurred not only Moses' wrath but also God's.

In this passage, one of several in which God and Moses negotiate a kind of reconciliation, we have a memorable statement of God's principles concerning sin and forgiveness, and Moses' response to it. On God's part, there is an utter abhorrence of evil, which has devastating consequences not only for the present but echoing along lines of descent into the future. This is matched by a moving summary of his own nature. We could say that God's 'default setting' is grace: to forgive sin, to show steadfast love, to be slow to anger, to be merciful.

Moses recognized this graciousness, which probably went further than he had expected. He accepted how unwilling the people were to yield to God's loving will, but he pleaded for their pardon, that they should not lose their 'inheritance' as the covenant people of the Lord.

There is an old cliché about 'hating the sin but loving the sinner'. Like many such sayings, it may be old but it enshrines an important truth.

4 October

THE HOLINESS OF GOD

In the year that King Uzziah died, I saw the Lord sitting on a throne, high and lofty… Seraphs were in attendance above him; each had six wings… And one called to another… 'Holy, holy, holy is the Lord of hosts; the whole earth is full of his glory.' The pivots on the thresholds shook at the voices of those who called, and the house filled with smoke. And I said: 'Woe is me! I am lost, for I am a man of unclean lips, and I live among a people of unclean lips; yet my eyes have seen the King, the Lord of hosts!' Then one of the seraphs flew to me, holding a live coal that had been taken from the altar… touched my mouth with it and said: 'Now that this has touched your lips, your guilt has departed and your sin is blotted out.' Then I heard the voice of the Lord saying, 'Whom shall I send, and who will go for us?' And I said, 'Here am I; send me!'

ISAIAH 6:1–8 (abridged)

I remember preaching on this passage a few days after the assassination of President Kennedy—an event comparable to the death of Uzziah, the 'good' king on whom the nation had pinned its hopes. At this moment of acute disappointment and anxiety, Isaiah went into the temple and had this astonishing vision of God's glory. When the smoke cleared, he had walked into a new vocation. Uzziah was dead but Isaiah lived—a new voice of challenge, rebuke and hope for God's people.

The vision is described in extraordinarily powerful terms. Anything that could 'shake' the doorposts of the temple must have been terrifying. The six-winged seraphs sang, their voices echoing through the vast building. Sunday by Sunday many of us sing the same words, but can we imagine their awesome impact on the young man as the whole place filled with smoke? He was in the presence of pure holiness, but was stained with human failure. Then, his sin purged by the touch of a fiery coal from the altar, came the moment of commissioning.

And they who fain would serve Thee best are conscious most of wrong within.

HENRY TWELLS (1823–1900)

5 October

THAT GLORY MAY DWELL IN THE LAND

Restore us again, O God of our salvation, and put away your indignation toward us... Will you not revive us again, so that your people may rejoice in you? Show us your steadfast love, O Lord, and grant us your salvation. Let me hear what God the Lord will speak, for he will speak peace to his people, to his faithful, to those who turn to him in their hearts. Surely his salvation is at hand for those who fear him, that his glory may dwell in our land. Steadfast love and faithfulness will meet; righteousness and peace will kiss each other. Faithfulness will spring up from the ground, and righteousness will look down from the sky. The Lord will give what is good, and our land will yield its increase.

PSALM 85:4, 6–12

This psalm is a prayer for public revival and renewal, based on the willingness of God to forgive the past. Once again it is an appeal to the 'steadfast love' that is his nature, and a longing for 'salvation'—'health' in the deepest sense of the word.

Mostly the psalmist wants to spell out the blessings that will follow such a restoration. The Lord will 'speak peace' to his people. His glory will 'dwell in the land', provided that people fear him—reverence him, respect him. 'Righteousness and peace will kiss each other'—a rare and precious combination of virtues. Usually 'peace' is threatened because each side in a given situation thinks it is in the right ('righteous'). Here, both sides find 'right' in making peace. The ground will yield not only crops but 'faithfulness', and the sky will drop not only rain but 'righteousness'.

Surely, the psalmist seems to be saying, all this gives good reason for turning back to the Lord? Surely the ensuing blessings would outweigh the humiliation of admitting that we were wrong and God was right?

In today's world, wouldn't it be wonderful if, in places of conflict, people turned again to the God of steadfast love, so that 'righteousness and peace would kiss each other'—a truly revolutionary reconciliation!

6 October

YOUR SINS ARE FORGIVEN

Having dug through [the roof], they let down the mat on which the paralytic lay. When Jesus saw their faith, he said to the paralytic, 'Son, your sins are forgiven.' Now some of the scribes were sitting there, questioning in their hearts, 'Why does this fellow speak in this way? It is blasphemy! Who can forgive sins but God alone?' At once Jesus... said to them, 'Why do you raise such questions in your hearts? Which is easier, to say to the paralytic, "Your sins are forgiven", or to say, "Stand up and take your mat and walk"? But so that you may know that the Son of Man has authority on earth to forgive sins'—he said to the paralytic—'I say to you, stand up, take your mat and go to your home.'

MARK 2:4–11 (abridged)

And of course that is, miraculously, what the man did: he got up and went home. The crowd dispersed, pondering on the significance of it all. Jesus—'the Son of Man', as he liked to call himself—had authority to forgive sins (a divine prerogative) as well as the power to heal.

The paralysed man had been let in through the roof by some friends, because the house was crowded. When Jesus saw him, his first words were not 'Get up and walk' but 'Your sins are forgiven'. Most onlookers might have thought his biggest problem wasn't his sin but his paralysis. But the teachers of the law had a bigger problem: how can a mere human forgive sins? These skilful heresy hunters smelt serious error!

Jesus dealt with their problem first. In true Jewish fashion, he answered a question (even a whispered one) with another question: Which is easier, to forgive sins or to heal a paralysed man? (Both are, of course, impossible.) All right, said Jesus, I'll do the easy bit first, to show that I have authority to do the difficult bit as well. The stunned crowd and scribes were left to reflect that if the body was healed by God's power, so were the sins forgiven by the same power.

No wonder the crowd said that they had never seen anything like this before (v. 12). The Son of God had not been on earth before!

7 October

FORGIVEN AND RENEWED

Bless the Lord, O my soul, and do not forget all his benefits—who forgives all your iniquity, who heals all your diseases, who redeems your life from the Pit, who crowns you with steadfast love and mercy, who satisfies you with good as long as you live so that your youth is renewed like the eagle's. The Lord works vindication and justice for all who are oppressed. He made known his ways to Moses, his acts to the people of Israel.
PSALM 103:2–7

We are all familiar with the idea of God blessing us, but there is a persistent call in the psalms for us to bless God. The Hebrew word 'to bless' can mean to bestow favour or goodness (as when God blesses us), or it can mean to give thanks or worship, as when we bless God. This passage is one of the great Old Testament songs of gratitude, and in it we are called to 'bless' God for all of his 'blessings' of us.

The psalmist called them his 'benefits', the good things that flow from his love and care for us. Forgiveness, healing, redemption, vigour and strength all come from the Creator. Above all, his nature offers us a constant experience of 'steadfast love' and mercy. We may think of health and strength as normal elements of life, and of sickness and infirmity as abnormal. The psalmist sees it differently. Good health, daily strength and life itself are gifts, for which we should be thankful and bless our Creator. Sickness and infirmity are opportunities for God to show his care in other ways—in healing, perhaps, or in mercy and love even in times of testing.

As so often, the psalmist roots this in past experience. They know God can be trusted, because he has proved it in the past, in the experience of Moses and the Israelites—and they have seen that he is a God of justice and of truth, who has cared for the oppressed.

Perhaps we are more adept at counting grievances than blessings. Nurturing a sense of gratitude can transform our approach to the world—and our understanding of God himself.

8 October

A BROTHER'S FORGIVENESS

But Esau ran to meet [Jacob], and embraced him, and fell on his neck and kissed him, and they wept. When Esau looked up and saw the women and children, he said, 'Who are these with you?' Jacob said, 'The children whom God has graciously given your servant.' Then the maids drew near, they and their children, and bowed down; Leah likewise and her children … and finally Joseph and Rachel… bowed down. Esau said, 'What do you mean by all this company that I met?' Jacob answered, 'To find favour with my lord.' But Esau said, 'I have enough, my brother; keep what you have for yourself.' Jacob said, 'No, please; if I find favour with you, then accept my present from my hand…' So he urged him, and he took it.

GENESIS 33:4–11 (abridged)

This is close to the end of one of the best-known biblical stories of family conflict, feud and eventual reconciliation. As we have read before, Rebekah, Isaac's wife, favoured their younger son, Jacob, and encouraged him to deceive his elderly and blind father and 'steal' the inheritance of his older brother, Esau. The plot worked well but, not surprisingly, Esau was outraged and Jacob had to flee the family home.

Eventually, after many years, Jacob was brought to the point where he knew he must be reconciled with his brother. God had spoken to him in various dramatic ways, and now the moment had come. Typically, Jacob felt that the way to his brother's heart would be a massive gift of cattle and wealth, but even as he set out he was terrified that Esau's reaction would be negative and violent. He had completely misread his brother's character, however. When they finally met, Esau 'ran to meet him'. They embraced, kissed, wept, as Jacob's wives and children drew near and respectfully bowed down to the older brother. Esau didn't want the gifts but he must have noticed how Jacob constantly called him 'my lord', which by right of birth he was.

Esau emerges from this story as the man of integrity, content with what he has, not envious of his brother—and willing to forgive.

9 October

THE UNFORGIVING DEBTOR

'For this reason the kingdom of heaven may be compared to a king who wished to settle accounts with his slaves… One who owed him ten thousand talents was brought to him; and, as he could not pay, his lord ordered him to be sold, together with his wife and children and all his possessions, and payment to be made. So the slave fell on his knees before him, saying, "Have patience with me, and I will pay you everything." And out of pity for him, the lord of that slave released him and forgave him the debt. But that same slave, as he went out, came upon one of his fellow slaves who owed him a hundred denarii; and seizing him by the throat, he said, "Pay what you owe." Then his fellow slave fell down and pleaded with him, "Have patience with me, and I will pay you." But he refused; then he went and threw him into prison until he would pay the debt.'
MATTHEW 18:23–30 (abridged)

This is one of the 'kingdom parables' of Jesus. It's important not to press the details too far, but such narratives are probably the only way we can begin to enter into any real understanding of life in 'the kingdom of heaven'—living in perfect harmony with God's purposes.

Two men are in debt. Both are 'slaves' of the king. One owes the king 10,000 talents, the kind of figure that would have had the first hearers whistling with amazement. It represented about 150 years' wages for a labourer—an unimaginable sum.

Faced with the threat of his whole family being sold into slavery, the man pleaded for forgiveness—and, perhaps to his surprise, received it. The massive debt was wiped out, not because he could ever hope to pay it off (which he ludicrously offered to do) but because the king was generous. Then, released from his own debt, he went out and found a fellow slave who owed a mere hundred denarii—about a hundred days' wages. When the man couldn't pay, he had him thrown into prison.

Our debt to God is so great that we could never hope to repay it ourselves. He forgives us not because we deserve it but because he is gracious.

10 October

FORGIVING AND FORGIVEN

'When his fellow slaves saw what had happened, they were greatly distressed, and they went and reported to their lord all that had taken place. Then his lord summoned him and said to him, "You wicked slave! I forgave you all that debt because you pleaded with me. Should you not have had mercy on your fellow slave, as I had mercy on you?" And in anger his lord handed him over to be tortured until he would pay his entire debt. So my heavenly Father will also do to every one of you, if you do not forgive your brother or sister from your heart.'

MATTHEW 18:31–35

Here is the sequel to the previous story, with an important message from Jesus, the storyteller, as a conclusion. The other servants, outraged at the behaviour of the man who had had his fellow slave and debtor thrown into prison, let the king know. He, too, was furious.

He sent for the offending man and tore into him: 'You wicked slave!' Not only did he withdraw his remission of the debt, but he had the man handed over to the torturers—his fate had to be worse than that of the other man who was merely locked up. The king also spelt out the nature of his offence: 'Should you not have had mercy on him, in the way I had mercy on you?'

The 'king' in the story is not meant to be God. Parables are stories, not news reports. Nevertheless, they are theological case studies. We're meant to read or hear them and draw profound conclusions. In this case, Jesus himself spelt out the central message of the story. Forgiveness has two faces: one says 'forgiven' and the other says 'forgive'. Those who have been forgiven by God are massively in his debt. They have been recipients of his mercy and generosity (just like the slave in the story). Such an experience of grace—for that is what it is—should and must change their hearts. Those who have been forgiven are those whose hearts are ready to forgive.

It is 'from the heart' that we learn to forgive.

11 October

THE FATHER HAS COMPASSION

The Lord is merciful and gracious, slow to anger and abounding in steadfast love. He will not always accuse, nor will he keep his anger forever. He does not deal with us according to our sins, nor repay us according to our iniquities. For as the heavens are high above the earth, so great is his steadfast love toward those who fear him; as far as the east is from the west, so far he removes our transgressions from us. As a father has compassion for his children, so the Lord has compassion for those who fear him. For he knows how we were made; he remembers that we are dust.
PSALM 103:8–14

Some people think that there is a separate 'God of the Old Testament', a God of wrath and vengeance, and of course there are times when the writers speak of God's anger at sin and intolerance of evil. It could hardly be otherwise, given the holiness of God and the constant failures of his earthly creatures. However, as in this passage, the writers are always at pains to balance that picture of a God of holiness and purity with an equally compelling emphasis on another fundamental aspect of his nature—his mercy. The God of Abraham, Isaac and Jacob is a God of mercy, a God of forgiveness, a God of grace. He is 'slow to anger', quick to forgive. Above all, he does not (praise be!) 'repay us according to our iniquities'. There is no 'little black book' of sins to be constantly brought out and thrown in our faces, as so often happens in human disputes. Where God is concerned, when he forgives, he forgets. Our transgressions have been dumped on the other side of nowhere, 'as far as the east is from the west'—a lovely image!

This flows from the profound truth that we are creatures, that our Father is our God. He has compassion on us even when we fail him. He 'knows how we are made'. Of course he does; he made us!

While this passage reminds us that we are 'but dust', that 'dust' is shaped by the hand of God; it is infinitely precious to him. He loves and values what he has made.

12 October

A DESPERATE FATHER

Jesus asked the father, 'How long has this been happening to him?' And he said, 'From childhood... but if you are able to do anything, have pity on us and help us.' Jesus said to him, 'If you are able!—All things can be done for the one who believes.' Immediately the father of the child cried out, 'I believe; help my unbelief!' When Jesus saw that a crowd came running together, he rebuked the unclean spirit, saying to it, 'You spirit that keeps this boy from speaking and hearing, I command you, come out of him, and never enter him again!' After crying out and convulsing him terribly, it came out, and the boy was like a corpse... But Jesus took him by the hand and lifted him up, and he was able to stand.

MARK 9:21–27 (abridged)

This story of the healing of the epileptic boy (as it is now usually called) immediately follows the account of Jesus' transfiguration in the Gospels. The contrast is stark—the glory of God revealed on the mountain, the tears and despair of suffering humanity at its foot. The disciples who had not accompanied Jesus had been confronted with this desperate father but had been unable to help him or heal his son. In the language of the day, he was 'possessed by a spirit' which sometimes caused him to fall or convulse or cry out, and, as the father said to Jesus, he had been like this since childhood. He had asked the disciples to 'cast it out', but 'they could not do so' (v. 18).

The dialogue between Jesus and the father is very revealing. The father asks Jesus to help 'if you are able', but the Lord turns the request round. No, if *you* are able: everything is possible for the one who believes. It forces the father to think about his own faith, and his reply is painfully honest: 'I believe; help my unbelief.' That faith was clearly enough. Jesus took the boy, spoke to his inner fears, dismissed the hideous darkness that was wrecking his life, and healed him.

Perhaps we can all echo the father's honest and heartfelt request, in many different situations: 'Lord, I believe; help me where faith falls short!'

13 October

THE MERCIFUL JUDGE

The Lord is king; let the peoples tremble! He sits enthroned upon the cherubim; let the earth quake! The Lord is great in Zion; he is exalted over all the peoples. Let them praise your great and awesome name. Holy is he! Mighty King, lover of justice, you have established equity; you have executed justice and righteousness in Jacob. Extol the Lord our God; worship at his footstool. Holy is he! Moses and Aaron were among his priests, Samuel also was among those who called on his name. They cried to the Lord, and he answered them. He spoke to them in the pillar of cloud; they kept his decrees, and the statutes that he gave them. O Lord our God, you answered them; you were a forgiving God to them, but an avenger of their wrongdoings. Extol the Lord our God, and worship at his holy mountain; for the Lord our God is holy.

PSALM 99

This psalm has as its refrain a reminder of the holiness of God: 'Holy is he!' the psalmist sings, and right at the end adds, 'for the Lord our God is holy'. The holiness of God is an elusive concept, perhaps best expressed in poetry and hymn. 'He sits enthroned upon the cherubim; let the earth quake!' It's quite hard for the human mind to comprehend a personal being who is not, as even the best of us are, a mixture of good and evil, of conflicting motives, of self and sin marring even our best intentions. To be 'holy' is to be wholly good. As John puts it, 'God is light, and in him there is no darkness at all' (1 John 1:5).

Yet, as always, the psalmist wishes to balance that picture of utter purity with a recognition of an equally fundamental characteristic of the Lord God. When his people cried to him in their time of need, 'you were a forgiving God to them'. The God of holiness is also a lover of justice and mercy—attributes of an ideal monarch.

Name Him, brothers, name Him with love strong as death;
But with awe and wonder, and with bated breath!

CAROLINE NOEL (1817–77)

14 October

SING A NEW SONG

O sing to the Lord a new song; sing to the Lord, all the earth. Sing to the Lord, bless his name; tell of his salvation from day to day. Declare his glory among the nations, his marvellous works among all the peoples. For great is the Lord, and greatly to be praised; he is to be revered above all gods. For all the gods of the peoples are idols, but the Lord made the heavens... Ascribe to the Lord the glory due his name; bring an offering, and come into his courts. Worship the Lord in holy splendour; tremble before him, all the earth.

PSALM 96:1–5, 8–9

'Above all gods' may sound a bit strange to our ears! Yet in the world of ancient Israel it was a necessary and important thing to say. The Lord was not like the gods of the nations around them, the powers that pressed as insidiously on them as materialism and secularism do on us. Egypt or Assyria might rule the nations and even conquer the armies of Israel, but Yahweh was the God of all the earth, the infinite, personal and invisible Creator. He could not be reduced to an image of wood or stone; he was not an arbitrary tyrant, but a just and merciful God. His purpose was 'salvation'—life in all its fullness—not the acquisition of offerings and sacrifices.

So he deserved a 'new song', and this idea is picked up through the pages of scripture, until finally the redeemed around the heavenly throne join their voices to sing it. It celebrates the 'glory' and the 'marvellous works' of the Lord. It echoes through his sanctuary in the great temple, to which the people gladly bring their freewill offerings. The beauty of the temple worship, the robes of the priests, the incense and mystery, spoke to the worshippers of this God of awe and might. Though they might 'tremble' before him, there was still deep gratitude and love for his salvation and the wonder of his creation.

The 'new song' is for everybody: 'sing a new song to the Lord, all the earth'. All we need to do is retune our hearts to the God of glory and strength.

15 October

THE SONG OF THE LAMB

They sing a new song: 'You are worthy to take the scroll and to open its seals, for you were slaughtered and by your blood you ransomed for God saints from every tribe and language and people and nation...' I heard the voice of many angels... and the living creatures and the elders; they numbered myriads of myriads and thousands of thousands, singing with full voice, 'Worthy is the Lamb that was slaughtered to receive power and wealth and wisdom and might and honour and glory and blessing!' Then I heard every creature in heaven and on earth and under the earth and in the sea... singing, 'To the one seated on the throne and to the Lamb be blessing and honour and glory and might forever and ever!'

REVELATION 5:9, 11–13 (abridged)

In this vision John 'sees' the inner sanctuary of heaven, with the throne of God and beside it a Lamb 'standing as if it had been slaughtered' (v. 6). This is the 'Lamb of God who takes away the sin of the world' (John 1:29), Jesus the Saviour. He alone is able to take a secret scroll and open its seals—the record, we may assume, of those who have been redeemed through the 'blood of the Lamb'.

When it is opened, the new song is sung, echoing through the courts of heaven. It is a song about the Saviour and about those he has saved from every nation. The song goes on, now being picked up by 'every creature in heaven and on earth', a vast and universal hymn of praise to God, 'the one seated on the throne', and to the Lamb.

It is always dangerous to treat such visions as though they were images from TV news reports. Rather, they are reflections of a greater reality, picked up by the prophetic gift of the seer. This is not a photographic image of what heaven will be like. Instead, sense the joy and triumph; thrill to the unity and fellowship and love of this vast crowd of the redeemed. That is what heaven will be 'like'.

The Lamb of God, sacrificed on earth for our forgiveness, will be glorified in heaven for our worship.

16 October

SALVATION FOR THE SWINDLER

[Jesus] entered Jericho... A man was there named Zacchaeus; he was a chief tax collector and was rich. He was trying to see who Jesus was, but on account of the crowd he could not, because he was short in stature. So he ran ahead and climbed a sycamore tree to see him... When Jesus came to the place, he looked up and said to him, 'Zacchaeus, hurry and come down; for I must stay at your house today.' ... All who saw it began to grumble and said, 'He has gone to be the guest of one who is a sinner.' Zacchaeus stood there and said to the Lord, 'Look, half of my possessions, Lord, I will give to the poor; and if I have defrauded anyone of anything, I will pay back four times as much.' Then Jesus said to him, 'Today salvation has come to this house, because he too is a son of Abraham. For the Son of Man came to seek out and to save the lost.'

LUKE 19:1–5, 7–10 (abridged)

This is one of Luke's magnificent literary cameos. Zacchaeus the chief tax collector, universally hated and despised, had his fair share of curiosity, and when he heard that the prophet from Nazareth was visiting the town he wanted to see him. It was no good being at the back of the crowd: being short of stature he would see nothing. So, abandoning dignity, he climbed a sycamore tree to get a good view.

In the event, he got a good deal more. Jesus stopped, looked up and—to the astonishment of both Zacchaeus and the Jewish crowd—invited himself to supper! The bystanders were shocked at the prospect of a prophet dining with a traitor to the national cause—and a swindler, to boot. Zacchaeus, for his part, had a fit of genuine repentance, confessed his financial wrongdoing and offered generous recompense to those he had defrauded. In reply, he was told by Jesus that 'salvation had come to his house', and that he also was a 'son of Abraham', whatever the crowd thought of him.

When people complained about Jesus welcoming 'sinners' (see Luke 15:2), he always answered the same: 'I didn't come for the "righteous", but for sinners.'

17 October

A LIVING HOPE

Blessed be the God and Father of our Lord Jesus Christ! By his great mercy he has given us a new birth into a living hope through the resurrection of Jesus Christ… and into an inheritance that is imperishable, undefiled, and unfading, kept in heaven for you, who are being protected by the power of God through faith… In this you rejoice, even if now for a little while you have had to suffer various trials, so that the genuineness of your faith—being more precious than gold that, though perishable, is tested by fire—may be found to result in praise and glory and honour when Jesus Christ is revealed. Although you have not seen him, you love him… and rejoice with an indescribable and glorious joy, for you are receiving the outcome of your faith, the salvation of your souls.

1 PETER 1:3–9 (abridged)

This letter was written, apparently as a kind of round robin, to Christians in various churches across what we would now call Turkey. When it was written, state persecution in that part of the world was in fact uncommon (though an ever-present threat), but the Christians, as a religious sect with very different ideals and principles from their neighbours, were permanent targets of abuse. So, 'for a little while', they might well be subject to vicious, even violent, local persecution.

In such circumstances, what was their hope? In eloquent terms, the glory of the gospel is laid out for them. They have a 'new hope' through the resurrection of Jesus: a new 'inheritance' awaits them and it is 'imperishable'. No opposition can touch it, because it is 'kept in heaven' for all who are being protected by the power of God through faith. The eventual goal is salvation, even though in its fullness it won't be seen until Jesus Christ is 'revealed'.

Meanwhile, they have to suffer various trials, but even these will have a good outcome. Through them they will be purified, like a precious metal in the fire, and will emerge glorifying Jesus.

'Although you have not seen him, you love him.' Could that be said of us?

18 October

REPENTANCE AND FORGIVENESS

Then he said to them, 'These are my words that I spoke to you while I was still with you—that everything written about me in the law of Moses, the prophets, and the psalms must be fulfilled.' Then he opened their minds to understand the scriptures, and he said to them, 'Thus it is written, that the Messiah is to suffer and to rise from the dead on the third day, and that repentance and forgiveness of sins is to be proclaimed in his name to all nations, beginning from Jerusalem. You are witnesses of these things.'
LUKE 24:44–48

It is generally thought that someone's 'last words' have particular significance: after all, there is no opportunity for the speaker to correct or amend them! In Luke's Gospel these are Jesus' final instructions before he leaves his disciples to carry on the work he has commissioned them to do. He reminds them that everything that had happened to him was in fulfilment of the law and the prophets, and then explains their task. They were to preach the gospel—which encompassed the cross and the resurrection of Jesus, and required repentance of those responding to it. Through that repentance, and in the name of Jesus, there would be forgiveness of sins. In Luke's sequel, the book of Acts, we can read how Peter preached precisely that message on the day of Pentecost a few weeks later (Acts 2:38).

'Repentance' is not a word much used today. We tend to think of it in negative terms—sackcloth and ashes, eccentric men with posters, miserable sinners weeping. In fact, it is a very positive word. The New Testament word is *metanoia*. 'Meta' means 'change' and 'noia' means 'thinking'. 'Repentance', then, is about radically changing our thinking. It is to stop pleading innocence and admit our guilt. It is to stop arguing and agree with God. It is to open our minds to the mind of the Creator, whose desire is to remake us in the image of Christ.

We shall never know the release of true forgiveness if we are unwilling to change our minds about our sin—and stop protesting our innocence.

19 October

THE SCAPEGOAT

[Aaron] shall take from the congregation of the people of Israel two male goats for a sin offering, and one ram for a burnt offering... He shall take the two goats and set them before the Lord at the entrance of the tent of meeting... When he has finished atoning for the holy place and the tent of meeting and the altar, he shall present the live goat. Then Aaron shall lay both his hands on the head of the live goat, and confess over it all the iniquities of the people of Israel, and all their transgressions, all their sins, putting them on the head of the goat, and sending it away into the wilderness by means of someone designated for the task. The goat shall bear on itself all their iniquities to a barren region; and the goat shall be set free in the wilderness.

LEVITICUS 16:5, 7, 20–22

This is part of the long account in Leviticus of the rituals involved in the annual 'Day of Atonement', when the Jewish people repented their sins (individual and collective) and sought God's forgiveness. At that time, the ceremony involved a complicated series of animal sacrifices, first to cleanse the high priest, then the holy place (the inner sanctuary of the temple) and then the people. Our reading concentrates on the strange ritual of the scapegoat—one of two goats chosen from the flock. The first was offered as a sacrifice; the other was intended symbolically to bear away the sins of the people. The high priest laid his hands on its head, confessing all their 'iniquities, transgressions and sins', before the animal was sent off into the desert, never to be seen again. It is hard to think of a more vivid way of demonstrating that what God forgives, he banishes—or of a more telling explanation of what John the Baptist meant when he said that Jesus was the 'lamb of God who takes away [literally, 'bears off'] the sins of the world' (John 1:29). (Lambs and goats were regarded as interchangeable in the temple rituals.)

What the divine scapegoat has carried away, I carry on my back no longer.

20 October

MOUNTAINS TO MOTORWAYS

Thus says the Lord: ... I have kept you and given you as a covenant to the people, to establish the land... saying to the prisoners, 'Come out,' to those who are in darkness, 'Show yourselves.' They shall feed along the ways, on all the bare heights shall be their pasture; they shall not hunger or thirst, neither scorching wind nor sun shall strike them down, for he who has pity on them will lead them, and by springs of water will guide them. And I will turn all my mountains into a road, and my highways shall be raised up. Lo, these shall come from far away, and lo, these from the north and from the west, and these from the land of Syene.

ISAIAH 49:8–12 (abridged)

Who is the 'you' in this oracle? That question has kept commentators busy for centuries! Is it Israel as a nation? Or is it the Servant of the Lord, the messianic figure who is 'despised and rejected' (53:3) yet through his suffering brings about salvation for God's people? Is it, as Christians tend to feel, a prophetic picture of Jesus, who did all of those things? Or is it, in some mysterious way, all of the above?

It doesn't really matter! What we have here is a vision of restoration, a promised golden age, in which prisoners are released, the hungry fed, the thirsty led to springs of water. Not only that, but the 'way'—the long journey—will be simplified, so that those from distant lands may also come to share in the messianic blessings. Mountains will be flattened, highways raised up, so that people from the north and the west—and from the 'land of Syene', in Egypt, to the south—could find their way to answer the call.

The language of prophecy and vision is not the language of the chronicler or reporter. The eye of faith will read the words, the ear of faith hear them, and the heart of faith will interpret what it is that God is saying through the words.

The obstacles will be laid low and the roads will be raised up so that the paths to blessing are clear. But however clear the road, we still have to travel it.

21 October

THE FAITH OF AN OUTSIDER

Jesus was going through the region between Samaria and Galilee. As he entered a village, ten lepers approached him. Keeping their distance, they called out, saying, 'Jesus, Master, have mercy on us!' ... He said to them, 'Go and show yourselves to the priests.' And as they went, they were made clean. Then one of them... turned back... prostrated himself at Jesus' feet and thanked him. And he was a Samaritan. Then Jesus asked, 'Were not ten made clean? But the other nine, where are they? Was none of them found to return and give praise to God except this foreigner?' Then he said to him, 'Get up and go on your way; your faith has made you well.'
LUKE 17:11–19 (abridged)

The Samaritans get a distinctly good press in the Gospels, though in the Jewish community they were despised and isolated—rather like 'lepers', in fact. The trouble was that the Samaritans were not Gentiles (you expected Gentiles to get it all wrong) but practised—as it was popularly judged—a corrupted version of Judaism. They worshipped in the wrong place (Mount Gerizim) and in the wrong way.

Lepers, too, were isolated in accordance with the rules in the book of Leviticus, usually driven away even from their families. Perhaps for this reason, the Bible sometimes seems to see the disease as a metaphor for sin, which also cuts us off from God and often from one another.

Jesus healed these ten lepers at a distance, we may notice—simply with a word. On other occasions, he touched lepers (Mark 1:41). So delighted were they to find the symptoms disappear that nine of the ten went charging off to find the priest who could give them a certificate of cleansing. But one (and he was a Samaritan) paused to give thanks to God. His reward was that he was not just 'made clean' (v. 14) but made 'well'—whole, truly and deeply 'healed' (v. 19).

Perhaps the fact that the Samaritan was an outsider, even in the lonely fellowship of the leper colony, made him even more grateful for the word of acceptance and healing.

22 October

PERFECT FORGIVENESS

And every priest stands day after day at his service, offering again and again the same sacrifices that can never take away sins. But when Christ had offered for all time a single sacrifice for sins, 'he sat down at the right hand of God,' and since then has been waiting 'until his enemies would be made a footstool for his feet'. For by a single offering he has perfected for all time those who are sanctified. And the Holy Spirit also testifies to us... 'This is the covenant that I will make with them after those days, says the Lord: I will put my laws in their hearts, and I will write them on their minds... I will remember their sins and their lawless deeds no more.'
HEBREWS 10:11–17 (abridged)

The chief concern of the writer of Hebrews is to show that the repeated sacrifices of the temple have been fulfilled in the one, complete sacrifice that Jesus made of himself on the cross. This sacrifice not only needs no repetition but, by its very nature, precludes it. What Jesus did was an adequate atoning sacrifice for the sins of the whole world, for all time (see 1 John 2:2), so the language is about 'completion'. When Christ had offered his sacrifice, he 'sat down' and 'waited' until the sin for which he had died was finally eliminated from his Father's creation—until his enemies were made a 'footstool for his feet'.

This is not just abstract theology. It actually affects our lives as believers here and now. Once we have accepted that the sacrifice of Jesus is sufficient for forgiveness, we can stop looking for other ways to find it. We shall not feel the need to 'earn' what is a gift, or to 'justify' ourselves when, in Christ, God has already done so.

In this same letter, that truth leads the writer to issue a warning: such a sacrifice should never be treated lightly or carelessly. If the price of my forgiveness was the death of the Son of God, then every sin I commit adds something to that price. Sin is serious, and we shall take it lightly at our peril.

Assurance of forgiveness without presumption: that is the message of Hebrews.

23 October

A HOPE THAT DOES NOT DISAPPOINT

Therefore, since we are justified by faith, we have peace with God through our Lord Jesus Christ, through whom we have obtained access to this grace in which we stand; and we boast in our hope of sharing the glory of God. And not only that, but we also boast in our sufferings, knowing that suffering produces endurance, and endurance produces character, and character produces hope, and hope does not disappoint us, because God's love has been poured into our hearts through the Holy Spirit.

ROMANS 5:1–5

'Therefore' (in the light of Paul's argument up to that point), 'since we are justified by faith, we have peace with God.' With remorseless attention to the scriptures, Paul has set out his case. 'Righteousness'—'being right with God'—is something we receive as a gift from him, what Paul calls 'grace'. And the way we receive God's grace is faith. As we turn to him and trust him, he plants the seed of faith in our hearts.

So we stand 'justified'—counted as righteous. That's how sinners (which is what we are) can be considered saints (which is what Paul constantly calls Christians). From that new status of being justified, we can be at peace with God, a peace brokered by Jesus Christ on the cross. We have access to God and we can have confidence one day of sharing his glory—that is 'our hope'.

Of course, we aren't there yet. There is a process of growth to go through, from suffering to endurance, from endurance to a stronger character, from character to hope—a hope that does not disappoint us. That last phrase captures very well the New Testament meaning of 'hope'. When we say 'I hope so', we mean we'd like it to happen but we can't be certain. 'Hope' in the New Testament is the absolute certainty that what God has promised he will do. That is why Paul can say that 'it does not disappoint'. How could it? It is God's gift poured into our hearts through the Holy Spirit.

To hope in God is simply to believe that he will do what he has said.

24 October

WHILE WE WERE STILL SINNERS

For while we were still weak, at the right time Christ died for the ungodly. Indeed, rarely will anyone die for a righteous person—though perhaps for a good person someone might actually dare to die. But God proves his love for us in that while we still were sinners Christ died for us. Much more surely then, now that we have been justified by his blood, will we be saved through him from the wrath of God. For if while we were enemies, we were reconciled to God through the death of his Son, much more surely, having been reconciled, will we be saved by his life… We even boast in God through our Lord Jesus Christ, through whom we have now received reconciliation.
ROMANS 5:6–11 (abridged)

Here is yet another example of Paul's use of the 'how much more' device. God didn't send his Son to die for us when we were good, but when we were bad. This goes against logic, he suggests. We can imagine someone giving their life to save someone dearly loved, but it stretches credulity to imagine someone willingly sacrificing their life for a scoundrel. Yet God did it. 'While we were still sinners' Christ died for us. He didn't wait until we had changed our ways and set out on a new life. Those changes followed his action, rather than preceding it.

Now, says Paul, if that is how God regards us, 'how much more' will he complete what Christ began. We have been forgiven ('justified') through his blood, and that will lead to our full salvation from the judgment that otherwise awaited us. We are saved, now, by Christ's death. We will be saved, in the final judgment, by his life—the new life which is his gift to those who trust in him.

Paul was trying to assure these Christians in Rome that their 'salvation' was everything the word implies: forgiveness, new life, wholeness, reconciliation with God. We are saved and we shall be saved. That, at heart, is the good news of the gospel.

'Reconciliation' is a wonderful word; Jesus came to be the 'one mediator' between God and humanity (1 Timothy 2:5) and so to reconcile us to God.

25 October

THE ONE WHO LOVED ME

For through the law I died to the law, so that I might live to God. I have been crucified with Christ; and it is no longer I who live, but it is Christ who lives in me. And the life I now live in the flesh I live by faith in the Son of God, who loved me and gave himself for me.

GALATIANS 2:19–20

A short reading today, but one that expresses with crystal clarity a key feature of Paul's teaching. For him, the Christian life was a matter of dying and then rising to a new life—being 'crucified with Christ' and yet living now a new life, the life of the risen Son of God.

He puts it quite bluntly in his letter to the church at Rome: 'Do you not know that all of us who have been baptized into Christ Jesus were baptized into his death?' (6:3). What he meant was that to be a Christian was to share in some way in the death of Jesus, through which sins are forgiven. Only then can we share in his risen life. This 'dying' and 'rising' were symbolized in the ritual of baptism, in which the new believer renounced the 'old' life and entered into the 'new' one.

This is one great truth: we 'die' with Christ in order to 'live' in him. The other truth expressed so powerfully here by the apostle is that all of this was a divine initiative *for me*. The emphasis is quite clear: the Son of God loved me and gave himself for me.

Christianity is not a set of rules or a formula of belief, but a living and personal encounter with the Son of God. He loved me, says Paul, the former persecutor of Christians—and he loved me so much that he gave himself to death for me!

26 October

THE LIGHT OF THE WORLD

[Jesus] saw a man blind from birth. His disciples asked him, 'Rabbi, who sinned, this man or his parents, that he was born blind?' Jesus answered, 'Neither this man nor his parents sinned; he was born blind so that God's works might be revealed in him. We must work the works of him who sent me while it is day; night is coming when no one can work. As long as I am in the world, I am the light of the world.' When he had said this, he spat on the ground and made mud with the saliva and spread the mud on the man's eyes, saying to him, 'Go, wash in the pool of Siloam' (which means Sent). Then he went and washed and came back able to see.

JOHN 9:1–7

One of the overarching themes of John's Gospel is light (see John 1:5; 3:19). Here, in this account of the healing of a blind man in Jerusalem, we have a kind of extended parable on the spiritual themes of blindness and sight.

The man healed had been 'blind from birth'. His disability was not, said Jesus, the consequence of his own or his parents' sin (a common idea at the time), but to reveal the glorious works of God. Jesus speaks of night and day, darkness and light, and then says, 'I am the light of the world.' At that point he restores the man's sight.

The Bible undoubtedly sees physical blindness as some kind of metaphor for spiritual blindness. This is not to imply that blind people are themselves sinful (a concept explicitly rejected by Jesus here), nor that their inability to see implies impaired spiritual understanding. It is simply to draw a parallel. The physically blind have not chosen to be so—but the spiritually blind are wilfully so. Those who cannot see physically are deprived, through no fault of their own, of some of the most satisfying experiences of life. Those who cannot (or will not) 'see' spiritually are deprived of the deeply satisfying experience of faith.

To meet Jesus, to trust him and to do what he says: that is the 'formula' for the recovery of spiritual sight.

27 October

ONE THING I KNOW

[The Jews asked] 'Is this your son, who you say was born blind? How then does he now see?' His parents answered, 'We know that this is our son, and that he was born blind; but we do not know how it is that now he sees... Ask him; he is of age...' His parents said this because... the Jews had already agreed that anyone who confessed Jesus to be the Messiah would be put out of the synagogue... So for the second time they called the man who had been blind, and they said to him, 'Give glory to God! We know that this man is a sinner.' He answered, 'I do not know whether he is a sinner. One thing I do know, that though I was blind, now I see.'

JOHN 9:19–25 (abridged)

This is the sequel to the story of the healing of the man born blind. For some reason this miracle (possibly because it took place practically under their noses in the centre of Jerusalem) seems to have especially angered the Pharisees. The man's parents were interviewed by them but would only confirm that he had been born blind. Out of fear, for they were being questioned by powerful religious leaders from the temple establishment, the parents suggested that as their son was 'of age' they should question him directly. So they did, for a second time.

Like his parents, the man must have realized the risk involved in suggesting that Jesus had acted like the Messiah, so his replies were canny. To their charge that Jesus was a 'sinner', his answer was, in its own terms, irrefutable. 'I don't know whether he's a sinner. I only know one thing for sure. I was blind, and now I can see.' When the questioning continued, he became bolder, openly ridiculing the idea that with all their professed 'wisdom' on the subject of Moses and the Law, they couldn't explain this one incontrovertible fact. 'If this man were not from God, he could do nothing,' he asserted (v. 33). For his pains—and his honesty—he was thrown out of the temple courts.

It is the simplest testimony of all, but very hard to refute: 'One thing I know. I was blind, and now I can see.'

28 October

FROM BIRTH TO OLD AGE

In you, O Lord, I take refuge; let me never be put to shame… Rescue me, O my God, from the hand of the wicked, from the grasp of the unjust and cruel. For you, O Lord, are my hope, my trust, O Lord, from my youth. Upon you I have leaned from my birth; it was you who took me from my mother's womb. My praise is continually of you… But I will hope continually, and will praise you yet more and more. My mouth will tell of your righteous acts, of your deeds of salvation all day long, though their number is past my knowledge. I will come praising the mighty deeds of the Lord God, I will praise your righteousness, yours alone. O God, from my youth you have taught me, and I still proclaim your wondrous deeds. So even to old age and grey hairs, O God, do not forsake me, until I proclaim your might to all the generations to come.

PSALM 71:1, 4–6, 14–18

This is obviously the psalm of an older man looking back over his life. As he does so, he is aware that right from his mother's arms he has been blessed and protected. He has put his hope and trust in God, and God has not failed him. Yes, there have been (and perhaps still are) enemies and opponents, 'unjust and cruel', but he still looks to the Lord to rescue him from them.

This is a psalm of quiet confidence, from a heart that brims over with praise and thanksgiving. Here is no 'grumpy old man'! As he considers his life, he can see that from his youth he has known the love and kindness of God. He has been taught about God's saving acts, and (wisely) he has 'leaned' upon him in times of need. Now, in the evening of life, his hair is grey but his hope and faith shine like silver. And there is still time to share with 'generations to come' the blessings that he has enjoyed.

There are two great advantages about advancing years. One is that we can look back with gratitude. The other is that we can look forward with the confidence of faith.

29 October

FORGIVE, AND RESTORE

'When your people Israel, having sinned against you, are defeated before an enemy but turn again to you, confess your name, pray and plead with you in this house, then hear in heaven, forgive the sin of your people Israel, and bring them again to the land that you gave to their ancestors. When heaven is shut up and there is no rain because they have sinned against you, and then they pray toward this place, confess your name, and turn from their sin, because you punish them, then hear in heaven, and forgive the sin of your servants, your people Israel, when you teach them the good way in which they should walk; and grant rain on your land, which you have given to your people as an inheritance.'

1 KINGS 8:33–36

This is part of Solomon's magnificent prayer at the consecration of the temple he had built. Much of it is an extended hymn of praise to the Creator, to whose glory the great house had been built—while admitting that no earthly dwelling could 'contain' the God of heaven and earth. The prayer is also an intercession for the nation and for its continued survival and prosperity. This section deals with more sombre matters, however. What happens when the people sin against the Lord, as they had done in the past and would do again?

The scenario the king draws in his prayer is familiar. The nation has sinned (perhaps flirting with foreign gods); they are defeated in battle; they connect the two events and recognize that the situation must be corrected. Solomon sets out the process: they 'turn again to you'; they 'confess your name' and pray; they 'plead with you in this house'. If that do that, he asks, will the Lord please hear them in heaven, forgive their sin and restore their fortunes. He then applies the same principle to other situations—famine and blight—with the same plea for mercy.

Solomon's prayer is both deeply spiritual and profoundly practical. Because everyone sins, everyone needs to know this path of turning back to God, confessing failure and pleading for forgiveness.

30 October

WALKING IN THE LIGHT

God is light and in him there is no darkness at all. If we say that we have fellowship with him while we are walking in darkness, we lie and do not do what is true; but if we walk in the light as he himself is in the light, we have fellowship with one another, and the blood of Jesus his Son cleanses us from all sin.

1 JOHN 1:5–7

Just as in his Gospel, so in this letter John uses images of light and darkness as metaphors for spiritual truth. God himself is 'light'. As if to emphasize the fact, we are given the negative form of the same statement: 'in him there is no darkness at all'. Most of what we experience is a blend of light and dark, whether in the physical realm (twilight, dawn, cloud and sunny spells) or in the area of morality. Most people, even the best and the worst, are essentially mixtures of 'light' and 'darkness'. The evil very often have some redeeming feature; the good would be the first to admit that they are not perfect. Yet in God there is no darkness at all. He is pure and unadulterated light.

Consequently, those who claim to be in 'fellowship' with God, to be living a life intimately bound to his, cannot walk in the darkness. There is no room in such a relationship for the intrusion of evil. We are called to 'walk in the light' as he, the Lord God, is 'in the light'. When we do, we are truly in 'fellowship' (communion) with him and one another. Yet how can this be? As we have seen, all human life is flawed. So are we cut off for ever from the God who made us and loves us? No, asserts John—because 'the blood of Jesus his Son cleanses us from all sin'. The tense is present continuous: the 'blood of Jesus keeps on cleansing us'. And because it keeps on cleansing us, we can keep on walking in the light with our God.

The Father and the Son live constantly in the light, but we have flaws that introduce darkness into our lives. If we, too, are to 'walk in the light' then we must root our faith in the blood of Jesus, which 'cleanses us from all sin'.

31 October

ROBED IN WHITE

Then one of the elders addressed me, saying, 'Who are these, robed in white, and where have they come from?' I said to him, 'Sir, you are the one that knows.' Then he said to me, 'These are they who have come out of the great ordeal; they have washed their robes and made them white in the blood of the Lamb. For this reason they are before the throne of God, and worship him day and night within his temple... They will hunger no more, and thirst no more... for the Lamb at the centre of the throne will be their shepherd, and he will guide them to springs of the water of life, and God will wipe away every tear from their eyes.'

REVELATION 7:13–17 (abridged)

In this visionary book of Revelation, the seer offers us a series of pictures of heaven, and here we see a 'great multitude that no one could count' as they stood before the throne of God and of the Lamb, Jesus Christ (v. 9). In this passage there is a conversation between an 'elder' and the seer about the identity of this vast crowd of worshippers.

Prompted by John, who was having these visions one Sunday on the island of Patmos, the elder explained that they were the people who had come out of the 'great ordeal'. They had suffered, but their robes, perhaps blemished by that ordeal or even through their own failures during it, have been washed and made white 'in the blood of the Lamb'. Obviously blood doesn't wash things white, so we are here in the realm of powerful metaphor. It was through the sacrifice of Jesus that they stood forgiven, 'robed in white' (v. 9).

So they are full of love and gratitude, and join in wonderful songs of worship around God's throne. Now, at last, they are released from suffering and can know security: 'the Lamb at the centre of the throne will be their shepherd'. Whatever the past has held (and this book was probably originally a message to a persecuted church), the present and future are in the hands of the God and Saviour to whom they belong.

It is in days of darkness that we need a vision of the light.

November: The future

As we approach the season of Advent, with its emphasis on 'the last things' and the second coming of Christ, it is natural to consider what the future holds for those who believe in God. The Bible sets out no detailed master plan of what lies ahead, but what it does do is to set the future firmly in the purposes of God. He knows the future, and will in due time reveal his loving purpose for the whole creation. The future—ours, and the world's—is the theme of this month's readings.

1 November

GOD'S YEARS HAVE NO END

'O my God,' I say, 'do not take me away at the mid-point of my life, you whose years endure throughout all generations.' Long ago you laid the foundation of the earth, and the heavens are the work of your hands. They will perish, but you endure; they will all wear out like a garment. You change them like clothing, and they pass away; but you are the same, and your years have no end. The children of your servants shall live secure; their offspring shall be established in your presence.

PSALM 102:24–28

The psalmist is having a midlife crisis! Worried that he will be cut off in his prime, he prays that God will at least let his servant reach old age. This thought stimulates him to reflect in a much more profound way on the mystery of time, as it relates both to the God of eternity and to mortal human beings.

He recognizes that God is the source of everything that exists. 'In the beginning', as the book of Genesis declares, there was God and nothing else. Creation is his work but, although it was created by the eternal God, the creation itself is subject to change and decay. One day, even the earth and the skies will perish (a remarkable insight for a man of his time). In a memorable comparison, they will 'wear out like a garment'. God made them but he didn't make them to be eternal like himself. They will change—indeed, perish—but 'you are the same, and your years have no end'.

From that stark contrast the writer draws a reassuring conclusion. The security of 'the children of your servants'—mortal, like the psalmist—is secure, because they live 'in your presence'. Those who live united to God share the life of God. As Jesus himself put it, 'Because I live, you also will live' (John 14:19).

Our times are in God's hands. Whether our lives are long or short, the children of the eternal God can dwell secure.

2 November

BROUGHT TO COMPLETION

I thank my God every time I remember you, constantly praying with joy in every one of my prayers for all of you, because of your sharing in the gospel from the first day until now. I am confident of this, that the one who began a good work among you will bring it to completion by the day of Jesus Christ. It is right for me to think this way about all of you, because you hold me in your heart, for all of you share in God's grace with me, both in my imprisonment and in the defence and confirmation of the gospel. For God is my witness, how I long for all of you with the compassion of Christ Jesus.

PHILIPPIANS 1:3–8

Some years ago, I was leading a retreat at a convent in Holland. Over the main entrance was a text in Latin, which read *Dominus qui incepit ipse perficiat*: 'What God has begun he will complete.' It's a sort of terse summary of verse 6 in this passage, and it's a reminder that God doesn't begin something that he can't finish. He had begun a 'good work' in the church at Philippi, and by the time of his return ('the day of the Lord Jesus') he would have completed it. It's a reminder that we are all 'work in progress'. The New Testament may call us 'saints', but only in the sense that we are on a journey towards that goal.

There is a warmth of love and concern in this letter, as well as an assurance that Paul is praying for them 'constantly'. They had shared with him in the work of the gospel; they had stood with him during his imprisonment and also in holding firm to the truths that he had taught them ('the defence and confirmation of the gospel'). They were his 'partners': in slightly disguised form, the word occurs several times —'partners' in the gospel (v. 5), partners in God's grace, and partners in the defence of the message (v. 7). No wonder, in his time of loneliness under house arrest, he longed for their company.

What was true for the Philippians is true for us. We are 'work in progress', but it is progress towards a destiny that God has already marked out for us.

3 November

SHORT- AND LONG-TERM RESCUE

We do not want you to be unaware, brothers and sisters, of the affliction we experienced in Asia; for we were so utterly, unbearably crushed that we despaired of life itself. Indeed, we felt that we had received the sentence of death so that we would rely not on ourselves but on God who raises the dead. He who rescued us from so deadly a peril will continue to rescue us; on him we have set our hope that he will rescue us again, as you also join in helping us by your prayers, so that many will give thanks on our behalf.
2 CORINTHIANS 1:8–11

This is a typical example of the apostle Paul in full flood. We must sympathize with the poor secretary who was trying to take it all down, because in literary terms it's a muddle. It probably suggests that Paul was speaking of something very painful, near the heart of his concerns.

Clearly he had been through a terrible time in 'Asia'—the area we now call Turkey. 'Utterly, unbearably crushed' is strong language, and, coming from an apostle who had frequently been arrested, beaten and imprisoned, it suggests an extremely painful and even frightening experience. So much so, Paul says, that he began to despair of survival and instead placed his hope in the resurrection from death.

However, God did 'deliver' him—we aren't told how. On the basis of that experience, Paul asserts his belief that the same God will deliver him in the future, in response to their prayers. What we then have is a little exercise in tenses! God has delivered him (past tense): his past experience is to be used as a ground of hope. God is delivering him (present continuous): his experience now is that the same God is with him, whatever the circumstances. God will deliver him (future): 'he will rescue us again'. On the basis of experience in the past, Paul builds his confidence for the present and the future. And over and beyond it all, there is the greatest hope: the 'God who raises the dead'.

Our hope for the future is often based on our experience of the past. For the Christian, that means cultivating a grateful memory of past blessings.

4 November

THE SECRET OF WISDOM

'Where then does wisdom come from? And where is the place of understanding? It is hidden from the eyes of all living, and concealed from the birds of the air. Abaddon and Death say, "We have heard a rumour of it with our ears." God understands the way to it, and he knows its place. For he looks to the ends of the earth, and sees everything under the heavens. When he gave to the wind its weight, and apportioned out the waters by measure; when he made a decree for the rain, and a way for the thunderbolt; then he saw it and declared it; he established it, and searched it out. And he said to humankind, "Truly, the fear of the Lord, that is wisdom; and to depart from evil is understanding."'

JOB 28:20–28

The search for wisdom is really the search for meaning and purpose—a search as relevant now as it was in the days of Job. What is its source? Where does it come from? How can we answer that most elusive of questions, 'Why does the universe bother to exist?' or the even more personal one, 'Why are we here?'

The answer, says Job, is not easily found. Human beings struggle with the questions. Death and destruction (*abaddon*) have heard no more than a 'rumour' of it. Until we have some answers, the future is unsure and life insecure.

Job is clear about one part of the answer: 'God understands the way to it.' He must do, because he 'sees everything under the heavens'. God, then, is the key to wisdom; he provides meaning and purpose. Because he is the Creator of wind, wave, thunder and rain, the universe itself is not meaningless. Consequently, Job can repeat what becomes a kind of refrain to this book: 'Truly, the fear of the Lord, that is wisdom; and to depart from evil is understanding.'

'Fear of God' is not terror but reverence; it is not subservience but worship, not grovelling but gratitude, not humiliation but humility. That kind of fear can begin to unlock for us the answers to many of those elusive questions.

5 November

THE SHIELD AND REWARD

After these things the word of the Lord came to Abram in a vision, 'Do not be afraid, Abram, I am your shield; your reward shall be very great.' But Abram said, 'O Lord God, what will you give me, for I continue childless, and the heir of my house is Eliezer of Damascus?' … But the word of the Lord came to him, 'This man shall not be your heir; no one but your very own issue shall be your heir.' He brought him outside and said, 'Look toward heaven and count the stars, if you are able to count them.' Then he said to him, 'So shall your descendants be.' And he believed the Lord; and the Lord reckoned it to him as righteousness.
GENESIS 15:1–2, 4–6

Abram left his home city of Ur, far to the east, and journeyed to Canaan at the prompting of a God he hardly knew yet trusted completely. His obedience to that prompting was to prove one of the decisive moments in the long story of humankind's relationship with God.

Today's passage comes quite early in Abram's story (God renamed him Abraham when he was 99 years old). The Lord had already told him that his descendants would be more numerous than the dust of the earth, but at this point he had no offspring—the 'heir of his house' was a slave, Eliezer. Now, however, he is promised that his descendants will outnumber the stars. Unlikely as it seemed, Abram 'believed God', and it was 'reckoned to him as righteousness' (see Romans 4:3).

In this way, Abraham became the epitome of faith. Throughout his life he exhibited an amazing gift for exercising faith, even in the face of the most daunting circumstances. Promised that his elderly wife would have a child, he believed it and was blessed with the birth of Isaac. Told by God to sacrifice his only son, he was reluctantly prepared to do it. And this all flowed from his first decision to follow God's urging and uproot himself and his family in order to settle in a strange land.

Faith is itself a gift of God. We can pray with the disciples of Jesus, 'Lord, increase our faith!' (Luke 17:5).

6 November

A FUTURE OF PEACE

In days to come the mountain of the Lord's house shall be established as the highest of the mountains, and shall be raised above the hills; all the nations shall stream to it. Many peoples shall come and say, 'Come, let us go up to the mountain of the Lord, to the house of the God of Jacob; that he may teach us his ways and that we may walk in his paths.' For out of Zion shall go forth instruction, and the word of the Lord from Jerusalem. He shall judge between the nations… they shall beat their swords into ploughshares, and their spears into pruning hooks; nation shall not lift up sword against nation, neither shall they learn war any more.

ISAIAH 2:2–4 (abridged)

This reads, as it stands, like a wonderful song of hope. The days are coming when all the nations will turn to Israel's God for guidance, and as a result there will be golden years of peace and prosperity: nations 'shall not learn war any more'. Of course it is well to hold such a vision of hope before us: God has not washed his hands of the human race in despair. Nevertheless, after this scenario of blessing, verse 6 sets it in a very different context: 'For you have forsaken the ways of your people, O house of Jacob. Indeed they are full of diviners from the east and of soothsayers like the Philistines.' The passage goes on in a similar vein. The land is full of idols; the people are more interested in acquiring riches than the approval of the Lord. It is in this setting that the word of hope is sounded, because anything else would simply be a kind of spiritualized wishful thinking.

God, as the arbitrator between nations and the agent of disarmament on a mass scale, is dependent on those same nations turning to him as their teacher. As people seek to 'walk in his paths', they will see the futility of war and the vanity of materialism.

It sometimes seems impossible that greed, envy, injustice and exploitation will ever be done away with. Perhaps one day the nations will accept that many of our problems are simply beyond us, and turn at last to God.

7 November

THE SUFFERING SERVANT

He had no form or majesty that we should look at him, nothing in his appearance that we should desire him. He was despised and rejected by others; a man of suffering and acquainted with infirmity; and as one from whom others hide their faces he was despised, and we held him of no account. Surely he has borne our infirmities and carried our diseases; yet we accounted him stricken, struck down by God, and afflicted. But he was wounded for our transgressions, crushed for our iniquities; upon him was the punishment that made us whole, and by his bruises we are healed.
ISAIAH 53:2B–5

These are among the best-known words in the Bible, but only because Handel set them to memorable music in *Messiah*. Their meaning, hotly disputed by biblical scholars, tends to elude the casual hearer. About whom is the prophet writing? Who is this 'man of suffering'?

As it happens, a character in the book of Acts asked almost precisely those questions. The Ethiopian eunuch was travelling back from Jerusalem and reading in his chariot this passage from Isaiah. He was joined, providentially, by the deacon Philip, who asked him if he understood what he was reading. 'How can I, unless someone guides me?' he replied—and then asked the key question: 'About whom does the prophet say this?' Philip's reply, which has become the classical Christian interpretation of the text, was to proclaim to him 'the good news of Jesus' (Acts 8:30–35).

The 'neutral' answer to the question would be 'the suffering servant of the Lord'—who, for Christians, is manifestly Jesus. That was how Jesus saw his own role, and that was the story of his life. It is uncanny to read this passage and to see how precisely the prophecy expressed in the sixth century BC was fulfilled in Jesus of Nazareth.

'He was wounded for our transgressions, crushed for our iniquities; upon him was the punishment that made us whole, and by his bruises we are healed.' How movingly those words apply to the Saviour, Jesus Christ.

8 November

LIKE A LAMB TO THE SLAUGHTER

All we like sheep have gone astray; we have all turned to our own way, and the Lord has laid on him the iniquity of us all. He was oppressed, and he was afflicted, yet he did not open his mouth; like a lamb that is led to the slaughter, and like a sheep that before its shearers is silent, so he did not open his mouth. By a perversion of justice he was taken away. Who could have imagined his future? For he was cut off from the land of the living, stricken for the transgression of my people. They made his grave with the wicked and his tomb with the rich, although he had done no violence, and there was no deceit in his mouth.

ISAIAH 53:6–9

'All we like sheep': Handel set the words to a frolicsome jig, and I suppose it might seem fun to a sheep to escape from its pen and scamper off over the hills… until it meets a hungry wolf! The rest of this passage provides an equally sombre context to the sin on which we humans embark all too lightly, and all too often: 'The Lord has laid on him [his 'suffering Servant'] the iniquity of us all.' Sin has consequences, and the Son of God bore those consequences on the cross. While we may speculate on how exactly the mystery 'worked', we should always remember that it was motivated solely by love—God's love for his fallen creatures, and the love of Jesus for the 'lost' he had come to seek and save. In an act of divine love, the Father and the Son worked together to free us from the consequences of sin.

Here in this vivid prophecy, there is a picture of totally undeserved suffering, borne for the sake of others: the lamb that was to be 'slaughtered'; the perversion of justice; the ignominy of a death shared with criminals—and all borne by one who was entirely innocent and honest. It is hard for a Christian to read this and not think of Jesus, pronounced innocent by his judge and yet led away to crucifixion.

There is no such thing as a victimless sin: the final victim is the Son of God who bears its burden to the cross.

9 November

THE FRUIT OF SUFFERING

Yet it was the will of the Lord to crush him with pain. When you make his life an offering for sin, he shall see his offspring, and shall prolong his days; through him the will of the Lord shall prosper. Out of his anguish he shall see light; he shall find satisfaction through his knowledge. The righteous one, my servant, shall make many righteous, and he shall bear their iniquities. Therefore I will allot him a portion with the great, and he shall divide the spoil with the strong; because he poured out himself to death, and was numbered with the transgressors; yet he bore the sin of many, and made intercession for the transgressors.
ISAIAH 53:10–12

This rather elusive passage may illustrate why commentators have pondered long and hard over the identity of this 'suffering servant' of the Lord. Some have thought that the servant is in fact God's people, Israel, out of whose suffering would come ultimate blessing. Some think that it was the prophet himself, predicting his own fate, borne for the sake of the people to whom he witnessed. Most, however, have seen this as a messianic prophecy, and therefore, for Christian readers, a pre-echo of the suffering and death of Jesus Christ.

This is our last reading from these 'servant songs', and we end them with the note of hope that finally emerges. Although God's servant was 'crushed with pain', out of this anguish he will see 'light'. Although he 'poured himself out to death', he will find satisfaction—he will 'prolong his days' and 'see his offspring'. As a literal prophecy about Jesus, the latter was not, of course, true. He wasn't married and he didn't have any children. But in a deeper sense he did have 'offspring' in all those who through him became 'children of God' (John 1:12). This is not a description of defeat but of victory.

Couldn't an almighty God have forgiven our sins without putting his Son through the appalling experience of crucifixion? The answer is, I suppose, 'yes', but how else could God have demonstrated the extent of his love for us?

10 November

THE LORD WHOM YOU SEE WILL COME

See, I am sending my messenger to prepare the way before me, and the Lord whom you seek will suddenly come to his temple... But who can endure the day of his coming, and who can stand when he appears? For he is like a refiner's fire and like fullers' soap; he will sit as a refiner and purifier of silver, and he will purify the descendants of Levi and refine them like gold and silver, until they present offerings to the Lord in righteousness.

MALACHI 3:1–3 (abridged)

Malachi was writing in the fifth century BC, so, although this is the last book of our Old Testament, it was probably not the last book of the Hebrew Bible to be written. However, his words have a peculiar relevance placed right at the end of the Old Testament, because they pick up the idea of the messenger who would precede the 'coming of the Lord'. 'Malachi' means 'messenger', and the whole book is a warning to the people to turn back to the Lord before it's too late. After all, when the Lord comes it will be 'suddenly', unexpectedly. It will be too late then for repentance and reformation.

It was widely believed among the Jews that Elijah would return to herald the coming of the Messiah: a cup of wine is kept for him at every Passover meal. The disciples of Jesus asked him why the scribes taught that Elijah must come first. Jesus' reply was that he had come (by implication, in John the Baptist: see Luke 1:17) and 'they did to him whatever they pleased' (Mark 9:13). In Malachi's time, the people would have said that they were hoping for the appearance of Elijah, and were 'seeking' the coming of the Lord. But, the prophet warns, 'who can endure the day of his coming?' It would be a day of judgment on those who had abandoned the Law and withheld their sacrifices.

However, the judgment would not be without blessing. Refined and purified, the people would again present their offerings to God with joy.

'A refiner's fire and fuller's soap'—both refer to purification with a purpose.

11 November

THE SUN OF RIGHTEOUSNESS

But for you who revere my name the sun of righteousness shall rise, with healing in its wings. You shall go out leaping like calves from the stall. And you shall tread down the wicked, for they will be ashes under the soles of your feet, on the day when I act, says the Lord of hosts… I will send you the prophet Elijah before the great and terrible day of the Lord comes. He will turn the hearts of parents to their children and the hearts of children to their parents, so that I will not come and strike the land with a curse.
MALACHI 4:2–3, 5–6

We saw yesterday how the prophecies of the return of the prophet Elijah were fulfilled, for the Gospel writers, in the coming of John the Baptist. There would be a messenger of the Lord, a voice 'crying in the wilderness', calling on the people to 'prepare the way of the Lord' (see Isaiah 40:3; Mark 1:2–3). John's father, Zechariah, was told that his son would 'turn the hearts of parents to their children' (Luke 1:17), which echoes these words of Malachi. This messenger would precede the 'great and terrible day of the Lord', a day of which Jesus spoke but which he saw as some time still in the future.

For the disobedient, the coming of the messenger and the Day of the Lord would be times of judgment. But for those who 'revere' God's name, the 'sun of righteousness' would rise like the dawn, bringing light and warmth. Again, it isn't hard to see why Christian writers and preachers have constantly thought of this 'sun' as the 'Son', Jesus. Luke seems to have had a special interest in these prophecies. Zechariah's song speaks of a 'dawn from on high' which will break upon us through the coming of the Lord. It will 'give light to those who sit in darkness and in the shadow of death, to guide our feet into the way of peace' (see Luke 1:76–79).

Hail the heav'n-born Prince of Peace! Hail the Sun of Righteousness! Light and life to all He brings, Ris'n with healing in His wings.
CHARLES WESLEY (1707–88)

12 November

THE PERFECT GIFT

Every generous act of giving, with every perfect gift, is from above, coming down from the Father of lights, with whom there is no variation or shadow due to change. In fulfilment of his own purpose he gave us birth by the word of truth, so that we would become a kind of first fruits of his creatures.

JAMES 1:17–18

Where does 'goodness' come from? What is the source of generosity, of light, of new life? James has a simple answer. It all comes from 'above', from one source, which he calls 'the Father of lights'. At first sight, this is a strange or, at any rate, unexpected title for God, yet it is full of profound symbolism. 'Let there be light!' was the first divine command, which brought into being the entire creation (Genesis 1:3). The 'Word', Jesus, was to be the divine light shining into the world's darkness, which 'did not overcome it' (John 1:5). Light, in the ancient world, was security, safety, guidance and hope, and the Father is the origin and provider of all those blessings—'the Father of lights'.

He can be this because he is himself pure light. Usually, when we experience light it is partial: there is some element of shadow, some dilution of the brightness. But in God, says James, there is no 'variation or shadow due to change'. As the Bible says elsewhere, he dwells in 'unapproachable light' (1 Timothy 6:16); 'God is light and in him there is no darkness at all' (1 John 1:5). It is from this glorious and perfect light that every 'generous act', every 'perfect gift' comes down, poured out from the 'Father of lights'.

Of those gifts, none is greater than the new life that he made possible through his Son, Jesus: a new 'birth' through the word of truth (the gospel), by which we can become the 'first fruits' of a wonderful harvest of redeemed humanity.

The 'perfect gift' is one given without strings, with generous intent, and out of a loving heart.

13 November

A CLEAR CONSCIENCE

Now who will harm you if you are eager to do what is good? But even if you do suffer for doing what is right, you are blessed. Do not fear what they fear, and do not be intimidated, but in your hearts sanctify Christ as Lord. Always be ready to make your defence to anyone who demands from you an account of the hope that is in you; yet do it with gentleness and reverence. Keep your conscience clear, so that, when you are maligned, those who abuse you for your good conduct in Christ may be put to shame. For it is better to suffer for doing good, if suffering should be God's will, than to suffer for doing evil. For Christ also suffered for sins once for all, the righteous for the unrighteous, in order to bring you to God.

1 PETER 3:13–18

Peter was writing to Christians in a period when persecution, at any rate at a local level, was beginning to affect the Church. He was aware that in those circumstances a consistent and godly lifestyle would be their best (and perhaps their only) defence against their enemies. So here, and elsewhere in this letter, he urges them to live in such a way as to evoke respect rather than suspicion or antipathy. His first concern is that they should not be fearful. But they are also not to be 'intimidated' by others: on the contrary, by making Christ the holy centre of their lives, they are to be ready to defend their faith to anyone. They should do it, however, not with arrogance or contempt but with gentleness and reverence (perhaps a better translation would be 'respect'). In this way, they will keep their consciences clear, and if they are abused, it will not be their fault.

Christ suffered undeservedly and, all through history, so have his followers from time to time. Peter's warning is against provoking enmity by rudeness, arrogance or insensitivity.

14 November

COMING WITH THE CLOUDS

John to the seven churches that are in Asia: Grace to you and peace from him who is and who was and who is to come, and from the seven spirits who are before his throne, and from Jesus Christ, the faithful witness, the firstborn of the dead, and the ruler of the kings of the earth. To him who loves us and freed us from our sins by his blood, and made us to be a kingdom, priests serving his God and Father, to him be glory and dominion forever and ever. Amen. Look! He is coming with the clouds; every eye will see him, even those who pierced him; and on his account all the tribes of the earth will wail. So it is to be. Amen.

REVELATION 1:4–7

Many people reading these words will hear in them the echo of the great Advent hymn 'Lo, he comes with clouds descending'. Indeed, the whole book of Revelation is set in the context of a Church waiting for the Lord to come and deliver it from the time of persecution which had suddenly broken upon it. The writer, John, is 'in the Spirit' on the island of Patmos on 'the Lord's day' (Sunday) when he receives a series of astonishing visions (1:9–11). In this opening passage he sets the context for the visions that are to follow. Jesus, who died, is alive, the 'firstborn of the dead'—the prototype, we might say, of all those who will share his risen life through faith in him. He was crucified with the mocking accusation 'Jesus of Nazareth, the King of the Jews' (John 19:19), but now he is 'the ruler of the kings of the earth'. Not only that, but by his death and resurrection he has freed us from our sins and made us a kingdom, 'priests serving his God and Father'. This same Jesus will come again. That will be the story of Revelation, unfolding through both grim and glorious images. And that is the great hope that will always sustain Christians through times of persecution, ridicule or rejection.

'Christ has died. Christ is risen. Christ will come again.' It is easily said, but there is a triumphant hope in those words.

15 November

THE BEGINNING OF THE END

Peter, James, John and Andrew asked [Jesus] privately, 'Tell us, when will this be, and what will be the sign that all these things are about to be accomplished?' Then Jesus began to say to them, '... Many will come in my name and say, "I am he!" and they will lead many astray. When you hear of wars and rumours of wars, do not be alarmed; this must take place, but the end is still to come. For nation will rise against nation, and kingdom against kingdom; there will be earthquakes in various places; there will be famines. This is but the beginning of the birthpangs.'

MARK 13:3–8 (abridged)

This is part of the 'little apocalypse'—a kind of summary of Jesus' teaching about the 'last things'. It appears to bring together prophecies about events in the immediate future (the sacking of Jerusalem and the dispersion of the Jews, which happened in AD70) and others relating to the second coming of Christ, in a more distant future.

These opening answers undoubtedly relate to events that lay in the more immediate future. Jesus had remarked that the temple itself would be destroyed, and the four disciples wanted to know when this would happen and what warning there would be. Jesus' answer was that there would be no immediate 'sign'. In fact, what some people would take as 'signs' would be nothing more than natural occurrences. There would also be an abundance of false 'messiahs'. These were not signs of the 'end', but simply the beginning of 'birthpangs'.

Birthpangs are signs that something good will be born out of present suffering. Eventually, the terrible events would unfold that would bring to an end the tortured history of biblical Israel. Following an abortive uprising against the Romans, Jerusalem was destroyed and people fled, first to the country and then across the whole of the Middle East. The era of the 'dispersion' had begun.

It is hard not to be 'alarmed' when we hear of war and rumours of war, but it helps if we see them as 'birthpangs' of a new order.

16 November

THE END OF THE BEGINNING

'After that suffering, the sun will be darkened, and the moon will not give its light, and the stars will be falling from heaven, and the powers in the heavens will be shaken. Then they will see "the Son of Man coming in clouds" with great power and glory. Then he will send out the angels, and gather his elect from the four winds, from the ends of the earth to the ends of heaven... When you see these things taking place, you know that he is near, at the very gates. Truly I tell you, this generation will not pass away until all these things have taken place... But about that day or hour no one knows, neither the angels in heaven, nor the Son, but only the Father.'
MARK 13:24–27, 29–30, 32

Now the discourse moves into more distant realms. 'After that suffering' there will be events of cosmic significance. With 'great power and glory' the Son of Man (Jesus) would come again, gathering his chosen people from the ends of the earth.

At first sight there seems to be an inbuilt contradiction between the call of Jesus to observe the signs of his coming, which will tell them that it is 'near, at the very gates', and his clear statement that no one except the Father knows when it will take place. However, this should simply warn the wise Bible reader that this kind of prophetic writing is not to be treated like straight reportage of future events. To take it literally, without regard to its images and idioms, is to invite error.

It's likely that here Mark is combining prophecies about the immediate future (the destruction of the temple and the scattering of the Jewish people) with ones about the future coming of Jesus in glory. In essence, however, the message about both is the same: the Father knows! No one else does, but the people then, and God's people now, are not at the mercy of casual or accidental events. And the one who knows, cares.

What is the value of such prophecies? Surely, as Jesus says, because when the events happen, we can say, 'He told us so'—and faith will be confirmed.

17 November

LISTEN TO HIM!

And while [Jesus] was praying, the appearance of his face changed, and his clothes became dazzling white. Suddenly they saw two men, Moses and Elijah, talking to him… Now Peter and his companions were weighed down with sleep; but since they had stayed awake, they saw his glory and the two men who stood with him. Just as they were leaving him, Peter said to Jesus, 'Master, it is good for us to be here; let us make three dwellings, one for you, one for Moses, and one for Elijah'—not knowing what he said. While he was saying this, a cloud came and overshadowed them; and they were terrified as they entered the cloud. Then from the cloud came a voice that said, 'This is my Son, my Chosen; listen to him!'

LUKE 9:29–30, 32–35

This is Luke's account of the transfiguration, when Jesus appeared in his glory before three of his disciples. A week or so earlier, they had confessed for the first time their belief that Jesus was the Messiah. Now that confession of faith was to be confirmed in the most dramatic way. Jesus took them up a mountain and suddenly shone with heavenly glory. Two figures appeared with him, identified by the disciples (perhaps in that strange way we identify people in dreams?) as Moses, the giver of the Law, and Elijah, the first of the great Hebrew prophets. So 'the Law and the Prophets' met with Jesus and talked with him.

As Luke recounts it, there is something trance-like about the narrative (they were 'weighed down with sleep'). Peter then made a fatuous suggestion—that they should erect tents, one each for Jesus, Elijah and Moses. In that way, perhaps they could catch this amazing moment for ever! He didn't know what he was saying, we are told.

Finally a cloud covered the mountain and there was a voice. Its message was clear and simple, not unlike the heavenly voice at the baptism of Jesus: 'This is my Son, my Chosen' (see Luke 3:22). But this time there was a significant addition: 'listen to him!'

The Law and Prophets spoke of God and for God, but the Son spoke as God.

18 November

THE GOD OF THE LIVING

Jesus said to them, 'Those who belong to this age marry and are given in marriage; but those who are considered worthy of a place in that age and in the resurrection from the dead neither marry nor are given in marriage. Indeed they cannot die any more, because they are… children of the resurrection. And the fact that the dead are raised Moses himself showed, in the story about the bush, where he speaks of the Lord as the God of Abraham, the God of Isaac, and the God of Jacob. Now he is God not of the dead, but of the living; for to him all of them are alive.'

LUKE 20:34–38 (abridged)

These sayings of Jesus follow a bizarre attempt by the Sadducees to discredit belief in the resurrection of the dead, which Jesus (like the Pharisees and most Jews of his time) believed in. They had concocted a hypothetical case in which a woman had had seven husbands, six of whom died before she also died. The seven men were all brothers, obeying the principle that they should marry their brother's widow and raise up children for him. The Sadducees wanted to know whose husband the woman would be 'in the resurrection'.

Jesus turned the argument against them on the evidence of the Pentateuch, the 'books of Moses', which were the only scriptures they regarded as authentic. First, however, he enunciated a fundamental principle, which it is very easy to overlook. The resurrection life is not simply a 'second innings' of this one. It is life on an entirely different plane—real, recognizable, but different. In heaven all such questions will be meaningless. Love will survive, but not the exclusivity of relationships. There will be no such thing as marriage (nor, of course, death and widowhood).

As for the resurrection principle, hadn't they noticed? It is enshrined in the books of Moses, where God is called the 'God of Abraham, Isaac and Jacob'. He couldn't be the God of corpses, could he?

'To him, all are alive'—yes, and so are we, and those we have loved.

19 November

GOD, THE PAST AND THE FUTURE

He has made everything suitable for its time; moreover he has put a sense of past and future into their minds, yet they cannot find out what God has done from the beginning to the end. I know that there is nothing better for them than to be happy and enjoy themselves as long as they live; moreover, it is God's gift that all should eat and drink and take pleasure in all their toil. I know that whatever God does endures forever; nothing can be added to it, nor anything taken from it; God has done this, so that all should stand in awe before him. That which is, already has been; that which is to be, already is; and God seeks out what has gone by.

ECCLESIASTES 3:11 — 15

The 'Teacher', or 'Preacher', who wrote Ecclesiastes, is often seen as something of a fatalist: 'What's going to happen will happen, and there's nothing you can do about it!' But in fact his message is not so much about fatalism as faith. Things happen—we can't predict them and we can't alter what has already taken place—but we can be confident that behind everything that happens is the eternal God, in whose hands we must rest our lives and before whose almighty will we can only bow in awe.

This sense of awe springs from our awareness of past and future. The past is gone but it profoundly influences our present lives. Some of us are slaves to it, reliving our past failures and disappointments or living our lives in a golden age (as we seem to remember it) which has gone for ever. For the Teacher, however, both our past and our future are located within God's glorious wisdom. We can neither change the past nor dictate the future. What we can know, he says, is the serenity of faith. If both past and future are in God's hands, then we can 'be happy and enjoy ourselves' in the present.

To live a fulfilled life now, we need to put the past into God's hands (past sins forgiven, memories healed) and trust him for the future (which he knows, and we don't).

20 November

THE DAMASCUS ROAD

Saul, still breathing threats and murder against the disciples of the Lord, went to the high priest and asked him for letters to the synagogues at Damascus, so that if he found any who belonged to the Way… he might bring them bound to Jerusalem. Now as he was going along and approaching Damascus, suddenly a light from heaven flashed around him. He fell to the ground and heard a voice saying to him, 'Saul, Saul, why do you persecute me?' He asked, 'Who are you, Lord?' The reply came, 'I am Jesus, whom you are persecuting. But get up and enter the city, and you will be told what you are to do.' The men who were travelling with him stood speechless because they heard the voice but saw no one. Saul got up from the ground, and though his eyes were open, he could see nothing; so they led him by the hand and brought him into Damascus.

ACTS 9:1–8 (abridged)

This is, of course, the 'original' Damascus road experience, when someone's life is completely turned around. The 'someone' in this case was Saul of Tarsus, to be known later as Paul, the apostle to the Gentiles and preacher of the Christian gospel. At this point, however, he was 'breathing threats and murder' against the emerging Christian community. Saul was a Pharisee, a man who had studied under the great teacher Gamaliel, and he saw this new 'Way' as a threat to the ancient religion of his people. Bearing letters of authority, he was on his way to the town of Damascus when this incident occurred.

The story is told with characteristic colour and detail by Luke—the conversation between the 'voice' and the astounded Pharisee, the reaction of his companions, and the result of it all—Saul, eyes open but blinded, being led by the hand into the city. The heresy hunter went meekly into Damascus, where a somewhat sceptical Christian leader, Ananias, laid hands on him, restored his sight and baptized him.

'Who are you, Lord?' Saul had enquired anxiously—to be told, 'I am Jesus'. Perhaps that question and answer offer the first steps to every true conversion.

21 November

WHERE WE COME FROM

The God who made the world and everything in it, he who is Lord of heaven and earth, does not live in shrines made by human hands, nor is he served by human hands, as though he needed anything, since he himself gives to all mortals life and breath and all things. From one ancestor he made all nations to inhabit the whole earth, and he allotted the times of their existence and the boundaries of the places where they would live, so that they would search for God and perhaps grope for him and find him—though indeed he is not far from each one of us. For 'In him we live and move and have our being.'

ACTS 17:24–28

Paul had been invited to address the Areopagus in Athens, a kind of cultural council, after disputing in the marketplace with the two main philosophical groups of the day, the Epicureans and the Stoics. Put crudely, the former thought that as this life is all we have, it should be lived to the full. The latter believed that as this life is all we have, it should be endured with patience and fortitude, thus demonstrating the nobility of humanity. Paul had preached to them 'Jesus and the resurrection' (v. 18). They seem to have missed the point rather fundamentally but were intrigued enough to offer this invitation, and Paul the evangelist was not one to pass up such a strategic opportunity.

Cleverly, he began his speech where they were, with the belief, shared by most if not all of his hearers, that 'the Lord of heaven and earth' was the source of everything that exists, including human life. Such an omnipotent being could hardly be confined to human shrines, because he was the source of the life and energy that erected them. All peoples were his creatures and his intention was that during their life on earth they should search for him and perhaps find him. In truth, however, he is not elusive. He is 'not far from each one of us'.

'In him we live and move and have our being': a Greek poet may have said it first, but in many ways it is the foundation of all faith.

22 November

WHERE WE ARE GOING

'Since we are God's offspring, we ought not to think that the deity is like gold, or silver, or stone... While God has overlooked the times of human ignorance, now he commands all people everywhere to repent, because he has fixed a day on which he will have the world judged in righteousness by a man whom he has appointed, and of this he has given assurance to all by raising him from the dead.' When they heard of the resurrection of the dead, some scoffed; but others said, 'We will hear you again about this.' ... Some of them joined him and became believers, including Dionysius the Areopagite and a woman named Damaris, and others with them.

ACTS 17:29–32, 34 (abridged)

While the Areopagus had listened politely to the first part of Paul's speech, appreciating its universalism, as he went on doubts began to arise. First, he appeared to pour scorn on the images, altars and temples that were such a feature of the city of Athens. These, he said, were products of 'human ignorance'—and we may imagine that this went down badly in the intellectual capital of the world! The time had now come for 'repentance', a fundamental change of heart and mind. Indeed, God had already fixed a day when the world would be judged 'in righteousness' by someone he had appointed. This universal judge was not named by Paul, but the one chosen for the task had been authenticated by the fact that God had raised him from the dead.

That was one step too far for most members of the Areopagus. Nevertheless, even from that august body there were converts: Dionysius (a member of the Areopagus, no less), 'a woman named Damaris' and some others. Some have suggested that there were few converts because Paul had preached a watered-down gospel. All I can say is that if I were invited to address the Royal Society, say, and achieved a similar response, I would be more than delighted!

Innocent ignorance is perhaps excusable; obstinately to resist what we know to be true is not.

23 November

TOGETHER, UNTIL THE HARVEST

'The kingdom of heaven may be compared to someone who sowed good seed in his field; but while everybody was asleep, an enemy came and sowed weeds among the wheat… So when the plants came up and bore grain, then the weeds appeared as well. And the slaves of the householder came and said to him, "Master, did you not sow good seed in your field? Where, then, did these weeds come from?" He answered, "An enemy has done this." The slaves said to him, "Then do you want us to go and gather them?" But he replied, "No; for in gathering the weeds you would uproot the wheat… Let both of them grow together until the harvest; and at harvest time I will tell the reapers, Collect the weeds first and bind them in bundles to be burned, but gather the wheat into my barn."'

MATTHEW 13:24–30 (abridged)

Sometimes only a story can illuminate the deepest mysteries. Here, in one of his kingdom parables, Jesus deals with one of the most intractable of them: how a loving Creator will deal with the presence of evil in his creation. He does it in a story of timeless relevance, but particularly so for a crowd who lived by sowing, growing and reaping.

A farmer sowed *good* seed, it is emphasized. There was nothing wrong with his initial project. However, in the night an 'enemy' came and sowed weeds in the same field, so that when the crop began to appear, wheat and weeds were growing alongside each other. The labourers had a suggestion—though a tedious and back-breaking one. They could go painstakingly through the field and remove the weeds. The farmer tells them not to do it, because in the process they would uproot the good wheat as well as the weeds. At harvest the reapers could separate the weeds from the wheat, the former for burning in a bonfire, the latter for gathering into the owner's barns.

Throughout the story, the owner is in charge of his field. In the end, the enemy's work will be frustrated and the owner's crops gathered into his barns. This is really a story of the ultimate triumph of good over evil.

24 November

A VISION OF GOD

Over the heads of the living creatures there was something like a dome, shining like crystal... And above the dome over their heads there was something like a throne, in appearance like sapphire; and seated above the likeness of a throne was something that seemed like a human form. Upward from what appeared like the loins I saw something like gleaming amber... and downward from what looked like the loins I saw something that looked like fire, and there was a splendour all around. Like the bow in a cloud on a rainy day, such was the appearance of the splendour all around. This was the appearance of the likeness of the glory of the Lord. When I saw it, I fell on my face, and I heard the voice of someone speaking.

EZEKIEL 1:22, 26–28 (abridged)

A few years ago I invited the children in our village junior school to listen to this passage from the prophet Ezekiel and then try to draw his vision of the glory of God. The result was startling—mainly because children like to think in pictures, and the whole of this opening chapter is simply full of pictures. There are mysterious creatures with wings, and faces that suggest human, lion, ox and eagle. There is a terrible machine with 'wheels within wheels' and eyes in the rims of them. There are thunder and lightning and burning coals of fire.

Then, as the vision clarifies, there is this magnificent description of the dome above it all, with a throne on the dome, and on the throne 'something that seemed like a human form'. The most vivid image is kept until last: 'like the bow in a cloud on a rainy day, such was the appearance of the splendour all around'. Ezekiel doesn't claim that, even in this vision, he actually saw God. What he believed he had perceived was 'the appearance of the likeness of the glory of the Lord'.

This wonderful vision, awesome yet beautiful, brought the prophet to his knees. He 'fell on his face', and then heard the voice of someone speaking. It was the voice of God; of that he never had any doubt.

Awesome and beautiful—those two words seem to sum up the nature of God.

25 November

THE GREAT MULTITUDE

I looked, and there was a great multitude that no one could count, from every nation, from all tribes and peoples and languages, standing before the throne and before the Lamb, robed in white, with palm branches in their hands. They cried out in a loud voice, saying, 'Salvation belongs to our God who is seated on the throne, and to the Lamb!' And all the angels stood around the throne and around the elders and the four living creatures, and they fell on their faces before the throne and worshipped God, singing, 'Amen! Blessing and glory and wisdom and thanksgiving and honour and power and might be to our God forever and ever! Amen.'
REVELATION 7:9–12

People often wonder what heaven will be like, and are a bit disappointed to hear that nobody really knows. All we're told about heaven in the Bible is that it is 'like' something else. Jesus would say, 'The kingdom of heaven is like…' and then add any one of a long list of similes: a net of fish, a field, a king going into a far country, a banquet, a farmer sowing seed, a priceless pearl. Then we have visions, like this one from Revelation, which in vivid language offer us pictures of a place of infinite beauty, worship, security and love.

If they seem a bit like dream sequences in a film, that's perhaps not a bad way to understand them. After all, it simply isn't possible for a human being, tied to earth, time and space, to begin to understand that 'other' dimension of living which is heaven. It is life lived in the presence of God but in the company of all his people from every age, every nation and every language. It is futile and potentially misleading to treat these visions as literal forecasts or descriptions, but we are entitled to look at them with the eyes of faith and to learn what we can from them. When we do, they can teach us truths that are beyond human reason.

The most striking thing about this passage is the utter centrality of God and of the 'Lamb', in heaven. At last, the Creator and his creation are at one!

26 November

THE FINAL VICTORY

Flesh and blood cannot inherit the kingdom of God, nor does the perishable inherit the imperishable. Listen, I will tell you a mystery! We will not all die, but we will all be changed, in a moment, in the twinkling of an eye, at the last trumpet. For the trumpet will sound, and the dead will be raised imperishable, and we will be changed. For this perishable body must put on imperishability, and this mortal body must put on immortality… 'Where, O death, is your victory? Where, O death, is your sting?' The sting of death is sin, and the power of sin is the law. But thanks be to God, who gives us the victory through our Lord Jesus Christ.

1 CORINTHIANS 15:50–53, 55–57

This is the climax of a long and complicated argument by the apostle Paul about the certainty of resurrection. He began it with a reiteration of the foundational truths of the gospel, which he was taught after his conversion—that Christ died for our sins, was buried, rose again and was seen by many witnesses. From this he moved on to the resurrection of those who are 'in Christ', his usual description of Christian believers. We too will be raised from death, as Christ was.

But what will the resurrection body be like? Paul's answer is a series of metaphors, including that of a seed being sown. What grows as a result bears a continuity of life with the seed, yet it is in other ways very different—better, more beautiful. Where human beings are concerned, the 'seed' of our dead bodies will produce an immortal resurrection body, sharing a continuity of life (we shall be the same 'persons'), yet different. What was 'sown' as physical is raised as spiritual.

From that point, this climax to the argument takes over. Flesh and blood can't inherit the kingdom of heaven, but 'we will be changed' into new people, living in new bodies, resurrection bodies, designed for life in God's eternal kingdom. Death will be swallowed up in victory, and the consequences of sin finally laid to rest.

That glorious victory is the work of Jesus Christ. 'Thanks be to God!'

27 November

THE MIND OF CHRIST

Let the same mind be in you that was in Christ Jesus, who, though he was in the form of God, did not regard equality with God as something to be exploited, but emptied himself, taking the form of a slave, being born in human likeness. And being found in human form, he humbled himself and became obedient to the point of death—even death on a cross. Therefore God also highly exalted him and gave him the name that is above every name, so that at the name of Jesus every knee should bend, in heaven and on earth and under the earth, and every tongue should confess that Jesus Christ is Lord, to the glory of God the Father.

PHILIPPIANS 2:5–11

This is probably a hymn from the early Church, quoted by Paul to make a particular point about the virtue of humility. We are, in short, to cultivate the 'mind of Christ'. Jesus had not grasped at the divine status which was his by nature, but for the sake of God's fallen creatures had 'emptied himself', accepting the status of human being—and not an ordinary, respectable one, either, but a 'slave'.

This passage is quite explicit about the divinity of Christ. The word 'form' translates the Greek word *morphe*, which means 'nature'. Jesus was in very nature divine. But when he came among us 'in the flesh', he became in very nature human. In one sentence the whole mystery of the incarnation is revealed. That was not the end of the story, of course. Jesus did not just humble himself to slavery, but to crucifixion—the shameful death of a common criminal. This was true humility, revealing the 'mind of Christ', which the Philippians should emulate.

But even that was not the end of the story. 'Therefore' (because he was prepared to accept this self-emptying for the sake of others) 'God highly exalted him'. He gave him 'the name above all other names'—'Jesus', the Saviour—and one day in the future every tongue will confess Jesus the Messiah as Lord, to God's glory.

'Let the same mind be in you,' Paul told the Philippians. May it be in us, too.

28 November

THE END OF THE RACE

As for me, I am already being poured out as a libation, and the time of my departure has come. I have fought the good fight, I have finished the race, I have kept the faith. From now on there is reserved for me the crown of righteousness, which the Lord, the righteous judge, will give me on that day, and not only to me but also to all who have longed for his appearing.
2 TIMOTHY 4:6–8

These may well be among the last words dictated by Paul before his execution: he was probably martyred in Rome in AD62. There is a true nobility about them, reflecting the confidence of his faith and memorably expressing the heart of the Christian's hope for the future.

Scholars have questioned whether this second letter to Timothy is Paul's own work, partly because the literary style is different from his earlier letters. This may be due to the use of a different secretary, or the letter may be someone else's compilation of the apostle's writings and sayings. However, the personal greetings at the end and the references to Mark, Luke and Tychicus suggest the hand of Paul.

In any case, it is hard not to be moved by these words. 'Poured out as a libation' refers to the practice, common in ancient Rome, of pouring a drink on the altar or on the floor as an offering of worship to a deity. That was how Paul now saw his life: an offering poured out for God. In the light of that, he was not apprehensive. He had 'fought the good fight'—the just war against evil and unbelief. He had 'kept the faith'—remained loyal to what had been revealed to him. Best of all (and there is much evidence that Paul was fascinated by the athletic games so loved by the Greeks), he had 'finished the race' and now awaited the 'crown' of laurel leaves given by the Master of the Games to the winner.

The 'crown' was for the winner, yet Paul says that it will be given to 'all who have longed for [Christ's] appearing'. In this race, there is not just one gold medal for one winner. All who finish the race receive the crown!

29 November

THE CITY OF GOD

I saw no temple in the city, for its temple is the Lord God the Almighty and the Lamb. And the city has no need of sun or moon to shine on it, for the glory of God is its light, and its lamp is the Lamb. The nations will walk by its light, and the kings of the earth will bring their glory into it. Its gates will never be shut by day—and there will be no night there. People will bring into it the glory and the honour of the nations. But nothing unclean will enter it, nor anyone who practises abomination or falsehood, but only those who are written in the Lamb's book of life.
REVELATION 21:22–27

The final triumphant vision in the Bible is of the city of God. This image is one that every human for the past three millennia would understand—a place of commerce, government, administration and (in ancient times, especially) security. Cities were walled, with stout gates, barred at night. Warriors guarded the entrances by day. People from the countryside would make for the cities in times of trouble, to find shelter. There was work in the city and worship in its temples.

This city, however, is different. It is the city of God, the final home of his people. Allow for the visionary language but then enjoy the images of security, peace, purity. The streets are not lit by lamps but by the glory of the Lamb, Jesus. This is a city without crime and without enemies, where the gates are never locked. Within its walls dwell people of many nations, each bringing their distinctive gifts.

When he first became aware of the onset of old age, Malcolm Muggeridge wrote, 'I see in the darkness and in the distance a glow in the sky... [and I know] a certainty surpassing all words and thoughts, that... I am a participant in his purposes, which are loving and not malign, creative and not destructive, orderly and not chaotic, universal and not particular. And in that certainty, a great peace and a great joy.'

'Nothing unclean will enter it.' Heaven would not be heaven if it included sin. The Lamb of God died to 'take away the sin of the world' (John 1:29).

30 November

THE BEAUTIFUL FEET

How beautiful upon the mountains are the feet of the messenger who announces peace, who brings good news, who announces salvation, who says to Zion, 'Your God reigns.' Listen! Your sentinels lift up their voices, together they sing for joy; for in plain sight they see the return of the Lord to Zion. Break forth together into singing, you ruins of Jerusalem; for the Lord has comforted his people, he has redeemed Jerusalem. The Lord has bared his holy arm before the eyes of all the nations; and all the ends of the earth shall see the salvation of our God.

ISAIAH 52:7–10

Feet aren't very beautiful, actually. A few years ago I washed the feet of a large congregation of people, and 'beautiful' would be the last word one would apply to the miscellaneous exhibition of knobs, bunions, blotches and misshapen toes that were unveiled before my eyes. Mind you, I couldn't really complain. My feet had been washed first, by a colleague, and I hardly think they offered a pretty sight. So the beauty here is spiritual. There is something intrinsically lovely about the journey of a messenger of good news. Their feet hurry and their message is welcome. As they make their way across the mountains with their wonderful tidings, they can't wait to share it with the people.

And what is this 'good news'? Why, it is of the victory of the Prince of Peace. The Lord has revealed his power (his 'holy arm'), not in judgment but in salvation. He has 'comforted his people'. At last the whole world will hear the good news; the 'ends of the earth' will celebrate the salvation of our God.

Paul quotes this very prophecy in his letter to the Romans (10:15), but now the message brought by the messengers is 'the word of Christ', the saving gospel. Everyone who calls on the name of the Lord shall be saved—but first they must hear the good news.

'Your God reigns.' That is the heart of the good news: God has acted, and his action is to bring healing and salvation to a stricken world.

December: Living in family

This month culminates in the feast of Christmas, which—even for those who are not religious—is a festival of the family. God's purpose from the very beginning was to create and bless families (as we shall see), and eventually the greatest of all families is that of his children, with himself and his Son, Jesus, as its joint heads. The Bible honours and cherishes the whole idea of family, but also teaches the responsibilities that that involves. 'Living in family' is our December theme.

1 December

A FAMILY AND A FLOOD

[And God said to Noah], 'For my part, I am going to bring a flood of waters on the earth, to destroy from under heaven all flesh in which is the breath of life… But I will establish my covenant with you; and you shall come into the ark, you, your sons, your wife, and your sons' wives with you. And of every living thing, of all flesh, you shall bring two of every kind into the ark, to keep them alive with you; they shall be male and female.
GENESIS 6:17–19 (abridged)

Everyone knows the story of Noah's flood, though they usually get it wrong! For a start, it wasn't Noah's flood, but God's, which immediately raises a problem. Why would God wish to destroy every living creature on the earth? Is this an example of the Creator behaving like a short-tempered human being and reacting in angry frustration? The story could be read that way but there is, of course, much more to it than that. Genesis has already brought us the story of the first act of human disobedience, by Adam and Eve, and then some of the ugly consequences—the first murder, for instance, committed by Cain. When the Lord saw that 'every inclination of the thoughts of (human) hearts was only evil continually' (6:5), he was sorry he had made humankind, and resolved to wipe it out and start again.

As usual with these biblical stories, we must ask, before anything else, what is the meaning of it? The answer, surely, must be that in the face of disobedience there were several options open to God, and one of them was to cancel what he had done and start again. In this story, we can see how a different and better 'Plan B' was instigated. Yes, there would be a flood and many would perish in it, but a 'remnant' would be preserved so that they could replenish the planet. For this he chose one God-fearing family: Noah, his wife, his sons and their wives. This one family would represent the entire human race, just as two chosen animals would represent each species of animal, bird and serpent.

Even in days of sin and confusion, God's love embraced the faithful family.

2 December

FAMILY LOVE

Be subject to one another out of reverence for Christ. Wives, be subject to your husbands as you are to the Lord. For the husband is the head of the wife just as Christ is the head of the church... Husbands, love your wives, just as Christ loved the church and gave himself up for her, in order to make her holy by cleansing her with the washing of water by the word, so as to present the church to himself in splendour, without a spot or wrinkle or anything of the kind... In the same way, husbands should love their wives as they do their own bodies. He who loves his wife loves himself. For no one ever hates his own body, but he nourishes and tenderly cares for it, just as Christ does for the church, because we are members of his body.

EPHESIANS 5:21–23, 25–30 (abridged)

As you read this, allow for the vast cultural differences between the first century and the 21st! In the world of that day, this was radical teaching, laying an equal (but different) obligation on both husbands and wives. All Christians were to 'be subject to one another' as a general rule. Wives would express this most evidently by 'submission' to their husbands. While husbands would share in the general obligation to be 'subject' to others, including their wives, they had a particular and demanding requirement to meet: they must love their wives 'as they do their own bodies'. Their conjugal love was to be as sacrificial as Christ's was for us. It's hard to argue, then, that the men got off lightly compared to the women!

The father is, Paul argues, the 'head' of the family, but this is qualified by the comparison that follows: 'as Christ is the head of the Church'. This is no endorsement of heavy-handed autocracy but, again, of self-giving love. Respect has to be earned, and so does headship. There will be occasions when, for various reasons, the man can no longer be head of the family, and the woman assumes that role: perhaps Lydia (Acts 16:15) falls into this category.

We are all subject to Christ, so why is it so hard to be 'subject' to one another?

3 December

THE HOUSE OF WISDOM

Wisdom has built her house, she has hewn her seven pillars. She has slaughtered her animals, she has mixed her wine, she has also set her table. She has sent out her servant girls, she calls from the highest places in the town, 'You that are simple, turn in here!' To those without sense she says, 'Come, eat of my bread and drink of the wine I have mixed. Lay aside immaturity, and live, and walk in the way of insight.'

PROVERBS 9:1–6

There are many 'houses' in the Bible: any name beginning 'beth...' means 'house of'. Here we have the house of wisdom—for the writers of Proverbs, probably the best kind of house to live in. 'Wisdom' means insight, understanding. The key to it isn't three years at a university or a library full of books, but 'the fear of the Lord'. That is the foundation and bedrock of true wisdom, in Jewish thought.

Wisdom is often seen as a wise woman. Here, her house has seven pillars, the number of perfection. She has been preparing a splendid meal, with freshly slaughtered meat and newly mixed wine. Everything is ready for Wisdom's guests. Who are they to be? Amazingly, they are the 'simple'—meaning those uncomplicated souls whose hearts and minds are open but uncluttered. They are 'without sense' but not without hope; and, because their disability is not wilful, they are 'immature' rather than stupid. In any case, they are welcome guests at Wisdom's table, and there, as they eat the meat and drink the wine, they can find 'insight'—true wisdom—for themselves.

The invitation comes to them from the highest places in town, even though they might be considered the lowliest of its residents. In terms that echo through the scriptures, they are called to eat bread and drink wine. They must, as an act of will, 'lay aside immaturity'. They have to want the gift of spiritual insight. When they receive it, they will 'live'.

The home that seeks true wisdom will be the one where the whole family learns and grows together in insight and understanding of the ways of God.

4 December

YOUTH AND AGE

Remember now thy Creator in the days of thy youth, while the evil days come not, nor the years draw nigh, when thou shalt say, I have no pleasure in them… In the day when the keepers of the house shall tremble, and the strong men shall bow themselves, and the grinders cease because they are few, and those that look out of the windows be darkened… and he shall rise up at the voice of the bird, and all the daughters of musick shall be brought low. Also when they shall be afraid of that which is high, and fears shall be in the way… and desire shall fail: because man goeth to his long home, and the mourners go about the streets… Then shall the dust return to the earth as it was: and the spirit shall return unto God who gave it.

ECCLESIASTES 12:1, 3–5, 7 (KJV, abridged)

This is probably one of the finest examples of Hebrew poetry, and the King James Bible magnificently captures its haunting, sad refrain. It is ostensibly a call to young people to be responsive to God while they are young, because the inevitable years of decline lie ahead.

Many of us will recognize the symptoms of ageing listed here, though the beauty of the language perhaps takes the edge off our regrets. Most will identify with the writer's metaphors—the 'strong men' for the failing limbs, the 'grinders' for the disappearing teeth, 'those who look out of the windows' for the fading eyesight. Others—especially men, I think—will relate to the early rising ('at the voice of the bird') at the call of nature!

Modern medicine means that people live longer, and with fewer distressing symptoms, than earlier generations, but nothing can stave off for ever the march of time. In the end, we shall go to our 'long home'. In a reversal of our creation, the dust will return to the earth as it was before God shaped it into a human being, and the spirit—the breath of his life—will return to the one who gave it (Genesis 2:7).

Although we should 'remember' our Creator when we are young, the wonderful truth is that it's never too late!

5 December

EVERYTHING IN ITS SEASON

To every thing there is a season, and a time to every purpose under the heaven: A time to be born, and a time to die; a time to plant, and a time to pluck up that which is planted; A time to kill, and a time to heal; a time to break down, and a time to build up; A time to weep, and a time to laugh; a time to mourn, and a time to dance; A time to cast away stones, and a time to gather stones together; a time to embrace, and a time to refrain from embracing; A time to get, and a time to lose; a time to keep, and a time to cast away; A time to rend, and a time to sew; a time to keep silence, and a time to speak; A time to love, and a time to hate; a time of war, and a time of peace.

ECCLESIASTES 3:1–8 (KJV)

If I ask my wife, 'What's the time?' she might answer, 'Ten past nine' or she might say, 'Time you changed that shirt!' 'Time' can mean the time on the clock and 'time' in the sense of the appropriate moment. The Greeks (of course!) had words to distinguish the two meanings—*chronos* for the first and *kairos* for the second. In this passage from Ecclesiastes, the 'time' is not connected with clocks but with human moments of choice. Time is a gift and we are called to use it wisely.

Life in community really depends on everyone having at least some grasp of this principle. There is a time to speak but there is also a time to hold our tongues—however justified an outburst might be. There is a time to laugh but there is also a time to weep, and it is woefully insensitive to get it wrong. We are, as Paul put it, to 'rejoice with those who rejoice, weep with those who weep' (Romans 12:15, NRSV).

These words were the lyrics of a very popular song 40 years ago, speaking to a generation living under the shadow of nuclear warfare. Their simple message of doing the right thing at the right moment is equally important now, but perhaps more readily ignored.

'It is now the moment for you to wake from sleep. For salvation is nearer to us now than when we became believers' (Romans 13:11).

6 December

ALL EQUAL IN THIS FAMILY

My brothers and sisters, do you with your acts of favouritism really believe in our glorious Lord Jesus Christ? For if a person with gold rings and in fine clothes comes into your assembly, and if a poor person in dirty clothes also comes in, and if you take notice of the one wearing the fine clothes and say, 'Have a seat here, please,' while to the one who is poor you say, 'Stand there,' or, 'Sit at my feet,' have you not made distinctions among yourselves, and become judges with evil thoughts? … You do well if you really fulfil the royal law according to the scripture, 'You shall love your neighbour as yourself.' But if you show partiality, you commit sin and are convicted by the law as transgressors.

JAMES 2:1–4, 8–9

The commandment to 'love your neighbour' is interpreted by most of us as 'don't be horrid to him/her'. But James, in his splendidly earthy letter, challenges this kind of compromise head on. To practise what he calls 'favouritism' is nothing less than a failure of belief in 'our glorious Lord Jesus Christ'. What on earth could he mean?

Favouritism is to prefer one person before another—to treat them differently. Of course we all love some people more than others, but that's not the same as giving preference to them. In the sight of Jesus, all stand equal in need of forgiveness and grace, equal in God's love.

The principle is not the problem, but the practice—and James' example of the two visitors to a church gathering just about sums it up. We might not, in our more egalitarian world, quite so openly fawn on the wealthy visitor or be quite so rude to the smelly vagrant. Nevertheless, we know in our hearts which visitor we should prefer to have. And in that preference, we unwittingly betray Jesus and his gospel. He came not for the 'righteous', but for sinners, showing the love of God to the unloved and unwanted. Thus the gospel turns the world's values upside down and challenges us to do the same.

God has no 'favourites' (Acts 10:34). Neither should we.

7 December

A FAMILY TRANSFORMED

About midnight Paul and Silas were praying and singing hymns to God... Suddenly there was an earthquake, so violent that the foundations of the prison were shaken; and immediately all the doors were opened and everyone's chains were unfastened. When the jailer woke up and saw the prison doors wide open, he drew his sword and was about to kill himself, since he supposed that the prisoners had escaped. But Paul shouted in a loud voice, 'Do not harm yourself, for we are all here.' The jailer... fell down trembling before Paul and Silas. Then he brought them outside and said, 'Sirs, what must I do to be saved?' They answered, 'Believe on the Lord Jesus, and you will be saved, you and your household.' They spoke the word of the Lord to him and to all who were in his house.

ACTS 16:25–32 (abridged)

We know nothing more about this jailer in Philippi, but the events of that momentous night earned him a place in the book of Acts and in the kingdom of heaven. He had been entrusted with two most unusual prisoners—a pair of preachers who had caused a local disturbance, Paul and Silas. They spent the night singing hymns—probably not the normal nocturnal soundtrack in the prison. When an earthquake caused the doors to fly open, the jailer assumed that his prisoners had escaped, which would mean the death penalty for him. He drew his sword, preferring suicide to execution, but Paul shouted to him not to harm himself. Astonished, the guard ran in and fell down trembling before them. His question presumably meant, what should he do to save his skin, but no honest evangelist could resist an invitation like that! 'Believe on the Lord Jesus', came the answer, to be followed by a promise. If he did so, he would be 'saved', and his household, too.

When their wounds had been washed and a meal eaten together, Paul and Silas 'spoke the word' to the jailer and his household and the whole family were baptized without delay (v. 33).

The gospel of Christ not only changes individuals, but whole households.

8 December

FAMILY LIFE: REST AND RESPECT

Remember the sabbath day, and keep it holy. Six days you shall labour and do all your work. But the seventh day is a sabbath to the Lord your God; you shall not do any work—you, your son or your daughter, your male or female slave, your livestock, or the alien resident in your towns. For in six days the Lord made heaven and earth, the sea, and all that is in them, but rested the seventh day; therefore the Lord blessed the sabbath day and consecrated it.

EXODUS 20:8–11

This is familiar as one of the Ten Commandments, the core principles of the Law which God revealed through Moses and which became the true heart of the Jewish religion. This law deals with what we would call the life–work balance, and it is as relevant in the 21st century as it was 3000 years ago.

The principle of 'sabbath' is deeply rooted in Jewish thought. It arose from the fascinating notion that even the Creator needed to rest after his work of creation. In six days, the universe was brought into being; on the seventh, its architect and maker rested: 'therefore the Lord blessed the sabbath day and consecrated it'. We don't have to believe in a literal six-day creation to see the wise principle being set out here. After work, rest; after rest, work. There is to be a balance and rhythm to life, which ensures that work does not become drudgery and rest is seen not as idleness but as 'holy'. We lose the principle of sabbath rest at our peril. God has not made us to be perpetual, ant-like busybodies. Into his scheme of things he has built rest, and while we may not observe it in the same way as those rural people long ago, our lives will be impoverished without it.

The Church moved the day of rest from the seventh day to the first to celebrate the day of the resurrection of Jesus, not to deny the sabbath principle. Christians also need to rest!

9 December

A SERVANT HEALED

A centurion… had a slave whom he valued highly, and who was ill and close to death. When he heard about Jesus, he sent some Jewish elders to him, asking him to come and heal his slave. When they came to Jesus, they appealed to him earnestly, saying, 'He is worthy of having you do this for him, for he loves our people, and it is he who built our synagogue for us.' … When [Jesus] was not far from the house, the centurion sent friends to say to him, 'Lord, do not trouble yourself, for I am not worthy to have you come under my roof… But only speak the word, and let my servant be healed. For I also am a man set under authority, with soldiers under me; and I say to one, "Go," and he goes, and to another, "Come," and he comes…' When Jesus heard this he was amazed at him, and… said, 'I tell you, not even in Israel have I found such faith.' When those who had been sent returned to the house, they found the slave in good health.

LUKE 7:2–10 (abridged)

Centurions (junior officers of the Roman occupying army) get a good press in the Gospels. Here one of them sends a message to Jesus, seeking healing for his slave. Clearly there was much more than simply domestic concern being expressed. He 'valued' the slave—perhaps a rather cool translation. To say that the slave was 'dear' to him might reflect the meaning better. The Jewish elders sent as his go-betweens also spoke of the centurion's respect for their people and religion.

Jesus agreed to go with them, but the centurion sent friends to tell him not to trouble himself. He was not worthy to welcome him into his house. If Jesus simply 'spoke the word', he knew that his servant would be healed. He gave his reason: authority. He himself was both under it and exercised it, and he recognized that Jesus, too, was under the authority of God and also wielded that authority on earth. Jesus' response was amazement: he had not seen such faith before, 'not even in Israel'. He spoke the word, and the servant was healed.

We should respect faith wherever we find it, even in unexpected places.

10 December

ALL ONE IN CHRIST JESUS

But now that faith has come, we are no longer subject to a disciplinarian, for in Christ Jesus you are all children of God through faith. As many of you as were baptized into Christ have clothed yourselves with Christ. There is no longer Jew or Greek, there is no longer slave or free, there is no longer male and female; for all of you are one in Christ Jesus.
GALATIANS 3:25–28

Readers may wonder what 'disciplinarians' have to do with the gospel! The word is actually *pedagogus*—'pedagogue', teacher, trainer. Having found faith, the believers no longer needed a 'trainer' or 'teacher': they were now children in God's family. That thought led Paul on. They had been 'baptized into Christ'; they were 'clothed with Christ'. This may be a reference to the white robe that was wrapped around the newly baptized. Being completely his, they are members of a family—and in a family there is no distinction of status. So, 'in Christ Jesus' they are all one: Jew, Greek, slave, freeman, man or woman.

To us this may seem obvious, though in practice we may still encounter class, ethnic or gender divisions in our churches. But in the first century it was revolutionary. When the church met in Corinth, for example, the Christians would sit together around one table—wealthy patricians, merchants and slave owners. Alongside them at the same table would be poor people, ex-criminals, slaves. There would be people of many nationalities—Romans, Greeks, Jews, North Africans and people from Asia Minor. And there would be men and women—not segregated, as they would have been in the synagogue, but side by side. As Paul thought of that motley collection, he must have realized that there had never, in the history of the human race, been a gathering like this. Astonishingly, they were visibly 'one in Christ Jesus'.

In a world still divided by culture, nationality, gender and status, it remains necessary to fight to maintain this 'freedom of the glory of the children of God' (Romans 8:21).

11 December

TELL THE CHILDREN

'You shall observe this rite as a perpetual ordinance for you and your children… And when your children ask you, "What do you mean by this observance?" you shall say, "It is the passover sacrifice to the Lord, for he passed over the houses of the Israelites in Egypt, when he struck down the Egyptians but spared our houses."'

EXODUS 12:24, 26–27

An important feature of Jewish life, as we know, is the value attached to the family. Even given the pressures of life today, their families are still generally strong, warm and united. Much of this seems to stem from the children's respect for their parents. It is reinforced by the mother's role as the teacher of the children and by their involvement from an early age in the sabbath prayers and rituals, and also by the powerful annual impact of Passover.

Today's passage comes at the end of the instructions given to the Israelites for the Passover, so that they would be spared the judgment meted out on the firstborn sons of Egypt, the final deadly plague. By God's powerful action his people would leave Egypt and begin their long journey to the land he had promised to their forefathers. The escape was to be endlessly commemorated in an annual ritual, the *seder* or Passover meal. At this they would solemnly recall those events of long ago, reciting the story as though it had happened to them, and eating unleavened bread and roast meat as their ancestors had done.

The ceremony begins with a child asking an apparently simple question: 'What do you mean by this observance?' By way of explanation, all that follows retells the story, speaks of the wonders of God, of the crossing of the Red Sea and the gift of manna and the Law. In this way, the children are involved thoroughly in the Passover. It might even seem that the whole observance is for their benefit!

'Teach it to your children'—perhaps Christmas dinner might be a good time, or when the Easter eggs are handed out.

12 December

A FAMILY PRAYER

For this reason I bow my knees before the Father, from whom every family in heaven and on earth takes its name. I pray that, according to the riches of his glory… you may be strengthened in your inner being with power through his Spirit, and that Christ may dwell in your hearts through faith, as you are being rooted and grounded in love. I pray that you may have the power to comprehend, with all the saints, what is the breadth and length and height and depth, and to know the love of Christ that surpasses knowledge, so that you may be filled with all the fullness of God.

EPHESIANS 3:14–19 (abridged)

This beautiful prayer, permeated with love for Christ and longing for the Christians in Ephesus, starts with Paul's own act of worship before the Father, 'from whom every family… takes its name'. That is a rather strange phrase: the Smiths, Morgans, Mackays and O'Donnells don't seem to 'take their names' from the heavenly Father. On the other hand, they all derive from families, and those families, in Jewish thought, had their roots in the 'seed' of their forefathers. It is actually the fatherhood of God that is being spoken about here. As our Creator, God is the Father of the human race. Through Christ, he is the particular Father of those who believe. All 'fatherhood', and therefore every family, owes its origin to him.

Paul's prayer is a model one, overflowing with warmth and longing that these people might be strengthened inwardly and that Christ might 'dwell in their hearts by faith' as they are 'rooted and grounded in love'. He wants them to know the all-surpassing love of Christ, so that through that experience they may know what he calls 'the fullness of God'. He didn't want them to be content with a 'survival level' of faith, but that they should know its 'breadth and length and height and depth'. For them, it should be nothing less than the best.

This is the prayer of a true pastor, who holds his flock before God and prays for their enrichment. It's also a family prayer—for the family of God.

13 December

THE VINE AND THE BRANCHES

'I am the true vine, and my Father is the vinegrower. He removes every branch in me that bears no fruit. Every branch that bears fruit he prunes to make it bear more fruit... Abide in me as I abide in you. Just as the branch cannot bear fruit by itself unless it abides in the vine, neither can you unless you abide in me. I am the vine, you are the branches. Those who abide in me and I in them bear much fruit, because apart from me you can do nothing. Whoever does not abide in me is thrown away like a branch and withers; such branches are gathered, thrown into the fire, and burned. If you abide in me, and my words abide in you, ask for whatever you wish, and it will be done for you.'

JOHN 15:1–2, 4–7

This is probably as clear a picture as the New Testament offers of the relationship between Jesus Christ and those who believe in him. Using an image applied in the Old Testament to the people of Israel, he calls himself the 'true vine'. Carved over the entrance to the temple in Jerusalem was the image of a vine. The people were meant to be a true vine bearing good fruit—but the Hebrew prophets tell us that they had failed. The vine was shrivelled. It produced only wild grapes (Isaiah 5:2). But now, says Jesus, the 'true vine' is here, in himself, the Messiah—and the vine grower is the Father himself.

So Jesus is the true vine. But his followers are its branches. They depend on the vine for their sustenance and growth. The sap flows from the tree into the branches, and thence into the fruit it produces. To be fruitful, the branch simply has to remain attached to the tree—to 'abide in me', as Jesus puts it. However, should the branch become detached—fail to 'abide'—then it will die and, as a useless encumbrance, will be thrown away and burnt. The secret of the fruitful Christian life, in other words, is to stay close to Jesus: to 'abide in him'.

'Apart from me, you can do nothing'—true. But 'if you abide in me... ask for whatever you wish, and it will be done for you.'

14 December

HE CARES FOR YOU

Humble yourselves therefore under the mighty hand of God, so that he may exalt you in due time. Cast all your anxiety on him, because he cares for you. Discipline yourselves, keep alert. Like a roaring lion your adversary the devil prowls around, looking for someone to devour. Resist him, steadfast in your faith, for you know that your brothers and sisters in all the world are undergoing the same kinds of suffering. And after you have suffered for a little while, the God of all grace, who has called you to his eternal glory in Christ, will himself restore, support, strengthen, and establish you. To him be the power forever and ever. Amen.

1 PETER 5:6–11

This letter was written to Christians scattered across the Middle East, at risk of suffering persecution. It marries two themes: the rewards of suffering faithfully endured in the name of Christ, and the grace and strength that God gives to those who turn to him. Here, Peter reassures the believers that whatever happens to them, they have not been abandoned by God. They may confidently cast their care on him because he cares for them. The Creator God knows and responds to the individual anxieties and needs of his people—an astonishing thought!

However, there are requirements of those people. They should 'humble themselves' under God's mighty hand: there is no help for those who help themselves. They should be disciplined in life, and alert. There are enemies, or, perhaps, one chief enemy—the devil, who 'prowls around like a roaring lion' seeking prey. The proud or undisciplined soul is most vulnerable to his attacks, which must be resisted with the weapon of faith and by the example of their fellow Christians already experiencing 'the same kinds of suffering'. This suggests that the lion stands for imperial Rome, which was starting to prove itself implacably opposed to all that Jesus' followers stood for.

Through his grace God will 'restore, support, strengthen and establish you' until he calls us to his 'eternal glory'. That is our true Advent hope.

15 December

KNOWING HIS VOICE

[Jesus said], 'I tell you, anyone who does not enter the sheepfold by the gate but climbs in by another way is a thief and a bandit. The one who enters by the gate is the shepherd of the sheep. The gatekeeper opens the gate for him, and the sheep hear his voice. He calls his own sheep by name and leads them out. When he has brought out all his own, he goes ahead of them, and the sheep follow him because they know his voice. They will not follow a stranger, but they will run from him because they do not know the voice of strangers.' … Again Jesus said to them, 'Very truly, I tell you, I am the gate for the sheep.'

JOHN 10:1–5, 7

A childhood spent in a remote village in central Wales taught me a lot about sheep—mostly that they were quite incapable of lateral thinking. What I certainly didn't learn was that sheep could recognize a shepherd's voice, though on reflection I realize that they did recognize the shepherd, charging across the field to greet him. I put that down to greed rather than affection, but in any case the result was the same.

Jesus here and elsewhere spoke of himself as a 'shepherd' and of his followers as his flock, his 'sheep'. In that way he was picking up an Old Testament metaphor (see, for instance, Psalms 23 and 100:3), in which God is the shepherd of his people, his flock.

The other metaphor here is of the gate of the sheepfold. The fold, usually built of stone, was the place where the flock spent the night, guarded by their shepherd. It might be shared by several flocks, so there was often a 'gate-keeper' in charge. However, Jesus also describes himself as 'the gate for the sheep'—their way into and out of the fold. That may refer to the way some shepherds would lie across the gateway as a human barrier to thieves or wild animals. Spiritually, it is a vivid expression of the truth that Jesus is the way into life and security.

Jesus knows who is in his 'flock', but the sheep also know him and recognize his voice. In that relationship lie trust, security and hope.

16 December

THE GOOD SHEPHERD

[Jesus said] 'The thief comes only to steal and kill and destroy. I came that they may have life, and have it abundantly… The hired hand, who… does not own the sheep, sees the wolf coming and leaves the sheep and runs away—and the wolf snatches them and scatters them. The hired hand runs away because a hired hand does not care for the sheep. I am the good shepherd. I know my own and my own know me, just as the Father knows me and I know the Father. And I lay down my life for the sheep. I have other sheep that do not belong to this fold. I must bring them also, and they will listen to my voice. So there will be one flock, one shepherd.'

JOHN 10:10, 12–16 (abridged)

This passage develops the theme of Jesus as the shepherd of his flock. In contrast to the sheep-thief, he is the 'good shepherd' who wants life, not death, for his sheep. In contrast to the hired hand, he is prepared to 'lay down his life for his sheep' in the face of danger. Not all shepherds are good ones, and even good ones have to overcome dangers and enemies. But the good shepherd has one overruling ambition for his flock: 'that they may have life, and have it abundantly'. What Jesus desires for his flock is not mere survival in the face of danger and disaster, but rich, satisfying life.

Some years ago I took the funeral of an elderly shepherd, who had plied his calling for a lifetime on the hills of the Ridgeway in Berkshire. People spoke of him as 'the last of a breed'. He lived for his sheep, spent days and nights with them, and was distraught if one died, happy when the lambs were safely delivered. He certainly didn't see himself as part of an industrial meat-production process. That is the kind of image I like to have in mind as I read these words of Jesus, the good shepherd, whose relationship to his sheep can be compared to the one he has with his Father—an indissoluble bond.

In the light of all this, it is encouraging that Jesus spoke of 'other sheep' who are 'not of this fold'—presumably, Gentiles—who must also be gathered in.

17 December

LIVING IN HARMONY

We who are strong ought to put up with the failings of the weak, and not to please ourselves. Each of us must please our neighbour for the good purpose of building up the neighbour... May the God of steadfastness and encouragement grant you to live in harmony with one another, in accordance with Christ Jesus, so that together you may with one voice glorify the God and Father of our Lord Jesus Christ. Welcome one another, therefore, just as Christ has welcomed you, for the glory of God.

ROMANS 15:1–2, 5–7

'We who are strong' sounds very proud! However, it might well be put in inverted commas: we who consider ourselves to be 'strong'. And Paul's point is a generous one: those with strong convictions ought to be tolerant of those who have doubts and hesitations. Not all of us can see the world as black and white all the time. That sets the tone for the passage, which is about living in harmony with one another. We please our neighbours in order to build them up, not to make them feel weak and dependent.

Two words stand out: 'steadfastness' and 'encouragement'. The first is a personal trait that we should seek by prayer and faith to cultivate. It's about reliability and loyalty, and it mirrors the nature of God. 'Encouragement' is an outgoing gift, one that we have for the benefit of others. Some people are natural 'encouragers'—like Barnabas, who took the new convert Paul, of whose conversion many of the disciples were sceptical, and presented him to the believers (Acts 9:27).

The final command in this passage is to 'welcome [or accept] one another, just as Christ has welcomed you'. How does Christ 'welcome' us? Openly, freely, without precondition beyond our true desire to belong to him. While we were still sinners, he died for us. When we fail him, he is still our Saviour, the one who brings forgiveness. Our welcome of others should mirror his of us.

'Live in harmony with one another'—it sounds easy, and is often so difficult.

18 December

WAITING IN SILENCE

For God alone my soul waits in silence; from him comes my salvation. He alone is my rock and my salvation, my fortress; I shall never be shaken… For God alone my soul waits in silence, for my hope is from him. He alone is my rock and my salvation, my fortress; I shall not be shaken. On God rests my deliverance and my honour; my mighty rock, my refuge is in God. Trust in him at all times, O people; pour out your heart before him; God is a refuge for us.

PSALM 62:1–2, 5–8

This is really a poem about the uniqueness of God: there is simply no one and nothing else that can replace him. In silence the psalmist 'waits' for God—attends to him, opens himself to him. God alone is the rock on which he can build his life, a sure and solid foundation. He alone is a fortress, a place of safety and security. He alone offers hope; he is the only source of 'salvation'—true and fulfilling life.

When I lead retreats, I often take the opening sentence of this psalm as a kind of refrain for participants: 'For God alone my soul in silence waits'. Sometimes there is no real substitute for excluding the noises and distractions of daily life and the world around and simply 'waiting' for God. There are many examples in the scriptures to support the idea that it is only when we are quiet that we can truly hear the voice of God. To 'wait' for him implies patience and discipline, and a deep desire to open ourselves o his will and purpose.

The psalmist uses his own testimony as an chance to encourage others to share in this blessing. He longs that they too should find that place of quiet trust for themselves. It will be a place where they can pour out the longings of their hearts and find refuge in his presence. Far from being a kind of desperate proof of weakness, it will be for them, as it has been for him, the way to deliverance and honour.

Is it possible today to find space and time to create an oasis of silence in which we can 'wait' on God and seek to hear his voice?

19 December

THE PERFECT LAW OF LIFE

The law of the Lord is perfect, reviving the soul; the decrees of the Lord are sure, making wise the simple; the precepts of the Lord are right, rejoicing the heart; the commandment of the Lord is clear, enlightening the eyes; the fear of the Lord is pure, enduring forever; the ordinances of the Lord are true and righteous altogether. More to be desired are they than gold, even much fine gold; sweeter also than honey, and drippings of the honeycomb. Moreover by them is your servant warned; in keeping them there is great reward.

PSALM 19:7–11

Just in case we're ever tempted to think that the Law—the Torah—was a terrible burden, we have a psalm like this one. It's an extravagant, fulsome tribute to the commandments of the Lord, setting out in poetic language the benefits that they bring. What Paul criticized in his letters to the Galatians and to Rome was never the Law of God itself—'the law is holy, and the commandment is holy and just and good' (Romans 7:12)—but the observance of rules and regulations: 'special days, and months, and seasons, and years' (Galatians 4:10). He was echoing the contempt of Jesus for those who tithed the mint in the garden but defrauded widows out of their property (Matthew 23:23).

That is certainly not the 'Law' as the psalmist sees it. This is something glorious and liberating, 'reviving the soul'; a source of wisdom that rejoices the heart; clear and true, opening up new ways of understanding—'enlightening the eyes'. This Law is not a burden but a delight, not a set of regulations and rules but a way of life.

Because they are 'true and righteous altogether', the 'ordinances of the Lord' are infinitely desirable—better than gold, sweeter than honey. They are a joy but also a warning. These are the commandments of the Almighty, yet for those who keep them 'there is great reward'.

'Let the words of my mouth and the meditation of my heart be acceptable to you, O Lord, my rock and my redeemer.'

20 December

THE WORSHIPPING COMMUNITY

I was glad when they said to me, 'Let us go to the house of the Lord!' Our feet are standing within your gates, O Jerusalem. Jerusalem—built as a city that is bound firmly together. To it the tribes go up, the tribes of the Lord, as was decreed for Israel, to give thanks to the name of the Lord. For there the thrones for judgment were set up, the thrones of the house of David. Pray for the peace of Jerusalem: 'May they prosper who love you. Peace be within your walls, and security within your towers.'

PSALM 122:1–7

'I was glad'—glad to be invited to join the throng of worshippers making their way towards the temple in Jerusalem. Perhaps they had come a long way and were only now approaching the hill on which it stood. For days they would have anticipated this moment: very soon their feet would be standing within the holy gates. On those Sunday mornings when the last thing we feel like doing is going to church it might be salutary to read this psalm, with its joyful expectation of blessing. Perhaps the secret lies in that expectation. If we drag ourselves off to Sunday worship expecting little, that is probably exactly what we shall receive.

The psalmist sings his joy, but he also considers the different aspects of what their worship in the city of God will entail. There will be gratitude, of course: they've got there, and they can see the very heart of the nation that the Lord had called to be his own. They are in the city of the king, the city of David—a place of government and rule. Reverence and respect will mark their visit.

They are also in a place of prayer, 'a house for prayer for all peoples' (Isaiah 56:7), so they prayed, and called on others to pray with them, for 'the peace of Jerusalem'. Over the centuries—indeed, millennia—the need for that prayer has not diminished.

Many of us will be in church over Christmas. Can we echo the psalmist's sense of joy and expectation at the prospect?

21 December

TO SUCH AS THESE

People were bringing even infants to [Jesus] that he might touch them; and when the disciples saw it, they sternly ordered them not to do it. But Jesus called for them and said, 'Let the little children come to me, and do not stop them; for it is to such as these that the kingdom of God belongs. Truly I tell you, whoever does not receive the kingdom of God as a little child will never enter it.'

LUKE 18:15–17

Jesus was constantly harassed by large crowds wanting his attention: people seeking healing or exorcism, others wanting teaching or advice, and some more intent on trying to trick him into an indiscretion. It's not surprising that the disciples tended to be rather protective. Here, however, they also displayed the dismissive attitude towards children that was a feature of the social climate of the day. It was not that children were unimportant or unloved—a large family was much to be envied—but their use and value came later, as breadwinners and supporters of the elderly members of their family.

So when mothers brought their children to Jesus for blessing, the disciples turned them away 'sternly'. The Teacher had weightier things to do than concern himself with a group of babies and toddlers. Jesus, however, had different ideas. First he ordered that the children should be brought to him rather than prevented. Then he laid his hands on them in blessing. His action was accompanied by an explanation given to the disciples: 'Whoever does not receive the kingdom of God as a little child will never enter it.' His point surely was that God's kingdom is for the pure and innocent, the trusting and needy, the helpless and dependent. The biggest barrier to entering it was the delusion that anyone had the 'right' to do so, or had 'earned' a place, or could claim it on grounds of social status, wealth or birth.

We do not ask for a childish faith, which is easily distracted, but for a child-like one, which is all about trust.

22 December

THE FAMILY OF FAITH

While [Jesus] was still speaking to the crowds, his mother and his brothers were standing outside, wanting to speak to him. Someone told him, 'Look, your mother and your brothers are standing outside, wanting to speak to you.' But to the one who had told him this, Jesus replied, 'Who is my mother, and who are my brothers?' And pointing to his disciples, he said, 'Here are my mother and my brothers! For whoever does the will of my Father in heaven is my brother and sister and mother.'

MATTHEW 12:46–50

When Jesus saw his mother and the disciple whom he loved standing beside her, he said to his mother, 'Woman, here is your son.' Then he said to the disciple, 'Here is your mother.' And from that hour the disciple took her into his own home.

JOHN 19:26–27

The second of these readings should help to correct any implication that Jesus was in some way 'anti-family'. The reading from Matthew emphasizes the 'new' family of the kingdom of heaven. The disciples of Jesus become part of his 'family'. Over history it has become a very, very large one! His love for them, and their love for him, is comparable to the love that dwells, or should dwell, in a human family. It is accepting, forgiving, generous, just as God's love is for us in Christ.

To read into these words of Jesus some kind of contempt for his mother and his brothers would clearly be wrong. If that were so, why, as he was dying on the cross, would he make loving provision for his mother, committing her into the care of his 'beloved disciple', John? That suggests a caring and thoughtful son, anxious that Mary (already, it is supposed, a widow) should be cared for in her old age. Taken together, these readings show how central to the teaching of Jesus and the principles of the kingdom of God is the notion of 'family'.

We should value both our earthly families and the family of God.

23 December

FAMILY RESPONSIBILITY

Honour widows who are really widows. If a widow has children or grandchildren, they should first learn their religious duty to their own family and make some repayment to their parents... The real widow, left alone, has set her hope on God and continues in supplications and prayers night and day; but the widow who lives for pleasure is dead even while she lives... Whoever does not provide for relatives, and especially for family members, has denied the faith and is worse than an unbeliever.

1 TIMOTHY 5:3–8 (abridged)

The situation of widows in the Bible was a peculiarly difficult one. In a patriarchal society the wife was simply the 'property' of her husband. When he died, she was left in a very exposed and vulnerable position. Consequently, there was special provision for widows. The whole Israelite community was expected to take them under its care (Exodus 22:22), although it is not clear whether this involved financial support. Certainly their children were to fulfil the obligations of the third commandment and 'honour' them, presumably by taking care of their needs. Much the same was expected of the Christian community, where there was a daily distribution of food for widows (Acts 6:1).

In our passage, describing the situation some decades later, we can see the way in which this had developed. Some (probably younger) widows were apparently taking advantage of the generosity of others, acting like the 'merry widows' of Shakespearean comedy. On the other hand, some children were neglecting their clear duty to their widowed mothers. The writer reserves particularly scathing language for such behaviour. To neglect to support needy parents was a denial of the faith, no less, making the offender 'worse than an unbeliever'. It's hard to think of a more damning verdict than that!

The problem of care for the elderly is still with us. The Bible urges us to consider our God-ordained duty to honour and care for our parents, over and beyond what welfare systems can do for them.

24 December

FAMILIES LIKE FLOCKS

He turns rivers into a desert, springs of water into thirsty ground, a fruitful land into a salty waste, because of the wickedness of its inhabitants. He turns a desert into pools of water, a parched land into springs of water. And there he lets the hungry live, and they establish a town to live in; they sow fields, and plant vineyards, and get a fruitful yield. By his blessing they multiply greatly, and he does not let their cattle decrease. When they are diminished and brought low through oppression, trouble, and sorrow, he pours contempt on princes and makes them wander in trackless wastes; but he raises up the needy out of distress, and makes their families like flocks.

PSALM 107:33–41

This is a psalm of contrasts, all reflecting the justice and mercy of God. On the one hand, the wicked find their lands turning from fertility to desert. By contrast, for the needy, God does exactly the opposite. Desert land provides pools of water and parched land fresh springs.

There follows a beautiful picture of domestic and family life as it was experienced by those who had been touched by God's generosity. The 'hungry' now live on fertile land, so they can sow fields, plant vines and gather fruitful crops. Their herds grow. They build towns to live in.

Sometimes, in the way of things, they will be 'diminished and brought low'. Oppression, trouble and sorrow have always been the lot of the poorest in our communities. The implication here is that such troubles are the consequence of unjust or insensitive rulers. However, while the 'princes' are condemned by God to 'wander in trackless wastes', the needy will again be raised up. The Lord will make their families 'like flocks'. God will bless them with many children, to provide labour, support and hope for the future.

We can see a contrast between the fortunes of the 'mighty' and the 'meek' in the song of Mary (Luke 1:46–55), and similar compassion for the poor in the ministry of her Son (4:18).

25 December

THE CHILD IN THE MANGER

'Glory to God in the highest heaven, and on earth peace among those whom he favours!' When the angels had left them… the shepherds said to one another, 'Let us go now to Bethlehem and see this thing that has taken place, which the Lord has made known to us.' So they went with haste and found Mary and Joseph, and the child lying in the manger. When they saw this, they made known what had been told them about this child; and all who heard it were amazed at what the shepherds told them. But Mary treasured all these words and pondered them in her heart.
LUKE 2:14–19 (abridged)

It's Christmas, and time once again to read the familiar story of the angels, the shepherds, and the baby lying in a manger. Out on the hills there had been a wonderful vision, songs of 'Glory to God!' and a promise that God's favour was being offered to all people. If the shepherds made their way into Bethlehem, they would find a newborn baby. How would they identify this particular child? He would be found 'lying in a manger' (v. 12).

We could think of many appropriate 'signs' to mark the identity of the newborn Son of God, but a wooden feeding trough wouldn't normally be one of them. Yet the sign was utterly in keeping with the whole event. Jesus was born to be a king, yet he was not to be found in a palace but among the cattle. One day every knee will bow before him, but his first worshippers were rough shepherds from the hills. His parents were not royalty but a working-class couple too poor to offer the usual sacrifice at the child's presentation in the temple. On the night of his birth, there was no room for his parents in the guest room, so they lay among the animals downstairs. When God became incarnate—when 'the Word took flesh'—he certainly did it thoroughly!

'Mary treasured all these words and pondered them in her heart.' The shepherds, with their story of a vision of angels, confirmed Gabriel's message. Hers was no ordinary child.

26 December

THE END OF AN ERA

In the time of King Herod, after Jesus was born in Bethlehem of Judea, wise men from the East came to Jerusalem, asking, 'Where is the child who has been born king of the Jews? For we observed his star at its rising, and have come to pay him homage.' ... Then [Herod] sent them to Bethlehem, saying, 'Go and search diligently for the child; and when you have found him, bring me word so that I may also go and pay him homage.' When they had heard the king, they set out; and there, ahead of them, went the star that they had seen at its rising, until it stopped over the place where the child was... On entering the house, they saw the child with Mary his mother; and they knelt down and paid him homage. Then, opening their treasure chests, they offered him gifts of gold, frankincense, and myrrh.

MATTHEW 2:1–2, 8–9, 11

The wise men ('three' is supposition, based on the number of gifts they offered) were actually 'magi', magicians, soothsayers. There is no suggestion here that they were kings. The soothsayers were people of enormous power and influence in the world of that time. Birth, death and every event of life fell under their rather sinister influence.

Christmas tradition presents them as benevolent old monarchs, faithfully searching for the Messiah. That was certainly not how the first Christians saw this story. For them, superstition, spells and the steaming entrails of a calf would never again determine the details of people's lives. From now on, it would be God's will and purpose that were paramount, and the events of life, good and bad, would be seen as the raw material of his loving will. That, for them, was the significance of the wise men falling down in worship before the child Jesus and offering him gifts. The old order was bowing the knee to the new. The age of superstition was over; the kingdom of God had come.

We all think we know the Christmas story, but behind the familiar characters and events lie truths that can surprise us and change our lives.

27 December

RESPECTING OUR PARENTS

Honour your father and your mother, so that your days may be long in the land that the Lord your God is giving you.

EXODUS 20:12

Children, obey your parents in the Lord, for this is right. 'Honour your father and mother'—this is the first commandment with a promise: 'so that it may be well with you and you may live long on the earth.' And, fathers, do not provoke your children to anger, but bring them up in the discipline and instruction of the Lord.

EPHESIANS 6:1–4

Two readings today, which deal with the principle of 'parenting'—as topical an issue now as it ever was in biblical times. To 'honour' our parents is to 'respect' them but, as Paul argues in the second reading, that respect has to be earnt, not simply demanded. Christian children are to 'obey their parents in the Lord', in obedience to this very commandment, but at the same time fathers should not 'provoke their children to anger'. Respect, Paul says, is a two-way thing.

Nevertheless, honouring parents is seen in both Jewish and Christian tradition as an essential element in a well-adjusted, secure and healthy society. We have certainly seen in Western society the bitter fruits of the breakdown of that respect. Lack of respect for parents is a contravention of the law of God, just as parental abdication of responsibility for their children is a denial of their God-given role. This is the first commandment with a promise: those who honour and respect their parents will enjoy long days 'in the land that the Lord your God is giving you'. For Paul, that had a universal application: 'so that it may be well with you and you may live long on the earth'. Our well-being, in other words, is tied up in the strength of our family ties.

Children—respect your parents. Parents—earn that respect. All of us, honour the family.

28 December

A FAMILY CRISIS

When he was twelve years old, they went up as usual for the festival. When the festival was ended… the boy Jesus stayed behind in Jerusalem, but his parents did not know it. Assuming that he was in the group of travellers, they went a day's journey. Then they started to look for him among their relatives and friends. When they did not find him, they returned to Jerusalem… After three days they found him in the temple, sitting among the teachers, listening to them and asking them questions… and his mother said to him, 'Child, why have you treated us like this? Look, your father and I have been searching for you in great anxiety.' He said to them, 'Why were you searching for me? Did you not know that I must be in my Father's house?' But they did not understand what he said to them… His mother treasured all these things in her heart.

LUKE 2:42–46, 48–51 (abridged)

This is the only story we have about the boyhood of Jesus, and its only possible source would have been Mary herself. It is the sort of event that parents never forget—the dreadful moment when they realize that a child has gone missing. So it's quite understandable that they were abrupt with him when they eventually traced him to one of the temple courts, where he was engaged in dialogue with the teachers of the law. 'Why have you treated us like this?' seems mild in the circumstances.

The answer of the twelve-year-old Jesus combines the very normal attitude of a boy of his age—'Why were you looking for me?'—with a slightly oblique rebuke: 'Didn't you know that I would be in my Father's house?' Luke comments that they didn't understand the significance of what he was saying in view of all that Jesus was to be and do over the rest of his life. 'The Father's house' was a phrase the Jews of the time used to describe the temple, but the subtle change of pronoun ('my Father's house') gives a different emphasis.

Again, 'Mary treasured all these things…'. Perhaps only years later did their full significance strike her. Her little boy was the 'Son of the Most High'.

29 December

YOUR LIGHT HAS COME

Arise, shine; for your light has come, and the glory of the Lord has risen upon you. For darkness shall cover the earth, and thick darkness the peoples; but the Lord will arise upon you, and his glory will appear over you. Nations shall come to your light, and kings to the brightness of your dawn. Lift up your eyes and look around; they all gather together, they come to you; your sons shall come from far away, and your daughters shall be carried on their nurses' arms. Then you shall see and be radiant; your heart shall thrill and rejoice.

ISAIAH 60:1–5A

There is a note of hope that runs right through the Advent and Christmas season. However dark things may appear to be, however impenetrable the clouds of despair, there is a light and one day that light will shine. For the prophet in today's reading, that light will break through the suffering of the people of Judah: the Lord God will 'arise' like the sun. They will lift up their eyes and see what great things God is doing for them, how the very nations that have despised and conquered them are coming towards the light that is shining on God's people. Their exiled sons and daughters will come streaming home. Kings and rulers will come, drawn by the light, and those who were once in despair will thrill and rejoice at the mighty acts of their God.

It's not surprising that Christians down the ages have seen in these words of the prophet a foretelling of the light that shone at Bethlehem—the 'light that shines in the darkness' (John 1:5), the coming of the one who described himself as 'the light of the world' (8:12). Both in the first coming of Jesus, marked by the shining of a star, and in his second coming in glory, the darkness of the world was and will be penetrated by the dazzling light of the Son of God.

Even a tiny candle can dispel a vast amount of darkness. What effect, then, must the light of God have on a darkened world?

30 December

THE FAMILY OF FAITH

They devoted themselves to the apostles' teaching and fellowship, to the breaking of bread and the prayers. Awe came upon everyone, because many wonders and signs were being done by the apostles. All who believed were together and had all things in common; they would sell their possessions and goods and distribute the proceeds to all, as any had need. Day by day, as they spent much time together in the temple, they broke bread at home and ate their food with glad and generous hearts, praising God and having the goodwill of all the people. And day by day the Lord added to their number those who were being saved.

ACTS 2:42–47

We can read in Acts 2:41 that 3000 people were converted on the day of Pentecost. Now Luke tells us how the newly baptized formed a new kind of community —and there had never been one like it before. Led by the apostles and the other original disciples—the witnesses of the risen Jesus—they devoted themselves to four primary pursuits. They sat at the feet of their teachers and drank in the truths of the life and teaching of Jesus. They created a powerful sense of 'fellowship' ('sharing' or 'partnership'). Following the command of Jesus, they regularly 'broke bread' in memory of him. And they prayed—the temple prayers, and (we later learn) spontaneous prayer together.

But this wasn't simply a holy huddle. To belong to Jesus meant following his priorities, and that included caring for each other in practical ways. So they shared everything they had, ensuring that the poorer members of their community were cared for. They sat lightly to their possessions, recognizing that need was a more important factor than want. Their homes were open to all. They were 'glad and generous' hosts. And in those homes, they broke bread in remembrance of the Saviour in whose name they had so recently been baptized.

There's no mention of evangelism here—just life in Christ. The sincerity and generosity of that life drew others to find out what made the difference.

31 December

THE GIFT OF PATIENCE

Be patient, therefore, beloved, until the coming of the Lord. The farmer waits for the precious crop from the earth, being patient with it until it receives the early and the late rains. You also must be patient. Strengthen your hearts, for the coming of the Lord is near... As an example of suffering and patience, beloved, take the prophets who spoke in the name of the Lord. Indeed we call blessed those who showed endurance. You have heard of the endurance of Job, and you have seen the purpose of the Lord, how the Lord is compassionate and merciful.

JAMES 5:7–8, 10–11

At the end of the year, patience is not always the most popular virtue. We want to get on with things, see what the new year brings, make new plans and tackle new challenges. That is all well and good. But, as the down-to-earth James reminds us, sometimes the gift we need more than any other is the priceless virtue of patience. As one year rolls away and another comes, we may wish things would move faster, but he would be the first to say that things move best at God's pace, not ours.

James links patience with endurance, and that's a very helpful way of seeing it. Patience sounds a rather negative virtue—don't do anything, just sit there and wait—but endurance introduces a more positive element. Those who endure will face and cope with whatever is thrown at them, without being victims of it. By their endurance, they overcome obstacles and transform situations.

As we come to the end of the year and of these readings, the call to 'patient endurance' might seem a rather low-key note on which to end. Yet for many of us it is the quality we shall need above all else to face the challenges and opportunities of the year ahead.

We do not and cannot foresee the future, but we know that there will be times ahead when what we need most of all is God's gift of patient endurance.

BIBLE INDEX

Genesis 1:1–3 (KJV) 8
Genesis 1:26–28 9
Genesis 2:4–7 107
Genesis 2:8–9, 15–17 10
Genesis 2:18, 21–23 11
Genesis 3:1–6 12
Genesis 3:8–13 13
Genesis 3:16–19 14
Genesis 6:17–19 358
Genesis 7:6–10, 17, 21 111
Genesis 8:15–19 112
Genesis 8:21–22; 9:11, 13 113
Genesis 12:1–3 15
Genesis 15:1–2, 4–6 330
Genesis 18:6–10, 12–14a 198
Genesis 24:63–67 232
Genesis 27:6–7, 9–17 199
Genesis 29:13, 15–20 233
Genesis 32:9–12 234
Genesis 33:4–11 301
Genesis 41:28–30, 32–33 152
Genesis 45:4–8 114
Exodus 2:1–8 65
Exodus 2:15–22 200
Exodus 2:23–25 70
Exodus 3:7–8, 10 71
Exodus 3:11–15 72
Exodus 4:10–13 73
Exodus 12:3, 5–8, 11–13 201
Exodus 12:24, 26–27 368
Exodus 13:3, 5, 8, 10 97
Exodus 13:20–22 76
Exodus 14:21–23, 26–27 77
Exodus 16:1–4 202
Exodus 16:9–12 203
Exodus 16:13–20 204
Exodus 20:8–11 365
Exodus 20:12 384
Exodus 30:25–31 158
Exodus 33:12–16 273
Exodus 34:6–9 296
Leviticus 16:5, 7, 20–22 312
Leviticus 19:13–18, 32–34 253
Leviticus 23:10–12, 21–22 205
Numbers 6:22–27 147
Deuteronomy 1:30–33 266
Deuteronomy 6:4–9 288
Deuteronomy 7:7–9, 12–13 235
Deuteronomy 8:2–5 227
Deuteronomy 28:1–6 206
Deuteronomy 30:15–20 176
Deuteronomy 33:26–29a (KJV) 87
Joshua 3:1–5 270
Ruth 1:11, 14, 16–17 (KJV) 22
Ruth 4:13–17 230
1 Samuel 16:11–13 136
1 Samuel 18:1, 3–5 236
2 Samuel 18:31—19:3 238
2 Samuel 23:1–4 139
1 Kings 8:33–36 322
1 Kings 10:1–7a 16
1 Kings 17:12–16 155
1 Kings 19:4–8 156
1 Kings 19:11–13 157
2 Kings 4:32–35 118
2 Kings 5:1, 10–13 121
2 Kings 7:8–10 215
Ezra 6:19, 21–22 208
Nehemiah 8:8–10 211
Job 19:23–27 175
Job 23:2–4, 8–11 267
Job 28:20–28 329
Job 42:1–6 60
Psalm 1 166
Psalm 6:4–9 41
Psalm 10:12–14, 17–18 148
Psalm 13 55
Psalm 15 182
Psalm 17:6–9 85
Psalm 19:7–11 376
Psalm 20:1–2, 4–7 74
Psalm 22:1–5, 23–25a 42
Psalm 23 (KJV) 46
Psalm 25:4–10 287
Psalm 27:1–6 285
Psalm 31:19–24 239

Psalm 34:3–6, 8 80
Psalm 34:15–19 88
Psalm 36:5–9 209
Psalm 40:1–4 61
Psalm 42:1, 3–8 50
Psalm 43:3–5 75
Psalm 46:1–5a 96
Psalm 46:8–11 149
Psalm 51:1–5, 17 294
Psalm 51:6–12 62
Psalm 56:2–3, 5–9, 11–13 265
Psalm 57:1–3, 7–10 291
Psalm 62:1–2, 5–8 375
Psalm 63:1–3, 5–7 49
Psalm 67:1–4, 6–7 192
Psalm 68:4–10 269
Psalm 69:1–3, 13–16 90
Psalm 71:1, 4–6, 14–18 321
Psalm 84:1–3, 5–7 110
Psalm 85:4, 6–12 298
Psalm 86:1–11 240
Psalm 89:1–4, 14 231
Psalm 91:1–6, 9–10 66
Psalm 92:1–5 130
Psalm 92:12–15 131
Psalm 96:1–5, 8–9 307
Psalm 99 306
Psalm 102:24–28 326
Psalm 103:2–7 300
Psalm 103:8–14 304
Psalm 104:10–15 225
Psalm 107:1–2, 4–13 224
Psalm 107:33–41 381
Psalm 108:1–6, 12–13 241
Psalm 112:1–9 174
Psalm 116:5–14 67
Psalm 121 53
Psalm 122:1–7 377
Psalm 125 181
Psalm 126 28
Psalm 127:1–2, 4–5 275
Psalm 130:1–2, 5–7 26
Psalm 138:1–2, 4, 6–8 282
Psalm 139:7–12 140
Psalm 139:13–18 280
Psalm 143:5–10 137
Psalm 145:13–19 122
Psalm 147:1–6, 8–11 242
Proverbs 2:1–9 167
Proverbs 3:19–26 168
Proverbs 3:27–34a 169
Proverbs 6:6–11, 16–19 170
Proverbs 8:12–17, 20–22 30
Proverbs 8:32–36 171
Proverbs 9:1–6 360
Proverbs 9:7–10 29
Proverbs 15:1, 3–4, 15–17 210
Proverbs 27:1–2, 5–6, 10 172
Proverbs 30:5, 7–9 173
Ecclesiastes 1:2–3, 5–9 17
Ecclesiastes 3:1–8 (KJV) 362
Ecclesiastes 3:11–15 344
Ecclesiastes 12:1, 3–5, 7 (KJV) 361
Song of Solomon 2:8, 10–14 178
Song of Solomon 8:4, 6–7 179
Isaiah 2:2–4 331
Isaiah 5:1–7 249
Isaiah 6:1–8 297
Isaiah 11:1–5 138
Isaiah 30:18–21 263
Isaiah 35:5–10 268
Isaiah 40:1–5 57
Isaiah 40:28–31 271
Isaiah 42:5–8 109
Isaiah 43:18–21 58
Isaiah 45:20–22 82
Isaiah 49:8–12 313
Isaiah 49:13–17 257
Isaiah 52:7–10 355
Isaiah 53:2b–5 332
Isaiah 53:6–9 333
Isaiah 53:10–12 334
Isaiah 55:1–3 126
Isaiah 60:1–5a 386
Isaiah 60:13–16 83
Isaiah 63:7–9 244
Isaiah 63:11–14 141
Isaiah 65:17–21 37
Jeremiah 18:1–6 23
Jeremiah 31:2–5, 8–9 245
Jeremiah 31:31–34 180
Lamentations 3:19–23, 25 18

Ezekiel 1:22, 26–28 349
Ezekiel 36:24–28 19
Ezekiel 37:1–6 108
Daniel 1:10–13, 15–19 212
Hosea 2:14–19 40
Hosea 6:1–6 43
Hosea 14:1–7 251
Joel 2:23–26a 59
Joel 2:28–32a 142
Amos 3:3–8 262
Amos 5:11–15 207
Micah 4:1–2 194
Micah 4:3–5 195
Habakkuk 3:17–19 250
Zephaniah 3:14–18a 272
Zechariah 8:16–19 252
Malachi 3:1–3 335
Malachi 4:2–3, 5–6 336
Matthew 1:18–21 78
Matthew 2:1–2, 8–9, 11 383
Matthew 5:3–9 183
Matthew 5:10–12 184
Matthew 5:13–16 115
Matthew 5:43–46, 48 33
Matthew 6:9–13 284
Matthew 6:19–21 116
Matthew 6:25–30 185
Matthew 6:31–34 186
Matthew 7:12–16a 276
Matthew 9:35–38 91
Matthew 11:28–30 56
Matthew 12:46–50 379
Matthew 13:24–30 348
Matthew 14:15–21 214
Matthew 14:22–27 48
Matthew 18:23–30 302
Matthew 18:31–35 303
Matthew 22:2–3, 5–10 213
Matthew 28:16–20 290
Mark 1:16–20 274
Mark 2:4–11 299
Mark 4:35–41 47
Mark 5:38–42 119
Mark 9:21–27 305
Mark 10:46–52 264
Mark 13:3–8 340
Mark 13:24–27, 29–30, 32 341
Mark 14:32–36 45
Mark 16:1–6 102
Luke 1:13–17 143
Luke 1:30–32, 34–35 144
Luke 1:68–75 79
Luke 1:76–79 (KJV) 27
Luke 2:8–11, 13–14 (KJV) 81
Luke 2:14–19 382
Luke 2:26–32 145
Luke 2:42–46, 48–51 385
Luke 3:15–17 146
Luke 4:16–21 31
Luke 5:27–32 221
Luke 5:36–39 20
Luke 7:2–10 366
Luke 7:11–15 120
Luke 7:44–50 248
Luke 8:44–48 84
Luke 9:29–30, 32–35 342
Luke 10:21, 23–24 191
Luke 10:34, 36–37 190
Luke 11:9–13 189
Luke 14:7–14 222
Luke 14:16–24 223
Luke 17:11–19 314
Luke 18:15–17 378
Luke 19:1–5, 7–10 309
Luke 20:34–38 343
Luke 23:39–43 100
Luke 24:28–32 289
Luke 24:44–48 311
John 1:25–27, 29 92
John 2:9–11 117
John 3:5–8 135
John 3:14–17 86
John 5:20–21, 23–24 105
John 6:48, 50–56 216
John 9:1–7 319
John 9:19–25 320
John 10:1–5, 7 372
John 10:10, 12–16 373
John 11:1–6 127
John 11:20–21, 23–27 128
John 11:41–44 129
John 12:1–5, 7–8 34

John 13:2–5, 12–15 260
John 13:33–38 21
John 14:1–6 51
John 14:15–18 134
John 14:25–28 54
John 15:1–2, 4–7 370
John 15:12–14, 16–17 (KJV) 32
John 16:31–33 64
John 17:11–15, 17 283
John 19:26–27 379
John 20:11–17 103
John 20:19–23 153
John 21:9–13 217
John 21:15–17 259
Acts 2:1–4 154
Acts 2:37–39, 41a 99
Acts 2:42–47 387
Acts 3:1–8 123
Acts 9:1–8 345
Acts 10:9–15, 19–20 218
Acts 10:34–38 159
Acts 16:25–32 364
Acts 17:24–28 346
Acts 17:29–32, 34 347
Acts 20:25–28, 31 243
Acts 20:32–35 247
Romans 1:1, 3–6 104
Romans 5:1–5 316
Romans 5:6–11 317
Romans 6:3–5, 7–8 24
Romans 6:5–9, 11 125
Romans 8:22–27 150
Romans 8:35–39 193
Romans 12:1–3 25
Romans 12:9–19 258
Romans 15:1–2, 5–7 374
1 Corinthians 10:9–12, 14, 16–17 ..219
1 Corinthians 10:11–13 286
1 Corinthians 11:18, 20–22 220
1 Corinthians 11:23–26 98
1 Corinthians 12:3b, 7–11 161
1 Corinthians 13:1–6 162
1 Corinthians 13:8–13 163
1 Corinthians 15:13–19 106
1 Corinthians 15:50–53, 55–57 351
2 Corinthians 1:8–11 328
2 Corinthians 4:16—5:1 52
2 Corinthians 5:17–20 36
2 Corinthians 8:7–12 255
2 Corinthians 12:7b–9 44
Galatians 2:19–20 318
Galatians 3:25–28 367
Galatians 5:22–25 160
Ephesians 2:4–9 95
Ephesians 3:14–19 369
Ephesians 4:29–32 35
Ephesians 5:21–23, 25–30 359
Ephesians 6:1–4 384
Philippians 1:3–8 327
Philippians 1:20–24 63
Philippians 2:5–11 352
Philippians 2:12–16 68
Philippians 3:7–12 177
Philippians 4:4–7 277
Philippians 4:10–13 281
Colossians 3:12–15 187
Colossians 3:16–21 188
1 Thessalonians 4:13–18 278
1 Timothy 2:1–6 94
1 Timothy 5:3–8 380
2 Timothy 4:6–8 353
2 Timothy 4:9–13, 19–21a 237
Titus 3:1–5 254
Hebrews 2:14–15, 17 93
Hebrews 4:14–16 151
Hebrews 10:11–17 315
Hebrews 13:1–6 279
James 1:17–18 337
James 2:1–4, 8–9 363
James 2:12–17 226
James 5:7–8, 10–11 388
1 Peter 1:3–9 310
1 Peter 1:22–25 256
1 Peter 2:9–10 124
1 Peter 3:13–18 338
1 Peter 5:6–11 371
1 John 1:5–7 323
1 John 1:8—2:2 295
1 John 4:13–16 89
1 John 4:17–21; 5:2–3 246
Revelation 1:4–7 339
Revelation 5:9, 11–13 308

Revelation 7:9–12 350
Revelation 7:13–17 324
Revelation 19:6–9 228
Revelation 21:1–5a 254
Revelation 21:22–27 354
Revelation 22:1–2, 17 164

★ ALSO BY DAVID WINTER ★

RETIREMENT

Bible Readings for Special Times

Each volume in the *Bible Readings for Special Times* series offers 24 undated reflections linking scripture to real-life experiences, especially for those times when we want to hear God's word speaking to us clearly, yet may not know where to start looking.

Retirement is an increasingly important part of modern life—some people spend almost as many years retired as they did employed. While facing it can be a daunting prospect, living as a retired person offers new challenges and opportunities. These Bible readings offer an honest but hopeful picture of what it can mean to be 'positively retired'.

ISBN 978 1 84101 430 2   £1.99

Available from your local Christian bookshop or, in case of difficulty, direct from BRF using the order form on page 397.

★ ALSO FROM BRF ★

ALONG THE DISCIPLESHIP ROAD

Following Jesus today

JAY COLWILL

By choosing to follow Jesus, setting off on the road of discipleship, we embark upon an adventure that will challenge us and take us into unknown territory. Along the way we will surely face all kinds of 'hills', times of struggle that present us with a stark challenge: do we press on, growing in strength and determination, or do we give up and turn back?

This book explores what we can learn from the stories of some of Jesus' disciples: Andrew, Peter, James, Mary Magdalene, Thomas and Matthew. Their experiences, their triumphs and failures of faith and, above all, their relationship with Jesus offer us help and guidance as we seek to follow him as disciples today.

ISBN 978 1 84101 401 2   £6.99

ORDER FORM

REF	TITLE	PRICE	QTY	TOTAL
430 2	*Retirement (Bible Readings for Special Times)*	£1.99		
401 2	*Along the Discipleship Road*	£6.99		

POSTAGE AND PACKING CHARGES				
Order value	UK	Europe	Surface	Air Mail
£7.00 & under	£1.25	£3.00	£3.50	£5.50
£7.01–£30.00	£2.25	£5.50	£6.50	£10.00
Over £30.00	free	prices on request		

Postage and packing:	
Donation:	
Total enclosed:	

Name ______________________ Account Number ______________

Address ____

____________________________________ Postcode __________

Telephone Number ______________ Email ________________

Payment by: ❑ Cheque ❑ Mastercard ❑ Visa ❑ Postal Order ❑ Maestro

Card no. ☐☐☐☐ ☐☐☐☐ ☐☐☐☐ ☐☐☐☐

Expires ☐☐ ☐☐ Security code ☐☐☐ Issue no. ☐☐☐

Signature ________________________________ Date __________

All orders must be accompanied by the appropriate payment.

Please send your completed order form to:
BRF, 15 The Chambers, Vineyard, Abingdon OX14 3FE
Tel. 01865 319700 / Fax. 01865 319701 Email: enquiries@brf.org.uk

❑ Please send me further information about BRF publications.

Available from your local Christian bookshop. **BRF is a Registered Charity**

You may be interested to know that David Winter is a regular contributor to *New Daylight*, BRF's popular series of Bible reading notes. *New Daylight* is ideal for those looking for a fresh, devotional approach to reading and understanding the Bible. Each issue covers four months of daily Bible reading and reflection with each day offering a Bible passage (text included), helpful comment and a prayer or thought for the day ahead.

Edited by Naomi Starkey, *New Daylight* is written by a gifted team of contributors including Adrian Plass, David Winter, Gordon Giles, Rachel Boulding, Helen Julian CSF, Margaret Silf, Anne Roberts, Stephen Rand, Tony Horsfall and Veronica Zundel.

NEW DAYLIGHT SUBSCRIPTIONS

❑ I would like to give a gift subscription
(please complete both name and address sections below)

❑ I would like to take out a subscription myself
(complete name and address details only once)

This completed coupon should be sent with appropriate payment to BRF. Alternatively, please write to us quoting your name, address, the subscription you would like for either yourself or a friend (with their name and address), the start date and credit card number, expiry date and signature if paying by credit card.

Gift subscription name ______________________________

Gift subscription address ______________________________

______________________________ Postcode ______________

Please send to the above, beginning with the next January/May/September issue: (delete as applicable)

(please tick box)	UK	SURFACE	AIR MAIL
NEW DAYLIGHT	❑ £13.35	❑ £14.55	❑ £16.65
NEW DAYLIGHT 3-year sub	❑ £30.00		

Please complete the payment details below and send your coupon, with appropriate payment to: **BRF, 15 The Chambers, Vineyard, Abingdon OX14 3FE**

Your name ______________________________

Your address ______________________________

______________________________ Postcode ______________

Total enclosed £ ________ (cheques should be made payable to 'BRF')

Payment by Cheque ❑ Postal Order ❑ Visa ❑ Mastercard ❑ Switch ❑

Card number: ❑❑❑❑❑❑❑❑❑❑❑❑❑❑❑❑❑❑❑

Expires: ❑❑❑❑ Security code: ❑❑❑ Issue no (Switch): ❑❑❑❑

Signature (essential if paying by credit/Switch card) ______________________________

❑ Please do not send me further information about BRF publications.

NB: BRF notes are also available from your local Christian bookshop. **BRF is a Registered Charity**

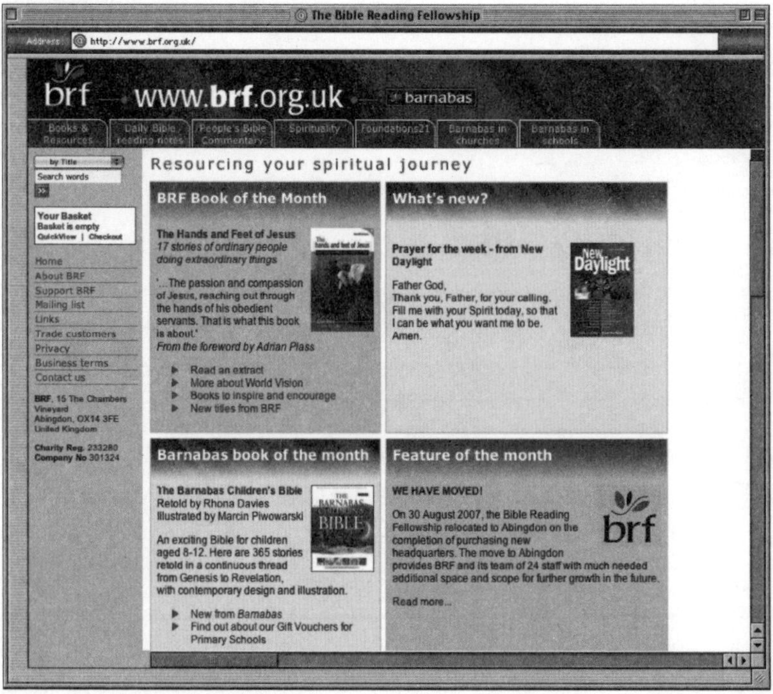